BTEC Level 2

edexcel
advancing learning, changing lives

SPORT LEVEL 2
BTEC First

Mark Adams | Paul Beashel | Julie Hancock | Bob Harris
Pam Phillippo | Alex Sergison | Iain Taylor

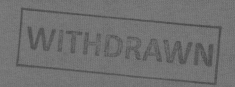

A PEARSON COMPANY

Published by Pearson Education Limited, a company incorporated in England and Wales, having its registered office at Edinburgh Gate, Harlow, Essex, CM20 2JE. Registered company number: 872828

www.pearsonschoolsandfecolleges.co.uk

Edexcel is a registered trademark of Edexcel Limited

Text © Pearson Education Limited 2010

First published 2010

13 12 11 10
10 9 8 7 6 5 4 3

British Library Cataloguing in Publication Data
A catalogue record for this book is available from the British Library.

ISBN 978 1 846906 22 0

Edited by Linda Mellor
Designed by Wooden Ark
Typeset by Tek-Art
Original illustrations © Pearson and Vicky Woodgate 2009
Cover design by Visual Philosophy, created by CMC Design
Picture research by Harriet Merry
Cover photo/illustration © Nice One Productions/Corbis
Back cover photos © David Madison/Getty, Eric Foltz/iStock
Printed in Italy by Rotolito Lombarda

Hotlinks
There are links to relevant websites in this book. In order to ensure that the links are up to date, that the links work, and that the sites are not inadvertently linked to sites that could be considered offensive, we have made the links available on the Heinemann website at www.pearsonschoolsandfecolleges.co.uk/hotlinks When you access the site, the express code is 6220V.

Disclaimer
This material has been published on behalf of Edexcel and offers high-quality support for the delivery of Edexcel qualifications. This does not mean that the material is essential to achieve any Edexcel qualification, nor does it mean that it is the only suitable material available to support any Edexcel qualification. Edexcel material will not be used verbatim in setting any Edexcel examination or assessment. Any resource lists produced by Edexcel shall include this and other appropriate resources.

Copies of official specifications for all Edexcel qualifications may be found on the Edexcel website: www.edexcel.com

Contents

About your **BTEC Level 2 First Sport Student Book**   vi

Unit	Credit value	Title	Author	Page
1	5	Fitness testing and training	Pam Phillippo	1
2	10	Practical sport	Mark Adams	33
3	10	Outdoor and adventurous activities	Alex Sergison	67
4	5	Anatomy and physiology for sport	Julie Hancock	93
5	10	Injury in sport	Julie Hancock	119
6	10	Sports development	Bob Harris	155
7	10	Planning and leading sports activities	Mark Adams	171
8	10	Technical skills and tactical awareness for sport	Mark Adams	205
9	10	Psychology for sports performance	Paul Beashel	219
10	10	Nutrition for sports performance	Julie Hancock	245
11	5	Development of personal fitness	Pam Phillippo	263
12	10	Lifestyle and the sports performer	Mark Adams	281
13	10	Work experience in the sports industry	Mark Adams	on CD
14	10	Exercise and fitness instruction	Bob Harris	309
15	10	Sport and leisure facility operations	Bob Harris	325
16	10	Leading outdoor and adventurous activities	Iain Taylor	341
17	10	Expedition experience	Iain Taylor	363
18	5	Effects of exercise on the body systems	Julie Hancock	387
19	10	Business skills in sport	Bob Harris	on CD
20	10	Planning and running a sports event	Pam Phillippo	399

Glossary   413

Index   417

Credits

The author and publisher would like to thank the following individuals and organisations for permission to reproduce photographs:

p.1 AP/PA Photos, **p.3** Pearson Education Ltd. Studio 8. Clark Wiseman, **p.4** ABACA/PA Photos, **p.5** AP/PA Photos, **p.6** AP/PA Photos, **p.10** Colin Read/Action Plus, **p.17** Eremin Sergey/Shutterstock, **p.29** Zuma Press/PA Photos, **p.31** Shutterstock, **p.33** Mike Egerton/EMPICS Sport/PA Photos, **p.35** Gareth Boden/Pearson Education Ltd, **p.38** Mike Egerton/EMPICS Sport/PA Photos, **p.41** Action Plus, **p.45** AFP/Getty Images , **p.47** Peter Dench/Corbis, **p.53** EMPICS Sport/PA Photos, **p.56** Eric Risberg/PA Photos, **p.61** Getty Images, **p.63** Corbis, **p.67** Harriet Merry, **p.69** Martin Beddall/Pearson Education Ltd, **p.71** Dorset Media Service., **p.79** Mark Hanauer/Corbis, **p.81** Photodisc. Karl Weatherly, **p.82** Harriet Merry, **p.84** Terje Rakke/Getty Images, **p.85** Photodisc. Karl Weatherly, **p.86** Photodisc. Bruno Herdt, **p.91** Gareth Boden/Pearson Education Ltd, **p.91** Jules Selmes/Pearson Education Ltd, **p.93** Science Photo Library, **p.95** Clark Wiseman/Studio 8/Pearson Education Ltd, **p.107** Science Photo Library, **p.108** Shutterstock, **p.117** Jules Selmes/Pearson Education Ltd, **p.119** Dave Thompson/PA Wire/PA Photos, **p.121** Gareth Boden/Pearson Education Ltd, **p.122** Photodisc. Jeff Maloney, **p.127** ABACA/PA Photos, **p.129** Dave Thompson/PA Wire/PA Photos, **p.132** SIPA Press/Rex Features, **p.137** Faye Norman/Science Photo Library, **p.143** Imagestate. John Foxx Collection, **p.145** PBNJ Productions/Getty, **p.148** © Image Source/Corbis , **p.154** Gareth Boden/Pearson Education Ltd, **p.155** David Davies/PA Archive/PA Photos, **p.157** Gareth Boden/Pearson Education Ltd, **p.158** Imagestate/Pearson Education Ltd, **p.161** David Davies/PA Archive/PA Photos, **p.163** PhotoDisc. Andy Sotiriou, **p.168** Getty Images, **p.171** Darren Walsh/Getty Images, **p.173** Gareth Boden/Pearson Education Ltd, **p.175** Luca Ghidoni/Getty Images, **p.177** Darren Walsh/Getty Images, **p.181** Glyn Kirk/Action Plus, **p.186** © Image Source/Corbis , **p.191** Neil Tingle/Action Plus, **p.195** © Image Source/Corbis , **p.201** Bongarts/Getty Images , **p.203** Gareth Boden/Pearson Education Ltd, **p.205** AP/PA Photos, **p.207** Gareth Boden/Pearson Education Ltd, **p.208** Corbis, **p.217** Stockdisc/Getty Images/Pearson Education Ltd, **p.219** Daniel Roland/AP/PA Photos, **p.221** Clark Wiseman/Studio 8/Pearson Education Ltd, **p.223** Daniel Roland/AP/PA Photos, **p.225** © MBI / Alamy, **p.229** © UpperCut Images / Alamy, **p.231** Digital Vision/GETTY, **p.233** Tony Feder/AP/PA Photos, **p.237** © Image Source/Corbis , **p.241** 2008 China Photos/GETTY, **p.243** Shutterstock, **p.245** Gareth Boden/Pearson Education Ltd, **p.245** Dennis Gray/Cole Publishing Group/Photodisc/PearsonEducation Ltd, **p.257** Dennis Gray/Cole Publishing Group/Photodisc/PearsonEducation Ltd, **p.259** © Image Source/Corbis , **p.261** Shutterstock, **p.263** Thinkstock/Jupiter Images/Alamy, **p.265** Clark Wiseman/Studio 8/Pearson Education Ltd, **p.267** JTPhoto/Brand X/Corbis, **p.272** Imagestate. John Foxx Collection, **p.276** © Image Source/Corbis , **p.276** Thinkstock/Jupiter Images/Alamy, **p.279** Mind Studio/Pearson Education Ltd, **p.281** Simon Bruty/Getty Images, **p.283** Rob Judges/Pearson Education Ltd, **p.285** David Madison/Getty, **p.287** Simon Bruty/Getty Images, **p.295** © Image Source/Corbis , **p.298** Rex Features, **p.301** Getty Images, **p.309** Image Source Ltd/Alamy/Pearson Education Ltd, **p.310** Jules Selmes/Pearson Education Ltd, **p.315** Image Source Ltd/Alamy/Pearson Education Ltd, **p.322** Gareth Boden/Pearson Education Ltd, **p.325** Getty, **p.327** Jules Selmes/Pearson Education Ltd, **p.333** Lindsay Lewis, **p.335** Diego Cervo/Shutterstock, **p.337** Action Plus, **p.339** Gareth Boden/Pearson Education Ltd, **p.341** © The Photolibrary Wales / Alamy, **p.342** Eric Foltz/istock, **p.344** Jules Selmes/Pearson Education Ltd, **p.347** Vitalii Nesterchuk/Shutterstock, **p.361** Jules Selmes/Pearson Education Ltd, **p.363** Jim DeLillo/istock, **p.365** Jules Selmes/Pearson Education Ltd, **p.367** Jim DeLillo/istock, **p.377** Photodisc, **p.385** Gareth Boden/Pearson Education Ltd, **p.387** Akira Suemori/AP/PA Photos, **p.389** Gareth Boden/Pearson Education Ltd, **p.395** Akira Suemori/AP/PA Photos, **p.397** Jules Selmes/Pearson Education Ltd, **p.399** Big Shots/Getty, **p.401** Gareth Boden/Pearson Education Ltd, **p.403** Photodic/Pearson Education Ltd, **p.411** Mind Studio/Pearson Education Ltd **unit 13, p.1** photolibrary **unit 19, p.1** Colin Hawkins/Corbis **unit 19, p.14** Shutterstock **unit 13, p.17** Jules Selmes/Pearson Education Ltd **unit 13, p.3** Gareth Boden/Pearson Education Ltd **unit 19, p.3** Clark Wiseman/Studio 8/Pearson Education Ltd **unit 13, p.5** Alamy/Neil Holmes Freelance Digital

The author and publisher would like to thank the following individuals and organisations for permission to reproduce their materials:
p.19 Forestry non-adjusted aerobic fitness values for males table. Adapted, with permission, from B.J. Sharkey, 1984, Physiology of fitness, 2nd ed. (Champaign, IL: Human Kinetics), 258
p.20 Forestry non-adjusted aerobic fitness values for females table. Adapted, with permission, from B.J. Sharkey, 1984, Physiology of fitness, 2nd ed. (Champaign, IL: Human Kinetics), 259
p.20 Forestry age-adjusted aerobic fitness values table. Adapted, with permission, from B.J. Sharkey, 1984, Physiology of fitness, 2nd ed. (Champaign, IL: Human Kinetics), 260–261
p.21 Forestry aerobic fitness values table. Adapted, with permission, from B.J. Sharkey, 1984, Physiology of fitness, 2nd ed. (Champaign, IL: Human Kinetics), 262
p.22 Lewis Nomogram. © Fox, Edward et al., The Psychological Basis of Physical Education and Athletics, 1988, McGraw-Hill. Material is reproduced with permission of The McGraw-Hill Companies
p.25 J-P Nomogram. Baun, WB, Baun MR and Raven, PB, Tenneco Health and Fitness Department
p.253 Table of energy expended by a person (weighing 60 kg) in 30 minutes. Information provided by the British Nutrition Foundation, www.nutrition.org.uk
p.372 Section of ordnance survey map. © Ordnance Survey OS 1:25 000 Scale Colour Raster ®

About the authors

Mark Adams is a Senior Verifier for Sport levels 1 to 3 and has worked with Edexcel for seven years. He has taught for ten years at schools and colleges across all qualifications. Mark is a consultant with the Premier League education and learning team. He is series editor for our BTEC National Sport books and is currently working on the new editions.

Paul Beashel is an Associate Consultant for Essex County Council and is responsible for the planning and delivery of innovative PE and sport-related initiatives in Essex and Jiangsu Province, China. He is a former Headteacher of an Essex Specialist Sports College and co-author of GCSE and A-level books on physical education and sport as well as being one of the authors of the previous edition of BTEC First Sport Student Book published by Heinemann.

Julie Hancock has worked with Edexcel for over 14 years and is a Senior Verifier for Sport and Sport and Exercise Science. She has taught for 20 years and helped develop a range of educational resources and publications as well as training for tutor programmes. Originally a PE teacher in secondary schools, then a lecturer in Further Education and Higher Education, she now delivers training to teachers and lecturers to in helping support the development of BTEC programmes.

Bob Harris has been in education for 30 years and has delivered BTEC Sports courses at all levels. He is an external verifier for Edexcel and an Examiner for other examining boards. Bob is the author of best-selling student books and teacher resources, including the previous editions of this book, BTEC First Sport Student Book published by Heinemann.

Pam Phillippo has played a key role in the redevelopment of Edexcel BTEC Sport qualifications and is an expert in psychophysiology. Formerly a lecturer in Further Education and Higher Education, and having worked with GB athletes, her specialist fields include fitness testing and training, exercise prescription, and experimental methods.

Alex Sergison has spent 12 years instructing and lecturing at all levels. He specialises in outdoor education and has provided management and advice for a number of outdoor activity centres including the Weymouth and Portland National Sailing Academy's water sport school. Alex is responsible for outdoor education course development for Weymouth College and has been working with Edexcel developing new watersports qualifications.

Iain Taylor has worked in education for 25 years and for Edexcel for the last 10. He has written bespoke BTEC short professional training programmes for the outdoor industry and worked for Outward Bound in both the UK and the USA. For the last 11 years he has been a Programme Leader in two Further Education colleges.

About your BTEC Level 2 First Sport

Choosing to study for a BTEC Level 2 First Sport qualification is a great decision to make for lots of reasons. More and more people are accessing the sports industry to improve their health, meet new people and learn new skills or support a local sports team. As the number of people using the sports industry grows then the demand for well-qualified people to work within it also grows. With the 2012 Olympic Games and Paralympic Games fast approaching there will be even more opportunities for people with sports related qualifications.

Your BTEC Level 2 First Sport is a **vocational** or **work-related** qualification. This doesn't mean that it will give you *all* the skills you need to do a job, but it does mean that you'll have the opportunity to gain specific knowledge, understanding and skills that are relevant to your chosen subject or area of work.

What will you be doing?

The qualification is structured into **mandatory units (M)** (ones you must do) and **optional units (O)** (ones you can choose to do). This book contains all 20 units, so you can be sure that you are covered whichever qualification you are working towards.

- BTEC Level 2 First **Certificate** in Sport: 1 mandatory unit and optional units that provide a combined total of 15 credits
- BTEC Level 2 First **Extended Certificate** in Sport: 2 mandatory units and optional units that provide a combined total of 30 credits
- BTEC Level 2 First **Diploma** in Sport: 2 mandatory units that provide a combined total of 60 credits

Unit number	Credit value	Unit name	Cert	Ex. Cert	Diploma
1	5	Fitness testing and training	M	M	M
2	10	Practical sport	O	M*	M*
3	10	Outdoor and adventurous activities	O	M*	M*
4	5	Anatomy and physiology		O	O
5	10	Injury in sport		O	O
6	10	Sports development		O	O
7	10	Planning and leading sports activities		O	O
8	10	Technical skills and tactical awareness for sport			O
9	10	Psychology for sports performance			O
10	10	Nutrition for sports performance			O
11	5	Athlete development		O	O
12	10	Lifestyle and the sports performer			O
13	10	Work experience in the sports industry			O
14	10	Exercise and fitness instruction			O
15	10	Sport and leisure facility operations			O
16	10	Leading outdoor and adventurous activities			O
17	10	Expedition experience			O
18	5	Factors affecting sports performance		O	O
19	10	Business skills in sport			O
20	10	Planning and running a sports event			O

*Learners may take unit 2 or unit 3, they may not take both.

How to use this book

This book is designed to help you through your BTEC Level 2 First Sport course. It is divided into 20 units to reflect the units in the specification. This book contains many features that will help you use your skills and knowledge in work-related situations and assist you in getting the most from your course.

Introduction

These introductions give you a snapshot of what to expect from each unit – and what you should be aiming for by the time you finish it!

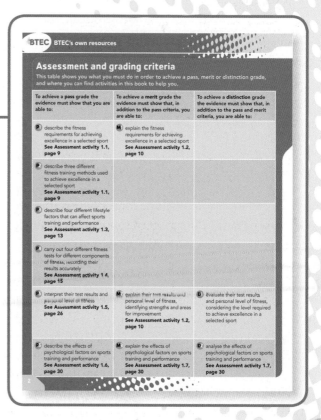

Assessment and grading criteria

This table explains what you must do in order to achieve each of the assessment criteria for each unit. Each unit contains a number of assessment activities to help you with the assessment criterion, shown by the grade button **P1**.

Assessment

Your tutor will set **assignments** throughout your course for you to complete. These may take the form of projects where you research, plan, prepare, make and evaluate a piece of work or activity, case studies and presentations. The important thing is that you collect evidence of your skills and knowledge to date.

Stuck for ideas? Daunted by your first assignment? These students have all been through it before…

How you will be assessed

This unit will be assessed by an internal assignment that will be designed and marked by the tutors at your centre. Your assessment could be in the form of:
- presentations
- case studies
- practical tasks
- written assignments.

Sarah, 16-year-old track athlete

This unit helped me to see that you need to focus on what you want to achieve, and it takes hard work, commitment and training to be successful.

I enjoyed looking at elite sports performers and thinking about the different fitness requirements and training methods they use. It was good to explore lifestyle and psychological factors and how they can affect sports training and performance because I could apply the things I learnt to how I perform on the track. I realised that mental fitness is just as important as physical fitness if you want to succeed.

There were lots of practical tasks and activities for this unit, which made it more exciting for me. The bit I enjoyed most was testing my fitness levels. I liked participating in different fitness tests and comparing my results to my peers. We looked at data tables and it was interesting to see what the results would be like for top sports performers.

Over to you!
- What areas of this unit might you find challenging?
- Which section of the unit are you most looking forward to?
- What preparation can you do in readiness for the unit assessment(s)?

Activities

There are different types of activities for you to do: **assessment activities** are suggestions for tasks that you might do as part of your assignment and will help you develop your knowledge, skills and understanding. Each one has **grading tips** that clearly explain what you need to do in order to achieve a pass, merit or distinction grade.

BTEC Assessment activity 1.1   P1 P2

1. Select a sport and describe the fitness requirements needed to achieve excellence. Rank the fitness requirements in order of importance and give your reasons. **P1**

2. Describe three different fitness training methods that could be used to achieve excellence in this sport. **P2**

Grading tips
- By selecting a sport that you participate in, you could draw on your personal experience to help you describe the fitness requirements and different training methods used.
- Include both the physical and skill-related components of fitness in your description.
- Think about the best performer in the UK and in the world in the sport you have selected. You can use the internet to research information on elite sports performers, the fitness requirements they have and the training they undertake.

There are also suggestions for activities that will give you a broader grasp of the industry, develop your skills and deepen your skills.

Activity: The work–life balance

In pairs or groups, discuss how work demands affect sports training and performance. For example, you may have a part-time job, and could discuss how the demands of work affect your sports training and performance. List the effects in a table, like the one below.

Work demands	Effect on sports training and performance
Part-time employment	Not enough time to train Increase in stress levels

Discuss how you try to maintain a healthy work–life balance and any further improvements you could make.

Personal, learning and thinking skills

Throughout your BTEC Level 2 First Sport course, there are lots of opportunities to develop your personal, learning and thinking skills. Look out for these as you progress.

PLTS

If you identify questions to answer and problems to resolve in your fitness testing, you can develop your skills as an **independent enquirer**.

Functional skills

It's important that you have good English, maths and ICT skills – you never know when you'll need them, and employers will be looking for evidence that you've got these skills too.

Functional skills

If you use ICT systems to record fitness test data and develop, present and communicate information you can develop your **ICT** skills in sorting data.

Key terms

Technical words and phrases are easy to spot. You can also use the glossary at the back of the book.

Key term

Eustress – a positive form of stress. Can occur when a sports performer enjoys testing their own sporting ability, pushing themselves to reach their full potential.

WorkSpace

Case studies provide snapshots of real workplace issues, and show how the skills and knowledge you develop during your course can help you in your career.

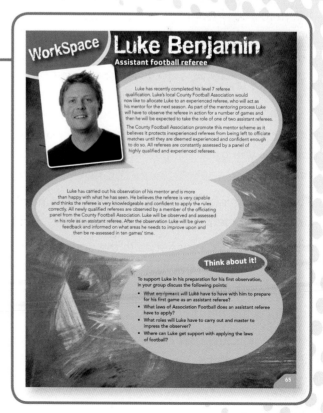

Just checking

At the end of each unit, you will find this activity there is an you will When you see this sort of activity, take stock! These quick questions are there to check your knowledge. You can use them to see how much progress you've made.

Edexcel's assignment tips

At the end of each unit, you'll find hints and tips to help you get the best mark you can, such as the best websites to go to, checklists to help you remember processes and really useful facts and figures.

Don't miss out on these resources to help you!

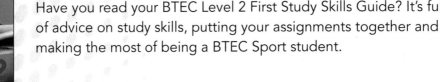

BTEC BTEC's own resources

Just checking

1. Define 'aerobic endurance' and state the units of measurement.
2. Describe two methods that can be used to determine the percent body fat of an individual.
3. Agility and co-ordination are skill-related components of fitness. Name the other three skill-related components of fitness.
4. What is eustress?
5. Describe how smoking can affect sports training and performance.
6. What does Fartlek training involve?
7. Name three side effects of anabolic steroids.
8. Why is it important to gain informed consent from participants prior to administering or undertaking fitness tests?
9. Describe the two types of motivation and give an example of each.

edexcel

Assignment tips

Research tips
- Get on the internet – the internet has a wealth of information on elite sports performance and the road that elite performers have taken to achieve excellence in their sport.
- Read sports magazines and their websites – Magazines like *Runner's World* or *Athletics Weekly* often contain profiles on elite performers, their training diaries and the training methods they use to enable them to perform at the highest of levels. See Hotlinks section on page ii for links to the websites for these magazines.

Get active!
- Try out a number of fitness training methods yourself. Experiencing training methods first hand will help you to understand why certain sports use certain training methods and techniques, and how these help the body to become more efficient in the sport to be undertaken, enhancing performance.
- Think about other ways of gaining information to support your assignment work. Speak to different sports coaches about the physical and skill-related fitness requirements they consider important, the training methods they use and their views and experience of how lifestyle and psychological factors can affect sports training and performance. Who is their most successful sports performer and why?

Practice makes perfect
- Make sure you are familiar with the pre-test procedures and fitness test methods before commencing your data collection. Observe an experienced practitioner administering tests, either live or on video.
- There is a wealth of published fitness testing data available for you to interpret your test results. Select data that will allow you to compare your results according to your age and gender.
- You could use your test results as a basis to help design a personal fitness training programme in the future. See links to Unit 11: Development of personal fitness – Be able to plan a personal fitness training programme.

32

Have you read your BTEC Level 2 First Study Skills Guide? It's full of advice on study skills, putting your assignments together and making the most of being a BTEC Sport student.

To accompany your book you'll find a CD Rom attached to the back cover. This contains a free video podcast that you can download on to your computer, for use at home or on the go via your mobile phone, MP3 player or laptop. Wherever you see the podcast icon in the book you'll know that the podcast will help you get to grips with the content. You can also access this podcast for free on the internet www.edexcel.com/BTEC or www.pearsonfe.co.uk/BTEC 2010 or via the iTunes store.

The CD Rom also contains units that have not been printed in the book. You can print these out or read them on screen. The units are:

- Unit 13 Work experience in the sports industry
- Unit 19 Business skills in sport

Ask your teacher about extra materials to help you through your course. You'll find great videos featuring the Premier League, activities, animations, and information about the Sport sector.

Your book is just part of the exciting resources from Edexcel to help you succeed in your BTEC course. Visit www.edexcel.com/BTEC or www.pearsonfe.co.uk/BTEC 2010 for more details.

Credit value: 5

1 Fitness testing and training

Most sports performers aspire to reach their full sporting potential. To achieve this, they must fully commit to their personal training plan, maintain a balanced, healthy lifestyle and possess the psychological skills and desire to succeed. Sports performers undergo regular assessments of their fitness to help predict their future performance potential. Regular fitness testing is essential to develop the performer's physical fitness and for the coach to identify areas for improvement and evaluate the success of a training regime. Fitness test results provide an objective view of performance and can be used to ensure training meets the needs of the individual and their sport.

In this unit you will look at the components of physical and skill-related fitness and explore why specific fitness components are necessary to achieve excellence in sport. Sports coaches ensure that training programmes are tailored to meet the specific needs of the sports performer, and through this unit you will gain an understanding of why different performers require different training methods in order to reach their full potential. The unit also looks at lifestyle and psychological factors and the effects that they have on sports training and performance. You will explore fitness testing and by participating in tests will be able to investigate your own levels of fitness.

Learning outcomes

After completing this unit you should:

1. know the fitness and training requirements necessary to achieve excellence in a selected sport
2. know the lifestyle factors that affect sports training and performance
3. be able to assess your own level of fitness
4. know the effects of psychological factors on sports training and performance.

1

Assessment and grading criteria

This table shows you what you must do in order to achieve a pass, merit or distinction grade, and where you can find activities in this book to help you.

To achieve a **pass** grade the evidence must show that you are able to:	To achieve a **merit** grade the evidence must show that, in addition to the pass criteria, you are able to:	To achieve a **distinction** grade the evidence must show that, in addition to the pass and merit criteria, you are able to:
P1 describe the fitness requirements for achieving excellence in a selected sport **See Assessment activity 1.1, page 9**	**M1** explain the fitness requirements for achieving excellence in a selected sport **See Assessment activity 1.2, page 10**	
P2 describe three different fitness training methods used to achieve excellence in a selected sport **See Assessment activity 1.1, page 9**		
P3 describe four different lifestyle factors that can affect sports training and performance **See Assessment activity 1.3, page 13**		
P4 carry out four different fitness tests for different components of fitness, recording the results accurately **See Assessment activity 1.4, page 15**		
P5 interpret their test results and personal level of fitness **See Assessment activity 1.5, page 26**	**M2** explain their test results and personal level of fitness, identifying strengths and areas for improvement	**D1** evaluate their test results and personal level of fitness, considering the level required to achieve excellence in a selected sport
P6 describe the effects of psychological factors on sports training and performance **See Assessment activity 1.6, page 30**	**M3** explain the effects of psychological factors on sports training and performance **See Assessment activity 1.7, page 30**	**D2** analyse the effects of psychological factors on sports training and performance **See Assessment activity 1.7, page 30**

How you will be assessed

This unit will be assessed by an internal assignment that will be designed and marked by the tutors at your centre. Your assessment could be in the form of:

- presentations
- case studies
- practical tasks
- written assignments.

Sarah, 16–year-old track athlete

This unit helped me to see that you need to focus on what you want to achieve, and it takes hard work, commitment and training to be successful.

I enjoyed looking at elite sports performers and thinking about the different fitness requirements and training methods they use. It was good to explore lifestyle and psychological factors and how they can affect sports training and performance because I could apply the things I learnt to how I perform on the track. I realised that mental fitness is just as important as physical fitness if you want to succeed.

There were lots of practical tasks and activities for this unit, which made it more exciting for me. The bit I enjoyed most was testing my fitness levels. I liked participating in different fitness tests and comparing my results to my peers. We looked at data tables and it was interesting to see what the results would be like for top sports performers.

Over to you!
- What areas of this unit might you find challenging?
- Which section of the unit are you most looking forward to?
- What preparation can you do in readiness for the unit assessment(s)?

1 Know the fitness and training requirements necessary to achieve excellence in a selected sport

Warm-up

How have they got there?

Think of a sporting role model: an elite sports performer, somebody who has achieved 'excellence'. Write down five factors that you think have contributed to their success. Think about their fitness levels, the training they have undertaken, their lifestyle and psychological factors.

Discuss in groups and compare the factors you have identified with those of other sporting role models.

1.1 Fitness requirements for achieving excellence in sport

Different people have different fitness requirements depending on their job, hobbies and the sports and leisure activities they enjoy. There are many definitions of fitness. In general, fitness is your ability to meet the demands of your lifestyle or environment.

Different sports require different fitness components. A sports coach can build a profile of a performer's sport-specific training needs in order to design a training programme to target and enhance fitness components that are important for their sport.

Components of physical fitness

The six components of physical fitness are:

- aerobic endurance
- muscular endurance
- flexibility
- speed
- muscular strength
- body composition.

Aerobic endurance is also known as cardio-respiratory fitness, cardio-respiratory endurance or aerobic fitness. It is the ability of the cardio-respiratory system to efficiently supply nutrients and oxygen to working muscles during sustained physical activity.

Jamaican sprinter Usain Bolt: the fastest man on the planet. What is his most recent time for the 100m?

Muscular endurance is the ability of a muscle to continue contracting over a period of time against a light to moderate load. It is the ability of the muscular system to work efficiently.

Flexibility means having an adequate range of motion in all joints of the body. It is the ability to move a joint through its complete range of movement.

Speed is calculated in the following way:

$$\text{Speed (m/s)} = \frac{\text{Distance (m)}}{\text{Time taken (s)}}$$

The faster an athlete runs over a given distance, the greater their speed. There are three basic types of speed:

* accelerative speed – sprints up to 30 metres
* pure speed – sprints up to 60 metres
* speed endurance – sprints with short recovery periods in between.

Muscular strength is the maximum force a muscle or muscle group can produce.

Body composition is the relative ratio of fat mass to fat-free mass (vital organs, muscle, bone) in the body.

A hockey player requires speed, aerobic endurance, flexibility, power, muscular endurance and strength. They use muscular endurance, strength and power when performing skills like shooting and defending. They also need to change direction quickly and efficiently and be able to respond rapidly to the position of their opponents.

Components of skill–related fitness

There are five skill-related fitness components:

* agility
* balance
* co-ordination
* power
* reaction time.

Agility is the ability of a sports performer to quickly and precisely move or change direction without losing their balance.

Balance is the ability to maintain your centre of mass over a base of support. There are two types: **static** balance and **dynamic** balance. A gymnast uses static balance when performing a headstand and dynamic balance to perform a cartwheel.

Co-ordination is the smooth flow of movement needed to perform a motor task efficiently and accurately.

One of the greatest gymnasts of all time: Ecaterina Szabo, Romanian gymnast, four times Olympic Gold Medallist at the 1984 Los Angeles Olympics. What skill-related fitness requirements does a gymnast have?

Power is the work done in a unit of time. It is calculated in the following way:

$$\text{Power (kgm/min or kgm/s)} = \frac{\text{Force (kg) x Distance (m)}}{\text{Time (min or s)}}$$

Reaction time is the time taken for a sports performer to respond to a stimulus and the initiation of their response. For example, a sprinter in the blocks responding to the starter's gun.

Body composition and sports performance

Body composition is assessed as the per cent body fat of an individual and is a health-related component of physical fitness. Different sports performers have different body types which makes them more suited to success in their sport.

The three body types are:

*   **Endomorph** – generally untrained individuals – non-athletes.
*   **Mesomorph** – well-suited to events such as swimming, gymnastics and sprinting.
*   **Ectomorph** – generally suited to events like long-distance running.

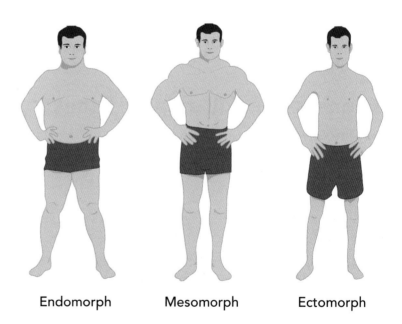

Endomorph   Mesomorph   Ectomorph

Figure 1.1 What is your body type?

1.2 Fitness training methods

There is a variety of fitness training methods which athletes and sports performers can use. The selection of a fitness training method depends on the training goals of the performer or athlete and their sport or event.

Table 1.1: Examples of fitness training methods for the different components of fitness.

Component of fitness	Training methods
Flexibility	• Static • Active • Passive • Ballistic
Muscular strength Muscular endurance Power	• Use of resistance machines • Use of free weights • Circuit training • Plyometrics
Aerobic endurance	• Continuous training • Fartlek training • Interval training
Speed	• Hollow sprints • Acceleration sprints • Hill sprints

Sport-specific training methods

The fitness training method selected should meet the needs of the performer and the fitness requirements of their sport. Here are two examples:

The basketball player

- **Fitness requirement:** To build anaerobic power and improve jumping ability.
- **Suggested training method:** Plyometrics.

Plyometric training involves completing specific exercises or activities to develop power and sport-specific skills. Plyometric training should be used carefully, because it can be physically stressful on the body and cause muscle soreness.

Plyometric exercises can be organised as part of a circuit, see figure 1.2 for an example.

1. Barrier hops
2. Incline push ups
3. Alternate bounding
4. Rim jumps
5. Lunges
6. Depth jump and stuff

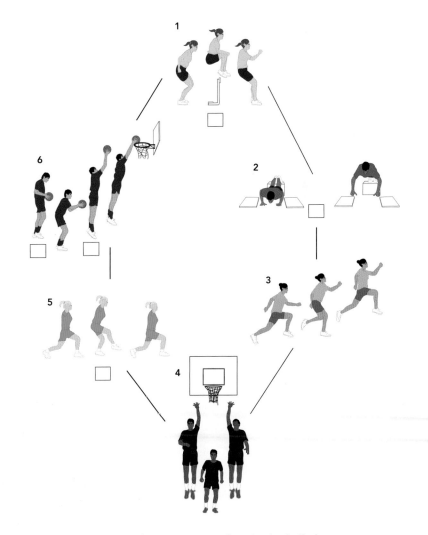

Figure 1.2: Plyometric circuit for a basketball player.

The netball player

- **Fitness requirement:** To improve aerobic fitness and sprinting ability on the court.
- **Suggested training method:** Fartlek training.

'Fartlek' comes from the Swedish word for 'speedplay' and is a training method that is used to enhance both the aerobic and anaerobic energy systems. Fartlek training is usually performed outdoors.

Fartlek training involves varying pace, from a fast sprint to a slow jog, and is beneficial in sports that involve using both the aerobic and anaerobic energy systems, like football, hockey and rugby. Here is an example of Fartlek training for netball:

1. Start with a 1.5–2 mile jog at a light to moderate intensity
2. Sprint 30m
3. Light jog 100m
4. Sprint 60m
5. Light jog 150m

Repeat steps 2–5 eight to ten times

6. Finish with a 6-minute jog for cool-down.

Sport–specific fitness requirements

Certain fitness components are particularly important to achieving successful sports performance. Table 1.2 shows the major fitness components for five different sports.

Table 1.2: Fitness components required for five sports.

Fitness component	Golf	Cycling	Gymnastics	Judo	Tennis
Aerobic endurance	✓	✓			✓
Muscular endurance	✓	✓	✓		✓
Flexibility	✓		✓	✓	✓
Speed		✓		✓	✓
Muscular strength	✓	✓	✓	✓	✓
Agility			✓	✓	✓
Balance	✓		✓	✓	✓
Co-ordination	✓		✓		✓
Power		✓		✓	✓
Reaction time		✓			

Tiger Woods' golf swing. What are the fitness requirements for a golfer?

For example, the fitness requirements for golf include the following:

- **Flexibility, balance and co-ordination** are needed to perform a co-ordinated, efficient and effective swing.
- **Muscular endurance and muscular strength** are needed to perform efficient trunk rotation and rotary movements of the swing. A golfer requires good muscular strength, particularly in the arms and legs. Good strength in the abdominal muscles is needed to prevent problems with the muscles of the lower back.
- **Aerobic endurance** is vital. Good fitness levels are required so that the golfer can perform well. Poor fitness levels could affect fine muscle control and concentration.

Some training methods that could be used for golf include the following:

- **Flexibility training,** e.g. Proprioceptive Neuromuscular Facilitation technique, to maintain and enhance golf swing.
- **Strength training,** e.g. use of resistance machines, to maintain and enhance golf swing.
- **Endurance training,** e.g. continuous distance swimming, to maintain optimum aerobic endurance levels.

Key term

Proprioceptive Neuromuscular Facilitation (PNF) – a stretching technique for developing flexibility. PNF is performed with a partner. If completed regularly, it can improve mobility and joint range of motion.

Assessment activity 1.1

BTEC

1. Select a sport and describe the fitness requirements needed to achieve excellence. Rank the fitness requirements in order of importance and give your reasons. **P1**

2. Describe three different fitness training methods that could be used to achieve excellence in this sport. **P2**

Grading tips

- By selecting a sport that you participate in, you could draw on your personal experience to help you describe the fitness requirements and different training methods used.
- Include both the physical and skill-related components of fitness in your description.
- Think about the best performer in the UK and in the world in the sport you have selected. You can use the internet to research information on elite sports performers, the fitness requirements they have and the training they undertake.

 Functional skills

Using ICT to research fitness requirements and training methods and present your information could develop your **ICT** skills.

What fitness components does a footballer need to consider?

Case study: fitness for football

Alex has gained a summer work placement in a local football club. He works alongside experienced coaches to assist with the coaching of the youth team.

Alex has been asked to create a presentation to give to the youth team which looks at the fitness requirements needed to achieve excellence in football. He has decided to use a 17-year-old centre forward as his case study.

1. What fitness components does a centre forward require to achieve excellence in football? Consider both the physical fitness and skill-related components of fitness.

2. What three different fitness training methods could Alex use to improve the centre forward's sports performance? Describe each method.

3. What four different lifestyle factors could affect the centre forward's sports performance? Consider factors like stress, smoking, drugs and diet.

Assessment activity 1.2

Explain the fitness requirements a goalkeeper needs to achieve excellence in football. In your explanation, consider any similarities or differences that might exist between the fitness requirements of a striker and a goalkeeper. **M1**

Grading tips

A goalkeeper's overall workload could be considered lower than for other players; goalkeepers don't have the same physical demands in terms of aerobic endurance. But, they still require similar fitness requirements to be able to perform well. You shoud consider:

- the physical fitness requirements for a goalkeeper, such as power, speed, strength (particularly leg, thigh and upper body) and flexibility
- the skill-related fitness requirements needed to be able to respond quickly and efficiently to game situations, such as agility, balance and reaction time.

2 Know the lifestyle factors that affect sports training and performance

2.1 Lifestyle factors

Lifestyle and well-being are important factors for sports performers. To succeed in their sport, performers must think about all aspects of their training and performance, including lifestyle factors.

All sports performers want to maintain good health and be injury free, so that they can train or compete in the sports they love.

Stress may occur if a sports performer thinks that they are unable to meet the demands of a sports performance or activity. Stress can have a positive or negative effect on training and performance. For example, a gymnast, enjoying the feelings created as they complete a complex vault, experiences **eustress**. Whereas, another gymnast, concerned about the technical aspects of the vault and worried about performing in front of a large audience, experiences negative stress, namely **anxiety**.

Drugs should not be taken. All drugs have side effects, they can reduce fitness levels and be harmful to health. Sports performers and athletes regularly undergo testing for illegal substances. The relevant National Governing Body of Sport and UK Sport are responsible for making decisions about which sports performer or athlete should be tested and when. Drug abuse is illegal. If a performer tests positive they can be banned from competing for life. Some examples of banned substances are shown in the table below.

Key terms

Eustress – a positive form of stress. Can occur when a sports performer enjoys testing their own sporting ability, pushing themselves to reach their full potential.

Anxiety – a negative form of stress. Can reduce a sport performer's level of confidence and concentration. Expectations of success are also reduced and the performer experiences a greater fear of failure.

Table 1.3: Examples of banned substances.

Drug	Effect	Examples of abuse in sport	Side effects
Anabolic steroids	Increases power by building up muscles Increases training time Used to help repair the body after training Increases competitiveness and aggression	• Power events, e.g., weightlifting • Sprint events	• Liver disease • Certain forms of cancer • Fluid retention • Infertility • Hardening of arteries • Skin disorders
Beta blockers	Used to steady nerves and improve fine motor control	• Shooting • Snooker • Darts	• Tiredness and lethargy • Low blood pressure • Breathing difficulties
Diuretics	Reduces body weight	• Horse racing • Boxing	• Dehydration • Muscle cramps • Kidney failure
Stimulants	Improves endurance Makes the performer more physically alert Reduces fatigue	• Endurance-based sports	• Increased blood pressure • Increased heart rate, palpitations • Paranoid delusions • Restlessness, sleeplessness • Anxiety • Shaking, sweating

Remember

Following a healthy, balanced diet helps the body to function properly. You need to make sure you eat the right amount and type of food, so that you have sufficient energy for your body to meet the demands of different sports.

- Make sure you maintain a healthy, balanced diet.
- Make sure you take part in regular physical activity.
- If you are healthy and active now, you are more likely to be healthy and active in adulthood.

Smoking narrows arteries, shortens breath and increases the risk of developing heart disease, respiratory disease and cancer. When someone smokes, carbon monoxide enters the body and this results in less oxygen being available for working muscles. Smoking can reduce aerobic endurance levels by up to 10 per cent, reducing efficiency.

Sleep is very important. Young athletes and sports performers should have at least 8 hours' sleep each night. It is important that the body has time for rest and recuperation. Insufficient sleep can reduce the positive benefits of training and can affect sports performance.

Diet is very important. Good nutrition helps reduce health risks such as heart disease, obesity, stroke and high blood pressure. A balanced diet is important for sports performers and athletes so that they can get the energy they need to perform well. A balanced diet consists of:

- carbohydrates
- fats
- proteins
- fibre
- vitamins
- minerals
- water.

Other lifestyle factors include:

- activity level
- sports participation
- work demands
- alcohol consumption
- medical history
- culture
- gender.

Did you know?

- Obesity is the accumulation of body fat above acceptable levels for an individual's age, gender and ethnic origin.
- Obesity leads to health problems, including diabetes and heart disease.
- The main causes of obesity are poor diet (eating too much) and inactivity.
- The number of young people in the UK who are clinically obese is rising at an alarming rate each year.

Activity: The work–life balance

In pairs or groups, discuss how work demands affect sports training and performance. For example, you may have a part-time job, and could discuss how the demands of work affect your sports training and performance. List the effects in a table, like the one below.

Work demands	Effect on sports training and performance
Part-time employment	Not enough time to train Increase in stress levels

Discuss how you try to maintain a healthy work–life balance and any further improvements you could make.

BTEC **Assessment activity 1.3** **P3**

Choose four different lifestyle factors and describe how they can affect sports training and performance. Use examples from your sports training and performance to support your description where appropriate.

Grading tips

• Outline your four lifestyle factors and then describe how each factor can affect sports training and performance.

• Think of your description as if you are 'painting a picture with words'.

Functional skills

Making contributions to discussions could help develop your **English** skills in speaking.

3 Be able to assess your own level of fitness

In this section you will follow the standard methods for different fitness tests, to assess your own fitness levels. In particular, you will look at the methods for the following tests:

• Sit and reach
• Grip dynamometer
• Multi-stage fitness test
• Forestry step test
• 35m sprint
• Vertical jump
• One minute press-up
• One minute sit-up
• Skinfold testing
• Body Mass Index (BMI).

3.1 Carry out fitness testing

Pre-test procedures

Before participating in fitness tests you should complete an informed consent form. This is documented evidence that shows that participants have been provided with all the necessary information to undertake the test. You will need to complete an informed consent form to confirm that you:

• are able to follow the test method
• know exactly what is required of you during testing
• have fully consented to your participation in the fitness tests
• know that you are able to ask your tutor/assessor any questions relating to the tests
• understand that you can withdraw your consent at any time.

Remember

Before you participate in, or administer any fitness test, it is extremely important that pre-test procedures are followed.

The consent form should be signed and dated by you (the participant), supported by a witness (usually your tutor) and if you are under 18 years of age a parent/guardian will also be required to give their consent to your participation.

INFORMED CONSENT FOR THE WINGATE TEST

1. The purpose of the test is to determine maximal anaerobic power and maximal anaerobic capacity.

2. This will be determined using the Wingate Anaerobic Cycling Test.

3. The participant will carry out standard warming-up and cooling-down procedures for the test.

4. The participant will be required to perform a 30-second all-out cycling test using a Monark 824E cycle ergometer.

5. All participants will receive method details in full.

6. The tutor/assessor is available to answer any relevant queries which may arise concerning the test.

7. The participant is free to withdraw consent and discontinue participation in the test at any time.

8. Only the tutor/assessor and participant will have access to data recorded from the test which will be stored securely. Participant confidentiality is assured.

I FULLY UNDERSTAND THE SCOPE OF MY INVOLVEMENT IN THIS FITNESS TEST AND HAVE FREELY CONSENTED TO MY PARTICIPATION.

Participant's signature   Date:

Tutor's/assessor's signature: Date:

I (insert participant's name), UNDERSTAND THAT MY PARENTS/GUARDIAN HAVE GIVEN PERMISSION FOR ME TO TAKE PART IN THIS FITNESS TEST, WHICH WILL BE SUPERVISED BY (insert tutor name). I AM PARTICIPATING IN THIS FITNESS TEST BECAUSE I WANT TO, AND I HAVE BEEN INFORMED THAT I CAN STOP THE TEST AT ANY TIME WITHOUT ANY ISSUES ARISING.

Participant's signature   Date:

Figure 1.3: Example of an informed consent form.

Your guide to recording test results

- Allow sufficient time to practise each fitness test method before you begin collecting data.
- Use an appropriate data collection sheet to record your results.
- Record each result as you get it, so you don't forget it.
- For reliable results, all fitness tests selected should be repeated. Depending on the tests chosen, these may be repeated on the same day (i.e., half day test-retest), or if a longer recovery period is required between trials, then a separate day test-retest.
- Use the correct units of measurement for your fitness tests. Some fitness tests will require the use of tables to process data and obtain the correct units of measurement. For example, the Multi-stage Fitness Test result is recorded as the Level and Shuttle achieved. You need to use a conversion table to look up the predicted aerobic fitness level (VO_2 max, ml/kg/min) for the Level and Shuttle obtained.

Calibration of equipment describes the process of checking (and if necessary adjusting) the accuracy of fitness testing equipment before it is used, by comparing it to a recognised standard. Prior to testing, equipment should be checked carefully. If equipment isn't correctly calibrated it could lead to inaccurate (invalid) results.

Issues with test methods – by completing different fitness tests, you will gain an understanding of why some tests might not be as valid and reliable as others, and factors which could affect test reliability and validity.

- **Reliability** is the ability to carry out the same fitness test method again and expect the same results. Reliability is repeatability – the results obtained should be consistent.
- **Validity** is the accuracy of the results. This means whether the results you have recorded from the fitness test are a true reflection of what you are actually trying to measure.

Example of issues with test reliability and validity

Jim wants to measure his body weight. He decides to use a set of scales, and weighs himself twice in 10 minutes (for reliability). However, before testing, he forgets to check whether the scales are correctly calibrated. Unfortunately, the calibration of the scales is incorrect – when there is no weight on the scales, the dial is **not** at zero. Jim, blissfully unaware, weighs himself.

Each time Jim weighs himself the result will be identical, so the test will be reliable. But Jim will not get a true measurement of his weight because the scales are providing an incorrect, invalid reading. This means the results will not be valid.

This example highlights how important it is to check calibration of equipment and practise test methods before collecting data to help ensure that final data collected is both valid and reliable, otherwise results are worthless.

Fitness testing methods

In this section you will explore different fitness tests covering each component of physical fitness.

> ### Key terms
>
> **Reliability** – consistency of results; repeatability.
>
> **Validity** – accuracy of results.

BTEC Assessment activity 1.4 (P4)

Carry out four different fitness tests for different components of fitness, accurately recording your results.

Grading tips
- Follow pre-test procedures carefully, design and complete your own informed consent form to participate in the fitness tests.
- Practise test procedures with your peers; being familiar with standard test protocol will help to ensure accuracy of results.
- Use a data collection form to record your fitness test results.
- Make sure you use the correct units of measurement.

  PLTS

If you identify questions to answer and problems to resolve in your fitness testing, you can develop your skills as an **independent enquirer**.

 Functional skills

If you use ICT systems to record fitness test data and develop, present and communicate information you can develop your **ICT** skills in sorting data.

Flexibility: sit and reach test

The aim of the sit and reach test is to measure trunk forward flexion, hamstring, hip and lower back range of motion. A standard sit and reach box is used.

1. Perform a short warm-up prior to this test. Don't use fast, jerky movements, as this may increase risk of injury. Remove your shoes.

2. Sit with your heels placed against the edge of the sit and reach box. Keep your legs flat on the floor i.e., keep your knees down.

3. Place one hand on top of the other and reach forward slowly. Your fingertips should be in contact with the measuring portion of the sit and reach box. As you reach forward, drop your head between your arms and breathe out as you push forward.

4. The best of three trials should be recorded.

Results

Table 1.4: Interpretation of results for the sit and reach test.

Rating	Males (cm)	Females (cm)
Excellent	25+	20+
Very good	17	17
Good	15	16
Average	14	15
Poor	13	14
Very poor	9	10

Strength: grip strength dynamometer test

The grip strength dynamometer test measures the static strength of the power grip-squeezing muscles, where the whole hand is used as a vice or clamp. A grip dynamometer is a spring device; as force is applied, the spring is compressed and this moves the dynamometer needle which indicates the result. Digital dynamometers are also available.

1. Adjust the handgrip size, so that the dynamometer feels comfortable to hold/grip.

2. Stand-up, with your arms by the side of your body.

3. Hold the dynamometer parallel to the side of your body, with the dial/display facing away from you.

4. Squeeze as hard as possible for 5 seconds, without moving your arm.

5. Carry out three trials on each hand, with a 1-minute rest between trials.

Results

Table 1.5: Interpretation of results for grip strength dynamometer test.

Rating	Males aged 15–19y (kg)	Females aged 15–19y (kg)
Excellent	52+	32+
Good	47–51	28–31
Average	44–46	25–27
Below average	39–43	20–24
Poor	<39	<20

Did your results surprise you when you did the dynamometer test?

Aerobic endurance: multi-stage fitness test

The multi-stage fitness test is used to predict your maximum oxygen uptake (aerobic fitness) levels and is performed to a tape recording.

1. The test should be conducted indoors, usually in a sports hall using two lines (or cones) placed 20m apart.

2. Perform a short warm-up.

3. Line-up on the start line and on hearing the triple bleep run to the other line 20m away. You must reach the other line before or on the single bleep that determines each shuttle run.

4. Don't get ahead of the bleep, you need to make sure you turn to run to the other line on the bleep.

5. You will find that the bleeps get closer and closer together, so you'll need to continually increase your pace.

6. Continue to run to each line. A spotter is used to check you have reached each line in time with the bleep. If not, you will receive two verbal warnings before being asked to pull out of the test.

7. Continue running until you are physically exhausted i.e., you have reached maximum exhaustion, at which point your level and shuttle reached is recorded and used to predict your maximum oxygen consumption (ml/kg/min) using a prediction table which accompanies the tape recording.

Results

Table 1.6: Interpretation of results of the multi-stage fitness test.

Rating	Males (aged 15–19y) (ml/kg/min)	Females (aged 15–19y) (ml/kg/min)
Excellent	60+	54+
Good	48–59	43–53
Average	39–47	35–42
Below average	30–38	28–34
Poor	<30	<28

 Did you know?

One of the highest aerobic endurance levels ever recorded was for former Olympic and World Champion Norwegian cross-country skier Bjorn Daehlie, who had a reported VO$_2$ max of 96 ml/kg/min.

Cyclists have achieved extremely high levels of fitness. Former three-times winner of the Tour de France, USA cyclist Greg LeMond, had a reported VO$_2$ max of 92.5 ml/kg/min.

Table 1.7: Interpretation of aerobic fitness results for elite athletes.

Rating	Males (aged 18–22y)	Females (aged 18–22y)
World class	80+	70+
Elite	70	63
Trained	57	53
Active	50	43
Untrained	45	39

Activity: Fitness results

Using the data tables provided, compare your aerobic fitness (VO$_2$ max ml/kg/min) results with normative data for your age group and to data for young elite performers.

- How do your fitness results compare?
- What improvements could you make to your current training regime to improve your aerobic fitness levels?

Discuss your results in groups.

Aerobic endurance: Forestry step test

The Forestry Step test was developed in 1977 by Brian Sharkey, and is a modified version of the Harvard Step test. The test is widely used in fitness selection procedures (for example, for police and fire service) and predicts aerobic endurance levels.

A different bench height is used for males and females. For males, the height of the bench should be 40 cm (15.75 inches), for females, 33 cm (13 inches). The stepping rate of 22.5 steps per minute is the same for both males and females, which means the metronome should be set at a cadence of 90 beats per minute.

1. Stand directly facing the bench and start stepping in-time with the beat of the metronome. As soon as you start stepping, the helper will start the stopwatch.

2. Keep to the beat of the metronome, which means you will put one foot onto the bench, then your other foot, then the first foot will be lowered to the floor, then your other foot i.e., 'up', 'up', 'down', 'down'.

3. Straighten your legs when you fully step up onto the bench.

4. Keep stepping for 5 minutes, at which point your helper will stop the metronome and you will need to sit down immediately and locate your radial pulse.

5. At 5 minutes and 15 seconds (15 seconds after sitting down) you will need to count your pulse for 15 seconds (stopping at 5 minutes and 30 seconds).

6. Record your 15-second pulse rate and perform a short cool-down.

Results

Use the tables to obtain your non-adjusted aerobic fitness level.
- In table 1.8a or 1.8b (depending on your gender), locate your 15 second pulse in the 'Pulse Count' column and find the value closest to your body weight (kg). The point at which these two values intersect gives you your non-adjusted aerobic fitness level (in ml/kg/min).
- Next, adjust your fitness level to take into account your age, which will provide a more accurate prediction of your aerobic endurance. In Table 1.9, locate your nearest age in years (left-hand column) and locate your non-adjusted aerobic fitness value (fitness score) along the top. The point where these two values intersect gives you your age-adjusted fitness level (ml/kg/min).
- Use table 1.10 to interpret your aerobic fitness level.

Table 1.8a: Forestry non-adjusted aerobic fitness values (ml/kg/min) for **males.**

Pulse count	Maximal oxygen consumption (VO$_2$ max)												
45	33	33	33	33	33	32	32	32	32	32	32	32	32
44	34	34	34	34	33	33	33	33	33	33	33	33	33
43	35	35	35	34	34	34	34	34	34	34	34	34	34
42	36	35	35	35	35	35	35	35	35	35	35	34	34
41	36	36	36	36	36	36	36	36	36	36	36	35	35
40	37	37	37	37	37	37	37	37	35	35	35	35	35
39	38	38	38	38	38	38	38	38	38	38	38	37	37
38	39	39	39	39	39	39	39	39	39	39	39	38	38
37	41	40	40	40	40	40	40	40	40	40	40	39	39
36	42	42	41	41	41	41	41	41	41	41	41	40	40
35	43	43	42	42	42	42	42	42	42	42	42	42	41
34	44	44	43	43	43	43	43	43	43	43	43	43	43
33	46	45	45	45	45	45	44	44	44	44	44	44	44
32	47	47	46	46	46	46	46	46	46	46	46	46	46
31	48	48	48	47	47	47	47	47	47	47	47	47	47
30	50	49	49	49	48	48	48	48	48	48	48	48	48
29	52	51	51	51	50	50	50	50	50	50	50	50	50
28	53	53	53	53	52	52	52	52	51	51	51	51	51
27	55	55	55	54	54	54	54	54	54	53	53	53	52
26	57	57	56	56	56	56	56	56	56	55	55	54	54
25	59	59	58	58	58	58	58	58	58	56	56	55	55
24	60	60	60	60	60	60	60	59	59	58	58	57	
23	62	62	61	61	61	61	61	60	60	60	59		
22	64	64	63	63	63	63	62	62	61	61			
21	66	66	65	65	65	64	64	64	62				
20	68	68	67	67	67	67	66	66	65				
Weight (kg)	54.5	59.1	63.6	68.2	72.7	77.3	81.8	86.4	91	95.4	100	104.5	109

Table 1.8b: Forestry non-adjusted aerobic fitness values (ml/kg/min) for **females.**

Pulse count	Maximal oxygen consumption (VO₂ max)											
45										29	29	29
44								30	30	30	30	30
43							31	31	31	31	31	31
42			32	32	32	32	32	32	32	32	32	32
41			33	33	33	33	33	33	33	33	33	33
40			34	34	34	34	34	34	34	34	34	34
39			35	35	35	35	35	35	35	35	35	35
38			36	36	36	36	36	36	36	36	36	36
37			37	37	37	37	37	37	37	37	37	37
36		37	38	38	38	38	38	38	38	38	38	38
35	38	38	39	39	39	39	39	39	39	39	39	39
34	39	39	40	40	40	40	40	40	40	40	40	40
33	40	40	41	41	41	41	41	41	41	41	41	41
32	41	41	42	42	42	42	42	42	42	42	42	42
31	42	42	43	43	43	43	43	43	43	43	43	43
30	43	43	44	44	44	44	44	44	44	44	44	44
29	44	44	45	45	45	45	45	45	45	45	45	45
28	45	45	46	46	46	47	47	47	47	47	47	47
27	46	46	47	48	48	49	49	49	49	49		
26	47	48	49	50	50	51	51	51	51			
25	49	50	51	52	52	53	53					
24	51	52	53	54	54	55						
23	53	54	55	56	56	57						
Weight (kg)	36.4	40.9	45.4	50.0	54.5	59.1	63.6	68.2	72.7	77.3	81.8	86.4

Table 1.9: Age-adjusted fitness levels.

Fitness score	30	31	32	33	34	35	36	37	38	39	40	41	42	43	44	45	46	47	48	49	50
Nearest age 15	32	33	34	35	36	37	38	39	40	41	42	43	44	45	46	47	48	49	50	51	53
20	31	32	33	34	35	36	37	38	39	40	41	42	43	44	45	46	47	48	49	50	51

(cont.)

Fitness score	51	52	53	54	55	56	57	58	59	60	61	62	63	64	65	66	67	68	69	70	71	72
Nearest age 15	54	55	56	57	58	59	60	61	62	63	64	65	66	67	68	69	70	71	72	74	75	76
20	52	53	54	55	56	57	58	59	60	61	62	63	64	65	66	67	68	69	70	71	72	73

Example 1: If your age is 16 years and you score 36 on the step test, your age-adjusted score is 38.

Example 2: If your age is 20 years and you score 65 on the step test, your age-adjusted score is 66.

Table 1.10: Aerobic fitness levels.

| Age and gender | Fitness category | | | | | | |
| | Superior | Excellent | Very good | Good | Fair | Poor | Very poor |
	Maximum oxygen consumption (ml/kg/min)						
15-year-old male	57+	56–52	51–47	46–42	41–37	36–32	<32
15-year-old female	54+	53–49	48–44	43–39	38–34	33–29	<29
20-year-old male	56+	55–51	50–46	45–41	40–36	35–31	<31
20-year-old female	53+	52–48	47–43	42–38	37–33	32–28	<28

Speed: 35m sprint

The 35m sprint test is best performed on an indoor athletics track, or use an outdoor track on a day when weather conditions will not affect test results.

1. Perform a warm-up.

2. Three people should keep time for the sprint, using stopwatches capable of measuring to one-tenth of a second.

3. Line-up on the start line, in a standing start position.

4. As soon as you start sprinting, the timers will start their stopwatches.

5. Sprint as fast as you can, crossing the 35m line.

6. When you cross the 35m line, the timers will stop their stopwatches.

7. Your time for the sprint is recorded to the closest tenth of a second. An average result can be taken from the three timers.

8. A maximum of 2 or 3 trials are performed in one day. Allow at least 3-minutes recovery between trials. A third trial should only be performed if the difference in times between your first and second trial is greater than 0.20 seconds.

9. The best time from your 2 or 3 trials is recorded as your 35m sprint result.

10. To prevent muscle soreness, perform a cool-down, followed by static stretching.

Results

Table 1.11: Interpretation of results for 35m sprint.

Rating	Males (s)	Females (s)
Excellent	<4.80	<5.30
Good	4.80–5.09	5.30–5.59
Average	5.10–5.29	5.60–5.89
Fair	5.30–5.60	5.90–6.20
Poor	5.60+	6.20+

Power: vertical jump test

The vertical jump test is a test of the anaerobic power of the quadriceps muscle group. A standard vertical jump board is used for the test, which may digitally record the jump height, or gymnast's chalk may be used instead.

1. Perform a short warm-up prior to the test.

2. Stand with your dominant side against the board, feet together, and reach up as high as you can to record your standing reach height.

3. Only one dip of the arms and knees is permitted. Make the jump and touch the vertical jump board at the peak of your jump.

4. Perform three trials. No rest is required between trials, the time taken to observe and record the height of the jump is all that is needed for recovery between consecutive trials.

Results

A nomogram is a diagram that can be used to obtain fitness test results. Use the Lewis nomogram (see figure 1.4) to predict the power of your quadriceps in kgm/s.

- Plot the difference (D) between your standing reach height and your best jump height (cm) on the nomogram line (D).
- Plot your weight in kilograms on the nomogram line (Wt).
- Using a sharpened pencil and ruler, join up the two plots, which will cross over the Power line (P) to give a prediction of the anaerobic power of your quadriceps muscles (in kgm/s).

Table 1.12: Interpretation of results for the vertical jump test.

Rating	Males (kgm/s)	Females (kgm/s)
Above average	105+	90+
Average	95	80
Below average	<85	<70

Muscular endurance: press-up test

The press-up test is used to assess the endurance of the muscles of your upper body.

1. Position yourself on a mat, with your hands shoulder-width apart and arms fully extended.

2. Next, lower your body until the elbows are at 90°.

3. Return to the starting position, with your arms fully extended.

4. Make sure your push-up action is continuous, with no rests in-between.

5. The total number of press-ups is recorded for 1 minute.

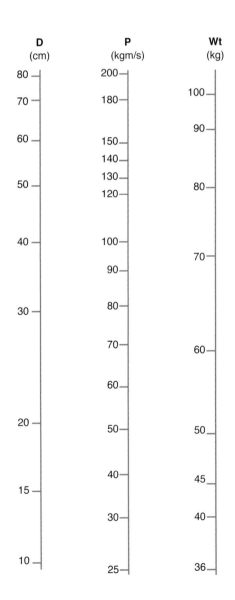

Figure 1.4: Lewis nomogram.

Due to reduced upper body strength, females may choose to use a modified press-up technique. The positioning is similar to the standard method, but in the starting position a bent knee position is assumed.

Results

Table 1.13: Interpretation of results for full-body press-ups.

Rating	Males	Females
Excellent	45+	34+
Good	35–44	17–33
Average	20–34	6–16
Poor	<19	<5

Table 1.14: Interpretation of results for modified press-ups.

Rating	No. of reps
Excellent	39+
Good	34–38
Average	17–33
Fair	6–16
Poor	<6

Muscular endurance: sit-up test

The sit-up test assesses the endurance and development of your abdominal muscles.

1. Lie on a mat with your knees bent, and feet flat on the floor, with your arms folded across your body. Your feet can be held by a partner if you wish.

2. Raise yourself up to a 90° position and then return to the floor.

3. Record the total number of sit-ups completed in 1 minute.

Results

Table 1.15: Interpretation of results for the sit-up test.

Rating	Males	Females
Excellent	49–59	42–54
Good	43–48	36–41
Above average	39–42	32–35
Average	35–38	28–31
Below average	31–34	24–27
Poor	25–30	18–23
Very poor	11–24	3–17

Body composition – skinfold testing

Skinfold testing can be used to predict percent body fat. In this section you will be using the Jackson-Pollock nomogram method to predict your percent body fat.

Following a standard method will help ensure your results are valid. You will need a tape measure and pen to mark each site and skinfold calipers (such as Harpenden or Slimguide) to take the skinfolds. Work in pairs or small groups for skinfold testing.

1. Measurements should be taken on dry skin on the right side of the body. Exceptions to this would be if the participant has a tattoo or deformity on the site location, which means the left side of the body would need to be used.

2. The participant should keep their muscles relaxed during the test.

3. Mark each skinfold site with a pen and use a tape measure to find the mid-points.

4. Grasp the skinfold firmly between your thumb and index finger and gently pull away from the body. The skinfold should be grasped about 1 cm away from the site marked.

5. Place the skinfold calipers perpendicular to the fold, on the site marked, with the dial facing upwards.

6. Maintaining your grasp, place the calipers midway between the base and tip of the skinfold and allow the calipers to be fully released so that full tension is placed on the skinfold.

7. Read the dial of the skinfold calipers to the nearest 0.5 mm, two seconds after you have released the calipers. Make sure you continue to grasp the skinfold throughout testing.

8. Take a minimum of two measurements at each site. If repeated tests vary by more than 1 mm, repeat the measurement. If consecutive measurements become smaller, this means that the fat is being compressed, and the results will not be accurate. If this happens, go to another site and then come back to the site to be tested later.

9. Make sure you record each measurement as it is taken.

10. The final value is the average of the two readings (mm).

It is important to practise the technique for skinfold testing to ensure that results are valid and reliable.

Skinfold site selection for males

Male participants will need to gain skinfold results (mm) for the following three sites:

- **Chest** – A diagonal fold, which is one half of the distance between the anterior auxiliary line and the nipple. (The anterior auxiliary line is the crease where the top of your arm, when hanging down, meets the chest.) The chest skinfold is used only for males.

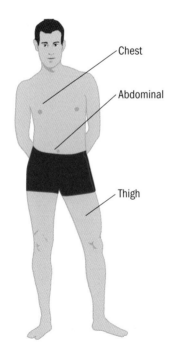

Figure 1.5: Location of skinfold sites for males.

- **Abdominal** – A vertical fold, which is 2 cm to the right side of the umbilicus (belly button).
- **Thigh** – A vertical fold, on the front of the thigh, halfway between the hip joint and the middle of the knee cap. The leg needs to be straight and relaxed.

Skinfold site selection for females

Female participants will need to gain skinfold results (mm) for the following three sites:

- **Triceps** – A vertical fold on the back midline of the upper arm, over the triceps muscle, halfway between the acromion process (bony process on the top of the shoulder) and olecranon process (bony process on the elbow). The arm should be held freely by the side of the body.
- **Suprailiac** – A diagonal fold just above the hip bone and 2–3 cm forward.
- **Thigh** – A vertical fold, on the front of the thigh, halfway between the hip joint and the middle of the knee cap. The leg needs to be straight and relaxed.

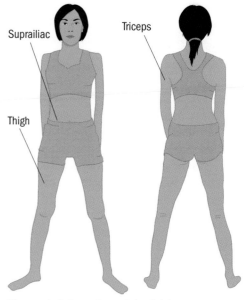

Figure 1.6: Location of skinfold sites for females.

Results

- Add up the sum of your three skinfolds (mm).
- Obtain your percent body fat result by plotting your age in years and the sum of the three skinfolds (mm) on the nomogram.
- Use a ruler and sharpened pencil to join up the two plots, which will cross over the percent body fat (wavy) vertical lines.
- Read your percent body fat result to the closest 0.5%, according to your gender.

Table 1.16: Interpretation of body fat results.

Rating	Males % body fat (16–29 years)	Females % body fat (16–29 years)
Very low fat	<7	<13
Slim	7–12	13–20
Ideal	13–17	21–25
Overweight	18–28	26–32
Obese	29+	33+

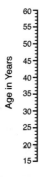
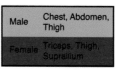
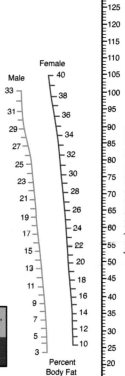

Figure 1.7: J-P nomogram.

Results

Table 1.17: Interpretation of BMI results.

Rating	BMI (kg/m²)
Desirable	20–25
Overweight	26–30
Obese and increased risk of CHD	31+

Body composition: Body Mass Index (BMI)

Body Mass Index is a simple measure of body composition and is used to check if a person is overweight. The test can determine if a person is at increased risk of developing Coronary Heart Disease (CHD) and other cardiovascular diseases.

Body Mass Index is widely used for the general population to determine the degree to which a person is overweight. However, the test is not always valid for elite sports performers and athletes, because it doesn't take into account frame size or muscle mass. For example, if a body builder were to have their BMI measured, they would be classed as obese; their potentially large frame size and high muscle mass would give an invalid test result.

Calculate your Body Mass Index:

- Measure your body weight in kilograms.
- Measure your height in metres.
- Carry out the following calculation to determine your BMI (kg/m²):

$$BMI = \frac{\text{Body weight (kg)}}{\text{Height (m) x Height (m)}}$$

PLTS

Generating ideas about your personal level of fitness can help you become a **reflective learner**.

Functional skills

Presenting fitness test results by using mathematics to obtain your fitness results, drawing conclusions and providing mathematical justifications, you could improve your **mathematics** skills.

BTEC Assessment activity 1.5 · P5

Interpret your test results and personal level of fitness. To do this, look at your results from four different fitness tests for different components of fitness and use data tables to determine your rating.

Grading tips

Use published data tables to interpret your test results. In your interpretation, think about the following:

- How do your results compare to your peers?
- How do your results compare to published data?
- How do your results compare to norms for your age and gender?

Find out what fitness levels are required for excellence. What fitness levels do county-level and/or international and professional performers achieve? How do your results compare?

3.2 Interpreting fitness test results

Fitness testing data collection form

Personal data – Recording test results						
Learner's name: Age (yrs/mths):			Height (m): Weight (kg): Body Mass Index (BMI kg/m²):			
Fitness component	Fitness test	Test 1	Test 2	Average result	Units	Interpretation of test results (rating)
Flexibility	Sit and reach				cm	
Strength	Handgrip dynamometer				kg	
Aerobic endurance	Multi-stage fitness test				ml/kg/min	
Aerobic endurance	Forestry step test				ml/kg/min	
Speed	35m sprint				s	
Power	Vertical jump				kgm/s	
Muscular endurance	1-minute press-ups				no. of reps	
	1-minute sit-ups				no. of reps	
Body composition	Skinfold tests				% body fat	

Figure 1.8: Example of a fitness testing data collection form.

4 Know the effects of psychological factors on sports training and performance

4.1 Psychological factors

Performing to the best of your ability requires physical fitness, skill-related fitness and mental preparation for the sports performance or activity. Sports performers need to be aware of psychological factors and the importance of maintaining their health and well-being so that their training and performance are not affected.

In this section you will consider psychological factors and the effects they can have on sports training and performance. For more on psychological factors, see Unit 9, Psychology for sports performance.

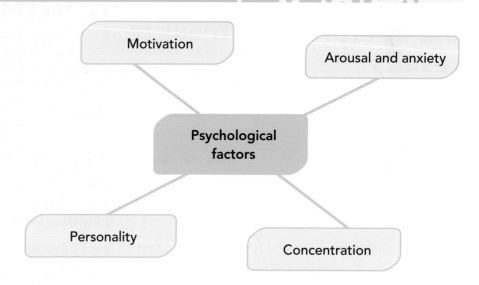

Figure 1.9: Psychological factors that affect sports performance.

Effects of psychological factors on sports training and performance

1. Motivation is the external stimulus and internal mechanisms which arouse and direct our behaviour. There are two categories of need which motivate us:

- **Intrinsic motivation** is the desire to challenge yourself and the enjoyment gained from sports participation and your sporting achievements.

- **Extrinsic motivation** relates to receiving external rewards such as praise from your sports coach or winning a trophy.

Sports performers need a balance between intrinsic and extrinsic motivation. Too many extrinsic rewards can reduce a performer's own intrinsic motivation, which is needed for long-term sports training and performance.

2. Arousal and anxiety. Arousal is the increased state of readiness of a sports performer in preparation for the performance or activity. To perform well, it is important that arousal levels are maintained at an optimal level.

Anxiety is a negative emotional feeling that occurs when arousal levels are too high and the sports performer starts to feel threatened by the situation or fears that they will fail. There are two main types:

- **State anxiety** is a type of anxiety that can occur when a performer is placed in a constantly changing situation. A sprinter may become anxious just before the start of a race as they are waiting for the starter's orders. The performer can experience somatic and cognitive anxiety during this period. However, anxiety reduces when they hear the starter shout 'on your marks', and the sprinter settles into their blocks.

Key term

State anxiety – a performer's response to a changing situation.

- ○ **Somatic anxiety** is how the body responds to the sports situation. A performer experiencing somatic anxiety can have a range of symptoms including increased heart rate and breathing rate, and they may feel physically sick.
- ○ **Cognitive anxiety** is the performer's general nervousness about the situation they are experiencing and their ability to perform well. Cognitive anxiety can reduce concentration levels.

- **Trait anxiety** relates to characteristics which a sports performer has which makes them react to certain situations in a specific way.

Arousal levels need to be kept at optimal (desirable) levels so that the sports performer can perform well. Failure to do so can cause anxiety and affect the performer's concentration levels and ability to make decisions. Anxiety questionnaires can be completed to determine a performer's level of self-confidence or tension in sporting situations.

3. Personality is the individual, unique characteristics or traits of a person, which determine behaviour.

Personality is unique to an individual, and sports performers should be aware of how their own personality could affect sports training and performance. Personality type can be determined by using a questionnaire. Sports coaches should treat performers differently according to their personality type and appropriate steps can be taken by the performer to prevent performance from being affected.

4. Concentration is the ability of a sports performer to process information and maintain focus.

To process information, a sports performer has to make sense of the information they are presented with and decide on the course of action to take. If a performer becomes overloaded with information it can negatively affect their performance.

Psychological factors and skilled performance

When learning a new skill, a performer can break it down into a number of sub-routines and concentrate on practising each task. For example, hurdling technique could be split into the approach run to the first hurdle, take-off, arm action, landing, and stride pattern between hurdles. As the hurdler becomes more efficient, less concentration is given to learning the skill of hurdling, and instead concentration is given to performing the race and reaching the finish line first.

Experienced sports performers are 'skilled' and can perform complex routines automatically, allowing more concentration to be placed on game situations and tactics.

> **Key term**
>
> **Trait anxiety** – a performer's response as a result of their own unique characteristics.

Gail Devers of the USA clears a high hurdle. How would you break down the components of hurdling technique?

29

Functional skills

Writing a report about your opinions on psychological factors could help develop your **English** skills in writing.

BTEC **Assessment activity 1.6** P6

1. Describe the effects of psychological factors on sports training and performance. **P6**
2. Describe the short-term and longer-term effects and what your own sports targets and goals might be.

Grading tip

Use examples from your own sports training and performance.

BTEC **Assessment activity 1.7** M3 D2

1. Provide an explanation of the effects that motivation, personality, concentration, anxiety and arousal have on sports training and performance. **M3** Give the details of 'how' and 'why'.
2. Analyse the effects that motivation, personality, concentration, anxiety and arousal have on sports training and performance. **D2**

Grading tips

- Support your explanation with reasons and personal sporting examples wherever possible.
- Cover both the short-term and long-term effects.
- In your analysis, think carefully about how the psychological factors are related and how each one can affect sports training and performance and the type of effects they can have.
- Apply knowledge and understanding gained from direct links to Unit 9 Psychology for sports performance.

William Shepherd
Health fitness instructor

William works in a busy health club and is responsible for:

- contributing to the daily running and operation of the club
- undertaking client health fitness assessments including analysis of lifestyle and psychological fitness
- ensuring the training that clients undertake will help them to reach their goals
- instructing clients in the gym
- planning and leading additional training sessions, such as aquaerobics and circuit training.

Describe your typical day

A typical day involves arriving at the club and carrying out checks on the gym equipment and swimming pool. Then I check the computer to see what clients are booked in for fitness/lifestyle assessments. We have a private room to undertake fitness measurements like heart rate, blood pressure and body fat, and then we use the gym to administer other fitness tests such as the step test and tests of muscular strength/endurance.

Depending on the client's needs and goals I usually administer a range of fitness tests to obtain results across the different fitness components. I can then advise on the best training methods for the client, and additional exercise classes that they would find beneficial.

What's the best thing about your job?

I enjoy meeting people and helping clients to reach their goals. Helping a client go from 'unfit' to 'fit' can be a long process. The process can involve overcoming issues that the client may have, like lifestyle or psychological factors which might prevent them from achieving their goals. It's extremely rewarding knowing that I've helped a client achieve their personal fitness goals. I've seen people turn their lives around by ditching bad habits and getting into shape.

Think about it!

1. What areas have you covered in this unit that provide you with the knowledge and skills used by a health fitness instructor?

2. What further skills might you need to develop? Think about how you would conduct a lifestyle/fitness assessment with a client and the skills needed. Write a list and discuss in groups.

Just checking

1. Define 'aerobic endurance' and state the units of measurement.
2. Describe two methods that can be used to determine the percent body fat of an individual.
3. Agility and co-ordination are skill-related components of fitness. Name the other three skill-related components of fitness.
4. What is eustress?
5. Describe how smoking can affect sports training and performance.
6. What does Fartlek training involve?
7. Name three side effects of anabolic steroids.
8. Why is it important to gain informed consent from participants prior to administering or undertaking fitness tests?
9. Describe the two types of motivation and give an example of each.

Assignment tips

Research tips

- Get on the internet – the internet has a wealth of information on elite sports performance and the road that elite performers have taken to achieve excellence in their sport.
- Read sports magazines and their websites – Magazines like *Runner's World* or *Athletics Weekly* often contain profiles on elite performers, their training diaries and the training methods they use to enable them to perform at the highest of levels. See Hotlinks section on page ii for links to the websites for these magazines.

Get active!

- Try out a number of fitness training methods yourself. Experiencing training methods first hand will help you to understand why certain sports use certain training methods and techniques, and how these help the body to become more efficient in the sport to be undertaken, enhancing performance.
- Think about other ways of gaining information to support your assignment work. Speak to different sports coaches about the physical and skill-related fitness requirements they consider important, the training methods they use and their views and experience of how lifestyle and psychological factors can affect sports training and performance. Who is their most successful sports performer and why?

Practice makes perfect

- Make sure you are familiar with the pre-test procedures and fitness test methods before commencing your data collection. Observe an experienced practitioner administering tests, either live or on video.
- There is a wealth of published fitness testing data available for you to interpret your test results. Select data that will allow you to compare your results according to your age and gender.
- You could use your test results as a basis to help design a personal fitness training programme in the future. See links to Unit 11: Development of personal fitness – Be able to plan a personal fitness training programme.

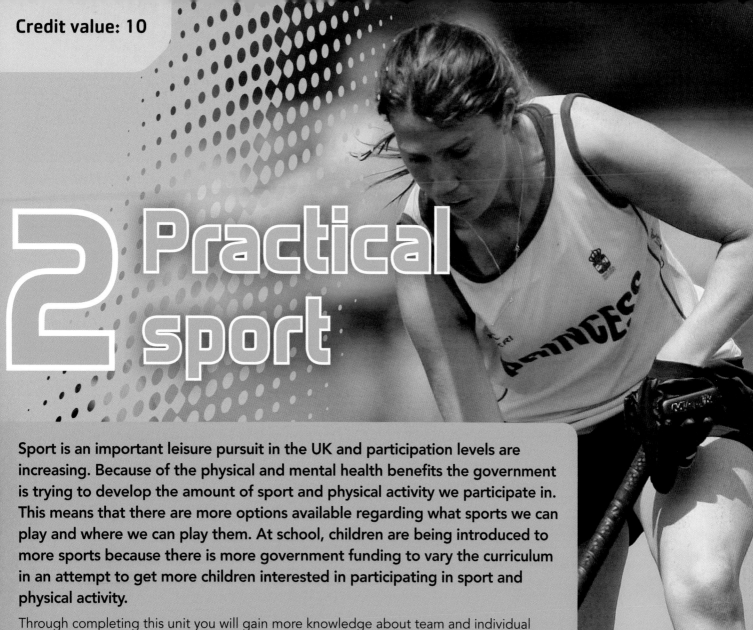

2 Practical sport

Sport is an important leisure pursuit in the UK and participation levels are increasing. Because of the physical and mental health benefits the government is trying to develop the amount of sport and physical activity we participate in. This means that there are more options available regarding what sports we can play and where we can play them. At school, children are being introduced to more sports because there is more government funding to vary the curriculum in an attempt to get more children interested in participating in sport and physical activity.

Through completing this unit you will gain more knowledge about team and individual sports and through developing your knowledge it is hoped that your own performance in sports will develop. This unit will provide you with an opportunity to play sports and learn about the application of skills, techniques, tactics and rules and regulations. In this unit you will learn how to analyse the performance of sports performers from team and individual sports and develop an understanding of how and why this analysis is important in developing individuals and helping teams to succeed.

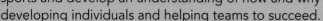

Learning outcomes

After completing this unit you should:

1. be able to demonstrate a range of skills, techniques and tactics in selected sports
2. know the rules, regulations and scoring systems of selected sports
3. know the roles and responsibilities of officials in selected sports
4. be able to review sports performance.

33

Assessment and grading criteria

This table shows you what you must do in order to achieve a pass, merit or distinction grade, and where you can find activities in this book to help you.

To achieve a **pass** grade the evidence must show that the learner is able to:	To achieve a **merit** grade the evidence must show that, in addition to the pass criteria, the learner is able to:	To achieve a **distinction** grade the evidence must show that, in addition to the pass and merit criteria, the learner is able to:
P1 demonstrate use of practical skills, techniques and tactics appropriate for one team sport **See Assessment activity 2.1, page 43**		
P2 demonstrate use of practical skills, techniques and tactics appropriate for one individual sport **See Assessment activity 2.1, page 43**	**M1** describe use of tactics appropriate for one team and one individual sport **See Assessment activity 2.1, page 43**	**D1** justify use of tactics appropriate for one team and one individual sport, identifying areas for improvement **See Assessment activity 2.1, page 43**
P3 describe the rules, regulations and scoring systems for one team sport **See Assessment activity 2.2, page 48**		
P4 describe the rules, regulations and scoring systems for one individual sport **See Assessment activity 2.2, page 48**	**M2** assess, using appropriate examples, the rules, regulations and scoring systems for one team and one individual sport **See Assessment activity 2.2, page 48**	
P5 describe the main roles and responsibilities of officials in one team sport **See Assessment activity 2.3, page 55**		
P6 describe the main roles and responsibilities of officials in one individual sport **See Assessment activity 2.3, page 55**		
P7 produce, with teacher support, an observation checklist that could be used to review the sports performance of an individual or a team **See Assessment activity 2.4, page 64**	**M3** independently produce an observation checklist that could be used to review the performance of an individual or a team **See Assessment activity 2.4, page 64**	
P8 use the observation checklist to review the sports performance of an individual or a team, identifying strengths and areas for improvement **See Assessment activity 2.4, page 64**	**M4** explain the strengths and areas for improvement of an individual or a team, in one individual sport or one team sport, justifying recommendations for improvement **See Assessment activity 2.4, page 64**	
P9 use the observation checklist to review own sports performance in an individual sport or team sport, identifying strengths and areas for improvement **See Assessment activity 2.4, page 64**	**M5** explain own strengths and areas for improvement in an individual sport or team sport, providing recommendations for improvement **See Assessment activity 2.4, page 64**	**D2** analyse own strengths and areas for improvement in an individual sport or team sport, justifying recommendations for improvement **See Assessment activity 2.4, page 64**

How you will be assessed

This unit will be assessed by an internal assignment that will be designed and marked by the staff at your centre. Your assessment could be in the form of:

- video recordings of you applying the appropriate skills, techniques and tactics for a selected team and individual sport
- practical log books with recording of your achievements and developments in each sessions
- observation records of your performance as a sports performer in team and individual sports
- video recordings of applying the rules and regulations from one team and one individual sport
- written summaries of the rules, regulations and scoring systems for one team and one individual sport
- observation record sheets
- oral interviews.

Kashif, 16-year-old basketball player

This unit gave me the opportunity to understand what skills and techniques are and how, once you've mastered them, your performance in sport can develop. Through participating in various sports in this unit I also developed more of an awareness about tactics in sports, what they are and how if applied correctly they can impact on success.

I also learnt the importance of performance analysis and how I can develop through reflecting on my own performance and analysing areas of strengths and weaknesses. Through learning more about this process I have now started to properly listen to the feedback of my peers and coaches. I am constantly seeking methods to improve my performance and see this as a personal challenge.

This unit introduced me to the rules and regulations of different sports and the roles of officials. We applied the rules whilst our friends played the sports.

Over to you!
- What are your favourite sports?
- Have you ever had your performance assessed, if so who by?
- Have you ever assessed anyone's performance? How did you go about it?

1 Demonstrate a range of skills, techniques and tactics in selected sports

Warm-up

Team vs individual

Select two sports and identify whether they are team or individual sports.

Make a list of the skills that are required to play each sport. For each sport describe how you score and how you win.

Produce a diagram of the area in which the sport is played, e.g. pitch, court.

Did you know?

The Concise Oxford Dictionary defines sport as, 'An activity involving physical exertion and skill in which an individual or team competes against another or others for entertainment'.

Key term

Team sport – a sport in which more than one player competes towards a set target or goal.

Through completing this unit you may be introduced to a variety of new sports or you may continue with sports which you have played for many years. You will learn about skills, techniques, rules and regulations and how to apply these in each sport you play. You are going to learn about what makes a sport a sport.

The term 'sport' is used for sports such as football, hockey, basketball and tennis but we can play these in different ways. We can play tennis with friends using an imaginary net with each player scoring at the end of each rally, but we could also play tennis in a highly organised competition with strict rules, and umpires applying the rules to each game, scoring each point and judging our performance.

Through completing this unit you are going to be introduced to specific techniques, skills and tactics that will develop your knowledge and possibly your ability to play sports.

Sports can be categorised in different ways but for the purpose of this unit you are required to categorise sports into individual and team sports.

Examples of **team sports** include:

- Association football
- Basketball
- Cricket
- Hockey
- Lacrosse
- Netball
- Rugby (league or union)
- Rounders
- Volleyball
- Wheelchair basketball.

Examples of **individual sports** include:

- Golf
- Trampolining
- Table tennis (singles)
- Archery
- Squash
- Judo
- Cross-country
- Boccia
- Athletics.

1.1 Skills and techniques

Every sport requires specific skills; mastering the application of these skills supports the development of a sports performer. The skills you require depends on the sport you play and in some sports the skills you need will be different. For example, a goalkeeper in netball will require different skills from a goal attack position.

To be successful in sports and master the skills of sports we must have certain abilities. In order to be a good tennis player a sports performer has to have good co-ordination, especially hand-eye co-ordination and high levels of speed. We are often born with these abilities, and our personal characteristics determine which skills we can and cannot master. A skill is learned and not something we can do without coaching, training or observation of others completing the skill. When we are first introduced to a skill it is often difficult to master and takes a lot of physical and mental effort.

Practice can help to develop a skill initially and at this stage a sports performer requires help with completing the skill correctly. As we develop our ability to perform a skill we begin to be able to perform it with very little conscious effort.

In sport we often use the word skilful to identify a quality which a sports performer displays when playing a sport. This can sometimes be confused with performance. A footballer who can complete a volley continually ('keepy uppies') can be seen as skilful but the skills are not a measurement of his ability to play football in a competitive scenario. A skilful player in sport should be someone who makes skills look easy and playing the sport look comfortable. A skilful performer should have mastered the sport and be in the right place to perform the appropriate skill to perfection.

A skilful player is not always a successful sports performer; for some sports the performance of an individual cannot always affect the outcome of the game. In team sports the outcome of a team's performance can depend on the success of both individual and team skills. Individual skills can include a performer's ability to pass, shoot and dribble, whereas team skills may include defending as a team, attacking as a team or the application of set plays in specific situations.

Key term

Individual sport – a sport in which a sole performer competes towards a set goal.

Figure 2.1: What techniques do you use in your preferred sport?

Remember

Think back to when you learned how to tie your shoe lace; at first the skill seemed complex and required lots of different movements and actions whereas now you do it without thought and with little effort.

Can you list three other open skills in hockey?

Different skills

Skills in sport can be categorised into different groups.

Simple skills: a simple skill is something like throwing, catching and striking. A key requirement for mastering these basic skills is the control of body movement – co-ordination. Performers must be able to fully control their body movement to perform a skill correctly.

Complex skills: these skills take a long time to learn because they involve a high level of co-ordination and control. A complex skill is a series of simple skills put together, which require complex movements and much more concentration. An example of a complex skill would be a tumble routine in gymnastics.

Skills can also be categorised as **open or closed skills**. Open skills are skills which are different every time they are carried out; factors that affect an open skill would be other players both on your own team and the opposing team. (For example, a rugby player running with the ball can be affected by the whereabouts of their own players and the position of the opponents, and this will change throughout the game and the players reaction in each situation.) A closed skill is a skill which when repeated is done the same way each time. The movement required to perform a closed skill should remain the same in all environments. An example of a closed skill would be a conversion attempt in rugby.

Through completing this unit you should be introduced to a variety of skills. For each skill you cover in each sport consider which category it would fall into.

Activity: Types of skills

Think about your favourite sport. Make a list of the skills required. Now do the same for a sport you are less familiar with which is in a different category (team or individual) from the sport you selected initially.

- Classify each skill required into simple and complex skills.
- Classify the skills into open and closed skills.

Techniques

A technique is often described as the *way* a sports performer performs a skill. In some sports, players perform the same skills in different ways. When doing this the sports performers are possibly using different techniques to provide the same outcome. For example, Andrew Flintoff and Monty Panesar will have a different bowling technique.

The best way to think about a technique is to consider how the skill can be broken down. A cricket bowling technique can be broken down into different elements: the run up, the positioning of the hands around the ball, the release, and the follow through. Breaking down the technique of each skill can help to develop a sports performer's knowledge and understanding of how to improve their application of each skill. Obviously the technical elements for each component required to complete the skill will be different for each performer, but the components of the skill will remain the same.

Activity: Bowling skills

Participate in a practical activity for cricket – the objective of the session is for everyone in the group to develop their bowling ability.

1. Break down each part of the skill of bowling and, working in small groups, consider methods of improving the technique.

2. Deliver your ideas to the group, demonstrating the effectiveness of your coaching.

3. As a group, discuss how many of your peers developed their skills after learning more about the skill of bowling.

4. Discuss what could be done to improve your own performance as a cricket bowler.

Now consider the techniques required for the skills needed in your sport.

1.2 Tactics

A **tactic** in sport is often a method used by a team or individual to attain the goal of winning. Tactics often depend on the opposition which a team or individual is competing against, the conditions which a sports performer finds themselves in and possibly the timing of the game in

Key term

Tactic – plan taken by sports coaches and sports performers to achieve a desired goal, which in sport is usually winning.

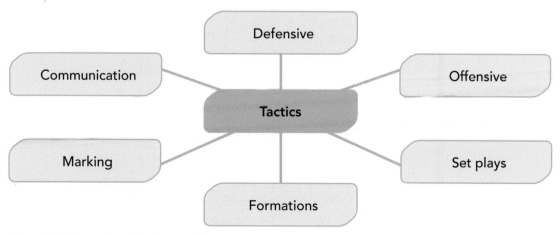

Figure 2.2: Examples of tactics used in sport.

a season. Some tactics are determined before the event starts – these often target a team or performer's weakness. For pre-event tactics, a sports performer must carry out research on the performer or team they are competing against.

An example of how we can apply tactics in team and individual sports is shown in marathon running and cricket. When running a marathon, the athlete may consider each stage of the race and the pace at which they run each stage. If the athlete does not have a strong sprint finish they may plan to increase their pace in the middle section of the race to try to break away from those athletes who have a much stronger sprint finish. However despite planning all these tactics, if on the day of the race the athlete is unable to break away from the pack in the middle of the race they will have to consider other tactics to ensure they do their best to win.

When playing cricket, the fielding team can place a varied amount of pressure on the batsmen at the crease. To do this the captain of the team will have to consider the strengths and weaknesses of the

Activity: Tactics

When Fabio Capello selects a team for an international game, he has to consider his tactical options. All the selections he makes will have to be considered against the following factors:

- strengths and weaknesses of the opposing team
- strengths and weaknesses of the available squad
- preferred positions of the players available
- a balance of players from all positions
- an appropriate balance of left- and right-footed players
- players who can contribute to set plays
- players whose strength is defending
- players who strength is attacking
- players who have equal strengths in defending and attacking.

1. In groups consider a selection of 22 players who you would chose to play in the next England international match. Justify your reasons for selecting each player.

2. For your squad selection pick a starting eleven, and select a formation – 4-4-2 or 4-3-2-1 etc. Justify your formation to the rest of the group and discuss the specific tactics you would ask the team to apply.

3. Consider the tactics for attacking – including set plays and defending, including marking.

4. Research which is England's next international match. (Check this information out on the FA's website. See Hotlinks section on page ii for a link to the website.)

5. After completing the selection, and considering the appropriate tactics, compare your outcome with the rest of the group.

Note This scenario can be changed and adapted to any national team manager for any sport.

batsman. The captain will then decide on the method of his attack. Some batsmen can play certain bowlers better than others so if a batsman is having success against an off-spin bowler the captain may change the bowler for the following over for a fast-paced swing bowler. A batsman may be more confident playing shorts at certain areas on the pitch. A captain may have a chat with his bowlers and change the location where they bowl to the batsman. Fielding positions may also change depending on where the bowler is bowling to and where the batsman's strengths are. The captain may also play to the strengths of his team, placing fielders in appropriate positions for their ability and plan a bowling attack around the team's strengths. In the final over of the game, if the batting team get a few runs the captain may also change the fielding positions of the full team to place pressure on the batsmen.

The main factors that will affect the application of tactics in team and individual sports are:

- attacking and defending
- the situation in the game – whether you are winning or losing
- your own/team's strengths – what parts of the race/game are you stronger in and which parts of the game are your own/team's weaknesses?
- your opponents' strengths and weaknesses.

The positioning of the fielders is one tactic that could be used to put pressure on the batsman. What else could be done?

Recording evidence

Throughout your practical performance in team and individual sports you should record your development. The methods that you use to keep a record may take different forms. The simplest method would be a written diary in which you record the skills, techniques and tactics covered in each session. You should use your diary to record your personal achievements and to record the specific areas of the sports you participate in for this unit which you think you need to develop and improve. When you select an area for improvement in one of your sports, consider the methods you would take to develop this element of the sport and include this in your diary. Keeping a practical diary will develop your understanding of the sport and highlight the areas in which you require development.

The other methods of recording your practical involvement in team and individual sports are:

- a video diary
- an audio log of your involvement (blog or podcast)
- obtaining feedback in the form of observation records and witness statements from your assessor, identifying your involvement in each session
- obtaining feedback in the form of observation records and witness statements from your peers identifying your involvement in each session.

Remember

In every session in which you participate you will be introduced to a new skill, technique and/or tactic, so make sure you update your diary for each session. At the end of the delivery of each sport you should have covered all skills and techniques required in the sport and some tactical considerations – these will be checked in your diaries – so keep them up to date!

Below is an example of a logbook that was completed by a student after a volleyball session.

Week One

Aims of the session: Introduction to the set and the ready position in volleyball.
Technical practices completed today: Ready position and set

Practice 1: Ready position

Outline of practice	Key technical requirements of practice
We paired off and got in the 'ready' position. Our coach told us to be ready to bounce. The aim of the practice was for each of us to try to touch our partner's knee with one hand – if we were in the correct position we could move away quickly and counteract the movement by touching their knee. The practice required us to be in the correct position and worked on our reaction time. After the practice we discussed the importance of being in the set position at all times when we did not have possession of the ball in volleyball.	The ready position is important in volleyball to ensure the player is ready to play a variety of shots and be ready to jump at any time. The position requires a sports performer to have their knees bent and their arms by their side to enable the player to move into any of the positions required to play any of the shots (set, dig, block). Also, having bent knees enables the player to jump if required.

Practice 2: The set

Outline of practice	Key technical requirements of practice
We starting with catching the ball above our heads using the 'W' hand position. Then we threw the ball in the air keeping our hands in the same direction as the ball travelled. We had to try to control the follow-through to get height. This gives you more time to decide what shot to play in a game. Then we progressed onto throwing the ball up in the air and carrying out a set using the W position and the follow through. Then we worked in groups setting the ball, initially to a partner and then around in a group of three. Our teacher said this demonstrated control and direction.	Start position: ready to bounce (ready position). Assess flight of ball – if possible our teacher said always set as this is the easiest shot to carry out. Position body – align body with the flight of the ball – always keep an eye on the ball. Get arms ready to set the ball – W position, arms above head with elbows bent. When ball lands in hands, extend elbows fully connecting the fingertips with the ball and pushing through the ball, leaving fingers fully extended in the direction the ball travelled. Be prepared to receive the ball again, but the player who carries out a volley can't re-hit the ball until another player on the team has touched the ball. Each team has only three hits when the ball comes into their half of the court.

How could the skills/techniques/tactics practised in the session be applied to a game situation?

Ready position – when a player does not have possession of the ball they should be in the ready position in case they have to play any of the required shots in volleyball

The set – this is the easiest shot to apply in volleyball and a player should use this whenever possible. A set is often used to set up a smash or move the ball up the court towards the net by passing the ball to another player.

In today's session we discussed methods of attacking in volleyball, we looked at using the three hits on our side of the court effectively to eventually set for a smash. We discussed the importance of getting the ball as high as possible on the first return shot, this should then provide an opportunity for one of the outside setters to set a smash opportunity for a hitter. I think this tactic is very effective in volleyball, however at the moment I need to work on the control and application of my sets to enhance the effectiveness of this tactic.

Do you feel that you have improved/not improved following the session?

Yes, I am now more aware of what stance to use in volleyball. I feel that through using the ready position my reactions and body are much more prepared for the variety of shots. I also feel that learning how to apply the set correctly has improved my performance. I now think about the position of my hands and body before carrying out a volley.

What were your strengths and weaknesses during the session?

I have developed my knowledge about the skills covered in the session, however, I feel that during a match I am still not getting onto the ready position at all times. I feel as if my strength today was my application of the set. I used it effectively throughout the drills and supported my team in the competition by using this skill effectively.

How did your strengths and weaknesses affect your performance during the game situation?

I was not in the ready position at all times, and I was caught out a couple of times, which cost my team a number of points. However, I used the set effectively to control the play and set the front line player on court to dig, which helped my team to win the final match.

Figure 2.3: Example of a student's logbook.

Assessment activity 2.1 P1 P2 M1 D1

1. Demonstrate use of practical skills, techniques and tactics appropriate for one team sport. **P1**

2. Demonstrate use of practical skills, techniques and tactics appropriate for one individual sport. **P2**

3. Describe how appropriate tactics are used in one team and one individual sport. **M1**

4. Justify the use of tactics for one team and one individual sport, and identify areas for improvement. **D1**

Grading tips

In order to meet the requirements of P1 and P2:

- Ensure that you visually record your application of various skills.
- Ask your teacher to keep a record of all of your practical achievements.
- Complete a practical diary that explains each of your practical achievements.

To meet the requirements of M1:

- Look back over your practical diaries and list all of the tactics used in each sport.
- Describe each tactic and how it can be applied in each sport successfully.

To meet the requirements of D1:

- Discuss which you think are the most effective tactics in each sport, saying why you think this to be the case.

PLTS

When playing as part of a team for your team sport you will develop your skills as a **team worker**.

Functional skills

Through completing a practical logbook for each practical session, and describing the tactics applied in each sport, you should develop your **English** skills in writing.

2 Know the rules, regulations and scoring systems of selected sports

2.1 Rules and regulations

All sports have rules and regulations which are governed by a national governing body. These rules and regulations determine the format of the game.

National governing bodies (NGBs) are responsible for organising their own sport in the UK. Their role is to ensure that the rules and regulations are applied and observed by officials, clubs and players in organised competition. The rules, laws and regulations are determined by the international governing bodies.

NGBs work closely with international governing bodies to ensure that the rules, structure and development of the sport are managed appropriately. In the past ten years a number of sports have undertaken some changes to the rules and regulations to make the sport more entertaining for the spectators. For example, in 2006 the Badminton World Federation adapted the method of scoring to ensure that for every rally won a point is awarded to the player or players who win the rally. In most sports rules and regulations are updated regularly, and it is the responsibility of everybody involved in a sport to have a thorough knowledge of these changes.

Table 2.1: Different sports have different national governing bodies.

Sport	National governing body
Association Football	The Football Association
Tennis	Lawn Tennis Association
Rugby union	The Rugby Football Union
Badminton	The Badminton Association of England
Athletics	UK Athletics
Rugby league	The Rugby Football League
Basketball	The English Basketball Association

Every sport must have a national governing body; if your sport is not listed in the table above, research it and add it to a table for your classroom.

Unwritten rules

As well as written rules there are also underpinning values associated with sport. These values, known as the unwritten rules, contribute towards fair play.

The concept of fair play includes:

- respect towards other sports performers
- respect towards coaches and spectators
- respect towards officials
- playing within the rules of the sport
- equality for all sports performers.

Applying fair play in sport, and promoting the concept of fair play at all levels, can help to reduce some of the negative elements of sport, such as cheating, gamesmanship, doping, violence, verbal abuse and physical abuse.

An example of how a sport has implemented these rules is the 'Respect' campaign. Respect was the FA's programme to address unacceptable behaviour in football – both on and off the pitch. This started in August 2008 and was aimed at players at all levels. This campaign included respect from parents and coaches towards officials and opposing sports performers and for players towards team members, opposing players and referees. The FA provided clubs at all levels of the game with resources to support this campaign and educate performers, spectators, club coaches and officials about the importance of respecting everyone through sport.

Players and participants

Different sports have different numbers of players participating in competitive situations. Sports like golf, tennis, gymnastics and athletics are usually considered individual sports (with some exceptions – e.g. doubles in tennis, relays in athletics). Other sports, such as rugby union, hockey, basketball and American football, are team sports. These sports have restrictions on the numbers of players allowed in a competitive situation at any one time.

What team sports are you involved with? How many people can be on the pitch, and in the whole team?

Activity: Sports teams

Complete the following table:

Sport	Number of players
Hockey	
Rugby Union	
Rugby League	
Lacrosse	
Basketball	
Water polo	

Playing space and facilities

One of the key regulations in sport is the court or pitch layout. It is up to the governing bodies to agree on the dimensions of the court or pitch in order for a competitive game to take place. Some sports are more flexible on the size of the playing area and its surface, whereas other sports are very strict regarding these dimensions. For example FINA (international Swimming Federation) state that all international competitions use a 50 metre Olympic style pool, whereas the FIFA (international football federation) state that football can be played on slightly different sized pitches as long as they are between 90m and 120m long and 45m and 90m wide, although the goals must be of a standard size.

Some NGBs will also dictate the surface types on which a sport can be played. Some sports can be played both inside and outside, and the requirements of the types of surfaces may differ. For example tennis can be played on a variety of surfaces in a variety of environments (both indoors and outdoors), however certain surfaces are generally only suitable for outdoor competitions, such as tennis and clay, whereas other surfaces are played both indoors and outdoors, e.g. hard court.

As with all major rules and regulations, players and officials must be aware of the rules regarding playing space and surfaces. It is the responsibility of the official to ensure that the facility where a sport is played is suitable for performance before the sport or event takes place. This is to safeguard the safety of players, spectators and officials.

Equipment

In some sports performers have to wear specific protective equipment. Often it is a requirement to wear specific equipment in sport to reduce or prevent injury; for example, footballers must wear shin pads. Sometimes the equipment requirements are to reduce injury to other players. In football, an official might consider the studs to be too long or too sharp and can ask for them to be removed.

Health and safety

Many rules and regulations have evolved to prevent the risk of injuries to sports performers who participate in competitions. In football the rule to wear protective shin pads at all times was introduced to reduce the number of injuries to footballers' lower legs. In addition to the requirements to wear protective clothing in sport, a number of other rules and regulations have been introduced to support the health and safety of sports performers.

Time

Most team sports have a restriction on the length of a competition. The time is often divided into equal periods. For example, rugby union and rugby league split the time dedicated to a competitive match for adults into two halves of 40 minutes each, whilst netball is played in four 15-minute quarters. This time is given to sports to provide teams with sufficient time to attempt to out-score the opposing team. Using the example of rugby union the team who has scored those points (from a combination of methods including tries, conversions and drop goals) will win the game, whilst in netball the team who scores the most goals wins.

For some sports there is an option to stop the clock and discuss tactics and make alterations, whereas in other sports the only time that tactical instructions can be given to the whole team is during the allocated breaks. An example of when a sport can stop the time, to provide players with tactical instructions and make changes, is in basketball when each team is given a number of opportunities to stop the clock and provide the team with appropriate instructions for a short period of time.

In certain sports competitions, when scores are even at the end of 'normal' time, extra time is played to determine a winner. If after extra time there is no clear winner some sports have a final method of concluding the match. For example, penalties are used in football when two teams are still tying after the completion of extra time. It is the responsibility of the tournament organisers with agreement of the international, national or regional governing body (as appropriate) to agree the method in which a final result will be reached.

For other sports, a winner can be confirmed before the allocated time has run out. A test match in cricket is allocated five full days; however each side is only given two innings each. So if one team scores five hundred runs in one innings after one day and on the second day the other team is bowled out for 50 and instructed to follow on and is bowled out again for 150 on the same day, the match is over as the team which bat first has won the fixture.

2.2 Scoring systems

Every sport has a different method of scoring. In most games the performer(s) who score the most points within a designated time period or through reaching a certain number of points is the winner; the main exception to this is golf, where the winner is the player who hits the lowest number of shots.

The methods of scoring for most games may involve invading an opponent's territory and targeting a specific goal, or target area. In some sports the number of points awarded may differ. In cricket, six runs are awarded for hitting the ball over the boundary, whereas four runs are awarded when the ball crosses the boundary without the ball bouncing before crossing the boundary. In most racket sports players are awarded points for hitting an object into the opponent's court.

Some sports require different methods of scoring, such as athletics where a performer is measured on times, distances and heights. Gymnastics events are scored using a subjective scoring method where performances are assessed against the perfect model through the eyes of judges.

The method of victory in sport is determined by what a sports performer has to do in order to win. This may be the number of points scored in a set period of time, or the fastest time over a certain distance. Every sport has clear rules which determine rules of victory. As a sport performer you must be aware of the requirements for winning, although it is also important to recognise that winning is not everything in sport.

How many different ways of scoring in sport can you think of?

BTEC Assessment activity 2.2 P3 P4 M2

1. Describe the rules, regulations and scoring systems for one team sport. **P3**
2. Describe the rules, regulations and scoring systems for one individual sport. **P4**
3. Assess, using appropriate examples, the rules, regulations and scoring systems for one team and one individual sport. **M2**

Grading tips

Include in your description of the rules and regulations of each sport for P3, P4:

- The major rules of each sport (applied by the NGB).
- The number of players required to compete in each sport.
- The required equipment for each sport (for participants and for general play).
- The dimensions and layout of the environment.
- The required facilities and playing surfaces.
- The time allocated to competition for each sport.
- The scoring systems for each sport.
- The requirements for victory in each sport.

To attain M2 you must consider the effectiveness of the rules and regulations for each sport – consider what rules you would implement to improve the game or make the game more exciting.

3 Roles and responsibilities of officials in selected sports

3.1 Roles

Officials

Different sports have different types of official, each with their own roles and responsibilities. Some sports require referees, umpires, judges, starters and timekeepers, and each official has clear roles and responsibilities regarding the application of the rules and regulations as stated by the governing body.

Umpires

Cricket uses umpires. Traditionally there will be two umpires per cricket match and they are in charge of all decisions made on the pitch. The umpires ensure that the game is played in accordance with the laws of cricket. The umpire makes the decisions regarding whether or not a batsman is out and whether a shot has been hit for four or six runs. The umpire uses signals to communicate with the scorers to ensure that the correct decisions have been recorded. It is important that the decisions made by the umpires are clearly communicated to the scorer. More recently for televised county and international matches the English Cricket Board and International Cricket Board have introduced a third umpire. The third umpire has been implemented to support the on-field umpires when making controversial decisions such as LBW (leg before wicket) decisions and controversial catches. The third umpire has access to television replays and this is used to support the on-field umpires and make appropriate judgements.

Activity: Off-the-field officials

Numerous sports have introduced off-the-field of play officials to support on-field officials. Do you think this has been effective? In your group discuss the advantages and disadvantages of off-the-field of play officials.

Referees

The role of referee is to ensure that all the laws of the game are followed by sports performers. The referee can apply the rules on the field of play, although a referee can manage the game from off the field of play. The referee makes decisions regarding the application of the laws of the sport.

An example of a referee who is on the field of play, and constantly making decisions that affect the end result, is a rugby referee. An example of a referee who is off the field of play is a tennis referee.

Judges

Sports such as gymnastics and boxing use judges to officiate. For gymnastics, the judge observes the performance of the athlete and makes a judgement regarding the demonstration of the skill or technique. The judgement is made against a criterion which is set against a perfect model of the skill/technique. A boxing judge will observe the performance of a boxer competing in a ring and award points for every clean punch connected or, at the end of each round, award one of the boxers the round. The judge makes decision from observations.

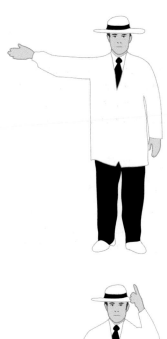

Figure 2.4: Examples of hand signals that a cricket umpire uses. Think of hand signals that officials from other sports use to communicate with other officials or spectators.

Judges can be found in other sports to make judgements on performance and determine whether a sports performer wins or not.

Starters

In sports like swimming and athletics the starter plays a vital role. It is the starter who tells the participants in a race when to start. The starter is in charge of monitoring false starts and sanctioning performers when the starting rules are broken by sports performers. In many sports the starter has the responsibility to verbally communicate with the performers and prepare them for the start of the race. An example of this would be the method of communication used by an athletic starter who will communicate, 'on your marks, get set' and then either shoot a pistol or blow a starter's horn.

In other sports a starter is given the role to tell on-field officials when play should begin; for example, a starter for a rugby match – the starter will blow a horn to ensure that the match referee knows when to start the game.

Timekeepers

Some sports have a restriction on the amount of time allocated to a match or competitive situation. For some sports there are official timekeepers to record the duration of the game and to start and stop the clock at specific points in the game. For some sports it is a requirement that every time the ball is out of play, or that play stops, time is stopped and not started again until play resumes. The timekeeper has the sole responsibility to stop and start the clock. It can also be the role of the timekeeper to inform the sports performers and on-field officials of any breaks in play and when the sport has concluded. This may require signalling to the on-the-field officials or by blowing a whistle or a horn to indicate the end of time allocated to parts of the game or the full game.

3.2 Responsibilities of officials

For each official in each sport there are defined responsibilities or obligations. These depend on a number of factors. These factors have to be learnt and understood by those taking the role of an official.

Appearance

For most sports it is a requirement that an official wears a specific uniform and should dress appropriately in their role. This uniform is often provided to differentiate the official from the players or performers and reinforces the importance of the official.

The uniform worn by the official should not clash with the colours of the sports performers. A football referee traditionally wears a black uniform. However if there is a possibility of this clashing with the kit

Figure 2.5: Officials' responsibilities.

of one of the team strips, or the goalkeeper's strip, the official should wear a strip of a different colour.

Effective communication

In some sports there are numerous officials involved in competitive situations and each official must be able to communicate clearly with the others. This may be through verbal or non-verbal communication.

The use of clear communication is important when enforcing the rules or laws of the sport. The official should clearly inform the players about each decision. An official who communicates effectively and confidently gains respect from sports performers. Those who are new to officiating in a specific sport should practice and develop their communication skills, to ensure that they can communicate openly and effectively when officiating in competitive situations. An official can reduce confrontation between officials, players, coaches and spectators by communicating effectively.

In some sports a referee is provided with a whistle which should be used by the official to control the game and as a method of controlling the performers and applying the rules. In some instances specific sanctions may require specific whistle usage. An official must learn how to use a whistle appropriately and confidently in a competitive situation to show control and knowledge of the rules and regulations of the sport.

Appropriate interpretation and application of the rules

One of the main responsibilities of an official in any sport is the ability to apply the rules and regulations appropriately. It is a requirement of all officials to observe participation of the sport and, if they spot that the rules have been broken, they must take appropriate action and sanctions as stated with the laws of the sport. When making these decisions an official needs to be in the best position possible, with the clearest view.

One of the roles of an assistant referee in football is to identify when a player is offside. Therefore the linesman must constantly ensure that they are in the correct position to view any possible offsides that could be committed by the attacking team. When the linesman spots an offside they must clearly signal that an attacking player is in an offside position and communicate this to the referee and the performers on the field of play.

When making any decisions it is important that the official is clear about the rules and understands what the sanctions are for when the rules are broken. Officials have to be confident in their decisions and stand by them. In a few sports, officials have an opportunity to seek support from television replays; but this is often only offered in elite competitions for elite officials.

Equipment

It may be a requirement for officials to be equipped with specific kit in order to carry out their role. This may be in addition to the uniform which officials are required to wear in some sports. If equipment is required to support the rules and regulations of the sport, it is each official's responsibility to bring the appropriate equipment to each competition/game. For example a netball umpire will need to come to a game equipped with appropriate kit, a whistle, a score card, a stopwatch, a coin and a pen.

Fitness

For some sports, officials need to be on the field of play and keep up with the play to ensure that they are close at hand to make decisions and sanction performers as necessary. This will require a high level of fitness for some sports as play can be very fast and the official may even do more running than some of the players on the pitch. For some of these sports the national governing bodies have made it a requirement to assess the fitness of officials in order to ensure that they have an appropriate level of fitness. In other sports, due to the impossibility of keeping up with the sports performers, officials will take a less active role. In rugby league, a match referee needs a high level of physical fitness to keep up with play in order to make appropriate judgements.

Qualifications

For some sports, the official must hold a recognised officiating qualification in order to officiate. All national governing bodies provide training and qualifications to educate and develop existing officials. This is often the case to ensure that the game is played within the laws stated but also to ensure that the sport is carried out in a safe and appropriate environment.

Activity: Officiating courses

For one team sport and one individual sport of your choice, visit the national governing body website, and carry out some research into officiating courses for each sport (this will often be found under education). Make a list of the different courses and the one which you feel would be most appropriate for you.

Control of players

An official will demonstrate control of the sports performers and ensure that they are safe during the competitive situation of the sport by applying the regulations correctly and confidently. Officials should also deal with injuries when appropriate and, if required, stop the competition to allow the sports performer to obtain medical treatment. In some sports, if the laws are broken because of serious foul play the officials have the power to discipline the players through sending the performers off the field of play. Control can also be applied through effective communication. In some sports officials have other forms of stopping and starting play, for example using whistles and starter's pistols. When players hear these noises they are aware that a rule has been broken and that performance should stop. For example, in hockey when a whistle has been blown by an umpire all players should stop playing and wait to hear the decision made by the official.

When play has stopped, officials should clearly verbally communicate – and when necessary signal – to the performers, spectators and coaches the rule which has been broken and the sanction that is to be carried out.

Accountability to spectators

When officiating, it is obvious that an official must be fair and not display bias towards a sports performer or team. Spectators who observe sports often come to watch a particular individual or team

When you next watch a sports event, look out for the techniques the official uses to maintain control.

and in these situations the official needs to demonstrate an unbiased opinion at all times. An official should apply the rules and laws of sport equally to all competitors and the methods of communication used to display which laws and rules have been broken must be clear.

Health and safety

A major responsibility for officials in sport is to ensure that every event is carried out with the safety of all sports performers, coaches and spectators as paramount. An official has the responsibility to carry out safety checks before the competition. These checks should include equipment checks, ensuring that the equipment that is required for the sport is suitable and that there is no chance of injury to sports performers.

Officials must also check the facility to ensure that the area where the competition is going to take place is safe. An official may carry out a risk assessment to reduce the risks to performers. A risk assessment might need to be carried out a couple of days in advance. Other checks may include area checks, just before the event, to ensure the area is safe and that there are no hazards like glass, standing water, or obstacles that may cause injury. If an official completes a safety check prior to a competitive situation and feels that the facility is unsafe then they have the authority to cancel the competition. The official could delay the start of the competition or game until the hazards have been removed or repaired.

Before a competitive situation or game an official should check the performers to make sure they are safe to start the sport. These pre-match checks should ensure that sports performers are wearing the appropriate equipment required to compete in the selected sport. In many sports it is a requirement that jewellery is removed and any other items of clothing that may be deemed dangerous. The officials of a sport should check that all equipment worn by sports performers is in accordance with the rules and regulations. These checks are not just for the safety of the individual performer but also for performers competing against them.

It is the responsibility of officials to monitor the health and safety of sports performers at all times. If an official feels that sports performers are under threat of injury or illness they have the responsibility to stop play and resolve the health and safety hazards. Hazards which could occur during play may include: damage to equipment during the competitive situation, the facility being made unsafe due to the weather or players becoming injured. In any of these instances, an official will have to assess the risk to the sport performer(s) and make a decision. The ultimate priority at all times is the safety of the sports performers; so if appropriate the official may have to abandon the competitive situation or game if they feel that there is no method of reducing the risk of injury to the sports performers. Before, during and after a sports event an official needs to assess the safety of:

- equipment
- facilities
- players.

Fair play

Earlier in this chapter we looked at the concept of fair play and how it is promoted through sport. Officials should promote fair play and follow the concept of fair play by respecting the sports performers who they are officiating, respecting the coaches and spectators observing the sport, applying the rules fairly and consistently to both teams, and treating all people involved in the sport equally.

Use of technology

As technology has developed in recent years, more sports have moved towards using technology to apply their laws consistently. For some, the introduction of technology is still under debate. However, other sports have embraced the use of technology to support officials in games who are on the field of play and require a second opinion. For these sports the introduction of technology has developed a further role. For example, due to technological advances in sport, cricket has introduced the third umpire; and rugby league has introduced a video referee, as has rugby union. The role of these officials is to assess the live situations observed by the officials on the field of play; they then make judgements through watching video replays over and over again and apply the advice of the officials on the field of play or the appropriate sanction in accordance with the laws of the sport.

BTEC Assessment activity 2.3 P5 P6

1. Describe the main roles and responsibilities of officials in one team sport. **P5**
2. Describe the main roles and responsibilities of officials in one individual sport. **P6**

Grading tips

In order to meet the requirements of P5 and P6 you have to:

- Make a list of all the officials in one team and one individual sport.
- Describe the responsibilities of each official involved in officiating each sport.

 PLTS

Researching the roles and responsibilities of different officials from team and individual sports will develop your skills as an **independent enquirer**.

 Functional skills

Through completing a written summary of the roles and responsibilities of different officials from one team and one individual sport you should develop your **English** skills in writing.

Even the world number one golfer, Tiger Woods, constantly reviews his own performance. The ultimate professional is always seeking new methods to improve their own performance.

4 Review the sports performance of an individual or team

In this section you will be required to review the sports performance of others who participate in sport and you will need to carry out an analysis of your own performance in either a team or individual sport.

As a sports performer you must develop the ability to assess your own performance. It is easy to assess the performance of others and to pick out their strengths and areas for improvement; however we often struggle to do this for ourselves. If we have the ability to analyse our own performance we can develop the areas which we need to improve and build on our strengths. Even those sports performers who are at the top of the game constantly seek to develop and improve.

Activity: Training and development

Discuss with your group the methods in which your coach assesses your performance in your sport. In groups discuss the training you have had as a sports performer to develop your skills and techniques.

4.1 Performance

Before you assess your performance in sport you must understand what it is you are measuring. Earlier in this unit different skills and techniques for different sports were examined. For example, rugby requires sports performers to be able to pass and catch – which are similar to those skills required in netball; however other skills required make these sports a world apart. Before analysing performance you need to be aware of the skills required for the sport and their correct application of these.

Sports performers who are reflective in their performance need to have the knowledge of the correct technique of each specific skill in their sport. The perfect model to compare our own performance of skills and techniques often comes from elite athletes in the sport in which we compete. If you were to analyse a footballer taking a free kick you will assess its outcome, possibly against a successful free kick taken by Cristiano Ronaldo or David Beckham and the technique which they used to create this perfect model.

Assessment

When assessing techniques and skills it can be important to break down the technique in order to assess each component. Many skills have a clear beginning and end; it is the part in-between that is difficult to assess.

When assessing performance and application of skills and techniques you should try to look at:

* the sports performer's starting position
* when appropriate the follow-through used
* the body position, before, during and after a skill
* the positioning of feet at each stage – footwork
* the end result.

You can also use statistics and data to measure the effectiveness of a performance. This may include the number of points or goals scored in a game, how fast you run, or swim, or how high or long you jump or throw. At elite level, in some sports, statistics are kept recording the success of every skill completed. For example, in hockey at an elite level every pass completed is recorded against every pass not completed, every tackle made is recorded against every tackle missed; at the end of the game each player will have a set of statistics which is used to analyse their performance. This information can be used to assess strengths and weaknesses of performance.

Performance is often measured based on how many games or competitions are won. This can be an effective way of measuring performance; however there can be a number of disadvantages to this method. When measuring your own performance against success you may not consider the level of those who you are competing against. For example, if an opponent is less able than yourself this may not be a good measure of your performance. This can also mean that you get driven by results rather than the correct application of the skill and technique and maximising skill levels within the sport played.

Analysis

There are a variety of methods to assess the performance of another player or team, including:

* observing them play to identify **strengths** and areas of **weakness**
* observing the performers and completing a checklist to monitor the ability of the player or team
* taking a video recording of a team or individual performing and then analysing the performance with the individual and their coach, or possibly the whole team.

Observation checklist

An observation checklist is used by many sports coaches and sports performers to generate a picture of a performer/team's performance. The performance is measured against the components of a top performance from the sport. An observation checklist is a tool to help a

Key terms

Strengths – personal attributes that you may have developed over the course of many years of playing the sport, specific skills, components of fitness that develop your ability to play a sport.

Weaknesses – flaws in your performance, the skills or components of fitness which require developing to enhance your performance.

sports performer to assess his/her own strengths and weaknesses. The information obtained from the checklist can then be used to develop an action plan for development. Before making decisions regarding such action plans sport performers need to discuss their findings with a coach or mentor.

Observation records should be used to prioritise the performance components for the future development of training programmes for sports performers and can also be used to monitor progress towards goals and targets. It is not a good idea for sports performers who are new to carrying out observational analysis to try this without support and guidance from experienced coaches.

The first requirement before completing an observation checklist is to identify the demands of a selected sport. These demands can be placed into four components of performance:

- physical (e.g. coordination, speed)
- technical (e.g. passing, serving)
- tactical (e.g. defending, attacking)
- mental (e.g. concentration and commitment).

If you are completing an observation record, you must have a clear understanding of the requirements for each component of performance for the sport. An example of how you would collate this information is shown in the table below.

Table 2.2: The requirements for each component of performance for a xhockey player.

Mental components	Physical components	Technical components	Tactical components
Motivation	Aerobic endurance	Passing/ receiving	Attacking
Relaxation	Speed	Dribbling	Defending
Control	Flexibility	Shooting	Creating space
Concentration	Agility	Tackling	Understanding the game
Commitment	Co-ordination	Flicking	Positioning
	Reaction time	Goalkeeping	
	Body composition		

When you have identified the key performance components for your sport, you need to assess your own standards (or those of another sports performer or team) against each component. How you assess each component will depend on the environment in which you carry out the observation. It is difficult to assess all components in a competitive environment. It may be the case that you will only carry out assessments on specific components in your observation.

In units 9, 11 and 18, you will examine how to assess fitness and psychological components. For your assessment in this unit you will be required to carry out an assessment of a sports performer or team's technical and tactical ability and the same components for your own performance, in either a team or individual sport.

The next stage will be to develop the checklist and for this you will have to consider an effective method of assessing each component of performance. This depends on whether you are assessing a team or an individual. You may choose to observe the full competition and make an overall judgement for each component of performance after the event for the player/team. This is called **performance profiling**. When using this method you need to have a clear scale that indicates the levels of performance you are measuring. If you use a 10-point scale, 1 on the scale may be unsuccessful application of the skill, technique or tactic whereas 10 may be faultless application of the skill, technique or tactic. Therefore if a performer scores 5 his application of the skill in question would be judged as average. Alternatively you may choose to complete a tally chart for the full duration of the competition to identify successful application of each component; you can then draw conclusions from the results obtained after the observation.

Below is an example of a performance profile that could be used as an observation checklist to assess the overall performance of each component of technical and tactical performance of a hockey player during competition.

Observation of Holly Benjamin – Hockey Player for Orkney Rangers											
Scale (1 limited ability – 10 perfect execution)	1	2	3	4	5	6	7	8	9	10	Comments
Technical components											
Passing/receiving						✓					
Dribbling					✓						
Shooting							✓				
Tackling			✓								
Flicking		✓									
Tactical components											
Attacking							✓				
Defending			✓								
Creating space					✓						
Understanding the game					✓						
Positioning					✓						

Figure 2.6: Example of a performance profile.

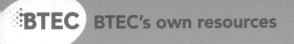

Here is an example of a tally chart observation checklist that can be used to observe the effectiveness of a hockey team.

Orkney Rangers Hockey Club – Match A	
Goals scored	II
Goals conceded	III
Technical components	
Completed passes (pass is received by a player from same team)	IIII IIII IIII
Uncompleted passes (pass in intercepted or is hit out of play)	IIII IIII IIII IIII IIII
Successful dribbles (player dribbles past a defender or moves into space effectively with the use of a dribble)	IIII IIII II
Unsuccessful dribbles (player attempts a dribble and is tackled before beating any players)	IIII
Shots on target (forces a save or scores a goal)	IIII
Shots off target (a clear attempt at a shot which is off the target of the goal)	IIII
Tackles completed (player successful wins the ball from the attacker whilst attacker attempts to dribble past the defender)	IIII IIII IIII III
Missed tackles (an attempt at a tackle that has resulted in the attacker passing the defender)	II
Successful flicks (a flick that has reached a player from the same team without the opposing team intercepting)	IIII III
Unsuccessful flicks (a flick that is intercepted or that does not reach a player from the same team)	IIII IIII
Tactical components	
Attacking	
Entries into the attacking third	IIII IIII IIII
Goals scored in open play	I
Number of short corners won	IIII II
Number of short corners converted in goals	I
Number of long corners won	IIII
Number of successful long corners (resulted in a shot on target at goal)	0
Defending	
Number of times defending their own third	IIII IIII IIII IIII
Goals conceded from open play	0
Number of short corners conceded	IIII III
Number of short corners successful defended (no goal scored)	IIII I
Number of long corners conceded	IIII III
Number of successful long corners defended	IIII II
Number of fouls conceded in own half	IIII
Number of penalties conceded	0

Figure 2.7: Example of a tally chart observation.

Activity: Strengths and weaknesses

Using the results from the two charts above, provide Holly with advice about her strengths and areas of weaknesses after the completion of the performance profile by the observer. Provide the team with support regarding their strengths and the team's areas of weakness after the completion of the tally chart by the observer. In your group discuss what could make these results less valid.

After completing the observation checklist the observer should then be ready to make judgements regarding the strengths and areas of weakness of the performer. Gathering the information and making the evaluations in the next process after the observation, the information collated must be interpreted and judgements made. When forming judgements you are giving your opinion on what you have seen as the observer; that is why it is important that when learning about the process of observation you seek the support of experienced coaches who may have more knowledge about the sport and the requirements of each performance components.

If a thorough observation has taken place the observer will also be able to comment on the following components of performance:

- respect towards other performers
- respect towards officials
- knowledge of the rules and regulations of the sport
- communication skills
- personal preparation for the competition
- an individual's contribution to the team (if appropriate).

Improvements

It is common practice for sports performers to want to develop their weaknesses and enhance their strengths to maximise their performance in a sport. An observation analysis gives a sports performer a basis on which to start this development. The analysis should provide the performer with specific areas where their performance may need development.

This development should not be conducted without support. All sports performers require support from experienced sports coaches, and to improve in any sport performers should seek support from these coaches and leaders. Sports performers may produce a development plan that each targets a specific area of weakness identified for their performance.

Areas of performance that need to improve ought to be prioritised. For example, if a striker in football identified that his weaknesses are heading, shooting and tackling, he may prioritise the improvement of the skills which are more appropriate for his position (heading and

Look at the observation sheet you created. Have you been impartial and fair in your notes?

shooting) and the other skill may be something which he may develop at a later stage.

Goal setting

A goal is an aim that you wish to achieve. For athletes, goals are the structure around which training programmes are developed to ensure they remain focused and motivated. When competing in a team, individuals will have their own goals, and the team will also have goals which will require individuals to work together – and this is an important part of the development of team spirit and team development. For example, at the start of the season a football team which is newly promoted to the Premier League may have a goal to finish outside the bottom three. To meet these targets the goalkeeper of the team may set a season goal not to concede more than 50 goals, and a striker at the club may have a target to score more than 15 goals in the league. If the targets of the players are met then it may be that the team goal can be achieved.

Goals are related to ability and every performer's goals will be different. Goals are set which generally fall into three categories:

Outcome goals are affected by the performance of the individual and their opponents:

- winning a race
- winning a medal
- making a final
- gaining selection for a team.

Performance goals focus on the quality of the performance:

- time
- height
- distance
- number of goals/points in a game
- number of goals/points in a season.

Process goals refer to an element of performance:

- skill
- technique
- application of tactics
- fitness.

The goal-setting process can provide a structure for improvement if a performer works with experienced coaches and instructors to set short- and long-term goals. When setting goals sports performers should use the SMARTER method of setting goals to ensure that the goals set are attainable.

All goals should be SMARTER:

- **S**pecific – avoid being unclear, make the target as precise and detailed as possible
- **M**easurable – define a method of measuring the success of the sports performer – set achievement targets – what by when?
- **A**chievable – goals should be able to be attained within a set period of time and should be relevant for the sports performer
- **R**ealistic – appropriate for the sports performer
- **T**imed – ensure you agree a timescale, even if the timescale includes mini-targets for athlete development
- **E**xciting – motivating for the performer
- **R**ecorded – ensure the targets are agreed with the performer and written down, record the progress towards the targets.

Short-term goals should be achieved by a sports performer in the near future (in a day, within a week, or possibly within a few months).

Long-term goals are set with the hope of them been achieved over a longer period of time (one month, one season, five years, or twenty years).

Sports performers need support to help attain these goals. This could come from people who could help with the development of the goals or specific courses which the performer or team could undertake. Performers could also be given specific exercises which they could undertake to attain a specific goal.

The feedback provided to sports performers should tell them who to seek help and advice from in achieving their goals, including:

- sport-specific sports coaches
- fitness instructors
- peer mentors
- teachers
- experienced sports performers
- parents and family
- sports rehabilitation specialists.

An athlete's performance and development are continually assessed and technology can help here. It can be used to analyse sports performance, and include video analysis and programmes like dartfish and candle technology which allow sports performers to slow down the skills and techniques that they carry out in real time. This enables coaches and performers to analyse techniques and help them develop.

A coach or fitness instructor can help you to achieve your goals. What do you need help with?

PLTS

Analysing the performance of an individual or team in this activity will develop your skills as a **reflective learner**.

Functional skills

Through summarising the strengths and weaknesses of an individual or team and identifying the strengths and weaknesses of their performance, you will develop your **English** writing skills.

BTEC **Assessment activity 2.4**

1. Produce an observation checklist that could be used to review the sports performance of an individual or a team from a sport of your choice. **P7** **M3**

2. Using the observation checklist that you produced, review the performance of an individual or team from your selected sport. After you have completed your observation of the performance of an individual or team, identify the strengths and areas for improvement of the performer or team. **P8** Provide recommendations for future development and improvement and justify why you think they are important. **M4**

3. Use your observation checklist to review your own performance in either a team or individual sport. After you have observed your own performance, identify and analyse the strengths of your performance and the areas that you feel require developing and improving. **P9**. Justify the recommendations for future development and improvement and say why you think each of these methods are important for your improvement in your selected sport. **D2**

Grading tips

1. You can ask your teacher for help, but to attain M3 you need to produce the observation checklist independently.

2. In order to achieve the M4 criterion in this task, in addition to the requirements for P8 you need to:
   - explain each of the strengths, and why you identified them to be strengths after your observation
   - explain each area of improvement that you identified, stating why you think the sports performer/team should improve this specific component of their performance.

3. In order to meet the requirements of M5 criterion in this task, in addition to the requirements of P9:
   - explain each of the strengths of your performance after the completion of your observation
   - explain each area which you feel requires developing and improving and provide recommendations for improvement.

Luke Benjamin
Assistant football referee

Luke has recently completed his level 7 referee qualification. Luke's local County Football Association would now like to allocate Luke to an experienced referee, who will act as his mentor for the next season. As part of the mentoring process Luke will have to observe the referee in action for a number of games and then he will be expected to take the role of one of two assistant referees.

The County Football Association promotes this mentor scheme as it believes it protects inexperienced referees from being left to officiate matches until they are deemed experienced and confident enough to do so. All referees are constantly assessed by a panel of highly qualified and experienced referees.

Luke has carried out his observation of his mentor and is more than happy with what he has seen. He believes the referee is very capable and thinks the referee is very knowledgeable and confident to apply the rules correctly. All newly qualified referees are observed by a member of the officiating panel from the County Football Association. Luke will be observed and assessed in his role as an assistant referee. After the observation Luke will be given feedback and informed on what areas he needs to improve upon and then be re-assessed in ten games' time.

Think about it!

To support Luke in his preparation for his first observation, in your group discuss the following points:

- What equipment will Luke have to have with him to prepare for his first game as an assistant referee?
- What laws of Association Football does an assistant referee have to apply?
- What roles will Luke have to carry out and master to impress the observer?
- Where can Luke get support with applying the laws of football?

Just checking

1. Define sport.
2. What is a complex skill?
3. What is an open skill?
4. Give three examples of closed skills.
5. Identify three different tactics used in individual and team sports.
6. Describe how tactics are applied in one sport of your choice.
7. Make a list of ten sports and identify the national governing body for each sport.
8. Identify the officials required to officiate a game of tennis and describe each official's responsibility.
9. Identify two different methods of analysing sports performance.

Assignment tips

- Produce your own observation checklist – do your research, then complete a checklist on a sport you know a lot about.

- KIS – 'Keep It Simple' – do not assess skills and techniques that are very rarely demonstrated in your selected sport; do not make it too hard for yourself.

- When completing your observation records try to record the performance, then you can go over the performance and make sure you have not missed anything.

- Ask a friend, teacher or coach to record your performance in a sport. Do not try to complete an observation record of yourself whilst playing – this is impossible!

- Identify each strength and area for improvement after your observation and write a number of sentences to explain why you made the decision that it was a strength or weakness. Refer back to your observation checklist as appropriate.

- When you are asked to analyse you should select the key points that you have been asked to look at and explain each point – providing reasons for each point and possible impacts.

3 Outdoor and adventurous activities

Outdoor activity offers challenge, excitement, and adventure. There are opportunities to learn new skills, meet new friends and discover a lifelong passion. Outdoor activities are varied and there are now more specialist training centres and multi-activity centres in different areas, meaning there are opportunities for everyone to participate.

However, with more people taking part in outdoor and adventurous activities, the chance of accidents and injuries happening can increase. Therefore it is important to consider the health and safety and precautions that must be taken by participants and training facilities. With due care and proper preparation, outdoor activity can offer a range of benefits to those taking part.

During this unit you will investigate the organisation and provision of various outdoor and adventurous activities and consider health and safety implications. You will look at the environmental impacts of outdoor activities and how to reduce them in order to protect our natural surroundings.

This unit will show you how to review your own performance and that of others, identifying strengths and areas for improvement.

Learning outcomes

After completing this unit you should:
1. know the organisation and provision of outdoor and adventurous activities
2. know health and safety considerations and environmental impacts associated with participation in outdoor and adventurous activities
3. be able to demonstrate techniques and skills associated with selected outdoor and adventurous activities
4. be able to review performance in outdoor and adventurous activities.

Assessment and grading criteria

This table shows you what you must do in order to achieve a pass, merit or distinction grade, and where you can find activities in this book to help you.

To achieve a **pass** grade the evidence must show that the learner is able to:	To achieve a **merit** grade the evidence must show that, in addition to the pass criteria, the learner is able to:	To achieve a **distinction** grade the evidence must show that, in addition to the pass and merit criteria, the learner is able to:
P1 describe the organisation and provision of two outdoor and adventurous activities **See Assessment activity 3.1, page 74**	**M1** compare the organisation and provision of two outdoor and adventurous activities **See Assessment activity 3.1, page 74**	
P2 describe the health and safety considerations associated with participation in two outdoor and adventurous activities **See Assessment activity 3.2, page 78**	**M2** explain health and safety considerations associated with participation in two outdoor and adventurous activities, identifying precautions and actions that can be taken, or used, in relation to them **See Assessment activity 3.2, page 78**	**D1** explain precautions and actions that can be taken, or used, in relation to health and safety considerations associated with participation in two outdoor and adventurous activities **See Assessment activity 3.2, page 78**
P3 produce a risk assessment for a selected outdoor and adventurous activity **See Assessment activity 3.2, page 78**		
P4 describe environmental impacts associated with participation in two outdoor and adventurous activities **See Assessment activity 3.3, page 80**	**M3** explain the environmental impacts associated with participation in two outdoor and adventurous activities, identifying precautions and actions that can be taken, or used, to reduce them **See Assessment activity 3.3, page 80**	**D2** explain precautions and actions that can be taken, or used, to reduce the environmental impacts associated with participation in two outdoor and adventurous activities **See Assessment activity 3.3, page 80**
P5 demonstrate techniques and skills appropriate to two outdoor and adventurous activities **See Assessment activity 3.4, page 87**	**M4** review and justify choice of techniques demonstrated in outdoor and adventurous activities **See Assessment activity 3.4, page 87**	
P6 review the performance of another individual participating in two outdoor and adventurous activities, identifying strengths and areas for improvement **See Assessment activity 3.5, page 90**		
P7 carry out a review of own performance in outdoor and adventurous activities, identifying strengths and areas for improvement **See Assessment activity 3.5, page 90**	**M5** explain identified strengths and areas for improvement in own performance in outdoor and adventurous activities, making recommendations for further development of identified areas for improvement **See Assessment activity 3.5, page 90**	**D3** justify recommendations relating to identified areas for improvement in own performance in outdoor and adventurous activities **See Assessment activity 3.5, page 90**

How you will be assessed

This unit will be assessed by an internal assignment that will be designed and marked by the staff at your centre. Your assessment could be in the form of:

- presentations
- case studies
- practical tasks
- written assignments.

Sam, 15-year-old kayaker

Studying this unit helped me focus on the skills I need to develop so I can get a job in the outdoor adventurous activity industry. I am certain now that I want to pursue a career in this field. I love being outside and active. This really looks like the perfect option for me.

Taking part in the sports was great fun. I learnt loads of new techniques that I hope to put into use in the future. It was also great to watch the instructors. They certainly knew what they were doing and made it really easy to understand what was needed of us. I hope I am able to explain things like that when I eventually teach.

Talking about reviewing our sessions was particularly useful. I found it helpful to look at what I had done well each lesson to give me motivation for next time, as well as what I needed to do to improve and get better.

Over to you

- What part of this unit do you think you will enjoy most?
- Is there anything you feel you may find quite challenging?
- How can you prepare yourself in readiness for the unit assessments?

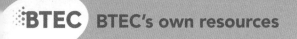
1 Know the organisation and provision of outdoor and adventurous activities

Warm-up

Outdoor activities

Think of an outdoor adventurous activity that you would love to try.

Now in small groups discuss the following.

- What is it about this activity that appeals to you?
- Can you do it locally and if not, why not?
- Do you think that you would be nervous taking part in this activity?

Key term

Outdoor and adventurous activity – physical activity that stimulates and challenges participants and is done outside, often in a hostile environment.

1.1 Organisation of outdoor and adventurous activities

Although the **outdoor and adventurous activities** industry is hugely varied and encompasses a wide range of sports, when you look at the organisation of these different sports it is easy to see a number of similarities within their structure.

National governing bodies

These are often at the top of the organisational chain for outdoor and adventurous activities. They help to regulate standards of quality and safety. Outdoor adventurous activity centres are usually affiliated with one or more governing bodies. However in order to gain the body's stamp of approval it is usual that the centre has to go through a vigorous inspection. National governing bodies have a wide range of responsibilities and roles, some of which are listed below:

- regulating safety and standards
- designing training schemes
- promoting the sport
- organising competitions and events
- providing grass roots opportunity.

Training centres and clubs

Training centres and clubs provide opportunity for training and participation. It is usual for both to be connected to a governing body. Training centres are usually staffed by professional staff paid either for a contracted number of hours or on a casual basis. They are usually commercially focused but may receive financial support from local

The Weymouth and Portland National Sailing Academy was completed in 2008. Which world-class sporting event was it built for?

authorities or other sources. Clubs may stand alone or be connected to a training centre. They may use paid staff but often rely upon volunteers for support.

Training schemes

Training schemes are usually set out by an activity's governing body. A full training scheme will provide structure from the first step into an activity at grass roots to elite performance training. Many activities distinguish between young people and adults and adapt their training schemes to reflect this.

Awards and certification

Participants who successfully complete a course are usually awarded certification. Certification is often issued or regulated by the governing body. Certification may be used to gain insurance, rent equipment from activity centres and act as evidence for those wishing to progress through a training scheme.

Competition

Competition is vital to help promote a sport. It provides a visual spectacle that may inspire those watching to have a go at the activity. Competition takes place at all levels – from junior amateur events right through to professional well-funded championships. This progression is vital to provide competitors with experience and give coaches the opportunity to spot those with potential to compete at an elite level.

Competition may be local, national or even international and organised by centres, clubs, or governing bodies.

Employment

Outdoor adventurous activity offers great opportunity for those wishing to pursue a career. As in any industry there are many jobs in the outdoor industry; for example, management, administrative, maintenance and instructional roles. However those wishing to supervise or teach an activity in a governing body affiliated centre must hold relevant certification. Progression within the outdoor adventurous activity industry is good. It is possible for cadet or volunteer instructors to gain experience from a young age. Qualified instructors may take on additional responsibility as chief or senior instructors supervising those with less experience.

Case study: Surfing

The British Surfing Association is the governing body for surfing in the UK. The BSA:

- regulate standards within their nationwide affiliated centres
- provide a clear structure for training and participation in the form of surf awards
- organise events and competitions at all levels
- promote the sport through their website and publicity.

Affiliated centres must employ BSA-qualified instructors who teach a well-structured scheme of training. Employment provides excellent opportunities to progress and take on further responsibilities.

The benefits of a career as a British Surfing Association instructor are great: lots of time on the beach, plenty of sun and working doing something you love. How would you go about gaining an instructional certificate?

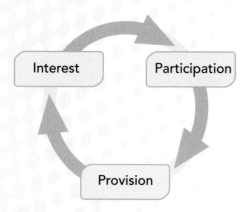

Figure 3.1: Provision, interest and participation are hugely reliant upon one another.

1.2 Provision of outdoor and adventurous activities

The provision of outdoor and adventurous activities is dependent on a number of factors. The provision of a sport determines how easy it is for us as participants to take part in it and thus provision locally and nationally can greatly determine the popularity of an activity. However, it is also important to remember that without demand for a sport it is not likely that provision will be developed and opportunities created for participation.

Local provision

Centres and clubs are responsible for providing local opportunity in an activity. The mainstay of many of these centres and clubs is grass roots participation. Therefore it is vital that they work closely with local councils and schools to promote and provide opportunity within their activity.

'Have a Go' days or taster days are a fantastic way to get people taking part in activities. However without a clear way of following up on an enjoyable experience, extended participation is unlikely to happen. Therefore it is important that schemes such as youth clubs and structured courses are available and easily accessible.

Unfortunately many outdoor adventurous activities are expensive to participate in. In order to make activities available for all, it is common for centres and clubs to apply for subsidies, grants or sponsorship.

National provision

National frameworks are usually reliant upon governing bodies to hold them together. Thanks to governing body certification and standardisation of teaching, it is relatively easy for participants to move between training centres and clubs.

As participants reach higher levels of performance, and elite athletes begin to emerge, it is common for training to take place at national camps or academies. Camps may revolve between venues whereas academies tend to be at a fixed location, but both require participants to travel to attend them.

Influences upon provision

There are many things that can affect the numbers participating in an activity and provision.

- Media portrayal: is an activity given much coverage? Is it shown in a positive way?
- Location: outdoor adventurous activities are likely to be reliant upon the environment. It is often simply not possible to participate in a sport locally if the environment does not allow it. Even with suitable areas available, it is not always accessible to local people. Public transport, for example, may not be in place to provide a suitable service.
- Finance: Many activities are expensive. Those with less disposable income are less likely to spend money on the expensive equipment that is often vital for participation. It may be vital that clubs are in place to offer an affordable opportunity to take part.

Activity: Local provision

Consider an outdoor adventurous activity. What is your local provision like? Is there anything that could be done to increase participation?

PLTS

If you compare similarities and differences of your chosen activities you can develop your skills as a **creative thinker**.

BTEC **Assessment activity 3.1** **P1** **M1**

1. Choose two outdoor adventurous activities that interest you. Describe their organisation and provision. **P1**
2. Now compare the two. Think about similarities and differences within their organisation and provision. **M1**

Grading tips

There are many different types of outdoor adventurous activity.

- Think about their structure, who governs them, to whom they may appeal, and how easy it is to participate in them.
- Choose two that are completely different to make the comparison easier.

2 Health and safety considerations and environmental impacts associated with participation in outdoor and adventurous activities

As with any other industry, outdoor and adventurous activity is subject to legislation, industry standards and guidelines to enforce and ensure adequate health and safety provision.

2.1 Health and safety enforcement

Adventurous activities licensing authority

The Adventurous Activities Licensing Authority (AALA) is a government-funded organisation that is responsible for the inspection of adventurous activity centres and providers. Any centre running adventurous activities for people under the age of 18 must have an annual or bi-annual inspection of its safety management systems.

On successful completion of an inspection, a centre is issued a licence to carry out activity. The AALA is designed to offer both help and advice to centres and so it is commonplace for action plans to be advised and recommendations made to centres for future development.

AALA falls under the responsibility of the Health and Safety Executive. The Health and Safety Executive is responsible for all standards of safety within all businesses nationally. Businesses which fail to meet HSE benchmarks or follow procedures risk immediate closure.

AALA also work very closely with a number of national governing bodies, such as the British Canoe Union, in developing safety systems and setting standards.

National governing bodies

It is in a national governing body's best interest to encourage excellent standards of safety within their respective sports. Sports with higher standards of safety are more likely to attract people to have a go and thus boost their overall participants.

Most governing bodies inspect their affiliated centres once a year and focus heavily upon safety management procedures. Centres that do not meet the required standards may either be given an action plan, with a timescale to complete and a date for re-inspection, or in worst cases, they may lose their affiliation. Centres that lose affiliation with governing bodies can still operate; however, they will find it more difficult to attract customers, harder and more expensive to get insurance and should expect to receive a very thorough inspection from AALA.

2.2 Health and safety considerations associated with participation in outdoor and adventurous activities

All outdoor and adventurous activities carry some level of risk with them. This can vary significantly from hill walking in the summer in the Black Mountains in Wales to climbing Mont Blanc in the Alps in the middle of the winter. However, regardless of the activity itself, it is important that participants are both aware of any potential **hazard** and of what can be done to limit **risk**.

Hazards can be considered in the following categories:

- Mechanical – any moving equipment or machinery. i.e. the chain and gears on a mountain bike or the rigging on a boat.

Key terms

Hazard – anything that has potential to cause harm to a person.

Risk – a risk is the chance that a hazard may cause harm to someone.

- Physical – such as slips, trips or falls, e.g. tripping over a tree root while orienteering or falling from a rock face while climbing. Another example may be burning from a camp fire during an extended hike or expedition.
- Chemical – fuel for quad bikes, cleaning products for any equipment or lubricants such as those used on mountain bikes.
- Environmental – the weather and terrain. i.e. extreme heat whilst fell running causing heat exhaustion and dehydration or avalanches whilst snow boarding.
- Biological – any bacteria or microorganisms that may cause infection, such as infection due to surfing in polluted water.
- Organisational – this may be from unreasonable timescales and rushing to complete a task. It could be participating without proper experience or skill or without appropriate support or back-up.

Case study: Sunsail

Sunsail is a British organisation that boasts centres all round the world. They run both yachting centres and beach holiday clubs that offer a range of water sports. All Sunsail centres are stringently inspected every year by the Royal Yachting Association, the sailing governing body. Sunsail has an excellent record for safety and offers first-class tuition and support.

In July 2003 an 11-year-old girl was killed at one of Sunsail's centres in Greece. She was out sailing with a friend in very light wind and hot and sunny conditions. Both she and her friend were wearing buoyancy aids and were sailing well within their capabilities. On the water there was safety cover in the form of rescue power boats manned by experienced staff. A lookout constantly monitored all the sailors from the beach.

When an unexpected gust of wind caught the boat, it tipped over and quickly went upside down. The rescue boats immediately attended the situation and on arrival realised that the girl was entangled and had been pulled under the boat. Despite great efforts to rescue her and then revive her, the girl was pronounced dead soon afterwards.

Subsequently the centre was found to have followed all guidelines set out to protect sailors. However, in response to this terrible accident the extra precaution of attaching a floatation device to sailing craft to prevent them going upside down is now practised by RYA centres.

Unfortunately accidents do happen. This level of incident is rare and must be learnt from.

1. Are you aware of any other outdoor adventurous activity sessions that have ended disastrously?
2. Was anything learnt from them?

2.3 Risk assessment in outdoor and adventurous activities

One of the best tools for understanding hazards and risks and controlling them is a risk assessment. A risk assessment allows people to look at the possible hazards of taking part in an activity, the likelihood of an incident or injury happening and precautions that may be taken to prevent said incident or injury occurring.

The following is an example of a risk assessment form.

Identify the hazard	Who may be affected?	Existing control measures	Risk rating: Severity times probability	Suggested measures for development
Low branches on mountain bike trail.	Instructor and clients	All participants wear helmets. Instructors warn clients before participation.	Severity: 2 Probability: 2 Risk: 4	Trim branches back to clear trail.

Figure 3.2: Example of a risk assessment.

Identify the hazard

We have already discussed the categories of problems that may be a hazard. However, you should be aware that it is not always easy to spot potential hazards. It is possible that hazards will emerge during participation in an activity. For this reason a risk assessment should be considered a working document and should be continually updated.

Who may be affected

Those who may be affected can be split into staff, participants and bystanders. Some hazards may affect all these potential victims and some might affect only one. For example, a learner or participant crashing into a tree whilst skiing is likely to hurt only him or herself. However, a learner or sailor crashing a sailing vessel into another craft may hurt themselves, their instructor if they are on board and the crew of the other craft.

Existing control meaures

Any existing measures in place to control the incident should be identified and recorded. This could be in the form of protective equipment or supervision and procedures. If no control measures are in place, this should be documented on the form.

Rate the risk

The following simple method may be used to rate a risk.

- Give the risk a severity rating between 1 and 3.
  1 is the lowest risk – where the outcome would be only a minor easily treatable injury.
  3 is the highest risk – where the outcome may be serious injury or death.

- Give the risk a probability rating between 1 and 3.
  1 is the lowest probability – where the incident is highly unlikely to happen.
  3 is the highest probability – where the incident is very likely to happen.
- Now multiply the severity by the probability to give you a figure between 1 and 9.
  If the result is between 1 and 3 it is likely activity can commence as long as adequate care is taken.
  If the result is between 3 and 6 it is likely that further precautions should be taken or the activity should be attempted only with extreme caution.
  If the result is between 6 and 9 it is unlikely the activity should take place and that further precautions should be implemented before this is reconsidered.

Suggested measures for development

This section is for any further actions that could be identified which would reduce the risk or control the risk. On completion or implementation of any of these actions, it may be that the risk rating can be reassessed.

PLTS

Considering and reflecting on the leaflets and risk assessment will help you develop your skills as a **reflective learner**.

Functional skills

Using the risk assessment formula could help you develop your skills in **mathematics**.

BTEC **Assessment activity 3.2**

1. Research participation in two outdoor adventurous activities. Design a leaflet that advises on the health and safety considerations for each. **P2**

2. Now produce a risk assessment for a selected outdoor and adventurous activity. **P3**

3. Consider the leaflets and risk assessment you created in Assessment parts 1 and 2. Explain highlighted health and safety considerations, identifying precautions and actions that can be taken, or used in relation to them. **M2**

4. Now explain these precautions and actions fully. **D1**

Grading tips

- Draw upon knowledge from experienced coaches and participants. Ask them about incidents they may have witnessed to help you assess any potential hazards or risks.
- Use the various headings – mechanical, physical, chemical, environmental, biological and organisational – to help you think about potential hazards or risks.

2.3 Environmental impacts associated with participation in outdoor and adventurous activities

The nature of participation in adventurous activity unfortunately means that there will be some impact upon our environment. It is important that participants make all possible attempts to limit this impact in order to preserve the environment for others and to prevent restrictions being enforced which could stop others from enjoying the activity.

Below, we look at some of the common ways in which adventurous outdoor activity can impact upon the environment.

Erosion

Erosion is the gradual destruction or reduction of something through continued wear and tear. Any terrain that we, as humans, come into contact with over time is eroded. The speed of erosion is determined by the numbers of people participating and the type of terrain and its resilience. For example a path that goes over rock is likely to erode more slowly than one that goes over soft peat marsh land.

Unfortunately, erosion caused by people often exposes the terrain to other forms of erosion. For example, eventually paths that are regularly used may be worn away to the point where they become small gullies. These new gullies allow a route for water to flow down and this water in turn causes its own erosion – aggravating the situation.

Erosion can be slowed or even stopped with simple precautions. Paths can be reinforced or treated by either laying gravel or having a raised wooden walkway built over them. Participants in outdoor adventurous activity should keep to paths whenever possible to limit the spread of erosion.

What can be done to limit erosion caused by mountain biking?

Wildlife disturbance

Wildlife of all sorts – whether plant or animal – is greatly affected by human activity. Disturbance is often unintentional and may be caused through walking over plant life or disturbing nesting birds whilst climbing. A little common sense goes a long way to protecting our wildlife. Think before you take part in an activity: 'Am I going to cause any disturbance and if so, could I come back at another time when this disturbance may be reduced?' (For example, this might be after birds have finished nesting.)

You will often find signs in place to warn when rare and protected plants and animals are present. Pay attention to these signs and always try to keep to marked paths and trails.

Pollution

Unfortunately as the numbers of people taking part in adventurous outdoor activity has increased so too has the amount of pollution caused. Pollution is caused in three major ways:

- Air pollution. This is caused by vehicles used to access areas suitable for activity. Participants should consider using other forms of transport such as bicycles whenever possible. Air pollution is also caused by some types of outdoor activity themselves, such as motor cross. When taking part in sports such as this, people must pay special consideration to others enjoying the environment. Some areas have banned sports like this due to complaints made about a minority of participants, disregarding both the environment and local people with reckless participation.
- Rubbish. Obviously it is impractical to have rubbish bins in some places of interest so all rubbish should be removed on departure. Rubbish visually ruins the environment for others and can be dangerous for animals and birds who may become entangled or eat it by mistake.
- Chemical products. These may be in the form of cleaning products used to protect equipment after use or lubricants designed to aid performance. Both should be used with caution and neither should be allowed to drain into the ground where they could potentially poison both animals and plants.

Construction of facilities

Facilities are sometimes needed to store equipment and provide a sheltered place to give training and feedback. Facilities must be sited with respect to the environment and, where possible, avoid disturbing plant and wildlife. Facilities need access in the form of a road or track, as well as the use of electricity, water and drainage. All of these things add to the overall disturbance caused by new and existing facilities.

PLTS

Observing and designing a presentation will help you develop skills as a **reflective learner**.

Functional skills

Using a computer to help you create your presentation will develop your **ICT** skills.

 Assessment activity 3.3

1. Observe participation in two outdoor and adventurous activities. Design a presentation for a local school interested in taking part in outdoor adventurous activity. The presentation should describe environmental impacts associated with these two activities. **P4**

2. In the presentation explain these environmental impacts fully and identify precautions and actions that can be taken, or used to reduce them. **M3**

3. Finally in the presentation explain these precautions and actions. **D2**

Grading tip

- Have you remembered to consider erosion, plant and wildlife disturbance, pollution, and facility construction?

3 Demonstrate techniques and skills associated with selected outdoor and adventurous activities

3.1 Examples of outdoor and adventurous activities

Snow skiing

Skiing is a predominantly mountain sport that involves the use of a ski for each foot. This is a long flat device designed to allow the user to slide over the ground. The skis are used in conjunction with bindings that connect to boots. Often poles are held in each hand to aid balance. Skiing has many disciplines, such as cross country or free style, and appeals to a wide range of participants.

Windsurfing

This is a sport which involves the use of a board with a sail attached to it that relies upon the wind for propulsion. Windsurfing can be done in a wide range of conditions, from waves to dead flat lakes. When the participant is travelling at speed, they are normally attached to the board with foot straps and to the sail with a harness. This helps them control the sometimes large forces acting on the equipment in windy conditions.

Mountain biking

Mountain biking involves the use of a bicycle that has been designed to cope with rough terrain and continuous punishment. The bike frames are reinforced; they have thicker tyres than road bikes to allow additional grip, and often utilise suspension to soften impacts. They usually have a large number of gears to allow maximum performance both uphill and downhill.

Orienteering

The aim of this sport is to navigate between a sequence of control points marked on a map in the quickest time. Competitors must decide upon the quickest route and the pace at which to compete. Orienteering can be done in a wide range of terrains from mountainside to beachside sand dunes.

Have you been on a mountain-biking activity? What skills did you use?

Where is the nearest place to you where you can learn to kayak?

Climbing

Climbing is the ascent of a prolonged incline or steep face, usually using both hands and feet to aid progress. Climbing is usually done with the aid of specialised equipment, such as ropes and technical shoes, and normally involves two people working together to support one another. Climbing is generally done on rock faces, however there are other disciplines such as ice climbing that rely on different terrains. Over the last few years, deep water soloing has become very popular. This is climbing above water without ropes or support equipment and relying upon the water to break your fall should you lose contact with the rock face.

Kayaking

Kayaking is the propulsion of a water craft with a deck, by one or more individuals, using a double-ended paddle. Kayaking is a hugely popular sport and is accessible for a wide range of people. Kayaking can be done on the sea or inland lakes and rivers. Kayaks differ in design to increase efficiency in various conditions. For example, a sea kayak designed for long journeys is long and pointed to allow it to cut through the water and travel at speed.

Caving

This is the exploration of or travelling through cave systems. Due to the obvious lack of illumination caving is reliant upon participants using torches and lamps. There are caves in all shapes and sizes and they offer a variety of challenges for those entering into them – from basic navigation in and out, to squeezing through tiny nooks and crannies. Although most caving is done in dry caves, it is possible to cave in flooded caves. One of the most extreme versions is cave diving which involves exploration with the aid of breathing apparatus.

Sailing

Sailing is the propulsion of an on-water craft or vessel using the wind harnessed by sails. The craft can vary in size considerably from dinghies no more than 2 metres in length to yachts over 20 metres long. Sailing can take place on inland lakes, coastal waters or upon the most exposed and wild seas. Sailing craft can be designed to be controlled by an individual or a crew. Due to the variety of vessels and venues, sailing is a popular sport that appeals to many people.

Other examples

Paragliding, snow boarding, kite surfing, mountain boarding, fell running, coasteering and water skiing are other examples of adventurous outdoor activities.

3.2 Techniques and skills associated with outdoor and adventurous activities

The wide range of outdoor and adventurous activities available means the **techniques** and **skills** needed are also wide and varied. Even within the actual sports themselves, different disciplines call for adaptation of these techniques and skills. Therefore it is important that learners are able to recognise the skills they must develop in order to participate at any level.

Skills can be considered as either:

- hard skills, sometimes called physical skills, for example co-ordination, balance and endurance, or
- soft skills: social, emotional or intellectual skills, for example, planning and organisation, perseverance, teamwork and communication.

You will often find that skills beneficial in one outdoor activity are also useful in another. Some skills often associated with outdoor adventurous activity are:

- Planning: because these activities expose participants to the elements, and are often reliant upon the correct conditions, it is vital that activities are planned to fit in with suitable conditions. Many activities are carried out great distances from support and civilisation. It is very frustrating to forget a vital piece of kit and so ruin a day.
- Health and safety awareness: as we have discussed above, many outdoor and adventurous activities carry some risk. Safety checks of both the environment and equipment should be conducted before any session and participants should remain 'safety aware' during the activity.
- Determination: adventure often means an individual is pushed outside comfort zones and forced to decide whether they can go on or should turn back. Those who are determined will often succeed where those who are not may fail.
- Teamwork: no outdoor adventurous activity is recommended to be undertaken alone. Having someone with you often increases your enjoyment and means that there is support on hand if needed. Many tasks are impossible on your own so effective teamwork is crucial for successful completion.
- Communication: as groups taking part in these activities are often reliant upon one another, it is vital that good communication is maintained.
- Endurance: many outdoor adventurous activities are physically demanding and take time to complete. Endurance and stamina must be developed to aid participation.

Techniques may rely upon multiple skills to achieve them. For example, the technique of climbing a steep hill on a mountain bike requires balance, endurance and determination.

Key terms

Skill – an ability that can be learned or developed to allow an activity to be completed.

Technique – the way in which a movement is performed, or equipment is used. Techniques are always specific to the activity and environment.

3.3 Climbing

Hard skills

Rock climbing is a very physical activity. Climbers must be strong and able to pull themselves upwards with both upper and lower body. They must have **endurance** as many ascents take time and muscles are worked constantly over long periods. Some routes involve huge amounts of **flexibility** to allow the climber to stretch to reach the next hold. In precarious situations where holds are limited it is often just balance that allows the climber to maintain contact with the face.

Crimping is a technique that helps climbers to apply extra pressure through their fingers aiding grip. Are there any training aids that can be used to improve a climber's grip?

Soft skills

Climbing should always be done in pairs or groups and should never be attempted on your own. Whilst you are climbing, it may take both perseverance and courage to get to the top. The person spotting and supporting is responsible for the climber's safety and can aid with motivation. Teamwork and communication are vital to make it to the top and both members of the climbing team must maintain this throughout the ascent.

Techniques

Climbing often relies on specialised equipment such as harnesses and rope systems. The climber making the ascent will either clip himself to points on the rock face as he goes or be protected by a pre-placed anchor point above him. He must understand the correct technique for securing himself whilst simultaneously utilising techniques that will aid both the grip of his hands and feet.

The climber who is supporting is attached at the other end of the rope and feeds the rope out during the ascent with a belay system. This relies upon a precise technique to prevent tangling and ensure that in the event of a fall the rope does not slip.

3.4 Windsurfing

Hard skills

Windsurfing relies upon the participant's ability to **co-ordinate** a board, a sail and themselves all at once. They must use large amounts of **balance** to stand on the board and allow them to lean against the sail harnessing the power of the wind. For some manoeuvres, **power** is needed to control the equipment and **endurance** is needed to allow sustained performance.

Soft skills

Like many outdoor adventurous activities, windsurfing can be tricky to learn and **determination** may be required to improve. However those who **persevere** will be rewarded by participation in a massively rewarding sport. Due to the sport being reliant upon the wind, it is vital that participants are **organised** and plan ahead by checking forecasts to ensure suitable conditions. Windsurfing is not recommended to be done on your own. Windsurfing with someone else present not only means that there is always someone there who you can **trust** to help you if needed, but it is more fun anyway, with each person on hand to offer encouragement to the other.

What other soft skills can you think of that might be needed when windsurfing?

Techniques

The windsurfer is a reasonably complex piece of kit until you get used to it. Performance can be severely hampered unless due care is taken and the correct technique used to rig it. Even when moving the equipment on dry land, the wind is liable to catch it, potentially causing harm to both the participant and bystanders. The correct technique must be used to secure and move the equipment to prevent the wind making it unmanageable. Once afloat, every manoeuvre from sailing in a straight line to jumping and flipping rely upon techniques that must be learnt over time and can be aided through explanation by experienced windsurfers and frequent practice in a simulated situation.

3.5 Snow skiing

Hard skills

Skiing relies upon strength in the legs and body core. It is an exciting sport that often calls for quick reactions. Some balance is needed at all levels; however as you progress and manoeuvres become more complex, this becomes more crucial. On long routes and runs, or over demanding terrain, endurance is required to allow good posture to be maintained.

Soft skills

For many beginners, skiing pushes them outside their comfort zones during their first few attempts. Courage is needed as well as determination to succeed. Some ski areas are complex and careful planning must be used to ensure that participants do not find themselves on a route beyond their ability. When ski areas are busy, and in order to avoid collisions, skiers must communicate with one another. When skiers leave the beaten track it is vital they do so with another person who they can trust and rely upon.

Techniques

There are no brakes on skis, so technique must be used not only to ski in a straight line and turn, but also to stop. There are various techniques that can be used for steering and stopping, depending on your level of ability. As you progress, these techniques allow manoeuvres to be done at greater speed and with more control. For example, when starting, a skier may use a 'snow plough' to slow themselves. This is a technique where the skis form a V-shape, creating extra resistance against the snow that can be used to slow progression. Later, a skier may learn to stop by sliding sideways which calls for extra balance and co-ordination, but means that the skier slows down much faster.

How can you improve your posture and balance to help you when skiing?

3.6 Recording evidence of participation

There are many ways of recording evidence; however you should choose one that is suitable for you and the activity you are participating in.

Evidence can be provided by:

- you (the participant)
- your peers
- your instructor, coach or tutor.

Evidence can be in the form of:

- Diary or logbook – this could be filled in after each activity session and should include notes on dates and times of the session, what skills and techniques you used and learnt, what you felt you did well in, and what you felt you may need to develop for the future.
- Visual – cameras or video cameras could be used to record participation. Video cameras are particularly useful as they also provide opportunity to see yourself perform. This can be used to show progression and pinpoint areas for improvement.
- Observation check lists – these may be completed by peers or tutors. They can be used to tick off correct use of techniques and then analysed by you, the performer, to see what you must do to develop.
- Portfolio – it may be that you wish to use a combination of these methods above and then present them in a portfolio of evidence.

Activity: Developing your technique

Ask someone to video you performing an activity. Are you performing as you visualised? What could you do to develop your techniques?

 BTEC ## Assessment activity 3.4 P5 M4

1. Demonstrate techniques and skills appropriate to two outdoor adventurous activities. Record participation and completion of said skills and techniques in an appropriate manner. **P5**
2. Review the techniques demonstrated during participation and justify why you chose them. **M4**

Grading tip

Watch your instructors and tutors during participation. How does their technique differ from yours? Could you copy them to improve your own performance?

 ### PLTS

Demonstrating skills and techniques appropriate to outdoor adventurous activities will develop your skills as a **self manager**.

 ### Functional skills

Recording the techniques could help your **English** skills in writing.

4 Be able to review performance in outdoor and adventurous activities

4.1 Reviewing performance in outdoor and adventurous activities

For sports people at any level, whether just starting out or as an elite athlete, an ability to review personal **performance** is essential to encourage improvement in skills. It is equally important for those with aspirations to instruct or coach outdoor adventurous activity to develop the ability to praise, critique and provide recommendations for further development of others.

4.2 Feedback

As with the collection of evidence in the previous section, feedback can come from:

- you (the participant)
- your peers
- your instructor, coach or tutor.

Feedback should be seen as an opportunity for development. It is a positive part of the learning process and, when acted upon in the correct way, can be invaluable for a performer's development.

Feedback can be:

- verbal – during participation or in a debrief situation
- written – in reports, feedback sheets or observation checklists
- visual – with video or photographic evidence.

Feedback is best given as close to the session as possible so that specifics are still fresh in the mind. Although sometimes there is opportunity for feedback during the session, normally to avoid distraction feedback should be given after an activity has finished. It may be that a session is split with breaks to give and receive feedback. Alternatively, a session may be completed and then feedback provided at the end, ready for the next session. A productive session will often use both these methods.

SWOT

The following analysis system can be used to structure feedback.

- **Strengths** – What do I do well? What am I good at?
- **Weaknesses** – What do I need to improve? What prevents me performing at my best?
- **Opportunities** – What resources do I have available to me that may assist my development?
- **Threats** – What could prevent me achieving my objective?

Key term

Performance – the level at which a skill or technique is completed.

Remember

It is vitally important that strengths and positive areas of performance are included in all feedback. Without these, motivation is unlikely to be maintained and development unlikely to be successful.

4.3 Target setting

Targets may be put in place by coaches, peers, governing bodies or even onlookers. You may be setting personal targets in relation to a pre-set format, such as a training scheme designed by a governing body; or you could be comparing yourself to your peers and setting targets on aspirations to perform like someone else. However, in order for a target to be achievable you must want to reach it.

To aid motivation and allow sensible target setting, the following format is often used:

SMART

- **Specific** – well defined and applicable to a precise element of the activity.
- **Measurable** – there must be a way of measuring development. Ideally a figure should be used, for example an improvement in speed of 10%.
- **Achievable** – the goal must be attainable.
- **Realistic** – consider all elements that may prevent achievement. Is the target now realistic?
- **Timed** – timescales are needed for completion of the target.

Development opportunities

Development can be encouraged and worked upon by different people in different ways.

- The individual may independently provide feedback and development suggestions. An individual wishing to develop personal performance like this must have a high level of motivation and an in-depth understanding of the skills and techniques required by an activity. They must have the ability to think about self-critiquing whilst performing. This is often a huge challenge, especially for novices who may need all their concentration and focus to complete relatively simple tasks.
- Peers are fantastic for providing motivation and support. Because they are often learning at the same speed, it is possible for them to compare experiences. When a peer is at a higher level, they may be in a position to provide beneficial knowledge, especially when development is focused around an element that is recently overcome or conquered.
- Coaches and instructors are obviously trained to pinpoint both strengths and areas for improvement. They should be flexible in their setting of targets. Targets, however, must be set with the assistance of the performer themselves to ensure they are SMART. They can assist with development plans that utilise specific training and courses designed by industry professionals and governing bodies.

PLTS

Observing and reviewing your performance will develop your skills as an **effective participator**.

Functional skills

By recording and reviewing performance in a log book you may provide evidence towards **English**.

BTEC ## Assessment activity 3.5

1. Observe one of your peers while they participate in two outdoor and adventurous activities. Provide support and motivation for them. Review their performance identifying both strengths and areas for improvement. **P6**

2. Keep a logbook and, after each practical session, carry out a review of your own performance – identifying both strengths and areas for improvement. **P7**

3. Explain these identified strengths and areas for improvement and make recommendations for further development of areas for improvement. **M5**

4. Justify any recommendations made for improvement. **D3**

Grading tip

Remember that feedback can be provided by yourself, your peers and your instructors and tutors. To ensure the best image of how you are performing, gather feedback from as many sources as possible.

Martin Rivers
Sailing Centre Manager

Martin manages a bustling sailing centre that caters for a wide range of clientele. His responsibilities include the following:

- Employing and training staff.
- Advertising courses and clubs.
- Advising potential clients about suitable products.
- Meeting governing body guidelines in health and safety and standards of teaching.
- Planning rotas and schedules.
- Motivating and disciplining employees through regular meetings and appraisals.

Describe your typical day

I normally arrive at around 8 a.m. I check emails and the weather forecast for the day before preparing for the staff to arrive for the morning meeting. I must brief them of the courses that are going on, the weather that is forecast and any maintenance that must be carried out prior to the clients' arrival.

When the clients arrive for the day, I ensure I am on hand to greet them, deal with any concerns they may have and make sure their day with us starts smoothly. During the course of the day, I am always on hand to supervise the instructors and offer assistance if needed.

We usually finish the day with some staff training. I help the less experienced instructors develop personal skills in sailing as well as looking at areas within their instructional skills that they could develop.

What do you look for in your staff?

Obviously a high level of personal ability is crucial. To get to this standard, individuals need motivation and commitment. However it is skills such as communication and resourcefulness that allow sports people to become great instructors.

Think about it!

- Do you think you could inspire and enthuse people about a sport in the way that Martin does?
- Do you think you have the skills and qualities to work in the outdoor adventurous activity industry? In small groups, discuss what skills and qualities you may need to develop to succeed in this industry.

Just checking

1. Define an outdoor adventurous activity.
2. Briefly describe the structure of one outdoor adventurous activity.
3. Who is responsible for enforcing health and safety guidelines?
4. Define a 'risk' and a 'hazard'. Give examples of each.
5. Why is a risk assessment an important tool?
6. Name two ways in which outdoor adventurous activity can affect the environment.
7. Identify three skills that would be useful in a variety of outdoor adventurous activities.
8. Choose an activity and identify two techniques vital to effective performance.
9. What does 'SWOT' stand for?
10. What does 'SMART' stand for?

Assignment tips

- When writing your assignments, ensure that you present them clearly and in a structured format. Title each assessment activity appropriately and in the correct order in your folder.

- When conducting research use the Internet, books and magazines, but don't forget that the instructors you may meet will have a wealth of knowledge as well. Probe them for information and ask them about any specific relevant experiences they may have had.

- When learning a new outdoor adventurous activity, try to relax and have fun. Work at your own pace and ensure you enjoy the experience. As you become more confident you can start to push yourself harder.

- Support your peers and they will support you. If you work as a group, you are likely to find the experience of taking part in an outdoor adventurous activity more rewarding and you are likely to improve more rapidly.

- Ensure that you complete any reviewing or recording of sessions at the first available opportunity. If you do not, you are likely to forget specifics and reduce the effectiveness of the exercise.

- Read the assignment briefs thoroughly before you start. If the brief says explain and you only describe, you will not fulfil the brief in full.

- Make sure that you attempt all parts of the assignment briefs. Do not just attempt the pass criteria. Think big and try it all.

4 Anatomy and physiology for sport

The body is a complex mechanism of living tissue. It is designed to be extremely efficient, helping us to live and function. It can be trained to improve in efficiency, which enables sports people to perform better in a vast range of activities including running, swimming, cycling, jumping, throwing, skiing and diving. A trained athlete can go from standing still to sprinting in seconds.

In order for us to be able to perform any activity well we need to understand how the body is structured. This is called **anatomy**.

We must also be able to understand how the body functions. This is called **physiology**.

Learning about anatomy and physiology can help us to understand how we can help the body adapt to improve certain functions and enable us to perform at a high level. We are able to train our systems to improve our performance and can understand how the body can cope with the stresses placed on it by sports participation.

Learning outcomes

After completing this unit you should:

1. know the structure and function of the skeletal system
2. know the structure and function of the muscular system
3. know the structure and function of the cardiovascular system
4. know the structure and function of the respiratory system.

Assessment and grading criteria

This table shows you what you must do in order to achieve a pass, merit or distinction grade, and where you can find activities in this book to help you.

To achieve a **pass** grade the evidence must show that the learner is able to:	To achieve a **merit** grade the evidence must show that, in addition to the pass criteria, the learner is able to:	To achieve a **distinction** grade the evidence must show that, in addition to the pass and merit criteria, the learner is able to:
P1 describe the structure and function of the skeletal system **See Assessment activity 4.1, page 105**		
P2 describe the different types of joint and the movements allowed at each **See Assessment activity 4.1, page 105**	**M1** explain the movements occurring at two synovial joints during four different types of physical activity **See Assessment activity 4.1, page 105**	
P3 identify the major muscles of the body **See Assessment activity 4.2, page 109**		
P4 describe the different types of muscle and muscle movements **See Assessment activity 4.2, page 109**	**M2** give examples of three different types of muscular contraction relating to three different types of physical activity **See Assessment activity 4.2, page 109**	**D1** analyse the musculoskeletal actions occurring at four synovial joints during four different types of physical activity **See Assessment activity 4.2, page 109**
P5 describe the structure and function of the cardiovascular system **See Assessment activity 4.3, page 116**		
P6 describe the structure and function of the respiratory system **See Assessment activity 4.3, page 116**	**M3** explain how the cardiovascular and respiratory systems work together to supply the body with oxygen **See Assessment activity 4.3, page 116**	**D2** evaluate how the cardiovascular system and respiratory system work together to supply the body with oxygen and remove carbon dioxide **See Assessment activity 4.3, page 116**

How you will be assessed

This unit will be assessed by assignments that will be designed and marked by the staff at your centre. Your assessment could be in the form of:

- verbal presentation
- visual display
- practical tasks
- written assignments
- report writing
- lab report.

Derik, 15-year-old BTEC student

I'm really enjoying this unit now I've started to learn the names of things. At first it seemed difficult but when you start to use the names all the time it becomes much easier. Our teacher got us to make posters of the skeleton and a clay model of a muscle which we painted in different colours to show how it's structured. We made models of the human body out of tissue paper, cardboard, straws and string to show how the rib cage protects the heart and lungs. Miss Brown brought in a pig's heart to one of our lessons and dissected it in front of us! It was gross but it showed us the structures inside the heart that we had been reading about. It helped me to remember things because I saw it for real rather than just a picture in a textbook or on the Internet. I now understand how the body works and, along with the other information I've got from my fitness and training unit, I've started to plan and follow my own training programme. I hope this will improve my sports performance and help get me selected for the first team!

Over to you!

- Why will knowing about the structure and function of the skeletal and muscular system help Derik undertake appropriate physical training?
- Why will knowing about the cardiovascular and respiratory system help Derik undertake appropriate physical training?

1 Know the structure and function of the skeletal system

Warm-up

Pick a simple sporting action, such as kicking or throwing a ball, or jumping up and landing. Try to identify the following:

* What are the main muscles that help produce the action?
* Which joints are moved?
* Can you name the bones that make up the joints you have identified?

1.1 Structure of the skeleton

An adult human skeleton has 206 bones but at birth the human body is made up of around 350 bones. As we grow and develop some of these bones fuse together to form solid plate-like structures (the skull, for example, is one of these).

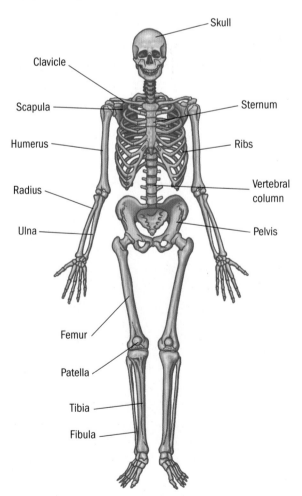

Figure 4.1: The bones of the skeleton. Try to memorise them all.

Skull

The skull consists of 8 bones that form the cranium, 14 bones that form the face and 6 bones that form the middle ear. The cranium is the part of the skull that protects the brain. The facial bones include the eye sockets, nose, cheek and jaw.

Sternum

Also known as the breast bone, the sternum is located in the middle of the chest.

Ribs

The rib cage is composed of 12 pairs of ribs which form a cage-like structure to protect vital organs, such as the heart and lungs. The first seven pairs of ribs attach directly onto the front of the sternum via costal cartilage. The next three pairs are attached to the seventh rib, also via costal cartilages. These are known as 'false' ribs. The remaining two pairs of ribs do not attach to anything other than the thoracic vertebrae, and are called 'floating' ribs.

Vertebral column

The vertebral column (see figure 4.2), also called the spine or spinal column consists of 33 bones. Of these, 24 bones are individual and unfused, while the remaining 9 are fused together. We rely on the spinal column for posture, movement, stability and protection. It helps to protect the spinal cord. There are five main areas to the vertebral column: cervical, thoracic, lumbar, sacral and the coccyx.

- **Cervical vertebrae (7 unfused bones)**
  The cervical vertebrae support the weight of the head by enabling muscle attachment through each of the vertebrae. The top two vertebrae, the atlas and the axis, enable the head to move up and down and side to side respectively.

- **Thoracic vertebrae (12 unfused bones)**
  The 12 thoracic vertebrae allow for the attachment of the ribs. These bones, together with the ribs, form the rib cage which protects the heart and lungs.

- **Lumbar vertebrae (5 unfused bones)**
  The five lumbar vertebrae are the largest of all the individual vertebrae. Their large structure offers a great deal of weight-bearing capacity, and secures the attachment of a number of muscles. This muscle attachment, together with the intervertebral discs of cartilage, enable flexion and extension (forward and backward movement) and lateral flexion (side to side movement) of the trunk.

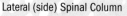
Lateral (side) Spinal Column

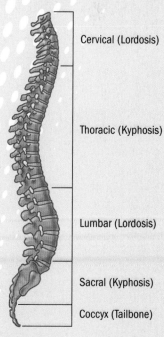

Cervical (Lordosis)

Thoracic (Kyphosis)

Lumbar (Lordosis)

Sacral (Kyphosis)

Coccyx (Tailbone)

Figure 4.2: Lateral view of the spinal column. How many bones make up the spinal column?

- **Sacral vertebrae (5 fused bones)**
  The five fused sacral vertebrae form the sacrum which fuses to the pelvis. The sacrum and the pelvis bear and distribute the weight of the upper body.

- **Coccyx (4 fused bones)**
  The coccyx forms the very base of the vertebral column, and acts as a base for muscle attachment.

Activity: Cause of back injuries

The lumbar region of the spine is the most common site of back injuries. Look at figure 4.2 on page 97 and suggest why this might be the case.

Clavicle

The clavicle or collar bone is classified as a long bone that makes up part of the shoulder girdle.

Scapula

The scapula or shoulder blade, is the bone that connects the humerus (arm bone) with the clavicle (collar bone).

Humerus

The humerus is the bone in the upper part of the arm.

Radius and ulna

The radius and ulna are the two long bones that sit side by side in the forearm. The inside bone is called the ulna, and the outside bone is called the radius.

Pelvis

The pelvis, also called the pelvic girdle or the hip girdle, is made up from two hip bones. These two bones meet on either side of the sacrum.

The pelvic girdle serves several important functions in the body. It supports the weight of the body from the vertebral column. It also protects and supports the lower organs, including the urinary bladder, the reproductive organs, and the developing foetus in a pregnant woman.

Femur

The femur is a long bone and forms the top part of the leg.

Tibia and fibula

The tibia and fibula are the two long bones that sit side by side in the lower leg. The inside bone is called the tibia, and the outside bone is called the fibula (commonly known as the shin).

Patella

The patella, or kneecap, is one of three bones, along with the tibia (shin bone) and femur (thigh bone), that make up the knee joint.

1.2 Axial and appendicular skeleton

One way to group the bones of the human skeleton is to divide them into two groups, namely the axial skeleton and the appendicular skeleton. The axial skeleton consists of bones in the **midline** (see figure 4.3) and includes all the bones of the head and neck, the vertebrae, ribs and sternum.

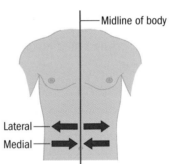

Figure 4.3: The appendicular skeleton consists of the clavicles, scapula, bones of the upper limb, bones of the pelvis and bones of the lower limb.

1.3 Function of the skeleton

The human skeleton has five main functions. These are: support, protection, movement, blood production and mineral storage.

- **Support** – Bones help to stabilise and support the framework of the body, as most muscles are attached to bones.

- **Protection** – Bones help to protect internal tissues and organs, for example the skull protects the brain and the rib cage protects the lungs.

- **Movement** – Bones enable movement to happen as the skeleton is jointed. Bones end in joints so the shape of the bones can dictate how we move.

- **Blood production** – Bones produce red blood cells in the bone marrow.

- **Mineral storage** – Bones help to store minerals such as calcium, phosphorus, sodium and potassium.

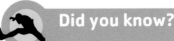

Did you know?

The longest bone in your body is the femur (thigh bone), which is about one quarter of your height.

Key term

Midline – direction referring to a vertical, invisible line through the middle of the body – see diagram.

Did you know?

99% of the body's calcium is stored in bones.

1.4 Tissues making up the skeleton

Cartilage

Cartilage is a soft, slightly elastic tissue. It does not possess a blood supply and receives nutrition via diffusion from the capillary network outside the tissue.

All bones start out as cartilage in the developing foetus, but this cartilage is gradually replaced by bone. There are three basic types of cartilage found in the body:

1 Hyaline or **articular cartilage** is a fairly resilient tissue and is found on the articulating surfaces of bones that form joints. The cartilage protects the bone tissue from wear and reduces friction between articulating bones.

2 White fibro-cartilage is a much denser tissue. It is tough, and its shock absorption properties means that it is often found in areas of the body where high amounts of stress are imposed. For example, the knee joint resists the huge amount of stress which is often a result of performing activities such as the triple jump.

3 Yellow elastic cartilage is a much more pliant and flexible tissue giving support and also flexibility. The external ear and the epiglottis are examples.

Bone

Bone differs from cartilage in that it is a rigid, non-elastic tissue and is composed of approximately 65% mineral components and 35% organic tissue such as collagen. Collagen is a protein which gives the bone some resilience and prevents the bones from breaking on the slightest of impacts. Bone tissue can be categorised into either compact or cancellous.

Compact bone or hard bone forms the surface layers of all bones and the whole of the cylindrical shaft of long bones. It goes some way to protecting bones from external forces or impacts and has great weight-bearing properties.

- Surrounding the compact bone is the **periosteum,** which is a fibrous and extremely vascular tissue. In addition to its vital role in bone development, the periosteum enables tendons to attach to bones, which transmit the muscular 'pull' and therefore allows movement to take place.

Cancellous or spongy bone lies beneath and inside to compact bone, and has a honeycomb appearance. In addition to this, the spaces of the cancellous bone are filled with red bone marrow, since the bony plates offer some protection for the manufacture of red blood cells here.

- Some bones, such as the flat bones of the skull, form directly in membranes.
- The short and long bones are formed by the gradual replacement of hyaline cartilage, from the foetal stage of development until full maturation in our late teenage years.

Bone structure

A living bone consists of three layers, all of which are honeycombed with nerves and blood vessels:

- the periosteum, or outside skin of the bone;
- the hard compact bone, supporting the weight of the body; and
- the spongy bone (bone marrow). Spongy bone occurs at the ends of long bones and is less dense than compact bone. The spongy bone of the femur, humerus, and sternum contains red marrow, producing red blood cells (which carry oxygen), white blood cells (which fight infection), or platelets (that help stop bleeding). Yellow marrow, at the centre, is used to store fats.

At about 3 months old the foetal skeleton is made up of cartilage. By 6 months old some of this cartilage has begun to harden. This process is called ossification.

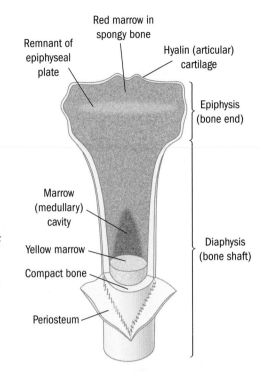

Figure 4.4: Cross-section through bone. Did you know bones contained all these parts?

1.5 Types of bones

Bones are designed to carry out a variety of specific functions. They fall into one of five categories, largely according to their shape:

Long bones

Long bones are cylindrical in shape and are found in the limbs of the body. Examples of long bones include:

- femur
- tibia
- humerus.

The primary function of long bones is to act as levers, and they are therefore essential in movement. Their other vital function is the production of blood cells, which occurs deep inside the bone.

Short bones

Short bones are small and compact in nature; they are often equal in length and width.

The short bones are designed for strength and weight bearing and include:

- the bones of the wrist (carpals)
- the ankle (tarsals).

Flat bones

Flat bones offer protection to the internal organs of the body. Examples include:

- the sternum
- the bones of the cranium
- the bones of the pelvis.

Flat bones also provide suitable sites for muscle attachment, with the origins of muscles often attaching to them. The pelvis, sternum and cranium also produce blood cells.

Irregular bones

Irregular bones are so named due to their complex, individual shapes and the difficulty in classifying them. They have a variety of functions which include protection. Examples include:

- the vertebrae (which protect the spinal cord)
- the bones of the face.

Sesamoid bones

Sesamoid bones have a specialised function: they ease joint movements and resist friction and compression. They exist where bones articulate or join. An example is the patella which is situated in the quadriceps femoris tendon.

1.6 Joints and movement

Usually the purpose of the **joint** is to allow some movement but the bones of the skull, for example, are joined so tightly that there is no movement. One way of classifying joints is by the quantity of movement permitted. The joints can be:

- fixed or immoveable, e.g. fused joints of the skull that provide no movement
- slightly moveable, e.g. between each vertebrae where a small range of movement occurs
- freely moveable or synovial, e.g. at the knee, a hinge joint, where a large amount of movement occurs.

Synovial joints

Synovial joints are further broken into groups according to shape and movement. These subgroups include the following:

A **hinge joint** only allows movement in one plane. For example: the knee joint only allows movement back and forth. Strong ligaments exist in order to prevent any sideways movement, just like the hinge on a door!

Key term

Joint – a joint, or articulation, is the interface (coming together) of two bones.

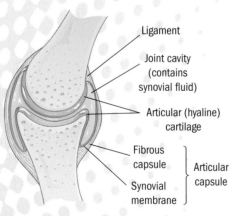

Ligament

Joint cavity (contains synovial fluid)

Articular (hyaline) cartilage

Fibrous capsule

Synovial membrane

Articular capsule

Figure 4.5: What type of joint is this?

A **ball and socket joint** allows the widest range of movement and occurs where a rounded head of a bone fits into a cup-shaped cavity; for example, in the hip and shoulder.

A **condyloid joint** allows movement in two planes – forwards and backwards and side to side, for example, in the wrist.

A **pivot joint** allows rotation only; for example, the cervical vertebrae where the axis rotates on the atlas.

A **saddle joint** occurs where concave and convex surfaces meet; for example the carpo-metacarpal joint of the thumb.

A **gliding joint** occurs when the flat surface of one bone slips over the other. It allows limited movement in a range of directions; for example in the hands or feet, i.e. intertarsal and intercarpal joints.

Did you know?

Synovial joints (freely moveable joints) make up 90% of our skeleton.

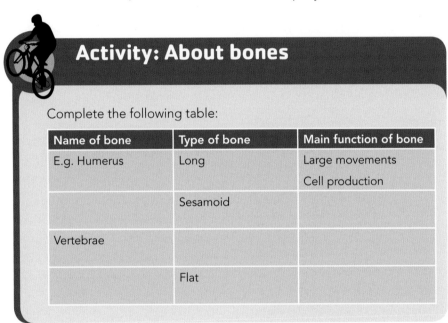

Activity: About bones

Complete the following table:

Name of bone	Type of bone	Main function of bone
E.g. Humerus	Long	Large movements Cell production
	Sesamoid	
Vertebrae		
	Flat	

Types of joint movement

Table 4.1 shows examples of where movement occurs in the body.

Table 4.1: Types of joint and their different movements.

Joint type	Movement at joint	Example
Hinge	Flexion/Extension	Elbow/Knee

Key terms

Flexion – bending the joint, i.e. decreasing the angle at a joint. For example, when a football player is preparing to kick a ball.

Extension – straightening the joint, i.e. increasing the angle at a joint. For example, a basketball player straightening their arm in order to block a shot.

Adduction – movement towards the body, i.e. bringing a limb towards the trunk. For example, arms pulled back together during breaststroke – adduction at the shoulder joint.

Abduction – movement away from the body, i.e. moving a limb away from the trunk. For example, when a gymnast pushes out their legs to do a star jump, abduction occurs at the hip joint.

Rotation – movement which moves a limb towards the body. For example, when a golf player performs a drive shot, the hip moves towards the body.

Circumduction – movement in which flexion, abduction, extension and adduction movements are combined in sequence. Any joint at which flexion, abduction, extension, and adduction may occur is a joint at which circumduction may occur. For example, the shoulder joint during an over arm bowling action in cricket.

Activity: Examples

For each of the types of movement in the key terms box can you identify another sporting example?

Table 4.1 (cont.): Types of joint and their different movements.

Joint type	Movement at joint	Example
Pivot	Rotation of one bone around another	Top of the neck (atlas and axis bones)
Ball and socket	Flexion/Extension/ Adduction/ Abduction/Internal and external rotation	Shoulder/Hip
Saddle	Flexion/Extension/ Adduction/ Abduction/Circumduction	Carpo-metacarpal joint CMC joint of the thumb
Condyloid	Flexion/Extension/ Adduction/ Abduction/Circumduction	Wrist joint Wrist/MCP and MTP joints
Gliding	Gliding movements	Intercarpal joint Intercarpal joints

Assessment activity 4.1  **P1 P2 M1**

With a partner verbally present to your class information that will describe the structure and function of the skeleton.

1. Do this by using some visual display so that you can point and explain each part in your presentation.

2. You could use a model of a skeleton or posters or point to each bone using your partner as the model!

3. Draw a poster to show the three main types of joints in the body and the movement produced at each.

4. For two of the synovial joints that you identify in task 2 select four sporting actions that shows clearly how this joint is used and also explain, either on the poster or verbally to your tutor, the type of movement that is occurring. **P1**, **P2**, **M1**

Grading tip

Make sure that you choose four different types of sporting actions for the two different synovial joints as this will help you to explain the different types of movement at each joint – check with your tutor before you start that your selection is appropriate!

 PLTS

Working with a partner to get all the information together and presented to the rest of your group will help develop your creative thinking, and team working skills. Also being able to explain why this topic is important will help you with your reflective learning skills.

 Functional skills

Presenting your research findings visually, and with an explanation, should develop your **English** speaking and listening skills.

2 Know the structure and function of the muscular system

2.1 Types of muscles

Muscle tissue

There are three types of muscle tissue:

1 **Skeletal or voluntary** muscle, which is external and used primarily for movement of the skeleton.

2 **Cardiac or heart** muscle, which is found only in the heart and used to force blood into the circulatory vessels.

3 **Smooth or involuntary** muscle, which lies internally and has several functions, including forcing food through the digestive system (peristalsis) and squeezing blood throughout the circulatory system.

 Did you know?

Muscles make up approximately 45% of the total body weight, and there are more than 600 muscles in the body.

It comprises about 40% of the body mass in men; less in women who have a greater proportion of connective tissue, mainly fat.

Apart from muscle tissue, and a rich supply of blood-vessels, muscles also contain a considerable amount of connective tissue to bind the muscle tissue together and transmit the forces to the bones so that they move.

Muscles are attached to bones (or other muscles) by tendons, which are composed of fibrous tissue.

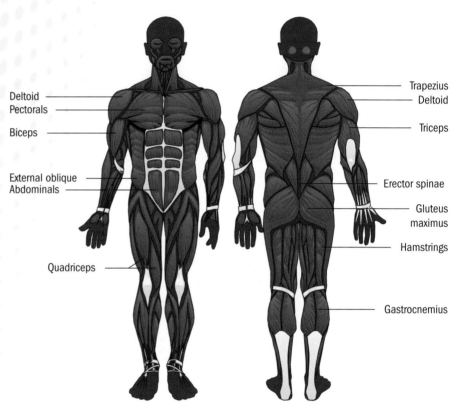

Figure 4.6: How many muscles not labelled on the diagram can you name?

Muscle movement

Muscle contraction on its own would produce very little, if any, movement in the body; however the muscles are attached to bones by tendons and therefore pull on the bones and cause movement at the joints of the body. This is one of the main reasons for the skeleton being jointed.

Tendons

Tendons, which attach muscle to bone, are extremely strong because they are formed from the **collagen** fibres of connective tissue that surround the different muscle layers (see diagram): the endomysium, perimysium and epimysium.

Key term

Collagen – the main protein in connective tissue, it is fibrous and its molecular structure provides strength and elasticity to tissue, skin, cartilage, ligaments, tendons and bones.

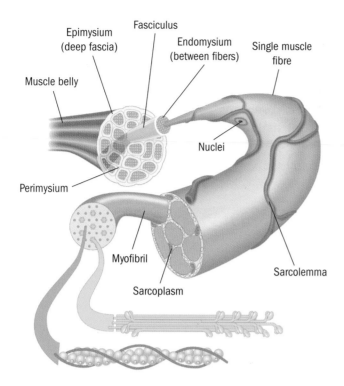

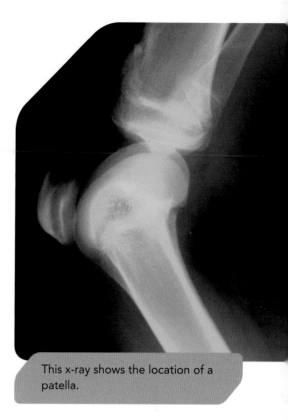

This x-ray shows the location of a patella.

Figure 4.7: Diagram of a tendon. Are you familiar with the names of all the parts shown?

Tendons (see figure 4.7) grow out of the muscle and gradually become more calcified as they approach bone. The collagen fibres lie lengthways in the tendon and this, combined with their poor blood supply, makes them difficult to repair when severed. Tendons have great strength and some elasticity but they are not compressible (they simply bend). Their main function is to transfer the force of tension from contracting muscles to bone but they also limit movement and provide support if the tendon crosses a joint (for example, see x-ray and diagram showing position of patella held in place by the patellar tendon).

Muscles are attached to bones (or other muscles) by tendons, which are composed of fibrous tissue. They are strong and flexible in order to allow movement to occur.

Properties of skeletal muscle

Skeletal muscle possesses three essential properties:

1 **Extensibility:** this is the ability of muscle tissue to lengthen when contracting.

2 **Elasticity:** this is the ability of muscle tissue to return to its normal resting length once it has been stretched. This can be compared to an elastic band that will always resume its resting shape even after stretching.

3 **Contractility:** this refers to the capacity of a muscle to contract or shorten forcibly when stimulated by nerves and hormones (excitability).

Figure 4.8: See how the muscle fibres are long and thin and wrapped up into bundles by the protective sheath. Do you know what this sheath is called?

There are three main types of muscle contraction:

1. concentric
2. eccentric
3. isometric.

 A **concentric contraction** happens when the muscle shortens as it contracts. An example of concentric contraction can be seen when we flex the biceps muscle.

Activity: Flexion movement

Can you name another flexion movement? Identify the muscle and its movement.

 Eccentric contraction is the opposite of concentric; the muscle lengthens as it gains tension – for example, the lowering of a weight after having performed a biceps curl.

An **isometric contraction** happens when there is tension on the muscle but no movement is made, causing the length of the muscle to remain the same, as in the arm muscles in a handstand.

Which of the gymnasts' muscles are contracting isometrically?

Antagonistic muscles

Muscles never work alone. In order for a co-ordinated movement to be produced the muscles must work as a group or team, with several muscles working at any one time.

Taking the simple movement of flexion of the arm at the elbow, the muscle responsible for flexion (bending of the arm) is the biceps brachii, and the muscle, which produces the desired joint movement, is called the **agonist** or **prime mover**.

In order for the biceps muscle to shorten when contracting, the tricep muscle must lengthen. The tricep in this instance is known as the **antagonist,** since its action is opposite to that of the agonist. The two muscles must work together to produce the required movement.

BTEC ## Assessment activity 4.2

1. Label a diagram of the muscular system.

2. Produce a poster that shows the three different types of muscle within the human body and give a brief explanation of their job in the body and then where they can be found.

3. With a partner produce a series of annotated photographs that show an exercise for each of the three different types of muscular contraction. **P3** , **P4** , **M2**

Grading tips

If you want to achieve D1 then you need to be able to combine the information you learned regarding the skeletal system with that of the muscular system.

If you do this, you will have to pick four different synovial joints and explain in detail, using different types of physical activities, how the skeletal system and the muscular system work together in order to produce the movement. **D1**

 ## PLTS

Working with your partner will develop your skills as a **team worker**.

 ## Functional skills

Presenting your research findings in the visual formats stated should help develop your **English** skills in writing.

3 Know the structure and function of the cardiovascular system

The cardiovascular system – sometimes called the circulatory system – consists of:

- the heart
- blood vessels and blood.

3.1 The heart

Structure of the heart

The heart (see figure 4.9) consists of two separate pumps. The right side pumps the blood to the lungs and the left side pumps the blood to the rest of the body.

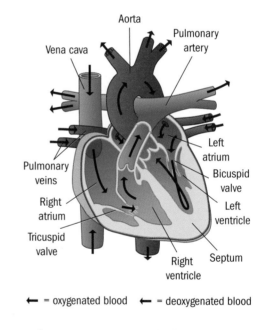

= oxygenated blood   = deoxygenated blood

Figure 4.9: Diagram of a cross-section through the heart. Why is the human circulation system called a double circulation system?

The heart is located in the cavity between the sternum and the lungs. It is made up of four chambers – two upper and two lower. The two upper chambers are called atria and the two lower are called ventricles.

The atria receive blood into the heart and the ventricles pump blood out of the heart. The right and left sides of the heart are divided by a muscular wall called the septum.

Remember

There are four chambered pumps forcing blood around the body:

- atria receive blood from veins
- ventricles pump blood into arteries.

Valves ensure the flow of blood in the correct direction.

The heart is located in the thorax, between and in front of the lungs.

A pacemaker (sino-atrial node) is in the wall of the right atrium and regulates the heartbeat

Did you know?

Your heart is about the size of your closed fist!

Blood flows through the heart and around the body in one direction only. This is maintained by special valves within the heart and the fact that veins also have valves which help control the flow of blood. Arteries have thick muscular walls and these are used also to direct the blood in one direction.

Blood circulates continuously via the heart, arteries, capillaries and veins. We have a double circulation system. The right side of the heart sends blood to the lungs to collect oxygen (pulmonary); it then returns to the left side to be pumped out to the body (systemic).

3.2 Structure and function of blood vessels

What are blood vessels?

Blood vessels are a complex network of hollow tubes that transport blood throughout the entire human body: capillaries, veins and arteries.

Types of blood vessels

Veins
Veins (see Figure 4.10, left) have walls that are thinner than arteries. They carry blood to the heart. The smallest of the veins are **venuoles.** They include semi-lunar valves to ensure direction of blood flow.

Arteries
Arteries are blood vessels with thick muscular walls (see Figure 4.10, middle) which carry blood away from the heart under high pressure. They are very elastic in their make up and have thick muscular walls to help control the pressure in them. Arteries branch repeatedly into smaller and smaller arteries – smallest of these are **arterioles** which have thinner walls than arteries.

Capillaries
Capillaries have walls made up of only a single layer of cells. This is where the exchange of oxygen and nutrients happens and the removal of waste products occurs. This exchange takes place by a process called **diffusion.** The smallest blood vessels link **arterioles to venules.**

Circulation

Blood vessels carry blood from the heart to all areas of the body. The blood travels from the heart via arteries to smaller arterioles, then to capillaries or sinusoids, to venules, to veins and back to the heart.

Microcirculation deals with the flow of blood from arterioles to capillaries to venules. As the blood moves through the capillaries, substances such as oxygen, carbon dioxide, nutrients and wastes are exchanged between the blood and the fluid that surrounds cells.

Figure 4.10: What do you think the diagram on the right shows?

Did you know?

Oxygen makes up about a fifth of the atmosphere.

Key terms

Thermoregulation – keeping the body at a constant temperature.

Vasodilation – when the blood vessels open.

Vasoconstriction – when the blood vessels close.

3.3 Function of the cardiovascular system

The function of the cardiovascular system is to ensure that there is sufficient blood flow through the heart, the body and the lungs.

Oxygen enters the body when you breathe in air through your mouth and nose and into your lungs. The oxygen is absorbed into your bloodstream by your lungs. Your heart then pumps the oxygen-rich (oxygenated) blood through the arteries, to tissues including organs, muscles and nerves, all around your body.

When blood reaches your tissues, it releases the oxygen, which is used by the cells to produce energy. In exchange, the cells release waste products – including carbon dioxide and water – that are, in turn, absorbed and carried away by blood.

This used, or 'deoxygenated' blood then travels along the veins back towards your heart. Your heart pumps this blood back to your lungs where carbon dioxide is breathed out and where, as you breathe in, the blood picks up fresh oxygen and starts the cycle once again.

Another function of the cardiovascular system is to make sure that a constant temperature of the body is maintained. This process is called **thermoregulation**.

Thermoregulation

Thermoregulation is the process used by the human body in order to regulate the flow of blood close to the body surface. The body temperature can alter because of the weather, the environment, through illness or participating in sport. As humans are warm-blooded, the body temperature must be kept relatively constant. Too hot or too cold and it can affect the body's ability to function normally.

In order to help the body cool down if it becomes too warm, the blood vessels 'open up' to help promote heat loss. This is called **vasodilation**.

In contrast, in order to help the body warm up if it becomes too cold, the blood vessels 'close down' to help conserve heat loss. This is called **vasoconstriction**.

Activity: Circulatory system

Starting with the heart and its left atrium, draw a basic diagram to show how the blood moves around the body. Make sure you finish back at the left atrium.

Try to show using different colour pens when the blood is oxygenated (red) and when it is deoxygenated (blue).

4 Know the structure and function of the respiratory system

The respiratory system includes: the nose and mouth, the epiglottis, the trachea, the lungs (the bronchus and bronchioles, the alveoli) the diaphragm and the intercostal muscles.

4.1 Structure of the respiratory system

Function of the respiratory system

Air enters the respiratory system through the nostrils and the mouth. It then passes over the epiglottis.

Air travels from the nasal passages and the epiglottis into the larynx, or voice box. The voice box is constructed mainly of cartilage, which is a flexible connective tissue. Food and liquids are blocked from entering the opening of the larynx by the epiglottis; this prevents people from choking when they swallow.

The larynx goes directly into the trachea or the windpipe. The trachea is a tube approximately 12 cm in length and 2.5 cm wide. The trachea is kept open by rings of cartilage within its walls.

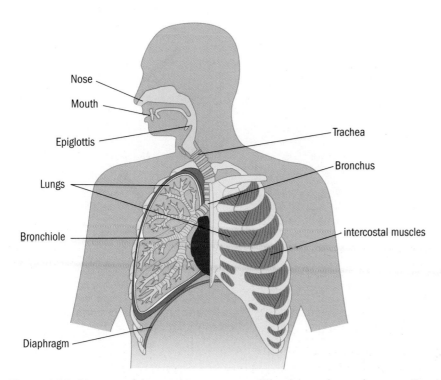

Figure 4.11: Diagram of the respiratory system. What keeps the trachea open?

Around the centre of the chest, the trachea divides into two cartilage-ringed tubes called bronchi. The bronchi enter the lungs and spread in a tree-like fashion into smaller tubes called bronchial tubes.

The bronchial tubes divide and then subdivide. By doing this their walls become thinner. Eventually, they become a tiny group of tubes called **bronchioles**.

Each bronchiole ends in a tiny air chamber that looks like a bunch of grapes. Each chamber contains many cup-shaped cavities known as **alveoli**. The walls of the alveoli, which are only about one cell thick, are the respiratory surface. They are thin, moist, and are surrounded by several numbers of capillaries. The exchange of oxygen and carbon dioxide between blood and air occurs through these walls – this process is called **gaseous exchange**.

4.2 The mechanics of breathing

Breathing in – inhalation

In order for us to take a breath in, the intercostal muscles have to contract, moving the ribcage up and out.

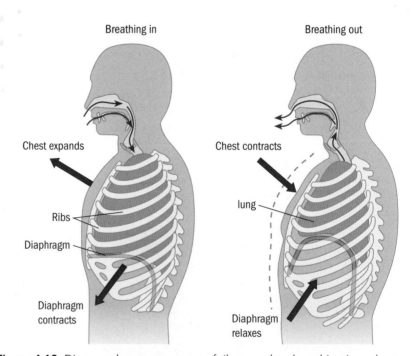

Figure 4.12: Diagram shows movement of ribcage when breathing in and out.

The diaphragm moves down at the same time, creating negative pressure within the thorax – this means it acts as a vacuum and sucks air in. The lungs are held to the thoracic wall by the membranes, and so expand outwards as well. This creates negative pressure within the lungs, and so air rushes in through the upper and lower airways.

Breathing out – expiration

Breathing out or expiration is created when the diaphragm (and the intercostal muscles) relaxes and it is returned to its normal position. This means the thorax gets smaller, increasing the air pressure in the lungs. The lungs deflate and we breathe out.

Activity: Breathing rate

How do you think your breathing rate will alter when you take part in exercise? Can you explain why?

Case study: The assistant coach

Jackie has recently started her Junior Sports Leaders Award (JSLA) while also studying for her BTEC First Diploma in Sport at school. When Jackie leaves school she would like to work coaching children of all ages. Her PE teacher told her about the JSLA course and suggested that once she has this qualification she could progress to the Community Sports Leaders Award (CSLA).

Part of the JSLA means that each person has to be involved in planning and leading a one-hour coaching session. Jackie already has some experience of coaching as she was completing the Sports Coaching unit on the BTEC First Diploma in Sport.

Having passed both her BTEC First Diploma in Sport and her JSLA, Jackie has been looking for summer work with her local Recreation and Amenities Department until term starts again and she returns to college to study for a BTEC National Diploma in Sport.

The department is running a series of sports events and she has been given an assistant's coaching role because she has her JSLA and her BTEC First. The coach who she is working with has asked her to think of some warm-up exercises that have to be suitable for 5-year-olds and teenagers. These two groups will be run on two different days.

- Can you think of some warm-up activities that are suitable for 5-year-old children and teenagers?
- Explain your reasons for choosing these activities.
- What are the similarities and differences between the two sets of activities?

Note: Think about the anatomical and physiological differences of very young children compared with teenagers!

Also how would these activities vary for an adult who was untrained? How would these activities vary for an adult who was trained?

PLTS

Producing a diagram and a poster for this activity will help you develop your skills as an **independent enquirer** and **creative thinker**.

Functional skills

Presenting your research findings should help to develop your **English** skills in speaking.

BTEC ## Assessment activity 4.3   P5 P6 M3 D2

1. Using PowerPoint, or another means of visual presentation, show and describe the function of the cardiorespiratory system.

   Make sure you explain that the two systems, i.e. the cardiovascular and the respiratory system, work together as one in order for the body to function normally. **P5**, **P6**, **M3**

2. Video a practical sports session that your group undertakes.

   Once you have done this watch it thoroughly and with a partner, or in a small group, pick out the following:

   • Signs that the cardiorespiratory system is being stressed but is working effectively and efficiently, such as hot flushed faces, sweating, increased rate of breathing etc.
   • Signs that the cardiorespiratory system is being overly stressed and is beginning not to work so effectively and efficiently, for example people struggling to keep performing at a comfortable level, cramp, having to stop or bend over to get their breath back etc.

   After doing this you should be able to reach an informed opinion of how and why the system worked well or started to struggle to function normally. This can either be recorded on your video or written and presented to your tutor separately. (Tip: you might even be able to produce a commentary on your recording! Ask your tutor for help and guidance.) **D2**

Grading tips

Remember to mention thermoregulation in order to fully achieve P5! Make sure that you evaluate the cardiorespiratory system in order to gain D2: this means you must gather as much evidence as possible from your video and your class work/notes and make your own judgement of how the system worked based on this.

Katie Gilbertson
Gymnastics coach

I work in a number of schools helping to deliver the National Curriculum as well as coaching gymnastics. My main responsibilities include supporting teachers to deliver PE lessons, after-school coaching sessions and running gymnastics clubs, which have children who take part purely for fun and also those who want to compete in local gymnastic competitions.

As I travel between schools I am not based at one place all the time, so I get to meet lots of different people and have access to a wide range of equipment and facilities. I enjoy seeing how children start to develop their co-ordination and are able to really express themselves creatively through taking part in physical activity and gymnastics. It's also nice to work with very competent children who undertake qualifications relating to their performance ability. They achieve certificates and get badges which they wear on their tracksuits very proudly!

As development of the human body is a slow process I have to be careful that I know how to coach the children in my care appropriately so they are safe from harm. Understanding the human body and how it functions is essential for my job. Knowing how it can be developed, coaching someone and seeing them be successful is a fantastic feeling.

I also help out at a gymnastics club which helps to develop teenage gymnasts who are performing at a high standard. This is a very different form of coaching from my day job of working with under-11s. However it is just as important that I am able to deliver training and coaching to match the ability of my gymnasts.

Think about it!

- Why is it important that Kate knows how the human body works for her job role as a gymnastics coach in schools and at the club?
- What qualifications do you think Kate will need for this job?

Just checking

1. What do the terms 'anatomy' and 'physiology' mean?
2. What are the five main functions of the skeleton?
3. What are the six synovial types of joints – give an example of each?
4. What is an antagonistic muscle?
5. What is the difference in structure between an artery and a vein?

Assignment tips

Research tips

- Use a wide range of sources in order to help you fully understand this unit and provide sufficient and well-referenced work for assessment.
- Look in the nursing/health, physiotherapy and human biology sections of the library for reference books to help you understand the basic concepts.
- Websites are useful but check in textbooks to make sure that the web material is reliable and valid.

Get active!

- When studying the skeleton and how joints move, do the movements yourself. This will help you identify the muscles that produce the movement. Feel how they contract and note what movement is produced. If you are aware of which muscles are responsible for specific movements you can start to understand and plan an appropriate training programme for a sport of your choice.
- Find someone who takes part in a different sport from you. What are the key movements for their sport? Can you identify the major muscles used to produce these movements?

Key points!

- Make sure you are familiar with the terminology used in anatomy and physiology – there are a lot to learn!.
- Make sure that you identify any gender differences, e.g. vital organs are larger in males than in females, as this will help you to explain norms produced and used in fitness testing and training (see Unit 1).

5 Injury in sport

Sport can be fun; it can improve your fitness levels and may be a big part of your social life. It is the focus of people working in the sports industry and elite sports performers. There are many health benefits related to taking part in sport.

However, although participating in sport is positive, sport also brings its own risks and hazards. Injury and exercise-induced illnesses can be an outcome of sports participation. It may not happen all the time to everyone involved in sport but it is common. Understanding the types of injuries that occur, the ways in which these can be prevented or reduced and the health and safety laws associated with the sports industry is essential for anyone involved in sports participation, particularly those working in the sports industry.

If you are involved in the sports industry you are likely to witness and deal with incidents regularly. It is vital that you know what to do if someone is injured or becomes ill because of participating in sport. You must know and abide by related health and safety laws. Whether you are a coach, teacher, instructor, attendant, supervisor or leader of a sports session, you should understand how and why risk assessment of a sports environment is vital to protect you and your participants from any risks and hazards.

Learning outcomes

After completing this unit you should:
1. know the different types of injuries and illness associated with sports participation
2. be able to deal with injuries and illnesses associated with sports participation
3. know the risks and hazards associated with sports participation
4. be able to undertake a risk assessment relevant to sport.

Assessment and grading criteria

This table shows you what you must do in order to achieve a pass, merit or distinction grade, and where you can find activities in this book to help you.

To achieve a **pass** grade the evidence must show that the learner is able to:	To achieve a **merit** grade the evidence must show that, in addition to the pass criteria, the learner is able to:	To achieve a **distinction** grade the evidence must show that, in addition to the pass and merit criteria, the learner is able to:
P1 describe four different types of injuries associated with sports participation and their underlying causes **See Assessment activity 5.1, page 134**	**M1** explain why certain injuries and illnesses are associated with sports participation **See Assessment activity 5.2, page 135**	
P2 describe two types and signs of illnesses related to sports participation **See Assessment activity 5.1, page 134**		
P3 demonstrate how to deal with casualties suffering from three different injuries and/or illnesses, with tutor support **See Assessment activity 5.3, page 140**	**M2** deal with casualties suffering from three different injuries and/or illnesses **See Assessment activity 5.3, page 140**	
P4 describe six risks and hazards associated with sports participation **See Assessment activity 5.4, page 149**	**M3** explain risks and hazards associated with sports participation **See Assessment activity 5.4, page 149**	**D1** give a detailed account of why participants are at risk of injury whilst taking part in sport **See Assessment activity 5.4, page 149**
P5 describe four rules, regulations and legislation relating to health, safety and injury in sports participation **See Assessment activity 5.4, page 149**	**M4** explain four rules, regulations and legislation relating to health, safety and injury in sports participation **See Assessment activity 5.4, page 149**	
P6 carry out and produce a risk assessment relevant to a selected sport **See Assessment activity 5.5, page 151**	**M5** describe contingency plans that can be used in a risk assessment **See Assessment activity 5.5, page 151**	**D2** justify the use of specialist equipment to minimise the risk of injury **See Assessment activity 5.5, page 151**

How you will be assessed

This unit will be assessed by assignments that will be designed and marked by the staff at your centre. The assignments are designed to allow you to show your understanding of the unit outcomes.

Your assessment could be in the form of:

- verbal presentation
- visual display
- case studies
- practical tasks
- written assignments
- report writing.

Anne, 16 years old

I play lots of sport and work at the local sports centre at weekends, so I'm aware of how sport injuries occur and sometimes how I could help. In class we worked with our group looking at injuries and illnesses linked to sport. I really enjoyed using role play to get a real idea of how I'd need to react to injuries and illnesses if I had to help a casualty. It was good fun and gave an insight into what might happen when I'm at work. When our tutor assessed us we had to work with another group and not people we knew. This was quite scary and really made me think as it made everything more real. We've just started looking at risks and hazards and different health and safety laws. I don't think this will be as much fun. I know I must understand it or I won't be able to work in the sports industry. If I don't follow the legislation and how it affects my place of work I could even be sued.

Over to you!

- What are you most looking forward to studying in this unit?
- What courses and qualifications could you study to help your future career?

1 Know the different types of injuries and illness associated with sports participation

Warm-up

Sports injuries

Think of one sports-related injury

Try to describe how this type of injury might commonly occur

Now try to think of ways in which you might help someone avoid this type of injury.

1.1 Causes of injuries

There are many reasons why sports injuries happen and, as a result, many different types of sports injuries. These are classified by identifying the cause of the injury:

- loading
- intrinsic factors
- extrinsic factors
- over-use
- alignment
- intensity
- effect of levers
- gravity
- resistance.

Key term

Loading – the overload principle is how the body adapts to stresses. The more you do, the more you are capable of.

Loading

The body can adapt to pressures and strains caused by the demands of physical exercise and sport, but this does not happen instantly. The body needs time to adapt to the demand and gain sufficient strength to cope with what is required. If this demand is placed on the body without it having a chance to adapt, then the body cannot cope. It may try to deal with what is happening but will eventually fail. This failure can result in damage to the body, i.e. a sports injury.

An example of a situation that might cause a loading injury is if you try to lift a heavy weight in the gym that is far heavier than you have lifted before. If over a period of time, you gradually build up the weight you are lifting then you will be able to lift the 'heavy' weight. But if you go from lifting 40 kg to trying to lift 80 kg then the stress placed on your body will be too much. The injuries caused may include muscle/tendon/ligament tears, strains and sprains.

Have you suffered an injury as a result of over-loading?

Overloading can be safely achieved by applying the **FITT principle**:

- **Frequency** – how often you train or take part in any physical activity.
- **Intensity** – how hard you exercise, or the amount of effort you put into your training programme.
- **Type** – type of exercise or activity you are doing.
- **Time** – the duration of your exercise session. It is recommended that you spend a minimum of 20–60 minutes training, but this will depend on fitness levels, goals and the time you have available:
    - For weight loss training, you should do 20–40 minutes of exercise.
    - For cardio-respiratory training you should do 40–50 minutes of specific exercise.

Intrinsic factors

Intrinsic factors come from inside the body and cause injury. Everybody has their own individual mechanics and some are better than others. Everyone has their own unique threshold of injury. There are injuries that can occur when stress develops within the athlete, for example an instant injury which is a sudden tear of muscle, rupture of ligament or tendon or sprained joint.

Extrinsic factors

Extrinsic injuries occur when an outside force is applied to the body which it cannot cope with. This might be, for example, body contact that could occur in a scrum, head-on collision or tackle; being hit by an object like a racquet, stick, hard ball or bat; a vehicular accident, which might involve a ski, car, hang-glider, boat or bicycle; and environmental factors like hitting a wall, post or floor, falling on a hard track or pitch, wet or hard ground, and injuries caused by weather conditions.

Over-use

Over-use injuries usually occur over time. They are the result of repetitively over stressing the body and can cause injury to the tendons, bones and joints. Common examples include tennis elbow (lateral epicondylitis), swimmer's shoulder (rotator cuff tendinitis and impingement), runner's knee, jumper's knee (infrapatellar tendinitis), Achilles tendinitis and shin splints. In most sports and activities, over-use injuries are the most common as a lot of sports require the performer to repeat a particular action over and over again, e.g. in the golf swing or rowing.

Alignment

Poor or incorrect posture, or body alignment, can result in injury. It is important that everyone has good posture as without this our body adapts to bad positions and this can make it difficult to perform everyday movements without pain or discomfort. The effect of incorrect alignment on sports participation means that performers cannot work at their best.

> **Key term**
>
> **FITT principle** – frequency, intensity, time and type.

> **Key term**
>
> **Over-use injury** – inflammation of tendons, muscles, joints or bones resulting from long periods of overuse.

Intensity

If you train at an intensity that your body is not used to this can result in similar problems to dealing with overload – the body is not able to cope and this results in injury.

Effect of levers

The skeleton is jointed to allow movement. These joints are covered by skeletal muscles which allow our bodies to work in a particular manner and make our joints a **fulcrum** when we lift a weight. If the weight exceeds what our muscles can cope with then it will result in damage to the soft tissue.

Gravity

Our body responds to the natural pull of gravity therefore if, for example, you are knocked off balance in a tackle you are likely to fall down. If you clip the top of the hurdle with your foot it throws you off balance. This is a common cause of injury.

Resistance

Resistance training is the term used to describe using weights, machines, and even your own body weight to effectively work your muscles. It is the term used to accurately describe all forms of resistance training, whether working with weights or not. However, as for intensity and overload, if the resistance is too great, then damage can occur; for example – lowering a weight too quickly because it is too great to control.

1.2 Types of injuries

As with causes of injuries, there are also many different types of sports injuries. Some are more common than others, e.g. bruises. Some are common in particular sports, e.g. a hamstring injury in football. Some are common to certain positions played within a game, for example head injuries to the forwards in a scrum in rugby.

Over-use injuries

Over-use injuries are described as tissue damage that results from repetitive demand or stress over a period of time (also see above). The types of injury commonly associated with over-use injuries include tendonitis, shin splints and dislocations.

Tendonitis – for example, Achilles tendonitis – is inflammation or irritation of a tendon. Tendons are the thick fibrous cords that attach muscles to bone. They function to transmit the power generated by a muscle contraction to move a bone. Achilles tendonitis is one of the most common tendonitis injuries in sport.

Key term

Fulcrum – the pivot point of a lever.

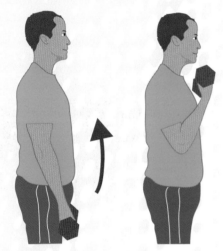

Figure 5.1: Which muscle contracts as the arm pivots at the fulcrum (the elbow)?

Did you know?

It is estimated that Achilles tendonitis accounts for around 11% of all running injuries.

The Achilles tendon is the large tendon at the back of the ankle. It connects the large calf muscles (**Gastrocnemius** and **Soleus**) to the heel bone (**calcaneus**) and provides the power in the push-off phase of running. The Achilles tendon can become inflamed through over-use or training too much, especially on hard surfaces or up hills. The Achilles tendon has a poor blood supply which is why it is slow to heal.

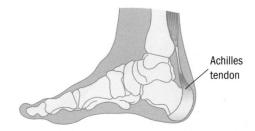

Achilles tendon

Figure 5.2: What can you do to try to prevent injury to your Achilles tendon?

Shin splints are the general name given to pain at the front of the lower leg. Shin splints are not a diagnosis but a description of symptoms, for which there could be a number of causes. Shin splints are common in people who do plenty of vigorous exercise, especially when the exercise is on a hard surface. Long-distance runners and ballet dancers are particularly susceptible.

The muscles in the front of the shin become swollen and enlarged. Because these muscles are contained and sealed within a tough membrane, it only takes a small amount of swelling before pain occurs because the muscles cannot expand. This pain gets worse as a person exercises. The muscles that help the foot bend upwards at the ankle are involved, which is why running and jumping contributes to the problem.

The specific area in front of the shin bone feels tender to the touch and may actually appear swollen too.

Dislocation is an injury in which the ends of your bones are forced from their normal positions. The cause is usually something like a blow or fall.

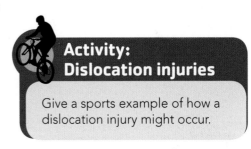

**Activity:
Dislocation injuries**

Give a sports example of how a dislocation injury might occur.

Dislocations are common injuries in contact sports, like football and hockey, and in sports that may involve falls, like downhill skiing and volleyball. Dislocations may occur in major joints, such as your shoulder, hip, knee, elbow or ankle or in smaller joints, like your finger, thumb or toe. The injury will temporarily deform and immobilise your joint and may result in sudden and severe pain and swelling.

Fractures

A fracture is a complete or incomplete break in a bone. There is no difference between a fracture and a break; it is the same thing. Fractures, like so many other elements of anatomy and physiology, can be classified in many different ways.

Open or compound fractures

An open fracture is a broken bone that penetrates the skin. This is an important distinction from a closed fracture because when a broken bone penetrates the skin there is a need for immediate treatment, and an operation is often required to clean the area of the fracture. Open fractures are typically caused by high-energy injuries such as car crashes, falls, or sports injuries.

Djibril Cisse's dreams of appearing in World Cup 2006 were over after he broke his right leg in the French team's final warm-up game against China (France 3-1 China).

Closed or simple fractures

A closed fracture is a broken bone that does not penetrate the skin and is therefore more difficult to diagnose immediately. The casualty may feel some pain and discomfort and possibly show some signs of bruising and swelling around the damaged area. However, this may not happen immediately depending on the severity of the fracture. Sports people have been known to continue performing and only later have been found to have been playing with a closed fracture.

Activity: Fractures

Stress fractures or closed fractures are difficult to identify from visual symptoms. How might a stress fracture be diagnosed accurately?

Soft tissue injury

The term 'soft tissue' refers to the tendons, ligaments, and muscles throughout your body. The injury is usually due to chronic stress placed on a joint, or over-use, but can also be caused by a single blow. Soft tissue injuries include strains, sprains, grazes and bruising but can also include injuries such as tendonitis and dislocations.

Sprains

The joints of your body are supported by ligaments. Ligaments are strong bands of connective tissue that connect one bone to another. A sprain is a simple stretch or tear of the ligaments. The areas of your body that are most vulnerable to sprains are your ankles, knees, and wrists. A sprained ankle can occur when your foot turns inward. This can put extreme tension on the ligaments of your outer ankle and cause a sprain. A sprained knee can be the result of a sudden twist. A wrist sprain often occurs when you fall on an outstretched hand. Most mild sprains heal with 'PRICE' (protection, rest, ice, compression, and elevation) and exercise. Moderate sprains may require a period of bracing. The most severe sprains may need surgery to repair torn ligaments. The blood 'pools' at the lowest point, following a sprain.

Strains

Our bones are supported by a combination of muscles and tendons. Tendons connect muscles to bones. A strain is the result of an injury to either a muscle or a tendon.. The strain may be a simple stretch in your muscle or tendon, or it may be a partial or complete tear in the muscle-and-tendon combination. The recommended treatment for a strain is the same as for a sprain: protection, rest, ice, compression and elevation. This should be followed by simple exercises to relieve pain and restore mobility. For a serious tear, the soft tissues may need to be repaired surgically.

Signs/symptoms of strains include:

- pain – sudden onset of severe pain, aggravated by movement
- tenderness at the site of tear
- local muscle spasm
- swelling of variable degree
- a gap is present in severe cases (total ruptures)
- bruising – which may be distant from the site of injury
- a lump – this is usually seen when the tear has been total, e.g. rectus femoris rupture
- pain on stretching muscle and contracting the muscle.

Treatment for sprains:

- rest – total for 24 hours/48 hours
- ice – to promote vasoconstriction of blood vessels
- stop bleeding as soon as possible
- compression – to slow bleeding
- elevation.

Bruising

Bruises are less commonly known as **contusions** or **haematomas**. Bruises occur due to direct trauma, often a blow to the outer part of the body, for example the thigh or back of the calf. This injury is commonly referred to as a 'dead leg'. It is a bruising of muscle tissue.

What causes a bruise to look as it does? The muscle is squashed between the object causing the impact and the underlying bone e.g. cricket ball or an opponent striking the muscles on the leg. Muscle fibres are squashed and the associated capillaries are torn. This results in bleeding into the area which causes a bruise or a haematoma formation.

Treatment

Contusions cause swelling and pain and limit joint range of motion near the injury. Torn blood vessels may cause bluish discoloration. The injured muscle may feel weak and stiff. To control pain, bleeding, and inflammation, keep the muscle in a gentle stretch position and use the PRICE formula:

- **P**rotect – protect the injured area from further harm by stopping play.
- **R**est – it is important that the injured area be kept as still as possible with no weight on it
- **I**ce – apply ice wrapped in a clean cloth. (Remove ice after 10 minutes.)
- **C**ompression – lightly wrap the injured area in a soft bandage or ace wrap.
- **E**levation – raise it to a level above the heart.

Most athletes with contusions get better quickly without surgery. Do not massage the injured area. During the first 24 to 48 hours after injury (acute phase) you will probably need to continue using rest, ice, compression bandages, and elevation of the injured area to

Did you know?

Football is the world's most popular sport with over 240 million registered players worldwide and many millions more who play just for fun. Footballers suffer more injuries than those involved in other sports like rugby, cricket, hockey, cycling and even boxing, however most football injuries are not very serious.

Key terms

Contusion – another name for a bruise.

Intramuscular haematoma – type of bruise where blood has not seeped very far away from the point of contact because the muscle bundle has not been disrupted, so the blood is retained in the muscle bundle sheath.

Intermuscular haematoma – type of bruise formed when blood has seeped some distance away from the point of contact. This shows that the muscle bundle sheath has been damaged and has allowed blood to seep out and away from the area.

control bleeding, swelling and pain. While the injured part heals, keep exercising the uninjured parts of your body to maintain your overall level of fitness.

Grazes

A graze, or abrasion, is an injury where the skin is scraped off against a rough surface, such as a fall on a hard surface or astro-turf. Most grazes only take off the surface layer of skin and leave a raw tender area underneath. However, some grazes can be much deeper and, in rare cases, the deeper layers of skin can be removed. Falls, scrapes and friction burns can all cause grazes.

Most cuts and grazes can be easily treated at home. However, more severe cases may need medical attention, such as stitches (sutures) to close the wound. The most common complication that can occur from a cut or graze is an infection, such as tetanus.

Blisters

Blisters typically develop due to friction on the skin. This can occur from the rubbing of clothing or sports equipment on the surface layer of the skin. Over time, the continued friction can cause the top layer of skin to separate from the layer of skin below.

One warning sign that a blister is about to develop is redness and warmth on the skin called a hot spot. Next, fluid fills the space between the top two layers of skin to provide protection from continued rubbing. When this happens you will see a blister that looks like a little bubble on the skin.

Most people get blisters on the heels, soles of the feet, and palms of the hands because they rub against shoes, socks or sports equipment.

Unbroken blisters that do not cause discomfort can be left alone to heal, because the best protection against infection is a blister's own skin. You can put a dry non-adhesive dressing over it to protect it until it is healed fully.

Cuts

Clean a cut with clean cold water if possible to help remove any debris that may be in it (this will also help to stop any bleeding). Dry and cover with a sterile dressing.

Serious injuries

Concussion

A concussion is an injury to the brain that results in temporary loss of normal brain function. It is usually caused by a blow to the head. This type of injury is common in contact sports like boxing or rugby. Cuts or bruises may be present on the head or face, but in many cases there are no signs of injury. Many people assume that concussions involve a loss of consciousness, but that is not true. In most cases, a person with concussion never loses consciousness.

People with concussion often cannot remember what happened immediately before or after the injury, and may be confused. A concussion can affect memory, judgement, reflexes, speech, balance, and muscle co-ordination. Any individual suspected of receiving a concussion-type injury should be advised to seek medical attention.

Even mild concussions should not be taken lightly. Neurosurgeons and other brain injury experts emphasise that, although some concussions are less serious than others, there is no such thing as a minor concussion. In most cases a single concussion should not cause permanent damage. A second concussion soon after the first one, however, does not have to be very strong for its effects to be deadly or permanently disabling.

Back injuries

Back injuries are quite common in sport, with most athletes suffering from them at some stage in their career.

Sports that use repetitive impact (e.g. running) or weight loading at the end of a range-of-motion (e.g. weightlifting) commonly cause damage to the lumbar spine (lower back). Sports that involve contact (e.g., football) place the cervical spine (neck) at risk of injury. The thoracic spine (mid-portion of the spine at the level of the rib cage) is less likely to be injured in sports because it is relatively immobile due to the rib cage.

Spinal cord injuries

A spinal cord injury is damage or injury to the spinal cord that causes a loss or impaired function resulting in reduced mobility or feeling. It is often caused by trauma, e.g. a car accident, a bad fall or a sports injury such as diving into a shallow pool, a rugby tackle or a fall in skiing or horse riding. The resulting damage to the cord is known as a lesion; any resulting paralysis is known as quadraplegia or tetraplegia if the injury is in the cervical region, or paraplegia if the injury is in the thoracic, lumbar or sacral region (see Unit 4, Anatomy and physiology for sport, page 97).

It is estimated that there are 40,000 people in the UK alone who are paralysed through spinal cord injury. The spinal cord is part of the central nervous system and carries signals to and from the brain, controlling almost every function of the body. When there is damage or trauma to the spinal cord it will result in loss or impaired function causing reduced mobility and/or feeling. The effects of spinal cord injury depend on the type and level of injury. These may be divided into two areas:

- **Complete** – means that there is no function (no sensation or voluntary movement) below the level of the injury.
- **Incomplete** – there is some function below the level of injury. A person may be able to feel parts of the body that cannot be moved, they may be able to move one limb more than the other.

Footballers often clash heads when tackling for a ball in the air – another example of how injuries can happen even when playing to the rules of the sport.

Did you know?

Up to 20% of all injuries that occur in sports involve the lower back or neck.

1.3 Types and signs of illnesses

Asthma

Asthma is defined as: a long-term condition in which over-sensitive airways become narrow and inflamed, making it difficult to breathe in and out normally. Its cause is not completely understood, but asthma is one of a group of allergic conditions, including eczema and hayfever, which often occur together.

Asthma attacks can vary in their severity and are sometimes relatively mild, but the condition is still a dangerous one. An asthma attack can spiral out of control at any time. One of the more common forms of this condition, exercise-induced asthma, affects many different people. As the name suggests, this is a condition that is brought about when someone starts participating in vigorous physical activity.

The most likely cause of exercise-induced asthma is the change in temperature or humidity that happens when beginning exercise. Often the breathing rate will go up naturally so if the air is a lot cooler this increases the flow of air into the lungs and can trigger an attack. The airways may become narrow and the result will include symptoms such as coughing, tightening of the chest, wheezing, feelings of fatigue and a shortness of breath.

Exercise-induced asthma may last for a period of between 5 and 20 minutes, or however long the individual tries to continue with the activity. After they stop to rest the symptoms will usually pass in about 5 or 10 minutes provided proper treatment methods are used.

Treatments can include preventative inhalers (usually red-brown in colour) and reliever inhalers (usually blue in colour). Preventative inhalers help to reduce inflammation in the airways and include becotide and flixotide. Reliever inhalers are used when airways become constricted. They make the airways bigger, but do not treat the cause of the inflammation. They are a good short-term measure, and relief will usually be instant. Everyone who suffers with asthma should have a blue 'rescue' inhaler, but should rarely need to use it. These inhalers contain ventolin and salbutamol. If a person needs to use their blue inhaler every day, they should see a GP because better treatment is available.

Heart attack

See diagram of heart in Unit 4, Anatomy and physiology for sport, page 110.

Heart attacks are triggered by different factors, including diet and genetic factors. Fortunately a heart attack is not a common sports-related illness. However, if someone does have a heart attack while taking part in sport you should know what signs and symptoms to look out for and what to do. A heart attack occurs when blood flow to a section of heart muscle becomes blocked. If the flow of blood is not restored quickly, the section of heart muscle becomes damaged from lack of oxygen and begins to die.

A heart attack, or myocardial infarction, can be eased by rest as this reduces the demands on the heart, but it will not help the pain. The blood supply to the affected heart muscles cannot be restored while the clot remains. Emergency help must be summoned immediately.

The most common heart attack signs and symptoms are:

- Chest discomfort or pain – uncomfortable pressure, squeezing, fullness, or pain in the centre of the chest that can be mild or strong. This discomfort or pain lasts more than a few minutes or goes away and comes back.
- Upper body discomfort in one or both arms, the back, neck, jaw, or stomach.
- Shortness of breath may occur with or before chest discomfort.
- Other signs include nausea (feeling sick), vomiting, light-headedness or fainting, or breaking out in a cold sweat.

Imbalance of heat

Training or competing in sport in extreme conditions can lead to an imbalance of heat and cause unconsciousness. The skin is the key to the body's ability to regulate its temperature (thermoregulation). Once the brain senses that there is an increase in temperature, it initiates thermoregulatory mechanisms. The skin is the main cooling organ. It maximises heat loss by using **radiation**, **convection**, **conduction** and **evaporation**.

Heat imbalance

Heat stroke, exhaustion and severe dehydration are risks in summer sports, especially in aerobic activities such as football and running.

Heat stroke is typically caused by a combination of a hot environment, strenuous exercise, clothing that limits evaporation of sweat, inadequate adaptation to the heat, too much body fat and/or lack of fitness. Early recognition and fast treatment of evolving heat stroke can save lives.

Early warning signs of impending heat stroke may include irritability, confusion, apathy, belligerence, emotional instability, or irrational behaviour. The coach may be the first to note that a player, heating up, can no longer think clearly. Giddiness, undue fatigue, and vomiting can also be early signs.

Heat imbalance can be a medical emergency. The life-saving adage is: cool first and transport second.

There are some things you should do for heat imbalance (e.g. heat stroke, exhaustion or dehydration) or while waiting for medical help:

- get professional medical help as quickly as possible
- move to a cool area as quickly as possible

Key terms

Radiation – heat is directly lost to the atmosphere.

Convection – heat loss is facilitated by moving air or water vapour.

Conduction – heat loss by direct contact with a cooler body.

Evaporation – heat is lost by turning liquid (sweat) into vapour (the skin's major heat loss mechanism).

 Did you know?

Serb tennis player, Novak Djokovic retired from a match due to 'heat illness'. Djokovic had a medical timeout after recovering a service break to lead 2–1 in the third set and complained of heat-related problems. The Serb draped towels packed with ice around his neck during changeovers, and lingered in the shade behind the baselines as long as possible.

- increase ventilation by opening windows or using a fan
- give the person water to drink if possible, but do not give medication such as aspirin or paracetamol
- shower the skin with cool, but not cold, water (15–18°C)
- alternatively, cover the body with cool, damp towels or sheets, or immerse in cool water
- if convulsions start, move nearby objects out of the way to prevent injury (do not use force or put anything in the mouth)
- if the patient is unconscious and vomiting, move them into the recovery position by turning them on their side and making sure their airways are clear. Continually monitor making sure that their airways are clear and they are still breathing.

Cold imbalance

In cold temperatures you begin to lose heat faster than you produce it. Prolonged exposure to cold may result in hypothermia, or abnormally low body temperature. Body temperatures that drop too low affect the brain and make it difficult to think clearly or move quickly. Hypothermia is dangerous because you may not realise that it is happening until it is too late.

The porters of Everest do not dress against the cold. Porters are prone to hypothermia and frostbite.

Hypothermia is more likely at very cold temperatures, but can occur even at cool temperatures (above 4°C) if a person becomes chilled from rain, sweat, or submersion in cold water. Victims of hypothermia are most often elderly or babies and those who are outside for long periods of time, such as long-distance swimmers or mountaineers.

Signs of hypothermia include:

- shivering/exhaustion
- confusion/fumbling hands
- memory loss/slurred speech
- drowsiness.

Severe hypothermia needs urgent medical treatment in hospital. Shivering is a good guide to how severe the hypothermia is. If the person can stop shivering of their own accord, hypothermia is mild; but if they cannot stop shivering, it is moderate to severe.

Things you should do for mild hypothermia or while waiting for medical help:

- move the person indoors, or somewhere warm, as soon as possible
- ensure that they change out of any wet clothing
- wrap them in blankets, towels, coats – whatever you have – protecting the head and torso as a priority
- increase activity if possible, but not to the point where sweating occurs, which cools the skin down again
- once body temperature has increased, be sure to keep the person warm and dry.

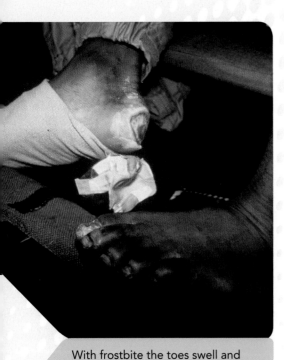

With frostbite the toes swell and have to be amputated

Viral infections

Viral infections, such as a cold or influenza, can have symptoms like high temperature, shivering, headache, dizziness and exhaustion. Be careful that infections are not confused with hypothermia as they have similar symptoms. Sports participation is not recommended for anyone suffering from a viral infection.

Hypoglycaemia

Most people will usually develop symptoms suggestive of **hypoglycaemia** when blood glucose levels are too low. They may have not eaten well or for a long time or have undertaken a lot of physical activity so that their natural body stores of blood sugar have been depleted. A person with low blood sugar levels may experience any of the following:

> ### Key term
>
> **Hypoglycaemia** – abnormally low level of sugar in the blood.

- nervousness
- sweating
- intense hunger
- trembling
- weakness
- palpitations
- trouble in speaking.

Most patients recognise the early warning signs of hypoglycaemia and counteract them by eating.

Diabetes is a blood sugar level disorder where a person's insulin is not adequately produced and so they may have to take more insulin via tablets or injection, on prescription from their GP. Insulin is normally produced in the pancreas and helps the cells in the body absorb glucose from the blood. Normally, the glucose level rises after a meal. Too much insulin in the blood and other diseases can cause hypoglycaemic episodes (also known as hypos).

Diabetes does not cause hypoglycaemia but there are various reasons why a hypo can happen:

- taking too much insulin
- missing a meal or delaying a meal
- vigorous exercise
- drinking too much alcohol.

Glucose is vital for brain function and the symptoms of hypoglycaemia occur to warn you to take in some food quickly. All too often these warnings are ignored – resulting in loss of consciousness. Some people with diabetes do not experience warnings. This is more common in people who have either had diabetes for a long time or those who have been tightly controlled with frequent hypos.

Activity: Considering sports injuries

Complete the following table with a partner.

Try to think of as many different sporting examples as you can for each section – not just the obvious ones.

Sport	Sports injury/illness	Cause
Running	Dehydration	Extrinsic factor – temperature
Football	Hamstring strain	Extrinsic factor – Slipped on wet field reaching for ball Intrinsic factor – Lack of flexibility
Skiing	Leg fracture	Extrinsic factor – environmental

PLTS

Thinking about how to design your poster to be clear in its message to the general public will help you develop your skills as a **creative thinker**.

Functional skills

Presenting your research findings in a poster format should help you develop your **English** and **IT** skills.

Assessment activity 5.1

A new local sports complex is about to open. You have seen some jobs for the complex advertised in the local press. One is for a fitness suite supervisor. The fitness suite will be used predominantly by the college students and staff during the day, however during lunch hours, evenings and weekends it is going to be opened to the general public.

You have applied for the supervisor's post to help manage this facility when being used by the public.

As part of the application process you have been asked to design a poster that can be used in the facility to warn people of 'what to do and what not to do' to avoid injury or illnesses while training in the suite.

Make sure you: describe four common injuries and two illnesses that relate to training in a fitness suite. Give as much detail as possible **P1**, **P2**

Grading tips

Ensure you use four examples of sports injuries and two examples of illnesses relating to fitness training in the fitness suite.

Try to be clear but succinct in your explanation of these issues on the poster.

Assessment activity 5.2

You have been shortlisted for the post you applied for in the new fitness suite because of your poster design. You now have to attend an interview.

The first part of the interview needs you to present your poster and explain with reasons and in detail the message you were trying to convey. You will be presenting to the Manager and the Deputy Manager of the suite who will ask you questions about the poster, your explanation of it and why you chose this particular topic as part of the interview process.

Explain how at least three of the injuries and illnesses you portray in your poster may be caused and suggest ways in which they can be prevented or minimised. **M1**

Grading tips

Make sure that you consider the following when preparing for your interview:

- specific issues relating to this environment
- fitness equipment used for training on
- fitness testing equipment
- temperature of the environment that the public are in.

In addition, as a member of staff you would need to understand what might go wrong and what to do if it did so did you consider:

- health and safety factors
- first aid resources
- emergency help if needed.

PLTS

Being able to explain why this topic is important will help you with your skills as a **reflective learner.**

Functional skills

Presenting your research findings in a poster format should help you to develop your **English** skills in speaking and listening.

2 Deal with injuries and illnesses associated with sports participation

Sport is more popular than ever before. Large numbers of people participate in a variety of school, college, university, professional, and recreational sports. As sport becomes more prominent in our lives, responsibility falls on the shoulders of people like coaches, supervisors, parents, teachers, clinicians, officials, and other workers involved in the sports industry to provide an environment that minimises the risk of injury in all sports. It is vitally important that you follow certain procedures when treating someone who is injured or who has become ill as a result of participating in sport.

2.1 Procedures and treatments

The procedures you follow may vary slightly depending on the organisation that you are working for or the qualification to treat people that you have. However the basic rules will stay the same.

1. Assess the situation carefully and as quickly as possible. This means looking at what has happened, how it happened, why it happened and the impact it has had on the individual (the casualty).

2. Always make sure you protect yourself first. Do not approach a casualty until any danger has been removed.

3. Once any danger has been removed and it is safe to approach the casualty you must protect them from any further injury.

4. Once this is done you can now assess the injury in detail.

Minor injury

Most minor sporting injuries can be treated by the PRICE treatment.

Table 5.1: The PRICE treatment is used for many sporting injuries.

P	Protection – injured player instructed to refrain from all painful positions/activities. Injured part should be immobilised by a pressure bandage or support bandage to assist this. If appropriate – injured player measured for crutches and taught non-weight bearing (NWB) walking.
R	Rest – in the first 48 hours after injury rest is a valuable contribution to the healing process. All activity or positions causing discomfort or swelling should be avoided. Move to active treatments as soon as possible by carrying out movements that do not produce pain.
I	Ice – apply ice or cold to the injured part. Ice will make local blood vessel's diameter narrower (constriction) causing a reduction in swelling and heat. It will cause sensory numbing of the area to reduce pain. Every precaution should be taken when applying ice. When icing a joint, the ice should be removed every 5 minutes and the joint moved gently in a pain-free range. Protect the skin over the injured part from 'skin burn' by putting the ice in damp towelling or by applying oil to the skin so that super-cooling does not occur as water escapes from under the pack and is trapped stagnant drawing salt and tissue fluid to the surface to cause a 'blister' or 'ice burn'.
C	Compression – apply a compression bandage. It may be worn for up to 24 hours before reapplication and offers counter-pressure to the injured site, reducing blood flow and controlling swelling. The patient's circulation should be checked prior to leaving the treatment area.
E	Elevation – the limb should be placed in an elevated position (above level of heart) which assists with the return of blood and fluid to the heart from the injury site. It reduces the formation of further swelling. Incorporate pain-free active (low level) non-weight-bearing movements in elevation to assist drainage.

Major/serious injury

If the incident is more serious and requires emergency treatment then it is important that you remain calm and follow the basic rules whilst getting professional help immediately.

Qualifications

Some jobs require you to hold a first aid qualification as there is a chance that first aid might have to be used in the work place at certain times. This is true in a sports environment if you are a coach, teacher, pool attendant or gym instructor. These types of jobs generally require a first aid qualification in addition to the qualification you may need to do the main aim of the job, e.g. teach or coach a particular sport.

First aid

If you hold a recognised first aid qualification then you might need to follow the aims and principles of first aid when treating a casualty:

Aims of first aid:

- to preserve life, and that includes your own
- to prevent further injury to the casualty
- to promote recovery of the casualty.

Principles of first aid:

Assess the situation – what's happened and why?

Get help – Calling the emergency services

If you call the emergency services for help it is vital that you give them accurate details of the incident that you are reporting (likewise, if you send someone to ring them while you deal with a casualty you will need to make sure that you give them all the necessary information to pass on).

You will need to let the emergency services know the following information:

- If the casualty is not breathing tell this to the emergency services first – this will make your call top priority.
- Who you are and why you are calling.
- Where you are – exactly – specific location is essential. Don't just tell them you are at the Sports Centre when actually the casualty is on number 8 rugby pitch that belongs to the centre but is half a mile away from the centre itself.
- What has happened to the casualty, e.g. collision with another player.
- When did the incident happen – how long ago?
- Number of casualties and details of their injuries.
- Details of any first aid given.

This person has been put in the recovery position. Make sure you are familiar with this position.

Did you know?

First aiders need to deal with the aftermath of a situation once it has been resolved and the casualty has gone to hospital or been treated for a minor injury. They need to keep records of what happened and what they did. This normally takes the form of an incident/accident book or form that is in the organisation where the injury occurred.

Case study: Basketball incident

A collision occurs between two players going for the ball in a basketball game.

Make the area safe – stop the game and make sure all equipment and people are away from the casualties.

Assess the casualties – approach the casualties and check their injuries in order of priority, i.e. if one is sitting up holding their head and talking to you, you know they are breathing and are not a serious casualty, at this time. However, if the other casualty is lying still on the floor not moving or speaking then they could possibly not be breathing and therefore should get priority of treatment. Talk calmly and shake their shoulders gently to see if they regain consciousness and respond to you.

The casualty may gain consciousness but will need to be kept safe. It is recommended that they get checked at a hospital as they have been unconscious and therefore may be suffering from concussion – see page 128.

If there is no response then make sure that the **airway is open**. This is done by making sure that the casualty is lying flat on their back. Tilt the head back and lift up the chin. Check inside the mouth to make sure nothing is blocking the airway, e.g. gum shield etc. Anything in the mouth that blocks the airway should be removed immediately.

Assess the casualty's breathing. Put your cheek close to their mouth and look down their body towards their feet. Listen for 10 seconds to see if you can:

- hear them breathing
- feel their breath on your cheek
- see their chest rising and falling as they breathe.

If the casualty is breathing – put them into the recovery position – see diagram.

It is essential to assess the casualty's breathing and state of injury in order to get the correct help.

The recovery position is used on an unconscious breathing casualty so that:

- they maintain an open airway
- if they vomit it will flow away
- the position is recognised by others who have attended first aid training.

If the casualty is not breathing: get help and then start Cardiopulmonary Resuscitation (CPR) (see figure 5.3).

- Check that the airway is open and there is nothing obstructing it such as the tongue or a gum shield.
- Make a seal over the mouth and pinch the nose. Give 2 vents – watching the chest rise and fall each time. (Start with 5 vents if resuscitating a child and then continue in the cycle of 2 vents to 30 compressions.)
- Then, placing the hands on the middle of the sternum, give 30 compressions. See diagram. (You may only need to use fingers if resuscitating a child.) You should keep repeating this cycle of 2 vents to 30 compressions until professional help arrives or you cannot continue without endangering your own life; remember the 3 P's from the aims of first aid (see above).

Get a player/official from the game to go and ring 999 for an ambulance – tell them to come back and tell you that they have done that and how long the ambulance will be. If the unconscious casualty is not breathing, then you, as a first aider, will need to give CPR until the ambulance arrives. If the unconscious casualty is breathing, you, as the first aider, will put them into the recovery position and keep checking that they are breathing. Keep talking to them to reassure them of what is happening if they do regain consciousness and keep them warm and comfortable.

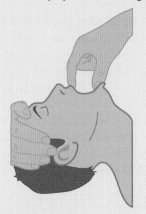

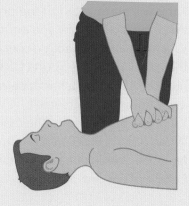

Figure 5.3: Make sure you are familiar with CPR procedures.

It is important to keep these records so that you can be sure that an accurate account of every incident is logged. They can then be viewed to help the organisation look at how these types of incidents are dealt with and if they can possibly be prevented in the future. (See example of a report form below.) Such records may also prove to be useful evidence if the casualties' conditions deteriorate at a later stage.

Incident/Accident Report Form

Name of club

1. Site where incident/accident took place: ....

2. Name of person in charge of session/competition: ....

Name of injured person: ....

Address of injured person: ....

Date and time of incident/accident: ....

3. Nature of incident/accident: ....

Give details of how and precisely where the incident/accident took place. Describe what activity was taking place, eg training game, getting changed, etc.

Give full details of the action taken including any first aid treatment and the name(s) of the first aider(s):

Were any of the following contacted: ....

Police:	Yes ☐	No ☐
Ambulance:	Yes ☐	No ☐
Parent/guardian:	Yes ☐	No ☐

4. What happened to the injured person following the incident/accident? (eg went home, went to hospital, carried on with session)

....

5. All of the above facts are a true and accurate record of the incident/accident.

SIGNED: .... DATE: ....

Name:.. Position...................................

Figure 5.4: Example of a sports incident report form.

2.2 Dealing with different types of casualties

As sport is a popular activity and everyone is encouraged to take part in exercise as a health benefit, it means that there is a great variety of people who may become a casualty and need help and assistance.

The types of people you may deal with as casualties include:

- adults
- children
- teenagers
- the elderly
- pregnant women
- participants with special needs – wheelchair participants, those with visual or hearing impairment.

Dealing with different types of injury and illness

Most sports injuries that are minor can be dealt with by using the PRICE treatment mentioned earlier in the chapter – see page 127.

Injuries and or illnesses that are severe always need emergency help.

PLTS

Undertaking a first aid assessment and showing how you would deal with three injuries or illnesses will help develop your skills as a **reflective learner**.

Functional skills

Identifying the injuries will develop your **English** skills in speaking and listening.

BTEC ### Assessment activity 5.3 P3 M2

You were successful in getting the job at the sports complex in the fitness suite. You are now undertaking your initial training in the job and as part of this you have to successfully complete a first aid qualification. In order to pass the part of the practical assessment of the first aid qualification you must:

Identify three different injuries or illnesses that may occur at work and clearly show your examiner how you would deal with these issues as a first aider. P3

If you do this on your own you will achieve M2 as well as P3! M2

Grading tips

Try to do the above activity on your own and without the support of your tutor.

Remember always to follow the basic first aid principles for any injury or illness.

Case study: Adam, semi-professional squash player

Adam is a semi-professional squash player. Whilst he was playing in the quarter finals of his local league annual men's competition he became conscious that the back of his left heel was hurting. He checked his heel at a break in play to see if there was any bruising but found nothing – no bruise, or cut or blister.

He decided to change his footwear to see if this helped, but it didn't.

1. What do you suspect could be the problem?

2. How could the problem be addressed?

3 Risks and hazards associated with sports participation

There are many known risks and hazards when taking part in sport. These depend on a number of factors which include people, equipment and the environment. However, there are specific rules, regulations and legislation which are set out by relevant health and safety organisations in order to help prevent and minimise the impact of risks and hazards on individuals.

3.1 Risks and hazards to people

Generally most people are aware of risks and hazards related to the sporting activities in which they participate. There are issues like being in physical contact with other participants, for example tackling someone in football. The rules and regulations of how the game is played are designed to prevent risks and hazards. Unfortunately, however, sometimes accidents happen and a tackle can knock someone off balance or hurt them through contact and cause an injury.

There are also some risks and hazards that are common knowledge but which still get forgotten.

Inappropriate warm-up/cool-down

Warm-up is very important when participating in sport for a number of reasons, including the following:

- preparing the cardiovascular and respiratory systems for the coming activity by progressive activity
- preparing the player psychologically for the coming activity
- helping to increase the core temperature of the body and that of the muscular tissues by increasing blood flow to muscular tissue

- stimulating reflex activity related to balance and co-ordination
- helping to achieve full joint mobility in the specific joints involved in the activity
- helping to achieve full soft tissue extensibility, muscles, tendons, ligaments.

A cool-down will help reverse these and brings the individual back to a normal state of function. A thorough cool-down helps to stop muscles becoming sore and stiff.

Physical fitness

To avoid injury and illness an individual should be physically capable. Their fitness level should be able to deal with the stresses and strains that the sporting activity demands of their body. If not, this can lead to problems – see FITT principle on page 123.

If you are leading a sporting activity or training session you must be aware of your participant's levels of fitness. Therefore you should make sure that they undertake some form of health screening before starting any type of activity, e.g. something like a PARQ (Physical Activity Readiness Questionnaire), and any problems highlighted should be discussed with a GP before it is safe to allow the individual to take part.

Physique

Appropriate physique for a particular sport or activity is crucial. No one who had the physique of a hammer thrower would consider being a gymnast. Physique is also crucial to the position a person plays in sport – how many football goalkeepers or basketball players do you see who measure 1.52m in height?

Food and chewing gum

Taking part in sport requires you to have good clear airways so if you are eating, drinking or chewing gum whilst playing the risk of choking increases. We looked at how to open an unconscious casualty's airway earlier – see page 138. If there is anything blocking the airway it must be removed; this includes gum shields and, of course, chewing gum, food, teeth and sometimes blood and vomit.

Skill level and incorrect technique

Skill development, and perfecting techniques to perform certain sporting actions, comes with time and practice. For example, hitting a good serve in tennis is a difficult technique to get right every time. It will take most people a lot of time, effort and good coaching to make sure that it is performed with accuracy regularly. If the player does not follow a coach's feedback then poor technique can develop and become normal. If incorrect technique is allowed to develop, this can increase the risk of injury. Getting correct feedback is essential so it is vital to find a tennis coach who is qualified to give information and feedback in coaching sessions.

Over training

If too much training happens then the body does not get time to recover and adapt appropriately – do you remember the overload principle from earlier in the unit? (Take a quick look at page 122 to refresh your memory.)

To prevent over training, make sure that you:

- notice and are aware of the signs and symptoms of fatigue – fatigue allows mistakes to happen
- have adequate rest periods between training sessions
- encourage brief periods of specific quality rather than long periods of quantity training
- vary the type of training activity in terms of intensity and task
- make sure that training resembles the game situation in terms of the number of repetitions of tasks
- when setting up coaching/training sessions with children take care to match them in terms of height, weight, maturity, experience and ability – not in terms of their chronological age.

Jewellery

Jewellery should never be worn when participating in sport for three simple reasons:

1. It could hurt someone else (a ring or watch can cut other participants).

2. It could hurt you (earrings can easily be caught by another player and rip your ear).

3. It could damage your jewellery. When we take part in sport our circulation increases and we try to reduce this by vasodilation which causes blood vessels to dilate and therefore our fingers to swell. This pressure can be increased by the pressure of a ring on a finger and if we damage this finger then the ring may have to be cut off to allow for the swelling from the injury.

Do you alway remove all your jewellery before participating in any sports activity?

3.2 Risks and hazards to equipment

Protective equipment

There are certain pieces of sporting equipment that are part of the sports governing bodies' rules and regulations, for example shin pads for mini soccer according to the National Governing Body for the Football Association.

> **Law 4: Playing equipment**
>
> - Players must wear shin guards and goalkeepers must wear a distinguishing playing strip.
> - Shin guards must be covered entirely by the stockings.

Not all rules and regulations specify equipment that has to be worn but plenty of players do so in order to avoid any unnecessary injuries, for example use of gum shields, pads, helmets, gloves and so forth.

Activity: Considering equipment

Draw up a list of different specialist equipment that is worn or used by sports participants to help protect them from injury. Against each example identify if it has to be worn because of the governing body's rules and regulations or because the participants choose to do so in order to prevent injuries.

Faulty or damaged equipment

Make sure that you never use specialist equipment inappropriately as this may cause an injury; for instance, running across a sports hall to get outside holding a javelin. You could trip and hurt yourself or bump into someone else and hurt them.

Do not try to use equipment you don't know about or have not been trained to use – again this could cause you or someone else injury. Make sure you never use equipment that is damaged or faulty. If you find it is damaged then do not use it but report it to someone in charge – either a member of staff at a sports centre or a coach or tutor. This is essential if you find that equipment is damaged or faulty and could put someone's life at risk – e.g. climbing ropes or harnesses, trampoline, parachute, etc.

3.3 Risks and hazards from the environment

Sports environments have to be checked consistently as their safety can easily be compromised. For example, a field that has a pitch marked out on it can be perfectly safe one day, but the next day it could be water-logged due to rain or even frozen solid due to extreme cold conditions. Before sport takes place the environment should always be checked and a decision made by someone in charge of the sporting activity as to whether or not it is safe to play on.

If participation is in a cold climate, for example mountaineering, then it is essential that appropriate clothing, equipment and safety mechanisms are in place as well and that the fitness levels of individuals are appropriate for the activity.

Extreme heat and extreme cold will have similar effects on the ground in that the surface will be difficult to play on because it will be too hard. If the activity is running, then running on a track or road that is an appropriate surface might be safe – but the temperature may cause heat imbalance for the individual. Participants should be encouraged to take care in heat by wearing protective sun shields, including creams and clothing and a cap, and to make sure that they keep well hydrated. The weather is an obvious example of how conditions can alter quickly outside.

Usually indoor facilities offer a little more consistency, given that they are not exposed to the elements; however it is still important to take care as other factors can have an impact. You must always check that nothing has been spilt on a floor that makes it slippery and therefore dangerous; for example, a bottle of water accidentally knocked over, or a leaky roof or a player landing on the floor who is sweaty. Check that equipment is not left out from a previous activity which could cause an obstructive hazard.

Lighting and temperature should both be considered for indoor facilities. Check that there is adequate lighting for the sport that is being undertaken. Badminton players need to see the shuttle clearly when it is hit high in the air. Make sure that the temperature is neither too warm or too cold so that any injuries, such as pulled muscles, do not occur and no one feels ill because of the heat.

How do you prepare for different weather conditions when participating in an outdoor activity?

3.4 Rules, regulations and legislation

Different organisations and facilities will have their own health and safety mechanisms in place, such as a dedicated accident/incident reporting system and how they conduct risk assessment of their facilities. There are some nationally recognised health and safety procedures which have to be followed by law – failure to do so could result in prosecution against either an organisation or an individual.

Legal action against someone who has not followed legal procedures is resulting in more and more court cases. Therefore if you are working in an organisation it is vital that you make sure you have appropriate training and are qualified in certain aspects of health and safety e g first aid and follow the procedures.

Should anything untoward happen and you have been trained or hold an appropriate qualification, and if you have followed the stated procedures, then you will always be protected by law against a prosecution because you have followed the legal requirements and accepted procedures.

Remember

If you do not become trained/qualified or fail to follow your training or the procedures in place then it could be you and not the organisation who faces legal action.

Table 5.2: Overview of legislation

Legislation	Content	Example in the sports industry
Health and Safety at Work Act (1994)	Revised from the original Act of 1974. Employers must ensure that all their employees and members of the public remain safe. Employers with five or more employees need to record the significant findings of the risk assessment.	Vitally important to the sports industry given that sport by its very nature has an element of risk to an individual's safety. All staff must be appropriately trained to help maintain safety within their working environment. For example, Lifeguard qualification for a pool attendant, First Aid qualifications held by appropriate staff on duty etc.
Health and Safety (First Aid) Regulations 1981	Reviewed in 2005. Employers must provide adequate First Aid provision for employees and the general public.	First Aid qualified staff on duty. First Aid facilities – First Aid box/room must be provided and checked regularly. Having basic first aid provision is a necessity for sports environments as accidents and incidents often occur here.
Control of Substances Hazardous to Health (COSHH) 2002	Employers must ensure that all employers are protected from exposure to hazardous substances.	Training of staff to utilise chemicals for cleaning and maintaining swimming pools. Pools etc. must be kept clean for health reasons and the use of hazardous chemicals controlled.
The Safety of Sports Grounds Act 1975	From 1975 building regulations had to conform to stringent standards for all sports ground developments.	Essential to eradicate disasters such as those at Ibrox and Bradford. Vital that sports grounds are constructed to the highest safety specifications in order to protect sports spectators.
The Children Act 2004	Children are protected by this law wherever they are. They should be able to grow up safely and positively.	Essential that all sports coaches, teachers etc. undergo Criminal Records Bureau checks before they are allowed to work with children. Children should be able to be educated, coached and allowed to play safely within a sporting environment. They should be guided by appropriately qualified people.

Table 5.2 provides an overview of some of the more well-known and commonly used laws and regulations that have to be followed when working in a sports environment.

Health and Safety At Work Act 1994

The basis of British health and safety law is the Health and Safety at Work etc. Act 1974. In 1994 The Health and Safety Commission (HSC) conducted a review of the Act and this is now the basis of all health and safety measures for employers who are responsible for the safety of their employees and members of the public.

It states:

'Your employer has a duty under the law to ensure, so far as is reasonably practicable, your health, safety and welfare at work. Your employer must consult you or your safety representative on matters relating to your health and safety at work.'

In general, your employer's duties include:

- making your workplace safe and without risks to health
- ensuring equipment and machinery are safe and that safe systems of work are set and followed
- ensuring articles and substances are moved, stored and used safely
- providing adequate welfare facilities
- giving you the information, instruction, training and supervision necessary for your health and safety.

As an employee you have legal duties too. These include:

- taking reasonable care for your own health and safety and that of others who may be affected by what you do or do not do
- co-operating with your employer on health and safety
- correctly using work items provided by your employer, including personal protective equipment, in accordance with training or instructions
- not interfering with or misusing anything provided for your health, safety or welfare.

In addition, Management of Health and Safety at Work Regulations 1999 requires employers to carry out risk assessments, make arrangements to implement necessary measures, appoint competent people and arrange for appropriate information and training.

Health and Safety (First Aid) Regulations 1981

This piece of legislation was reviewed in 2005. It states that:

'The Health and Safety (First Aid) Regulations 1981 place a duty on employers to provide adequate first aid equipment, facilities and personnel to their employees.'

The review supports the regulations and says:

'In its guidance, Health & Safety Executive (HSE) will continue to strongly recommend that employers should consider the public when conducting their first aid needs assessment and provide first aid for them. This is particularly important where a workplace has a large public presence such as educational establishments, places of entertainment, fairgrounds and shops etc.'

This is very important for people employed in sporting environments such as sports halls, sports centres, and stadiums as they will have to deal with large numbers of the public and people participating in potentially risky and hazardous activities.

Control of Substances Hazardous to Health (COSHH) 2002

COSHH requires employers to control exposure to health from hazardous substances to protect employers and those who may be exposed from work activities.

Employers must be aware of what hazardous substances are used in the workplace and the risks to health. Precautions and controls must be put in place. Employers must ensure that employees are properly trained and/or supervised when dealing with hazardous substances.

In the sports industry this is closely linked to toxic or harmful substances used whilst maintaining swimming pools or jacuzzis and when cleaning and disinfecting facilities. The following should be adhered to:

* Correct storage and handling of substances is closely monitored and made secure at all times.
* Staff should be regularly trained to ensure that correct storage and use of chemicals involved in the sports environment are maintained.
* Protective clothing must be provided by the employer for every employee who has to handle any hazardous substance in the course of their work.
* All staff should have appropriate first aid training to cope with any emergency situation that could occur whilst using hazardous chemicals.

The Safety of Sports Grounds Act 1975

The Wheatley Committee was set up in 1972 partially in response to a large number of spectators who died in a disaster at Ibrox Park, Glasgow. This was because of structural failure; the steel barriers on stairway 13 gave way – 66 people were suffocated to death and many more were injured in the crush.

Following the recommendations of this committee the Safety of Sports Grounds Act 1975 was established. Up until then there was no law about sports grounds, though building regulations had references to specific buildings. Accidents at sports venues were dealt with on the basis of common law principles about occupiers and their visitors.

The Safety of Sports Grounds Act 1975 applies to all sports grounds with accommodation for spectators. Safety controls are imposed through safety certificates issued by local authorities for sports grounds designated by the Secretary of State, currently:

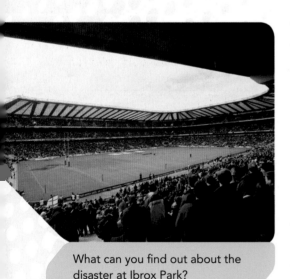

What can you find out about the disaster at Ibrox Park?

- those grounds occupied by FA premier and football league clubs with accommodation for over 5,000 spectators

- those with accommodation for over 10,000 spectators where other sports are played, which in practice means rugby, cricket and other football matches including internationals.

A 'stadium' is defined as a sports arena 'substantially surrounded' by spectator accommodation. The Act was aimed at a stadium if it had a capacity for 10,000 or more spectators.

Despite this some accidents still occur. The Bradford City Fire Disaster occurred on Saturday May 11, 1985 when a flash fire consumed one side of the Valley Parade football stadium in Bradford, England.

The fire broke out during a football match between the home team (Bradford City), and Lincoln City, on the day that Bradford City were supposed to have celebrated their winning the Football League Third Division trophy: 56 people lost their lives. A stray cigarette butt, discarded in a plastic cup, ignited rubbish that had piled up underneath City's antiquated main stand and, within four minutes, flames had engulfed the wooden structure.

Activity: Incidents at sports grounds

The Ibrox Park disaster of 1972 is by no means the only sports ground disaster to occur. Can you identify two other incidents – one from this country and one from another country? What measures should be taken to make sure these incidents are not repeated?

BTEC ## Assessment activity 5.4

You have settled into your job at the fitness suite and after having received appropriate training you have been asked to start helping clients with their fitness suite induction. First you must explain to them some of the risks, hazards, rules and regulations that operate within the fitness suite for health and safety reasons.

Produce a leaflet that highlights six risks and hazards that are associated with fitness training and identify four specific rules and/or regulations that are in place in the fitness suite. **P4**, **P5**

Give a clear and detailed explanation of why it is important to each individual that they are aware of the risks and hazards and the specific rules and regulations outlined in the leaflet. Make sure they fully understand what the risk could be to them if they do not undertake their training in the suite with due care and attention to the information given to them. **M3**, **M4**, **D1**

Grading tips

Make sure that when you have identified the six risks and hazards and the four rules and/or regulations that you *show why* and *clearly explain* how an individual can be at risk of injury when taking part in sport.

Make sure you identify how injuries could be prevented or at least minimised.

PLTS

Creating a leaflet will develop your skills as a **creative thinker**.

Functional skills

Demonstrating this should develop your **English** skills in speaking and listening.

The Children Act 2004

The Children Act 2004 places a duty on services to ensure that every child, whatever their circumstances, has the support they need to:

- be healthy
- stay safe
- enjoy and achieve through learning
- make a positive contribution to society
- achieve economic well-being.

As children participate in sport in so many different environments, such as summer schools, after-school clubs and coaching sessions, then employers who have employees working with these children are bound by the Children Act of 2004. This means they must ensure that every employee must:

- gain a police and a Criminal Records Bureau check and clearance before they allow an employee to work with children
- be appropriately qualified to do the work they are employed to do with the children
- be trained to recognise signs of possible abuse
- be trained in methods of dealing with abuse and how to report this appropriately. (See further information on this in Unit 7 Planning and leading sport activities.)

4 Risk assessment relevant to sport

Throughout this unit we have constantly referred to risk and how to prevent or minimise the risk of injury and illnesses related to sports participation. We can only rely on participants themselves to some extent to help prevent incidents happening.

There is legislation in place to help prevent an incident or accident occurring but we need to know about it and follow if we are to avoid prosecution. It is absolutely necessary that we make sure we do follow all of the guidance available to us.

A number of the pieces of legislation that we have considered already acknowledge the use of 'risk assessment'. So what is a risk assessment? What is its purpose and how do we do one?

4.1 Risk assessment – what is it?

As defined by the Health and Safety Executive (HSE), a risk assessment is a careful examination of what, in your work, could cause harm to people. It is the overall process of identifying all the risks involved in an activity and assessing the potential impact of each risk. Accidents and ill health can ruin lives and affect businesses if output is lost, machinery is damaged, insurance costs increase or you have to go to court. You are legally required to assess the risks in your workplace so that you put in place a plan to control the risks.

4.2 Purpose

The purpose of a risk assessment is to identify the level of risk posed. You must make sure any hazards are removed or minimised so that there is a safe environment to work in – or, in your case, for individuals to be able to safely participate in sport.

4.3 How to do a risk assessment

A risk assessment system will vary depending on the organisation and the environment (just like the incident/accident reporting systems covered earlier). However, the procedure for doing a risk assessment – just like the managing injury – will always be the same whether it's conducted by a manager, a tutor, coach, instructor or pool attendant.

There are two examples of risk assessment forms for you to look at – one has a risk judgement filled in. Both examine how a risk may occur and how high the risk factor is. Both identify how this might be minimised or prevented by asking for controls to be put in place and look at what actions should be taken if the risk is not prevented.

Activity: Risk assessments

The example looks at a slippery or wet floor on a squash court. It identifies what controls could be put in place – can you add any more for this example? What if the risk considered was a spillage of chemicals while cleaning the swimming pool? The controls suggested and the actions taken would vary enormously from a simple spillage. How?

Assessment activity 5.5   P6 M5 D2

You have been working for several weeks in the fitness suite and your duty manager is very impressed with your attention to health and safety. She has therefore asked you to help her review the risk assessments produced for a number of other areas within the sports complex.

Produce a risk assessment report of the sports hall using one sport as a worked example.

Produce a risk assessment report for the outdoor pitches using one sport as a worked example. **P6**

In order to explain your report findings to your duty manager, produce contingency plans for both areas assessed and explain in detail where and what specialist equipment could be used to minimise the risk of injury to anyone taking part in the sports activities identified. **M5**, **D2**

Grading tip

Make sure that you look at suitable contingency plans for *both* areas that you have assessed. This will make sure that you are able to identify appropriate specialist equipment and justify appropriate safety precautions with plenty of scope for discussion.

PLTS

Undertaking the risk assessment will help to develop your skills as a **reflective learner**.

Functional skills

Demonstrating this should develop your **IT** skills.

SPORTS DEPARTMENT			
RISK ASSESSMENT 2008/2009			**Date**
Activities usually carried out by The Sports Complex. List activities here. A thorough programme of warm-up exercises should be carried out at the beginning of every practice. All members of the club must read the Sports Complex Risk Assessment and Code of Conduct. All injuries/accidents must be reported by a member of The Sports Complex and to The Sports Complex Manager on duty, who will provide First Aid Cover and complete an accident report form as required.			
HAZARD	**CONTROL MEASURES IN PLACE**	**RISK FACTOR**	**FURTHER CONTROL MEASURES**
Squash Court Playing surface. A slippery or wet floor can lead to injuries to players during the course of the game.	Please ensure that the correct footwear is used by all players. The floors should be cleaned by the Sports Department on a regular basis so that dust is removed. The floors should be unsealed, with red painted lines and regularly checked for split boards.	Severity: High Likelihood: Infrequent	Please refer to The Sports Complex handbook sheet number 12 for 'guidelines for safety on Squash Courts'

Figure 5.5: Carry out a risk assessment for one of the activities you participate in.

Activity type	Identify hazards	Identify consequences	Implications	Identify the control measures	Identify action if incident occurs	Person responsible
Please list all the different types of activity	Please list the potential and real hazards associated with each activity type and who will/might be effected	Please list the consequences of each hazard and the possibility that this hazard will occur (high, medium, low)	How severe are its implications if the hazard does occur? (high, medium, low)	that are in place to reduce the risk of the hazard happening	What action will you take if the hazard does occur?	for ensuring that measures are implemented

Figure 5.6: Complete an activity registration and risk assessment for an activity you participate in using this form.

Chrissie Joseph
Leisure attendant

I work in a team of 30 leisure attendants who report to the Duty Officer. We work shifts with different people every day. The leisure centre is in a busy town and well used by the public. My main duties are to:

- Ensure that the safety and behaviour of the public is controlled to prevent injury, misuse and damage to facilities.
- Provide trained assistance in the form of lifesaving skills when necessary.
- Assist members of the public with the use of equipment as necessary.
- Carry out general cleaning duties (including internal and external areas).
- Set up and dismantle equipment in line with operational programmes as well as other general labouring duties.
- Assist where necessary in routine maintenance work.
- Undertake any other duties as directed by the Centre Supervisor/Duty Officer.

Describe your typical day

A typical day for me starts with reporting for work on time and finding out from my colleagues and the Duty Officer what happened on the previous shift. I then collect my schedule for my shift, which identifies what I need to do and what time I'm on duty and where. Some of the things I need to do include setting up any equipment needed in the main hall. I may have to check the pool chemical and pH rates and be on pool attendant duties or reception. I really like that part of my job – not knowing the order I'll be doing my tasks – it changes every shift. Also I like getting to work with different people every time.

What's the best thing about your job?

The best part of my job is meeting the different visitors to the centre. They ask for my advice and help. I understand the importance of safety so I'm keen to help them participate as safely as possible. However, accidents do happen, and as I am a qualified First Aider I have to deal with all sorts of issues – you never know what might happen.

Think about it!

- Why should Chrissie find out what happened on the previous shift before starting her shift?
- What does this unit cover that provides the knowledge and skills used by a Leisure Attendant? Write a list and discuss with your group.

Just checking

1. What is the difference between an intrinsic injury and an extrinsic injury? Give examples to help explain your answer
2. What key things do you always have to do when treating a casualty who is injured or ill?
3. Can you identify two pieces of legislation which are in place in order to help protect the public when participating in sport? Try to fully explain your answer.
4. Hopefully, risk assessment helps prevent injury. Other than making sure the playing areas are safe and clear of any obstructions, what else should someone consider before participating in sport to help prevent injury?
5. What qualifications would help someone working in the sports industry?

edexcel ▦

Assignment tips

Research tips

- There's a lot of information about sports injuries. Make sure you choose information appropriate to the level of study you are undertaking.
- If you use or refer to data and statistics, make sure you check where the information has come from. Treatment and recognition of the type and severity of some injuries depends on the country that has produced the information.

Get active!

- Understanding sports injuries is essential to their prevention as well as their treatment. Taking a first aid qualification can help with this.

Key points!

- Do not give first aid unless you hold a current first aid certificate.
- If you do become qualified, remember that you are only qualified to the level of the course you studied. Never go beyond what your course covered.
- When you take part in sport minimise, wherever possible, factors that can lead to injury. If you are going to lead a sports session remember to risk assess prior to the session!

6 Sports development

Are you interested in sport? Do you like organising things? Do you like working with different people? A career in sport development could be for you.

There are now many opportunities for people to be active and sport development is an increasingly important part of the sports industry. It is a fast-moving industry involving a variety of different people, sports facilities and organisations, both local and national, all trying to encourage us to lead healthier and more active lifestyles. Sports development involves looking at issues that affect sport today and which may affect your participation. For example, what will the legacy of the 2012 Olympics be for your country once the games have finished? How does coverage of sport in the media affect what you play?

This unit covers topics that answer these questions. What is sport? Where and how do you take part? What factors make participation difficult or impossible?

You will investigate a range of organisations trying to increase participation, from local organisations to those that operate at a national level.

Finally, you will investigate issues that affect sport today. What do you think the Olympic Games should mean to us today? What do you feel about the Olympic motto of 'Citius, Altius, Fortius' ('swifter, higher, stronger')?

Learning outcomes

After completing this unit you should:

1. know the nature of sports provision
2. know how and why people participate in sport
3. know the role of local and national organisations responsible for sports development
4. know the impact of different key issues on the sports industry.

Grading criteria

In order to pass this unit, the evidence that the learner presents for assessment needs to demonstrate that they can meet all the learning outcomes for the unit. The criteria for a pass grade describe the level of achievement required to pass this unit.

To achieve a **pass** grade the evidence must show that the learner is able to	To achieve a **merit** grade the evidence must show that, in addition to the pass criteria, the learner is able to:	To achieve a **distinction** grade the evidence must show that, in addition to the pass and merit criteria, the learner is able to:
P1 describe local voluntary, public and private sector sports provision for three different sports	**M1** compare local and national provision of sport, identifying areas for improvement	**D1** evaluate local and national provision of sport, explaining ways in which provision could be improved
P2 describe three different types of national sports provision that support elite performance		
P3 describe ways in which people participate in sport and reasons for participation		
P4 describe factors that affect participation in sport		
P5 describe strategies used to encourage participation in a selected sport **See Assessment activity 6.1, page 167**	**M2** explain strategies used to encourage participation in a selected sport **See Assessment activity 6.1, page 167**	**D2** evaluate strategies to encourage participation in a selected sport, making recommendations for future strategies **See Assessment activity 6.1, page 167**
P6 describe the role of one local and one national organisation responsible for the development of sport	**M3** explain the role of one local and one national organisation responsible for the development of sport	
P7 describe four key issues in sport and identify their impact on sport	**M4** explain the impact of four key issues on sport	

How you will be assessed

By completing a number of assessments you will develop the required knowledge and skills.

These assessments might include:

- practical activities
- PowerPoint presentations
- essays and reports
- multiple choice tests
- case studies
- role plays, etc.

Steven, 17–year-old casual sports coach

Using my own experiences was really useful. I thought about the issues that affected me each day, and then related this to other groups of individuals and how they might be affected when they took part in sport. I looked at what was being offered in my local sports centres to see how they tried to encourage as many people as possible to take part in some form of activity. I looked at the types of activities offered, when they were put on, what prices were charged and I asked different people about what factors made it difficult for them to be active. Talking with friends and family also helped me to understand a number of other topics, such as why people play sport at all, in what ways they got involved as well as the reasons why they were unable to, or stopped completely from taking part in an activity they wanted to.

Finally, I made sure I read the newspapers and watched sports coverage on the television as this was really helpful in developing my understanding of how sport is changing and developing at a national level.

Over to you!

- Are you interested in providing access to sport for people?
- Why?
- What do you need to know if you intend to follow a career in sport development?

1 Know the nature of sports provision

Warm-up

What factors might make taking part in sport more difficult? Can you think of five different things that would make taking part harder?

Imagine having a job where you are responsible for helping people to take part; responsible for creating opportunities for a range of different people. How could you achieve this?

Why should people be active? Why is sport important to all of us and the country? Actively developing sport is relatively new. Many people are now employed whose job it is to encourage more participation in sport and physical activity and to provide the right conditions to encourage and make this participation possible. This unit will look at why this aspect of the sports industry is important and who is involved. You will also look at what methods are used to achieve increased participation.

Key term

Sport – an activity involving physical exertion and skill that is governed by a set of rules or customs and often undertaken competitively.

The sports industry has many faces. But what do we mean by **sport**? Can you think of what makes an activity a 'sport'?

Sport includes a wide range of different types of sport – team, individual, winter, summer, invasion etc.

Sport can take many forms, for example:

- ball game
- team sport
- invasion game
- summer or winter game
- indoor or outdoor game
- net game
- bat and ball game
- target game.

Can you think of others? Can you give some suitable examples for each of the categories above?

Different people will play different sports for a variety of reasons.

But why does society think sport is important? Millions of pounds have been spent on sport in recent years. The 2012 Olympics, for instance, has already cost £9.3 billion pounds – a vast sum of money. Some people might argue that this is money which *could* be spent on other things such as schools or hospitals.

However, it is believed that sport also offers many benefits. For example:

- Sport has positive health benefits.
- Sport has positive social benefits.
- It provides jobs for many people.
- Sport teaches people team work, to play by the rules and to accept winning and losing in the right way.
- Success in sport raises national prestige and pride. Remember how you feel when your favourite football team wins!

Sport provides money to the government through taxes raised. What do you think?

1.1 Provision

Sport and sport-related products and services are generally provided by three types of organisations.

1. **Private organisations** such as David Lloyd, JJB, William Hill or private members' clubs which provide activities and services to make a profit for the organisation.

2. **Public organisations** such as local councils or authorities whose aim is to provide a range of services for local people to improve their standard of living.

3. **Voluntary organisations** such as local sports clubs and associations which offer sports activities etc. often to small groups of people who share similar interests such as playing netball or running.

Local sports provision

The area where we live is governed locally by elected officials called councillors and they make decisions that affect us all, including the level and nature of the provision for sport. You will find that your local council operates a range of sports facilities including sports fields and pitches, local sports centres and swimming pools. Your local council will organise these facilities, often using a management company to carry out the day-to-day running. You could speak with the manager of your local sports centre to find out more about this.

National sports provision

In addition to those organisations which tend to operate at a local level (although they may be a branch of a national chain of stores or clubs such as William Hill bookmakers or the Leisure Connection Group), there are a number of national organisations which are responsible for sports provision at the higher levels of performance. This includes the elite level – the level at which the international performers are found. These organisations may be responsible for a range of national factors involved in sports provision including funding, for instance Sport

Key terms

Private organisations – businesses and private clubs who undertake their business for profit for either the owners of the business or for the benefit of the business and its members.

Public organisations – organisations whose role is to benefit the general public.

Voluntary organisations – people or groups who undertake activities for no payment.

England or UK Sport, coach development through Sports Coach UK, the running of a particular sport such as the Football Association or UK Athletics, or in providing support to elite athletes such as the various English Institutes of Sport in Sheffield and Bath for example.

All of these organisations have important roles to play. They ensure that:

- there are facilities for everybody to participate, develop and progress in sport
- people who coach and lead sport are properly qualified
- sport is adequately funded
- the country is represented at all international competitions around the world
- sport is able to provide jobs and other benefits to the country and the population.

2 Know how and why people participate in sport

2.1 Ways to participate in sport

Sport offers people the chance to participate in a number of different ways. So:

- How?
- Why?
- What's stopping you from taking part?
- How do we get involved?

Activity: Taking part

Working in pairs, make a list of as many different reasons as you can why a person might take part in sport.

Getting a team of athletes fit enough and skilled enough to take part in the Olympic Games requires a huge team of people performing many roles. How many different roles can you think of?

Reasons

How many of the reasons given below did you think about?

Generally people take part in sport for one or more of the following reasons.

- developmental reasons – learning new skills
- social reasons – enjoyment, meeting new people, fun and enjoyment
- health and fitness benefits – reducing weight for instance.

Most people will take part in sport for one particular reason. It is important that sports providers are able to meet these various customer needs.

Activity: Meeting needs

In pairs, describe how your local sports centre meets three different reasons for taking part in sport. Use the information above and try to find different ways that your chosen centre helps people to meet a specific need.

Factors that affect participation

For example: 'I want to play but can't!' So what **barriers** will stop or prevent a person taking part in sport? Which of these reasons have you heard of?

* time
* money
* disability
* age and gender
* facilities
* cultural background or ethnicity.

> **Key term**
>
> **Barriers** – factors which prevent or make participation more difficult.

Activity: Factors affecting participation

Think about how each factor might affect participation. Try to match the example with the reasoning in the table below.

Reason	Example
Time	Having to travel long distances.
Cultural differences	Having commitments such as a mortgage, young family, car loan etc.
Disability	Individual health and interests change with this factor.
Money	Working shifts, weekends of starting early/ finishing late.
Location	Participant requires adapted game or equipment.
Age	Religious festivals or adherence to a particular form of dress.

These reasons will affect different people in different ways. For instance, a person who is unemployed has lots of time but lacks the money, whereas someone who holds down a well-paid job might have to work long hours including evenings and weekends.

A person who has some sort of disability may have both the time and money to take part but finds that local providers do not provide the types of activities or specialist access or facilities that they need.

Someone from a different cultural group may find difficulties because local providers do not provide suitable activities for them or activities provided in a way which takes into account specific religious requirements. The Muslim faith says that women dressed to take part in sport must not be seen by men.

Growth in sports participation

Sports participation continues to grow in this country. This may be due to a number of reasons.

Even the time of year affects participation. For example, when Wimbledon starts every June, what do you notice lots of people doing?

2.2 Increasing provision

But how do we increase participation in sport? In what ways can we encourage more people to take part? This will start when people are in school. School physical education and sport are the foundations on which the rest of sport is built. School sports can provide young people with the skills and abilities to become positive members of society. They shape lifelong attitudes to our health and fitness and are the starting point for developing potential sports performers on the ladder of sports performance.

Some sports are now trying to develop more participation within their own sport. For instance, the Football Foundation is committed to developing football at grass roots level – the level at which we start in sport, learning basic skills. Visit Football Foundation's website to find out more about how and why they are involved in developing football. See Hotlinks section on page ii for a link to the website.

Other methods come from the top. The government places a great deal of importance in sport and looks to develop sport in a number of ways. This includes funding sport and a range of initiatives designed to achieve certain targets.

Another method of encouraging participation in sport is by appointing Sport Development Officers. Many local councils appoint staff whose role is to engage with local people and organisations with the aim of increasing the number of people who take part in physical activity. This includes:

- increasing the number of places where activities take place
- carrying out research to find out what different members of local communities want to do and then taking steps to make these activities happen

Did you know?

To learn more about current sports initiatives you can visit the Youth Sport Trust website. See Hotlinks section on page ii for a link to their website.

- providing advice and training for individuals, such as training sports leaders
- supporting local people and organisations to develop activities through training, funding and advice and guidance.

However, for every benefit of a scheme or initiative, there is a disadvantage. For instance, schemes and initiatives may well increase the number of people becoming more active, but they cost a lot of money. How can it be shown that the benefits that might arise are worth the money that has been invested? For instance, improvements in health might take several years before they become apparent, although these benefits may save the country much money in the future in addition to the lives saved or given better quality of living. The drive to address the problem of childhood obesity will save money spent in the NHS on tackling the problems it may cause in later life such as diabetes and heart disorders as well as lost days at work.

In general, schemes to develop greater participation in sport have the following strengths:

- improved health for those involved
- a range of social benefits such as improved community spirit, less crime and anti-social behaviour
- increased success in international sport and thus increased international standing
- improved standard of living for many communities
- groups and individuals learn valuable lifelong skills
- there are savings in areas such as the health service, policing etc. as people become healthier and engage in less anti-social behaviour
- increased employment opportunities for those in the sports industry.

Disadvantages include:

- the costs involved in setting up the schemes – staffing, promoting etc.
- the time taken for schemes to have an effect
- the high costs of schemes for developing sport at an elite level – for instance the new Olympic facilities are likely to cost £2 billion
- competition with the ever-increasing demands for funding from other areas – schools, hospitals, social services and so on.

Can you find out how much money is invested by the government to encourage participation in sport in your local area?

3 Know the role of local and national organisations responsible for sports development

When we consider the provision of sport in this country, it is important to understand the various levels at which provision is made, i.e. at either a local or national level.

3.1 Local organisations

There are many different organisations that will try to develop sport and improve some aspect of sport in this country, for example:

- sports development officers who work for your local council
- school Sport Co-ordinators and Further Education Sports Co-ordinators
- county sports partnerships.

Sports development officer

Case study: Barry, Sports development officer

Barry, 25, is a Sports Development Officer who works for Peterborough City Council. His job is to increase the opportunities for sport, both recreational and competitive, for the population of Peterborough and the surrounding area, including:

- males and females
- adults
- those with specific needs
- people from different cultural and ethnic groups
- children
- families.

These activities take many different forms and include the following.

- Specific provision at facilities that the council operates such as swimming pools and sports centres. This includes swimming lessons for children and adults, fitness activities for a range of people, basic coaching in a range of sports for children, training for school teachers and potential sports leaders.

- Activities in local schools to increase the number of children taking part such as after school clubs, etc.

- Courses to develop existing coaches and sports club administrators such as child protection courses, how to develop volunteers, etc.

Many of these activities use permanent sports staff employed by the council. Other provision might be staffed by training volunteers and leaders who then take sessions, or if school teachers can be trained as leaders then they are able to provide sports activities in their own schools.

1. In what ways do Sports Development Officers in your school, college or local community develop sport?

2. In what ways are the barriers to people taking part in sport tackled?

School Sport Partnerships

A recent development are the new School Sport Partnerships. These are groups of schools working together to develop sport for all young people. Visit the Youth Sport Trust website for more information. See Hotlinks section on page ii for a link to this website. If you are a student in a college, you may find you have a FESCO somewhere (Further Education Sports Co-ordinator). Try to find out what they are employed at your college for.

County Sports Partnership

In addition, you will probably find that there is a County Sports Partnership near to you. These partnerships involve groups of different organisations in a local area which aim to provide one single system for sport for local people to benefit from. If your school or college has an SSCO or FESCO they will be a part of this system. Visit the SportEngland website to find out more. See Hotlinks section on page ii for a link to this website.

3.2 National organisations

It is also important to consider sport at a national level. How does the UK develop sport at the top level? There are many national organisations that look to develop sport at a national level. These include the governing bodies of each sport, such as the Lawn Tennis Association or the Rugby Football Union, organisations involved with specific groups of people, such as the Special Olympics or the British Paralympics Association, and also organisations involved with specific events such as the British Olympic Association.

Each has an important **role** to play in developing sport at a national level. Look at the following list and discuss what each might involve. Can you think of an organisation that adopts this role? Can you say how they carry out this role?

> ## Key term
>
> **Role** – something that is expected of a group or individual.

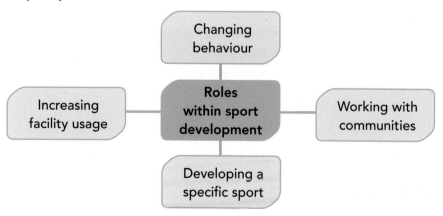

Figure 6.1: Roles within sport development.

In pairs, suggest ways that each role above might be carried out. For instance, 'Drink-Drive' TV campaigns at Christmas and in the summer attempt to change our attitudes to drinking and driving.

4 The impact of different key issues on the sports industry

The **impact** of sport and associated issues has become much more prominent with developments in technology. Sport is viewed by billions of people around the world. Satellite television means that almost any sports event can be viewed anywhere in the world. The news we see and hear is not confined to our own country any more.

Some of the issues that currently affect sport are as given in Figure 6.2.

Each of these issues will have an impact on the sport or on individuals or groups of people. For instance, the increasing awareness of people with disabilities through increased coverage of events such as the Paralympics has made us all more aware of the need to provide equal opportunities for everyone in society.

What effects might these types of issues have on sport?

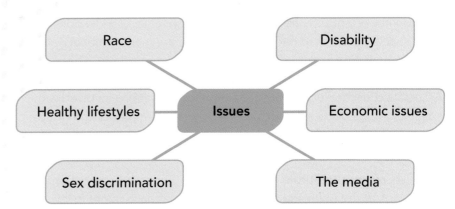

Figure 6.2: Issues that impact on participation in sport.

Activity: Role plays

Now try the following role plays.

1. You are a parent of a child who wishes to take part in sport but you have concerns about stories in the press linking the sport to drug taking.

2. You are a person with a disability who wants to participate. What issues and problems might you come up against?

3. Imagine you are a young, successful and attractive female tennis player. How is female sport covered by the media?

4. You are a political refugee and very talented at athletics. Do you think sport should be used for political ends, such as protesting about one country invading another?

Sports coverage is a major part of most newspapers. It is what a lot of people want to read about. We see and hear sport on the television and radio every day. Football can be viewed live every day of the week. Is this a good thing?

You may be able to access the Internet and news services on your mobile phone. Again, can you think of advantages and disadvantages of this?

The media coverage of sport can have a major effect on the way a sport is perceived – fair or dishonest, clean or tainted by drugs, good or bad for you. This also applies to those who take part as well as those who watch sport. Football supporters in the 1970s were generally regarded as hooligans. Many body builders might be viewed as people who take drugs in order to be successful. It is often said that what children see happening on televised sport on Saturday is repeated on the local field on Sunday.

Sport can have many important long-term benefits for a country. All the countries which have hosted the summer Olympic Games have facilities that can be used by people for many years. The 2012 Olympic Games in London will leave a legacy of facilities, accommodation and a different attitude to sport for many years after the Games have finished. But at what cost to the nation?

PLTS

Researching the changes in participation levels will develop your skills as an **independent enquirer**.

Functional skills

Using a PowerPoint format will develop your **ICT** skills.

BTEC **Assessment activity 6.1** P5 M2 D2

You have been asked by the manager of your local sports centre to give a presentation to the team. You have been asked to present information to outline the different ways that your chosen sport has encouraged and developed more participation. Explain to the team how these strategies encouraged more people to take part and then evaluate the success of these strategies.

Grading tips

To ensure success, make sure you do the following.

- Focus on one sport only.
- Discuss a number of different ways that have been used to increase participation.
- Give lots of detail about how each strategy works.
- Provide some facts and figures to show how the changes in participation have been achieved.

Activity: Sporting issues

Discuss as a group the following questions. Record your thoughts and those of others. Try to think of both positive responses and negative ones

1. Have the changes to football in this country in terms of when it is played (i.e. no longer only on Saturdays at 3pm and Wednesday evenings) been good or bad for the game? Give reasons.

2. Leaving televised sports events for a commercial break is damaging to sport

3. Most sporting competitions have a sponsor in the title, such as the Barclays Premiership or the Guinness Premiership in rugby union, and are dependent on this sponsor. This means that other sports which are not as attractive to a sponsor can struggle to develop.

4. Some sports events are only available on a 'Pay per view' basis.

5. Should some sporting events such as Wimbledon or the FA Cup final be available to all those who want to watch rather than only those who can afford to pay?

6. All sports performers are role models to others and so should be positive ones at all times.

7. Televising sport decreases participation.

8. Women's sport is slow and boring and should not get as much media coverage as men's sport.

9. The influx of huge sums of money into some sports, especially football, increases the pressure on players, managers and match officials and is leading to poor standards of behaviour, increases in drug taking and cheating, plus other illegal behaviour.

Look at each issue and put yourself in the position of each of the following:

- a sports fan who watches from home or by going to live events
- a male participant
- a female participant
- a sports provider
- Did your views change at all? If so, why?

Does this women's football match look 'slow and boring'?

Sharena Elliott
Sports Development Officer for Ethnic Minorities

Sharena works for a City Council Sports Development Team. She is responsible for:

- developing and increasing the range of sports opportunities for people from ethnic minorities
- working with the rest of the team to increase the quality of sports provision in the city
- providing data on the success of the activities she is responsible for leading during the day and evening
- developing leaders and instructors within the ethnic minority community to lead clubs and classes.

Describe a typical day

My typical day is not a 9–5 day but can involve evening activities as well as work at weekends. My work involves liaising with a variety of people regarding a variety of subjects, including providing activities, funding and staffing. I meet weekly with my line manager to discuss a variety of strategies to increase the provision for sport within the city. A typical day will also involve ensuring that activities planned are suitably staffed and equipped and that activities planned for the future are promoted in a suitable manner so that local people are aware of what activities are available.

What's the best thing about your job?

The best thing is knowing that I am improving the lives of a lot of people. I am providing activities that help people to help themselves and others – junior school children, mums and toddlers, families, a wide range of people. Two days are never the same – one day I might be in the office planning activities or arranging funding, coaches and so on; the next I might be coaching a sports activity to a group of children, adults or people with special needs.

Think about it!

- What aspects of this unit could be applied to the different activities Sharena has described?
- Looking at the activities that Sharena undertakes, what skills do you possess that would help you to be a successful Sports Development Officer
- What skills and knowledge do you need to develop or improve?

Just checking

1. Can you name three different groups of people who are targeted for sports development?
2. Can you name three different providers of sport activities?
3. Can you name a national sports facility for five different sports?
4. List three reasons why a person plays a sport of your choice.
5. Why has the provision of sport increased over recent years?
6. What is a School Sports Partnership?
7. List three roles of Sport England.
8. In small groups, choose a current issue that affects sport and discuss the effects it has on a sport of your choice.
9. Draw a spiderdiagram showing the positive and negative effects of one of the following: increased television coverage, performance-enhancing drugs, the celebrity status of top sports performers.

Assignment tips

You might use the following to help you achieve better grades.

- Know what is provided in your local area in terms of sports activities, clubs, events etc. Collecting price guides, programmes of activities from your local centre will all help.

- A map which shows what is provided and where is also a very useful aid to success. In addition, a map of the country which shows where the major sports facilities etc. are will be very useful.

- Keep up to date. Make a point of reading the sports section of a range of papers and collect articles about important events in sport. This might include stories about the 2012 Olympics, a person found to be taking performance-enhancing drugs, or a local sports scheme organised for a particular group of people. Successful students are able to talk about current issues affecting sport either generally or more specifically. For instance, television money has had a massive effect on football. Can you say why? But why does television not show sports such as badminton or squash as often? Why is drug use bad for sport?

- Get to know the sports and activities provided where you live. Could you tell someone new to your area where to go for a particular sport or activity?

- Visit the websites of a range of national organisations involved in sport such as – Sport England, Sports Coach UK, the governing body of a range of sports you are interested in, your local authority and so on.

- Talk to your local sports development officers about what they do, how they do it and why. They will have a great deal of information on current schemes and initiatives.

- There are links to Units 2, 3, 13 and 19 from this unit on Sport development.

- Talking to a range of people – friends, family, staff at your school or college, other students about what they play, why, where and so on. Are there activities that they would like to take part in but cannot? Why not? What would help them to take part, or even take part more often?

- When you attempt Merit grading criteria, you will need to explain. This means telling the reader why something has happened, will result in or similar. For instance, explaining how a particular barrier prevents someone taking part in sport might mean using examples or a case study to show the reasons why this happens.

7 Planning and leading sports activities

An effective sports leader should be able to develop sport and physical activity sessions to help the development of the skills and techniques of participants. A good sports leader should be able to plan and lead a session around clear aims and objectives. It is often the sports leader who is the 'unsung hero', the person who does not pick up the trophies, money, or awards. But without the dedication of effective sports leadership the majority of sport performers would have not had the same opportunities.

Often it is the influence of the sports leaders who we first meet in a particular sport or at a venue that affects our attitude towards sport and physical activity. A positive experience engages us in a particular sport and this is often influenced by the individual leading the sports session. Despite the majority of sports leaders creating positive attitudes towards sports there are some who generate negative attitudes towards sport and physical activity.

This unit looks at ways in which you can develop your skills and qualities as a sports leader and provides you with the ability to affect sporting opportunities for others through leading sports and physical activity sessions and events.

Learning outcomes

After completing this unit you should:

1. know the skills, qualities and responsibilities associated with successful sports leadership
2. be able to plan and lead an activity session
3. be able to review your planning and leadership of a sports activity
4. be able to assist in the planning and leading of a sports event
5. be able to review your planning and leadership of a sports event.
   N.B. Learning outcomes 3 and 5 are covered together in section 4 of this unit.

171

Assessment and grading criteria

This table shows you what you must do in order to achieve a pass, merit or distinction grade, and where you can find activities in this book to help you.

To achieve a **pass** grade the evidence must show that the learner is able to:	To achieve a **merit** grade the evidence must show that, in addition to the pass criteria, the learner is able to:	To achieve a **distinction** grade the evidence must show that, in addition to the pass and merit criteria, the learner is able to:
P1 describe the skills, qualities and responsibilities associated with successful sports leadership, using two examples of successful sports leaders **See Assessment activity 7.1, page 187**	**M1** explain the skills, qualities and responsibilities associated with successful sports leadership, giving comparisons and contrasts between two successful sports leaders **See Assessment activity 7.1, page 187**	**D1** evaluate the skills and qualities of two contrasting leaders in sport, commenting on their effectiveness **See Assessment activity 7.1, page 187**
P2 plan and lead a sports activity with teacher support **See Assessment activity 7.2, page 198**	**M2** independently plan and lead a sports activity **See Assessment activity 7.2, page 198**	
P3 carry out a review of their planning and leading of a sports activity, identifying strengths and areas for improvement **See Assessment activity 7.2, page 198**	**M3** explain strengths and areas for improvement in their planning and leading of a sports activity, making suggestions relating to improvement for their own development **See Assessment activity 7.2, page 198**	
P4 contribute to the planning and leading of a sports event describing own role within the event, and producing evidence that this has been effective **See Assessment activity 7.3, page 202**		
P5 Carry out a review of their performance whilst assisting the planning and leading of a sports event, commenting on their own effectiveness and identifying strengths and areas for improvement **See Assessment activity 7.3, page 202**	**M4** explain strengths and areas for improvement in assisting in the planning and leading of a sports event, making suggestions relating to improvement **See Assessment activity 7.3, page 202**	**D2** evaluate own performance in the planning and leading of a sports activity and event, commenting on strengths and areas for improvement and further development as a sports leader **See Assessment activity 7.3, page 202**

How you will be assessed

Your assessment could be in the form of:

- video recorded presentations of you describing the skills, qualities and responsibilities of successful sports leaders
- session plans completed for various physical activity sessions and sport
- observation records of your performance as a sports leader produced by your teacher
- video recordings of you delivering a sports activity session
- team meeting notes of the planning of your sport physical activity session
- written plan of your sports event
- observation record of your involvement in the sports event
- video evidence of your involvement in the sports event.

Holly, 16–year-old netball coach

This unit helped me to develop my knowledge about the requirements of planning, leading and reviewing sports activities and sports events. I enjoyed examining the different skills, responsibilities and qualities required to be an effective sports leader. I developed my own understanding of what is required to fulfil each skill, quality and responsibility through examining how successful sports leaders have fulfilled each area.

The unit was very practical and initially we were introduced to the requirements of sports leadership through observing effective leadership. It did not take long until I was planning and leading small parts of sports sessions. The most enjoyable part of this unit for me was supporting my friends in planning a sports day at a local primary school. It was after this experience that I decided that I wanted to be more involved in coaching and leadership.

Over to you!

- What do you think are the most challenging components of planning and leading physical activity sessions?
- What areas of this unit do you think you are most prepared for?
- What do you think you can do to prepare yourself for the requirements of this unit?

1 Know the skills, qualities and responsibilities associated with successful sports leadership

Warm-up

Good and bad sports leadership

- Make a list of things you think contribute to good sports leadership.
- Make a list of what you think contributes to being a bad sports leader/coach.

As a group discuss the examples each member of the group has agreed to be good and bad forms of sports leadership.

Leadership in sport is not always conducted from the sidelines or off the court, sometimes leadership can be from performers themselves. Often the leader of a team is called the team captain; however the team captain is sometimes not the only leader on the pitch. In 2008 John Terry was the captain of the England football team, but the selection of other experienced internationals such as David James, David Beckham, and Rio Ferdinand (who have all been the captain of the England football team) provided excellent support, advice and leadership for John Terry.

Figure 7.1: Skills required to be a successful sports leader.

1.1 Skills for sports leadership

The role of sports leader can involve many different forms, from leading an activity session, supporting the delivery of a sports coaching session, to a captain of a sports team playing alongside team mates. A sports leader's main aim is to encourage and increase young people and adults' participation in sport. Sports leaders are often required to support the development of sport at a grass roots level, ensuring that sports teams and coaches are organised and provide appropriate opportunities for participation. In order to develop sports participation, sports leaders need to develop skills to support them whilst leading sport and physical activity sessions.

Communication

If you can use different forms of communication effectively you can support the development of sports performers. The more effective your methods of communication, the easier it is to get messages across to players, spectators, other coaches and officials. There are a variety of methods used by sports leaders when communicating, these are:

- **verbal communication**, e.g. giving technical instructions to sports performers
- **non-verbal communication**, e.g. facial expressions and bodily gestures
- **listening**, e.g. after asking a sports performer a question.

Communication is one of the most effective skills if used correctly by a sports leader to communicate to sports performers. A successful sports leader has a clear voice and uses the correct technical language that is appropriate for the sports performers. If a sports performer needs to improve on a specific component of their game, a sports leader with effective verbal communication skills should be able to communicate this – clearly explaining what needs to be done to enhance and improve their performance or the performance of the team.

Non-verbal communication is often used by sports performers to read the mood of the sports leader. The sports leader should try to ensure that they provide positive body language all the time. Non-verbal communication may also be used when there is a lot of external noise occurring during a session and the sports leader needs to communicate a message to the sports performers. This could be done in the form of pointing to a specific position on the pitch or court.

A sports leader should listen to sports performers as well as talking to them. Sports performers can often support the sports leader in understanding their own needs and requirements regarding development, and clarify areas of difficulty during competitive situations for sports performers. Communication between the sports leader and the sports performer should be a two-way process to support the development of knowledge for both of them.

Key terms

Verbal communication – communication using words e.g. team talks, shouting instructions to players/team from the side line.

Non-verbal communication – communication not using words e.g. pointing, signals, body language.

This is an example of non-verbal communication – can you think of any other situations where non-verbal communication is used in sports? Do you think this form of communication is effective and when is it best used in sport?

Organisation of equipment

As a sports leader you must have a clear understanding of what equipment you are going to need before delivering your sport or physical activity session or event. As well as preparing the required equipment for the sports session you should ensure that it is in full working order and that you know how to use the equipment safely and effectively. The equipment used in your session should be checked to ensure that it is safe. These checks should take place before the session. You should ensure that as a sports leader you are insured to use the equipment required in the session (see page 185 on responsibilities and insurance).

Activity: Five-point equipment check

Produce a five-point guide that you should follow to ensure that a sports leader's equipment is organised prior to a sports or physical activity session.

Knowledge

When leading specific sport sessions a sports leader should have a high level of knowledge about the sport they are delivering. This helps in providing the sports performers involved in the session with reassurance that the sports leader has a wealth of knowledge in the sport and can support the development of their performance. A good sports leader should have a high level of knowledge about:

- the technical and tactical demands of the specific sport
- the specific fitness requirements of the specific sport
- laws, rules and regulations of the specific sport
- the treatment of basic sports injuries and first aid techniques as appropriate (an appropriate first aid qualification may be beneficial and required, depending upon the level of responsibility of the sports leader).

As a sports leader develops, their knowledge will increase. It is a requirement in many sports that people involved in the organisation and planning of sports activity sessions attain sport-specific leadership and coaching qualifications. Qualifications attained by a sports leader will increase their knowledge about how to develop sports performers in a specific sport.

Activity structure

When delivering a sports leadership session it is important that you deliver the session following the correct structure. You should ensure that the sessions that you lead have a clear structure and that each component of the session consists of the appropriate activities to ensure the participants are safe and secure, as well as developing their technical ability or tactical knowledge. Sports sessions should follow the following format: warm-up; main body; cool-down; feedback/debrief.

Target setting

When planning a session a sports leader will set specific goals which he/she would like to achieve within the session. These goals are called the aims and objectives of the session. When planning a series of sessions a sports leader will develop these aims and objectives for each session; as the sports leader develops their own knowledge of the participants involved in the session they may choose to develop individual targets for specific sports performers within the group. These targets may be short-term targets – things that will need to be achieved by the end of the session; medium targets or long-term targets which may be achieved by the end of a series of sessions or possible even by the end of a season/period of time. The sports leader should measure these medium- and long-term goals by setting short-term goals for each performer in each session.

Use of language

Effective sports leaders are also successful communicators and a measure of a successful communicator is the language used by an individual. The language used by a leader is very important as it can affect what the performers do. Through using language effectively a sports leader will develop:

- a rapport with the performers
- a high level of sport-specific knowledge
- a respect for performers
- sports performance of individuals and teams
- knowledge of the sport (including technical and tactical knowledge and rules and regulations of the sport).

As a sports leader you must communicate with sports performers in a clear and concise manner and ensure that you use the correct technical language. It is important to consider the level of the sports performers; for example, the language used for a hockey coaching session for a group of beginners will be different from the language used for a sports session for a group of elite hockey players. The language used for the beginners will need to be very basic and explain what they are doing and how to do each activity. The language used for the elite performers will be very technical.

The language used by a sports performer should always be appropriate and a good sports leader will always think before they speak to ensure that the communication they have with sports performers, spectators, officials and other coaches demonstrates respect for all people involved

The managers of some premiership football teams do not speak English as their first language. This can be a barrier when communicating with players. Can you think of two ways to overcome this problem?

in the session or sports event at all times. A good sports leader will increase the learners' knowledge of sport through their communication, clearly explaining the techniques, tactics and rules and regulations of the sport to the performers and passing on constructive and positive feedback appropriately. The language used should be appropriate for the group, as inappropriate language could offend.

Evaluating

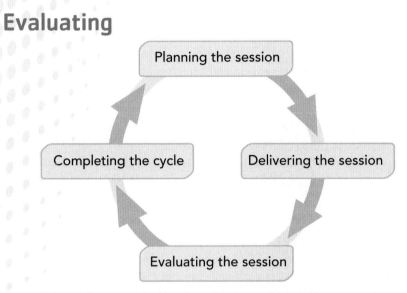

Figure 7.2: A reflective cycle. Use the reflective cycle to evaluate a session you have lead.

Sports leaders should be able to provide the performers who participate in their session with feedback on their strengths and areas for improvement in their performance. However, they are rarely prepared to reflect on their own performance. It is probably the case that, when you reflect on your performance, you find it easy to say what you do well but hard to comment on what did not work well. Effective evaluation of any sports leadership session should be impartial and identify strengths and areas to improve on in the performance of the sports leader. The key to good evaluation is honesty, and this will enable the sports leader to develop their weaknesses and enhance their performance. When new to leading sports and physical activity sessions, try to get as much support as possible from experienced sports leaders and sports coaches; this will develop your ability to assess your own performance and analyse good and bad leadership.

1.2 Qualities for successful sports leadership

A good sports leader demonstrates a number of positive qualities. These qualities support the development of respect with the participants and the relationship the sports leader creates with the group that they lead.

Appearance

It is important that, as well as having the technical and tactical knowledge of a sport and brilliant ideas for how to deliver each component of the session, the coach also demonstrates a positive appearance to the sports performers.

Activity: Key to success

Think of three successful sports coaches. For each sports leader, identify the key characteristics of their appearance – what do they wear, how do they look? For each of your selected successful sports coaches, discuss with your group whether or not you think they demonstrate a positive or negative appearance to the sports performers they influence and develop.

A sports leader should dress appropriately when delivering sports sessions as this could affect the session they are delivering. As a sports leader you are a role model, and therefore a coach should 'talk the talk and walk the walk' and look the part as well. For example, when delivering a football session to a group of children in a school sports hall (wooden floor) it would not be appropriate to wear football boots; however, if you were delivering the same session outside on a muddy football pitch football boots would be essential.

Leadership styles

The way you deliver your session will establish how successful you are as a sports leader. The method of leadership that you use may also have an effect on the performers that you are leading in your session. Different sports performers require different methods of leadership. When leading sports it is often the case that you are measured against achieving set targets and goals; these goals will be set by you through your session plan but when delivering the sessions you must ensure that you select the correct leadership style. A sports leader may have to develop their leadership style to support the development of sports performers.

There are various forms of leadership associated with sports leadership. To be a successful sports leader you will need to use all of these effectively. Different types of leadership suit different types of performers and different activities. The leadership style you choose to use can depend on a number of factors, including the aim of the session (what is required to be achieved within the session), the performers within the session (how the performers work together) and how the performers react to different leadership styles (this may depend on the level of the performers within the session).

You must consider how every individual is going to be enhanced by the sport or physical activity session.

There are three leadership styles identified in the table below.

Table 7.1: Advantages and disadvantages of different leadership styles.

Leadership style	Characteristics	Advantages	Disadvantages
Autocratic	The leader makes all of the decisions within the session. The leader tells the sports performers what to do and how to do it.	Good for beginners when delivering basic skills and techniques. Good method of controlling a group and keeping large groups safe.	Only works on single skills in isolation. Very difficult to examine prior knowledge and understanding of performers as session controlled solely by the leader.
Democratic	The leader decides what is to be delivered within the session but involves sport performers in the decision-making process.	Good for developed sports performers. Develops close relationships with sports performers. Develops communication and confidence of sports performers.	Time-consuming. Problems may occur in large teams when everyone has different opinions and ideas.
Laissez-faire	The performers are in control of the session and make the decisions. The sports leader is used as a mentor for the performers when appropriate.	Helps develop self-confidence. Can increase understanding and develop decision-making of sport performers. Can increase motivation of sport performers.	Lack of structure to the session. Can develop bad techniques without leader's intervention. Can take time to meet a desired goal or target.

Personality

Personality is what makes each person unique – their different characteristics. Every sports leader has their own characteristics and methods; these make every sports leader different. Sport leaders should be confident in their own ability to plan and lead sport and physical activity sessions. In order to have a positive impact on sports performers a sports leader should have positive personality characteristics.

Personalities fall into two categories, **extrovert** and **introvert**. Introverts are individuals who do not actively seek excitement and would rather be in calm or quiet places; in the world of sport introverts tend to prefer sports that require low levels of excitement but require high concentration levels and accuracy in their delivery. Extroverts are inclined to get bored quickly and are often poor at tasks that require a great deal of concentration. They constantly seek stimulation and excitement. Extroverts are often associated with team sports where situations are always changing and the decision-making process of the performer changes depending on the outcome of external forces (opponents, weather, spectators, and team mates). However, it is important not to think that extroverts just play team sports and introverts just participate in individual sports.

Key terms

Extrovert – loud, excitement-seeking, easily distracted.

Introvert – quiet, not seeking excitement, high concentration levels.

Activity: Introvert or extrovert?

Make a list of ten famous sport performers. Place each one of these sports performers into categories of introvert or extrovert. Next to each name in the table place the sport which they play, following the example given.

Introvert	Extrovert
Rodger Federer (tennis player)	Rio Ferdinand (footballer)

Make a list of ten of your friends and complete the exercise again. Think about the major characteristics of your friends and discuss with the group what you think makes your friends introverted or extroverted.

Do you think Tim Henman is an introvert or an extrovert?

As a sports leader, personality can be important in determining your success. The leadership style that a sports leader uses will depend on their personality. When leading a sports session you must create positive relationships with the participants which will help you to gain knowledge about their personality and understand what styles of leadership works for them. A sports leader needs to get to know the performers and what motivates them to achieve goals and targets. For example, Sue Hawkins (the England Netball National Coach), when selecting a new player for the senior squad, will develop a relationship with them to learn about the personality traits of the new player and what motivates them. Sue Hawkins will then ensure that within every coaching session the needs and targets of each member of the squad (including the new member of the team) are fulfilled using a variety of leadership techniques and coaching styles.

Enthusiasm

Good leaders must combine innovative ways of delivering sports and physical activity sessions, knowledge of the sport or activity they are delivering, effective communication and leadership skills with high levels of enthusiasm. Enthusiasm can often be infectious. When a sports leader is smiling and happy, the feeling and emotion rubs off on the performers in the session. An enthusiastic, knowledgeable sports leader will create a good image for the sport or physical activity and can often leave a lasting impression on sports performers.

Activity: Influences

Think back to the people who have influenced your sports performance in positive and negative ways (teachers, sports leaders, coaches etc.) Who are they and why do you think they have influenced your sporting performance and experience of a specific sport?

Motivation

Motivation affects the way we behave. Motivation determines what we do (and possibly what we don't do). As a sport leader you need to understand what motivates sports performers to participate in sport. A sports leader also has to understand what motivates his or her sports performers to ensure that they remain focused and achieve the desired goals of the session.

When leading sessions, the leader of the session must keep the sports performers motivated. For a complete novice to a sport it is often the first session that affects future participation. Sports performers who have been participating in a sport for a long period of time will require motivation to keep them engaged in the session. Therefore a role of the sports leader is to motivate all sports performers in all sessions, whilst understanding motivational needs of the performers.

There are two major forms of motivation: **intrinsic motivation** and **extrinsic motivation**. Intrinsic motivation is when a sports performer participates in an activity or sport for its own sake. They are motivated by the pleasure of the activity and the satisfaction or sense of accomplishment they feel from playing or participating in the sport or activity. It is the choice of the sports performer. Intrinsic motivation

Key terms

Extrinsic motivation – external rewards such as trophies, external praise or money.

Intrinsic motivation – internal rewards (self), love of the game or health benefits.

is considered to be a more positive form of motivation for sports performers as it helps them to participate in sport and physical activity and supports performers to push themselves to the limit.

Extrinsic motivation concerns the influence of things outside the athlete or activity and this includes external rewards. To be extrinsically motivated a sports performer is motivated by external factors and not by the sport or activity. When a sports performer is extrinsically motivated they play the sport with a desire to achieve something. Examples of rewards include prizes, trophies, medals, celebrity status and external praise, and even money.

Humour

A successful sports leader has to have a sense of humour; this enables them to relate to their sports performers. Obviously it is important that laughter is used at appropriate times and timing is key. Sports performers increase their enjoyment when they know that their sports leader can share a laugh and a joke with them.

Confidence

Confidence is a key quality of a leader. A leader should have the confidence to stand in front of performers and direct them towards achieving a target or goal. A sports leader should have the confidence to demonstrate and communicate at an appropriate level with the performers to whom he or she is delivering a sport or physical activity session. Confidence will develop as a sport leader improves their own experiences and knowledge.

1.3 Responsibilities of a sports leader

Sports leaders have responsibilities in the following areas:

- professional conduct
- health and safety
- insurance
- child protection
- legal obligations
- equality.

Can you think of any other responsibilities a sports leader might have?

Professional conduct

Conduct is the way we behave. In any position of authority or leadership the individuals who are being led must see that their leaders conduct themselves in an appropriate manner. For every leader there is an expectation of how they should behave and this is the same for sports

Did you know?

It is a requirement to gain a recognised qualification to be insured to plan and lead sport activities independently. Without a recognised and appropriate qualification you are only allowed to support a recognised qualified sports leader/coach.

leaders. Sports leaders should encourage participation in physical activity through providing participants with positive experiences. Sports participation should be promoted through fair play and by playing within the rules of the sport.

Activity: Code of conduct

Produce a ten-point guide that clearly states how a coach should behave.

Health and safety

Sport is a physical activity and carries an element of challenge to all who participate. Achieving the challenges and targets set will demand a mixture of skill, fitness and co-ordination. The risk of accidents is a threat, but the skill to identify the hazards that could cause accidents or minimise them is a key requirement when planning and leading sport and physical activity sessions.

The sports leader has responsibility for the sport performers and for their safety during the session. An effective sports leader will constantly check on the performers throughout the session, ensuring that they are safe and healthy at all times. The sports leader will also have to be aware of risks and hazards that could cause injury to the performers throughout the session.

Sports leaders should ensure that the equipment that performers will use is checked at three stages: before the set up, once assembled and then just before use. The sports leader should check for damage to the equipment which could cause injury or pose a risk to the sports

Case study: Carly, leisure attendant

Carly is a leisure attendant at Highfield Leisure Centre, carrying out a session to a group of fifteen 10-year-old girls. She has decided to deliver a uni-hockey session. The girls have never played hockey before and are not aware that they will be participating in a hockey session.

The session will be run within the sports hall at the leisure centre. However before the session a trampoline session has taken place, and the trampoline coach is not trained or insured to put the trampolines down at the leisure centre. This session

finishes at 12.00 and Carly's session is due to start at 12.15 as soon as the girls have all finished their swimming lessons.

1. What considerations does Carly have to take before setting up her activity?

2. Prioritise her actions prior to delivering the sports session.

3. What actions can Carly take to reduce injury to the performers who are going to be involved in her session?

performers or sports leader. If you spot any damage to the equipment to be used in your sport session report it to the senior coach or member of staff and do not use it in your session. Even if the equipment was required to meet the aims that you have set in your session you should not put the sports performers in your session at risk of injury.

Insurance

Sports leaders must have appropriate insurance cover to participate in physical activity as well as leading a sport or physical activity session. The sports leader has control over a group of performers and the responsibility that comes with this is that the sports leader is **liable** for their safety whilst they are under his or her supervision. If a sports performer had an injury under the supervision of a sports leader the sports leader is responsible for the accident and could be deemed **negligent**.

> ## Key terms
>
> **Liable** – required according to the law.
>
> **Negligent** – failing to produce the care expected of a sports leader.

Legal obligations

There are legal requirements that can affect the work of a sports leader. It is your responsibility to know and understand the relevant legislation and what you have to do to enforce it. Laws and legislation are passed by the government to support the safety of people who may wish to undertake physical activity. The following Acts have been established and are relevant to sports leaders at the time of publication.

Disability Discrimination Act 1995

This Act makes it illegal for anyone providing a service to discriminate against disabled people. This includes accessibility and provision in sport and physical activity.

Activity Centre Act (Young People Safety Act) 1995

This Act requires that all centres offering adventure activities for children under the age of 18 are registered and licensed to HM Government's Adventure Activities Licensing Service. The Act applies to facilities run by local authorities and private sector organisations. The requirements of registration and licensing are:

- staff should possess specific qualifications (these are listed and updated)
- specific operation procedures and emergency procedures are used at the centre
- to ensure that the centre is aware of and has the correct ratio of staff to children participating in any activity.

By holding this licence centres are providing an assurance that they will give all children who attend the centre a high level of service and ensure their safety at all times. This benefits children because they have greater opportunities to experience outdoor adventurous activities. Through gaining the licence facilities the centres will gain a good reputation in the delivery of adventurous activities to everyone – not just children.

Child protection

Child protection in sport and physical activity has become an important concern. It is essential to protect all children. When children are introduced to new people in new settings it is vital that a sport club keeps children safe and adheres to their statutory duties set out in legislation such as the Children Act (1989) and more recently the Children Act (2004). It is the duty of sports clubs to fulfil this responsibility.

Many sports clubs now complete police checks and ensure that sports leaders undertake child protection training via workshops on a regular basis. This helps to ensure that they are fully aware of the child protection and welfare issues surrounding coaching and leading sports performers under the age of 18. Child protection training is important for sports clubs to ensure that they are adhering to the government's Safer Recruitment drive. This means that all adults who are employed to work with children and young people undergo rigorous checks as part of their recruitment process.

The Children Act (2004)

This Act provides a framework for services working with children and young people to improve their health, development and well-being. This covers services such as leisure, recreation and play services. The Children Act (2004) makes it a responsibility of all agencies working with children and young people to work together and adopt a multi-agency approach when offering services to them. The Act enforces specific duties which must be carried out by the service providers. These duties include:

- providing care, planned and supervised activities for children at all times
- publishing adequate information about the services
- reviewing and monitoring the services on offer and consulting with the appropriate bodies, for example professionals who deal with the protection of children
- ensuring that registration is completed for all organisations which supervise activities for children under the age of eight years.

Before a service can be registered, the suitability of the organisation, all its employees and its premises have to be assessed.

How do you make sure the children are safe and enjoying themselves?

Equality

As a sports leader you will deliver sports and physical activity sessions to a range of performers with different abilities. Whatever their differences, you must provide the learners with equal opportunities to develop and improve their performance. Sports leaders should lead sport and physical activity sessions without any inequality or prejudice and ensure all participants are treated equally and included in all of their sessions.

Rules and regulations

When leading sport sessions you must promote the rules and regulations of the sport. As well as developing an individual's technical ability the session should develop their knowledge of the game. Sports leaders should ensure that participants learn to follow the rules and respect the officials who uphold the rules and regulations. Participants should be made aware of the consequences of breaking the rules and regulations of sports.

Ethics and values

Ethical practice can be described as conduct and actions that are honest, fair and responsible. Values are ideas on which we place worth or importance. These are vital when delivering sports sessions. Effective sports leaders should develop good sportsmanship and fair play in all performers. A sports leader should develop ethics and values within their sports sessions.

The following principles should be encouraged and promoted within every session:

- friendship
- respect for others
- playing with the right spirit
- equal opportunities
- fair play.

Did you know?

In 2008–09 the Football Association and the Premier League ran a campaign to promote fair play and respect towards officials – this campaign was called the Respect Campaign.

Assessment activity 7.1

You have been asked to participate in a discussion with your tutor, who has asked if you could lead the discussion and **describe** the skills, qualities and responsibilities associated with successful sports leadership, using two examples of successful sports leaders. **P1**

If you would like to attain M1 during your discussion you will have to **explain** the skills, qualities and responsibilities associated with successful sports leadership, giving comparisons and contrasts between two successful sports leaders. **M1**

Finally, if you would like to attain D1 criteria in this assessment you will have to **evaluate** the skills and qualities of two contrasting leaders in sport, commenting on their effectiveness. **D1**

Grading tips

- Ensure you use two examples of successful leaders when describing each of the skills, qualities and responsibilities.
- How has each of your selected sports leaders been successful? Provide examples of how they have used each skills, qualities and responsibilities to develop their success.
- What could they do to improve their application of each of the skills, qualities and responsibilities?

PLTS

Thinking about how other sports leaders have become successful will help you develop your skills as a **creative thinker**.

Functional skills

Through contributing within this discussion about the required skills, qualities and responsibilities required by sports leaders you will develop your **English** skills in speaking and listening.

2 Be able to plan and lead an activity session

To ensure that participants develop fully, a sports leader should plan every session thoroughly. When planning a sport or physical activity session a sports leader must be inclusive and flexible. It is often the case that what you plan for your session will need to be changed. The number of people you plan for can also change as can the levels of performers who attend your session.

The session plan that you design should incorporate a lot of information and detail. You will need to consider the following:

- clear aims and objectives and specific targets for performers' development within each session
- specific requirements for participants within the session, including medical needs, and or educational support
- the requirements of the facility – the set-up and equipment you will need
- the order of the activities – ensuring that the session progresses the learners
- safety checks (including performer checks and equipment and facility checks).

There are several considerations when planning a sport or physical activity session.

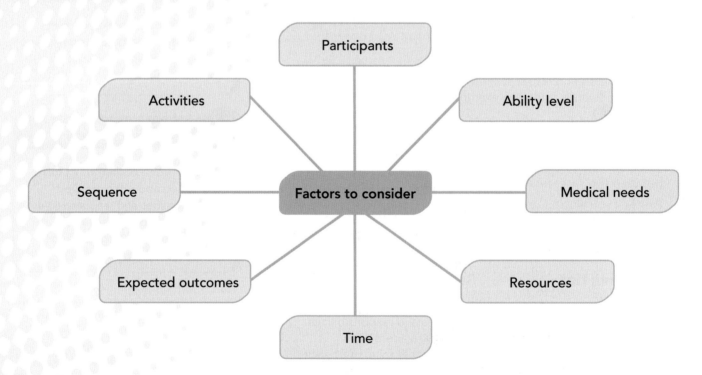

Figure 7.3: Factors to consider when planning a session. Think about how each factor would affect your planning. For example, what would you need to take into consideration when planning a session outdoors, and how would this differ from planning an indoor session?

2.1 Plan

Participants

Before starting to plan your sport or physical activity session, you must collect certain information about your group. This should include:

- group size
- age
- ability of performers
- gender mix
- interests and previous experience
- medical information
- specific needs of participants.

The session plan that you design will have to be realistic for the needs and aspirations of the performers to whom you will be delivering your session. Sports leaders will deliver sessions to a range of participants, including children, young adults, the elderly and disabled performers. When planning sessions you must consider the needs and aspirations of the different groups involved. Usually when you begin leading and planning sports and physical activities you will be leading your peers and young children.

Age of participants

Sports leaders should consider the requirements of different age groups when planning a sports leadership session. Planning a session for 7-year-olds will be very different from planning a session for teenagers. When planning sport and physical activity sessions the emphasis must be on enjoyment and that all participants are targeted for development and enjoyment.

When coaching young children you will need to be aware of the physiological factors that must be considered as well as motivational strategies and the selection of appropriate activities. A sports leader should think about child development when planning a sports session for young children. Children grow and develop at different rates. This means that two young sports performers of the same age may be at very different stages of their development – physically, emotionally, socially, and intellectually.

When developing sessions for children it is essential to consider the best methods to use to enhance learning. Children generally learn best from copying others – friends, parents, family members and sports leaders. You must consider which leadership style you choose to ensure that children's needs are met. Children are more willing to try new things and accept constructive feedback than adults. Children are also generally less afraid of failure and this fearless approach to sport provides sports leaders with an opportunity to develop sports performers' techniques at an early stage; through supportive leadership you can leave a long-lasting memory of the correct techniques and application.

It is believed that children have endless energy and can run around for unlimited periods of time. However, children do not breathe as slowly or deeply as adults, which means they work much harder than adults to provide the oxygen that their muscles need. It is not until children reach puberty that their energy systems (two aerobic and one anaerobic) is as efficient as adults. Due to these differences children do not take exercise as efficiently as adults. Temperature regulation is difficult to control and children can get dehydrated faster than adults do. It is therefore important that children should take lots of short breaks to allow time to take on fluids and for recovery.

Strength gain occurs mainly during puberty. Children of all ages can benefit from general fitness training and physical activity but strength and conditioning should not be given until the body has fully formed.

Initially young children will develop their co-ordination and ability to produce complex skills very quickly and sports leaders should use this co-ordination and attempt to develop basic skills and then build more complex skills as children develop. Concentration levels are generally low so sessions should have a variety of activities to keep the performers interested throughout the session.

As children develop into teenagers they become physiologically stronger. Body shapes increase in size and their energy systems become more efficient. They develop a clearer perception about the physical activities they are participating in and the concept of competition. They start to judge their own performance and the performances of those around them. As teenagers develop and their needs change sports leaders will adapt the sessions to ensure that success is attained in every session they take part in. Sports leaders need to maintain the interest of the sports performers, because lots of performers at this age stop participating in sport because of loss of interest. As a leader you should have methods to ensure that all performers remain motivated in all sports sessions and, although sessions can become more technical and complex, it is still important to maintain the element of fun.

When producing specific sessions for children and teenagers remember why these groups are attracted to sport and physical activity. The things that attract children to sport include:

- fun
- competition
- accomplishment
- socialising
- independence
- release of energy and emotion
- escapism
- challenge.

The benefits of exercise for children are endless but fall into three main categories:

- physical development
- personal and social development
- intellectual development.

As teenagers get older, the development of females is more significant than males. Some sports recognise these changes by preventing girls from continuing to compete against boys when they reach a certain age. When working with mixed-sex groups you should be aware of the considerations. A sports leader should never discriminate against gender. There are some sports that have been thought of as just for boys and some sports that are traditionally more for girls. However, such barriers are now being broken as 'traditional' male and female-dominated sports so that more people get the chance to take part in more sports.

Activity: 'Male' and 'female' sports

Make a list of sports that are predominantly male dominated. Now do the same for female-dominated sports. In a group, select one of the sports from each list and discuss what you would do to overcome the gender barriers and increase participation for females in the traditional male sports and vice versa for males.

Ability levels

Often the ability and age of your participants will determine the session you deliver and the activities you choose. When you have a clear idea of the ability and age of the performers in your session you will then have to develop an objective for what you wish your participants to achieve by the end of your planned session. Clear aims and objectives for your session will help you develop ideas about what activities you can use to meet the aims of your session.

Specific needs

Specific needs could refer to medical information about your sports performers that you will need to obtain prior to the session. This could refer to any disability or special educational needs (SEN). It is important that you include everyone in your session and that their needs and requirements are met. This may require adaptation to your session plan. Ensure that the plan you complete is flexible and can be changed at any time to take into account the needs of the participants.

What strategies can you come up with to overcome gender barriers in sports?

Aims and objectives

All sports leadership sessions should have a clear **aim**. Your aims should be stated on your session plan. This should be agreed before the start of the session. An aim is something that you want to achieve or that is an overall goal for the session, e.g. 'I want everyone in the session to be able to throw a ball by the end of my session'.

In order to achieve your aim you need to have **objectives**. These will have to be clearly written on your session plan and should express how you will meet each of your aims (if you have three aims you will need to have three objectives) e.g. in order for everyone in the group to throw a ball I must introduce, demonstrate and develop the required technique for throwing a ball.

Resources

When planning any sports or physical activity session it is often the equipment that you use which is essential to meeting the aims and objectives of your session. When using equipment and facilities in physical activity sessions the sports leader should check the availability of the equipment and facility and make sure that the equipment is safe prior to use. When using a new venue the sports leader needs to know the emergency procedures and the location of the changing rooms and toilets.

Target setting

Sports leaders must use targets to develop sports performers. These targets should be set around the sports performer's strengths and areas for improvement. The targets should be realistic and achievable. Sports leaders could use the SMARTER model for setting targets for participants in their session – see Unit 2, page 63.

Expected outcomes

Even when your session seems to be going to plan you must still have alternative ideas of what you could do if it needs changing because of external influences. These could include:

- double booking of the facility
- more people turning up to participate in your session than planned
- required equipment not available on the day
- extreme weather conditions
- facility closed.

A good sports leader should always ensure that they are prepared for every circumstance. This is known *as* contingency planning. When undertaking a contingency plan:

- Think through every possible thing that could go wrong.

- Before the event, check everything that you planned – check all equipment, availability of the facility, number of participants and specific needs of participants at least the night before the event.
- Make sure you have an alternative back-up plan and you are fully prepared in case something does go wrong.

2.2 Lead an activity session

Skills, qualities and responsibilities

When leading an activity session or sports event, a sports leader will demonstrate the skills, qualities and responsibilities described in the previous sections of this unit. The sports leader should ensure that the session flows and provides a variety of activities for the sports performers, ensuring that all participants are safe at all times. This should be measured through effective planning and preparation, pre-activity checks and through the sports leader monitoring the performance of the athletes during the session.

The sports leader should set out the aims and objectives of the session at the start of the session and for each activity clearly state the rules and regulations. The sports leader should relate these to the rules and regulations of the sport being coached to reinforce knowledge and develop the participants' understanding.

An important skill that sports leaders have to master is communication. Sports leaders will have to communicate effectively to ensure that their group understands the instructions provided and can follow them to support their development.

Demonstration

A sports activity session should be delivered using methods that are as visual as possible. Sports leaders should demonstrate to learners what they want them to do. The sports leader should have sufficient knowledge of the technical requirements of the skills to demonstrate the correct method to the learners. If the sports leader is unable to carry out the demonstration because of injury, or for another reason, they should carry out a demonstration using another member of the group, or another coach or sports leader who is available. If the sports leader is unable to carry out the demonstration he or she should describe each key factor of the technique and discuss its importance in the application of the skill.

The sports leader should ensure that the session is aimed at the correct level and that the language used in the session is appropriate for the participants. The session must be exciting and enjoyable for the performers but must also develop them. Sports leaders should aim to develop the performers by providing them with appropriate feedback. The leader should ensure that all participants are monitored throughout the session and positive feedback is used continually to encourage performers.

Remember

Do not allow children to pick their own teams – this can lead to weaker performers being left out and feeling isolated.

Activity structure

The structure of a sports session should be generic. Once you have developed the aims of the session, each element of the session should develop the participants towards the overall target of the session. A session should always start with a **warm-up** that needs to prepare the sports performers for the impending activity both physically and mentally.

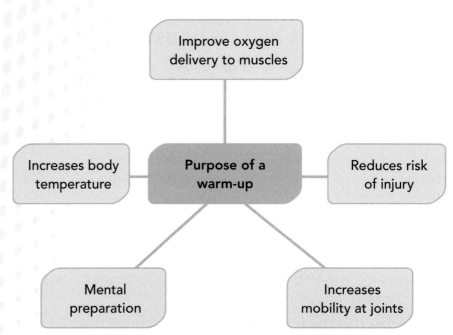

Figure 7.4: Purpose of a warm-up. Do you warm-up every time before doing any sporting activity?

The next part of the session should be the **skill introduction**. This should be related to the aims of your session and how you introduce the skills will depend on the ability level and experience of the group. When introducing the skill, the sports leader should demonstrate the requirements and discuss the key points of the technique with the participants.

After a skill has been introduced and the participants have developed an understanding of how to carry it out correctly, the sports leader should look at how the skill can be developed. In the **development of the skill** component the sports leader should try to progress the use of skill into a **conditioned game** or activity. For example, when working on short passing in football, a sports leader may condition a game of five versus five and to score a point a team must complete five short passes without the opposing team touching the ball. After the skill has been developed within a conditioned game the sports leader could then progress the participants into a competitive scenario. The sports leader should ensure that the aim of the session has been developed and observed during the **competitive** game. This could take the form of a full competitive game or a small sided game where players have more space and time to demonstrate the reflective use of the skill/technique covered in the session.

Finally the session should conclude with a **cool-down**. It is important that exercise does not simply cease but does so gradually. This will allow the heart to reduce speed slowly and allows the body to recover after exercise and prevent the delay of onset muscle soreness (DOMS).

Recording

As you develop as a sports leader, you should record your ideas and observations. It is useful to observe as many different sports leaders as possible to support your development. This can be done in a number of ways.

You can use any of the following methods to record evidence:

- diary
- logbook
- portfolio
- video
- audio
- observation record
- witness testimony
- feedback sheets.

What tips, techniques and methods have you noticed when observing sports leaders?

Session Planner

Date:	Time:	Venue:	Resources:	Ability levels: Age:

Aims and objectives of the session	Leadership style Leadership points

Component	Activity	Safety	Organisation
Warm-up (mins)			
Skills introduction (mins)			
Skill development (mins)			
Competition/ conditioned games (mins)			
Cool-down (mins)			
Evaluation of session			

Figure 7.5: Do you use a session planner like this one?

3 Be able to assist in the planning and leading of a sports event

N.B. This is learning outcome 4.

There are many different types of sports events. Here are some examples:

- sports days, training camps, and sports tournaments
- festivals
- charity events and competitions
- field trips
- outdoor education.

3.1 Planning a sports event

When organising a sports event it is important that you carry out certain tasks to ensure that the event is planned correctly. It is important that everyone in the group has a clear role when planning a sports event. The roles that people can take are:

- co-ordinator
- chairperson
- secretary
- finance officer
- publicity officer
- marketing officer
- steward
- specialist coach or trainer
- referee or official
- health and safety officer.

With each role there are responsibilities. The ultimate aim of your session will be to meet the agreed objective and ensure that participants have an enjoyable experience and are safe at all times.

Activity: Health and safety

Complete a ten-point safety checklist that you should carry out before your event.

Complete a five-point emergency procedure that you would follow if a minor injury occurred during your event (assuming that you do not hold an appropriate first aid qualification).

Complete a five-point emergency procedure that you would follow if a major injury occurred during your event (assuming that you do not hold an appropriate first aid qualification).

Health and safety

Health and safety is the most important responsibility a sports leader will have when planning and leading sport activity sessions or events. Unit 5 (Injury in sport) examines the importance of health and safety in much greater detail. Appropriate checks must be carried out before you complete your event to ensure that it runs as smoothly as possible without risk of injury to any of the participants. Risk assessments and constant safety checks should be carried out to ensure safety is paramount.

When planning an event where there may be large numbers of participants every possible occurrence should be considered. Sports leaders must have knowledge of basic first aid, and how to treat basic injuries, and what action to take if serious injury or harm is caused to a sports performer. It is your responsibility to ensure that someone who has a relevant first aid certificate is available during the delivery of your event and that they have appropriate equipment and resources.

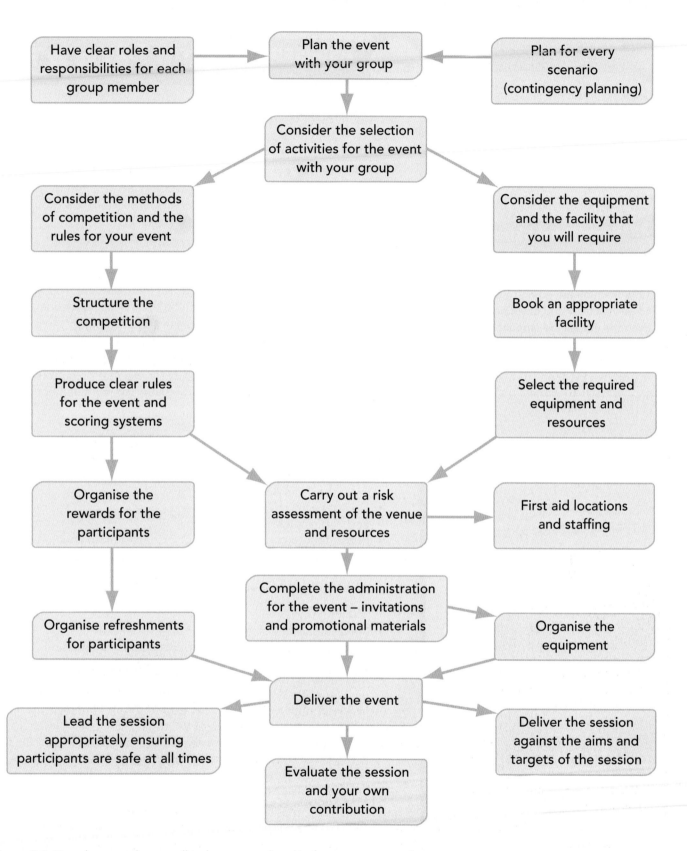

Figure 7.6: How do you make sure all tasks are completed before a sports event?

PLTS

Thinking about the activities you are going to include in your sports activity session and the correct sequencing of these activities will help you to develop your skills as a **self-manager**.

Functional skills

Through planning the amount of time that you are going to dedicate to each activity and ensuring that the total equals the amount of time provided for your session will help you develop your **mathematics** skills in problem-solving.

 Assessment activity 7.2

In order to meet the requirements of P2 you must plan and lead a sports activity session for a group of Year 7 students at a local school, using the session plan on page 195, with teacher support when required. **P2**

In order to meet the requirements of M2 you are required to independently plan and lead a sports activity session for a group of Year 7 students at a local school. **M2**

After the completion of your sports activity session you have been asked to provide your teacher with a review of your planning and leading of the sports activity to the Year 7 students at your local school, identifying strengths and areas for improvement. You will be asked to undertake your review in the form of a one-to-one interview. The interview will be recorded. **P3**

In order to achieve the requirements of M3 in this activity, you must also explain the strengths and areas for improvement in your planning and leading of a sports activity for the Year 7 students at your local school, making suggestions relating to improvement for their own development. **M3**

Grading tips:

- Try to plan to lead the sports activity session on your own to meet the requirements of M2.
- Do not forget to set clear aims and targets for your session and participants.
- Remember to consider contingency plans in case your expected outcomes change.
- When leading the session make sure you communicate clearly and use demonstrations when appropriate.

After your event:

- Make a list of the strengths of your session (use information obtained from the participants in the session and observers).
- Make a list of the areas which you think you could improve upon after the completion of your sports activity session (use information obtained from your teachers' feedback and observers).
- Speak clearly and, for each strength and area of improvement, tell the teacher why you think it was a positive point or a negative point and say what you could do to improve the weakness or enhance the strength.
- Research some courses that you could complete to support your development as a sports leader.

4 Be able to review your planning and leadership of a sports activity and event

4.1 Review

After the completion of a session or event a leader should invite participants to give feedback. This feedback can then be used by the sports leader to identify components of the session that went well and components of the session that may require development in the future.

During the developmental stage of leading sports activities, sports leaders should obtain feedback from more experienced supervisors and observers of the session. The feedback obtained from the experienced sports leaders/coaches can be used to improve and develop their performance. Eventually it may be that the more experienced leader/coach will learn from you – as you have done from them.

The methods of feedback should be different for the performer and the observer. When you are planning your session a sports leader should consider the methods of generating the feedback.

When completing a practical session the sports leader could just ask the performers how they felt the session went and this information might be useful; but this method of evaluation may not generate honest feedback from the performers. The sports leader could generate a questionnaire to obtain genuine opinions.

The method of feedback produced by a supervisor or observer will be significantly different and for the session and event that you complete, the assessor will produce an observation record of your performance which may look something like figure 7.8 (see p. 200):

Strengths and areas for improvement

After receiving feedback from participants and observers you should conclude, using the feedback and your own thoughts, what you felt were the strengths of your session/event and what parts of the session you would like to develop and improve upon for future sessions.

When you have identified your strengths you should look at areas for improvement. You might need to ask yourself:

- What went wrong in the session?
- Why do I think this component of the session needs developing?
- What did other people say (feedback) about this part of the session?
- What can I do to develop this part of the session and make it work?

After you have asked yourself these questions after a session or sports event you can start to consider how you are going to develop as a sports leader and set yourself targets for future development as a sports leader.

Please tick your answers

Did you enjoy the session?

Did you enjoy the warm-up?

Did you enjoy the drills in the session, e.g. dribbling between cones, shooting into the hockey net?

Did the sports leader communicate clearly?

Did the sports leader demonstrate clearly what you had to do in the session?

Did you feel that your performance improved in the session?

What extra activities would you like to have done in the session?

Figure 7.7: After a sports event you could obtain feedback from performers using a questionnaire. What other information would it be useful for you to find out?

Assessment

Name of Student:

Session Plan

Did the learner produce a lesson plan (prior to the start of the session/event?) **YES/NO**

Was the session planned appropriately for the needs of the participants? **YES/NO**

Will the session/event meet the aims and objectives of the session? **YES/NO**

Targets

Did the learner set targets for participants? **YES/NO**

Where these targets met during the session/event? **YES/NO**

Before the session

Did the learner carry out a safety check of the participants and of the venue and equipment prior to the session/event? **YES/NO**

Did the learner produce a risk assessment for the event/session? **YES/NO**

Delivery

Did the coach communicate effectively throughout the session/event? **YES/NO**

Did the learner organise the session effectively? **YES/NO**

Did the learner demonstrate appropriate knowledge and language of the sport and the techniques and skills covered in the session **YES/NO**

Did the coach wear appropriate clothing for the session? **YES/NO**

Did the coach motivate the performers throughout the session? **YES/NO**

Did the coach apply the correct rules and regulations as appropriate? **YES/NO**

Which components of the session/event were good? ....

Which areas could be improved? ....

Signed _____
(assessor)

Date _____

Figure 7.8: Assessment of student. What other information might be useful here?

Set targets for improvements

After you have carried out your initial assessment of your performance whilst planning and leading sports events/activity sessions, it is important that you consider methods to improve your leadership. When you are new to sports leadership you do not have to tackle your personal development alone. There are lots of courses you can attend and other sports leaders and sports coaches will be able to support you through attaining the targets you have set yourself. When setting yourself targets you should use the SMART model; see Unit 3 page 89.

Development plans

In order to continually develop as a sports leader, you should use the information gained from your session and event evaluation to make a plan for future development. A good sports leader will consider the different ways in which they can develop. As a sports leader you need to realise that you will never stop learning and, through working alongside other sports leaders and completing various coaching and leadership awards, your experience and abilities will be enhanced. In time your areas for improvement will become strengths. Your development should have one major goal – to develop your planning and leading ability. Development plans can be an extension of the targets that you set when identifying areas for improvement and should be devised to enhance your abilities.

Development plans could include developing individual skills, qualities or responsibilities or they could involve carrying out specific coaching and leadership courses. A sports coach has to have clear reasoning about why they want to pass a specific course or improve a specific component of their leadership. The aim of the development plan is to justify this and develop methods of achieving these goals. As a sports leader it is often your responsibility to produce your own development plan; however at the very early stages of development as a sports leader it is advised that you work alongside experienced coaches until your own knowledge of leadership increases and you obtain appropriate qualifications to lead independently.

Which successful sports coach do you most admire? How could you learn from them to develop your own coaching style?

PLTS

Working as part of a group and planning a sports activity event will develop your skills as a **team member**.

Functional skills

Taking part in team meetings and discussions about the sports event with your group should help to develop your **English** skills in speaking and listening.

BTEC Assessment activity 7.3 P4 P5 M4 D2

You should work in groups to assist in the planning of a sports event for this assessment activity.

You should contribute to the planning and leading of a sports event, describing your own role within the event, and producing evidence that demonstrates your involvement in the event planning process. **P4**

After the completion of your sports event you have been asked to carry out a written report that reviews your performance whilst assisting in the planning and leading of a sports event; you have to comment on your effectiveness and identify your strengths and areas that you think will require improvement. **P5**

In order to achieve M4 you must explain strengths and areas for improvement for whilst assisting in the planning and leading of a sports event, making suggestions relating to improvement for your own performance and the performance of the whole group. **M4**

In order to achieve D2 you must evaluate your own performance in the planning and leading of a sports activity and event, commenting on strengths and areas for improvement and further development as a sports leader. **D2**

Grading tips

- Ensure that at every stage of the planning process you and your group record your ideas and actions taken towards completing the event plan. Make a list of the strengths of your event (use information obtained from the participants in the session and observers and other group members).
- Make a list of the areas which you and your group think you could improve upon after the completion of your sports event (use information obtained from your teacher's feedback, group members' thoughts and from observers).
- Research some courses that you could complete to support your development as a sports leader.

Bridie Robbins
Leisure Centre Assistant

Bridie's role as a leisure assistant includes:

- lifeguarding
- general cleaning
- facility operations (preparing equipment for customers)
- planning and leading birthday parties.

In the past Bridie has supported one of her colleagues whilst leading birthday parties for young children. However she has been informed by the duty manager at the leisure centre that in two weeks' time the leisure centre is very busy and they will need both Bridie and her colleague to lead their own birthday parties for two different groups of children. This will mean that, for the first time, Bridie will have to plan and lead her own party.

The duty manager has told Bridie that she will be planning a party for 15 boys and girls. The ages of the children in the group will be between 9 and 10 years old. The parents who are organising the party would like a sports activity session that is fun and exciting for the children, however they have specifically asked for no football as the child whose birthday it is does not like football. Bridie has been told that she has to plan for 30 minutes of activities then the party will be taken to the swimming pool for a fun swim with parents before having the buffet in the leisure centre cafe.

The duty manager has told Bridie that she has the use of a full sports hall for the full duration of the party.

Think about it!

What other information do you think Bridie may need before starting to plan the sports activity session for the party?

Consider how Bridie should start to plan the sports activity session.

What activities should Bridie include in her activity session?

Think about what final checks Bridie will need to carry out before the party starts. What checks might Bridie have to carry out during the activity session?

How will Bridie know if her session has been a success?

Just checking

1. Make a list of four skills required to be a successful sports leader.
2. Make a list of four responsibilities required to be a successful sports leader.
3. Make a list of four qualities required to be a successful sports leader.
4. Identify the different types of communication and provide examples of how sports leaders use these effectively.
5. What are extrinsic and intrinsic motivation?
6. What are the components of a sports or physical activity session?
7. What is an aim?
8. What is an objective?
9. What checks should be carried out before a sports or physical activity session?
10. Describe five different sports events.
11. Make a list of the courses that you could carry out to develop your sports leadership experience.
12. Describe five methods of assessing your own performance whilst leading a sports or physical activity session.

Assignment tips

- Take the opportunity to observe and support experienced sports coaches/sports leaders whilst delivering sports events whenever possible.
- Maintain a diary of your activity sessions and specific activities which you like for each part of the sport session/event.
- There is a lot of useful information on the internet, but make sure you back it up with research from textbooks.
- Keep track of where you source your research from.
- Independently plan a sports activity session using the ideas gained from your observations of sports leaders.
- After you have delivered a session, makes notes straight away. This will help jog your memory when you need to evaluate the effectiveness of the session at a later date.
- When identifying strengths and areas for improvement, make sure you give reasons why. For each area of weakness provide suggestions relating to improvement and evaluate your overall performance commenting on long-term development targets.
- Set SMART targets for your development as a sports leader.
- Look out for opportunities to assist sports leaders. Volunteer wherever you can.

Credit value: 10

8 Technical skills and tactical awareness for sport

All sports performers need to be aware of the technical and tactical demands of their sport. Many people believe that it is the role of a sports coach to develop the technical or tactical ability of a player or teams; however those performers who develop their own technical and tactical ability are often those who succeed at the highest levels. For example, the world number one golfer, Tiger Woods, is famous for his dedication to practising and mastering the techniques and applying them in competitions. Although it is sports coaches who support development, it is important that as a sports performer you are aware of the demands of your sport.

Elite sports performers are constantly training and trying to develop their performance. The method that you use as a sports performer to improve your performance is a transferable skill and one which can be used to coach others when a playing career is over.

Learning outcomes

After completing this unit you should:

1. know the technical and tactical demands of a selected sport
2. understand the technical skills and tactical awareness in a selected sport
3. be able to plan and undertake a programme to develop own technical skills and tactical awareness
4. be able to review own technical and tactical development and set goals for further development.

Assessment and grading criteria

This table shows you what you must do in order to achieve a pass, merit or distinction grade, and where you can find activities in this book to help you.

To achieve a **pass** grade the evidence must show that the learner is able to:	To achieve a **merit** grade the evidence must show that, in addition to the pass criteria, the learner is able to:	To achieve a **distinction** grade the evidence must show that, in addition to the pass and merit criteria, the learner is able to:
P1 describe the technical and tactical demands of a chosen sport	**M1** explain the technical and tactical demands of a chosen sport	
P2 assess the technical skills and tactical awareness of an elite performer, identifying strengths and areas for improvement	**M2** assess the technical skills and tactical awareness of an elite performer, explaining strengths and areas for improvement	
P3 assess own technical skills and tactical awareness, in a chosen sport, identifying strengths and areas for improvement **See Assessment activity 8.1, page 216**	**M3** assess own technical skills and tactical awareness, in a chosen sport, explaining own strengths and areas for improvement **See Assessment activity 8.1, page 216**	**D1** compare and contrast own technical skills and tactical awareness with those of an elite performer and the demands of a chosen sport **See Assessment activity 8.1, page 216**
P4 produce a six-week training programme, with tutor support, to develop own technical skills and tactical awareness	**M4** independently produce a six-week training programme to develop own technical skills and tactical awareness, describing strengths and areas for improvement	**D2** evaluate the training programme, justifying suggestions made regarding improvement
P5 carry out a six-week training programme to develop own technical skills and tactical awareness		
P6 review own development, identifying goals for further technical and tactical development, with tutor support	**M5** independently describe own development, explaining goals for technical and tactical development	**D3** analyse own goals for technical and tactical development, suggesting how these goals could be achieved

How you will be assessed

This unit will be assessed by an internal assignment that will be designed and marked by the staff at your centre. Your assessment could be in the form of:

- presentations
- written assignments
- observation records and witness statements
- written training programmes
- video diaries and practical observation.

Jimmy Robinson, 17-year-old professional footballer

This unit helped me to understand the technical requirements of all the skills of football, and provided me with a greater appreciation of tactics and how, if carried out correctly, they can be used to improve a team's performance. I now understand that in order to develop my performance as a footballer it is important to develop my technical and tactical skills.

I feel as if I now have a greater appreciation of what the coach is saying to me when giving me feedback about my performance. Through analysing the performance of John Terry when completing this unit at school I realised that even the best footballers have to work on their game and they can always improve. I think that this has given me the motivation to listen to the coaches at the club when they give me feedback and I find myself working even harder to develop my weaknesses.

Over to you!

- Can you list five technical demands that are required to play football?
- Can you make a list of the strengths and weaknesses of your performance in your sport?

1 Know the technical and tactical demands of a selected sport

Warm-up

Developing a sports career

Think of a professional sports person – someone you consider to be a role model. List the honours they have gained during their career. What is their greatest achievement?

Write down the technical factors needed in their sport. Discuss the strengths and weaknesses of their performance.

Discuss who you think has supported the development of their career.

In Unit 2 Practical sport you were introduced to the skills, techniques and tactical demands in one team and one individual sport; for this unit you are required to examine the technical and tactical demands for one selected sport.

1.1 Technical demands

Technical demands can be applied to sports performance. In gymnastics the technical ability of a sports performer is very important – if a gymnast fails to carry out a specific skill using the incorrect technique they lose points.

The photograph below shows an example of a gymnast executing a handstand.

Activity: Judging technique

In small groups discuss what you think the perfect technique of a handstand is.

Now in your groups give this performer a mark out of ten for the execution of the handstand.

What could the performer do to improve their performance of this skill?

Technical demands in a sport are the actions that are required to play and participate in a sport. For example, in basketball the technical requirements include the basic requirements of the sports such as running, catching and jumping, and then more complex requirements and skills, such as shooting, dribbling, passing, tackling, pivoting, and receiving.

Skills are learned (see Unit 2, page 37). Skills can be classified into many different forms; skills can also be classified as:

- continuous skills
- serial skills
- discrete skills.

Activity: Technical demands in sport

1. Make a list of the technical demands in three sports.
2. Categorise each of the technical demands into serial, discrete and continuous skills in a table like the one below.

Serial	Discrete	Continuous

1.2 Tactical demands

The tactical demands in sport are the methods which a sports performer or team use to defeat their opponents in a competitive situation. For example, a basketball team may consider which player in a team will be marking a specific member of the opposing team; a formula one racing team may consider which tyres to use on a specific track and how much fuel to start the race with; a marathon runner will decide at what pace to run specific stages of a race to out-wit other competitors. Effective application of tactics in sport can include the correct selection of skills and techniques and their application in appropriate situations.

Tactical demands relate to various components of a sport such as:

- attack and defence – what methods to use when you have control of the ball, court, or race
- the situation a performer or team is in – if winning or losing, and the time or distance left until the end of the competitive situation in your sport
- the performer's or team's preferred style of play or performance – own strengths and weaknesses
- the opposition – what are the strengths and weaknesses of your opponents and what methods you or your team use to overcome the strengths and exploit the weaknesses.

Activity: Tactical demands

Create a list of the different tactics used in three sports by sports performers to achieve success, consider methods of defence and attack in each sport, and use a table like the one below to record the information.

Defensive tactics	Attacking tactics

2 Understand the technical skills and tactical awareness in a selected sport

2.1 Performance analysis

The simplest and most frequent form of analysis of performance is observation analysis (performance analysis). Analysis is important for sports performers and coaches. A performer's analysis of performance should be used to plan the next phase of development for them or their team. The coach will use the performance analysis to plan and develop the improvements for the team or performer.

Analysis of sports performers in competitive situations enables coaches to monitor the progress of the team or sports performers and compare them to other players, and to assess their strengths and weaknesses in their sport. Analysis can be of skills and techniques and application of tactics. Some coaches will analyse each element individually to allow them to assess each technical and tactical component of the sport in full.

Video analysis

Video analysis is one of the most popular ways to analyse performance. In order to carry out video analysis a video recording of the performance is made and then the sports performer or coach observes the performance in real time and, when required, uses slow motion to analyse the physical application of the skills and techniques. Video analysis allows the coach or sports performer to go over and over the performance of the team or individual.

Notational analysis

In Unit 2 Practical sport you were introduced to different forms of observation checklists to review your performance in a practical sport; these checklists are methods of recording and analysing performance. The completion of these forms during live performance or video analysis will support the sports coach or sports performer when assessing their tactical and technical application for their specific sport.

2.2 Performance analysis model

The performance analysis model (shown opposite) demonstrates how analysis of performance should be used as a starter stimulus for performance development. Analysis should be used to evaluate performance and generate strengths and weaknesses in an individual's or team's performance. It can then be used to inform subsequent planning for development. The planning stage of this model should be agreed by both performer and sports coach. Without the planning stage of this model your development as a sports performer can plateau. After the planning stage you should undertake the required action and training and should then be observed again performing in a competitive situation where further analysis can take place. After the cycle has been completed it is expected that the performance analysis starts again as it is a continuous process.

For **elite sports performers** every competitive performance is analysed and their technical and tactical demands are assessed. This is done by coaching staff but also by the media. Performance analysis and performance profiling is now a common part of competitive sport.

After completing an **objective analysis**, those observing should make generalisations about the performance and also list specific strengths and weaknesses. These should relate to the technical and tactical demands for the sport. For example, when observing the performance of a footballer the observer could make generalisations about the technical requirements of the sport through assessing the number of completed passes, tackles, shots on target etc. and could make generalisations regarding the individual's or the team's technical ability through assessing the number of set plays successfully converted, the success when in the attacking third and the success of defending when in their own third. In addition to using notational analysis the observer could make a **subjective analysis**.

Figure 8.1: Performance analysis model.

Key terms

Elite sports performers – those who compete at sports at a professional level or the highest level available in their sport; this includes professional athletes, national representatives, national record holders, world record holders, national champions and Olympians.

Objective analysis – analysis based on the measurement and comparison of numbers and performance data.

Subjective analysis – analysis based on observational judgements, personal interpretations, and opinions.

Activity: Observation checklist

Produce an observation checklist that you can use to assess the skills and tactical awareness of a sports performer from a specific sport. You will need to know each technical and tactical demand from the sport which you have selected. If you look back to Unit 2 Practical sport there are some different examples of how you could record the performance of a sports performer.

Did you know?

Prozone is a video analysis service used by elite sports performers to analyse their performance in detail. It was introduced to football to analyse the performance of sports performers by Sam Allardyce at Bolton in 1999. Allardyce used the programme to evaluate Bolton's performance and, through the support of the analysis and his coaching team, developed the performance of the team. The team went from one which had bounced from the Championship back to the Premier League, and then were relegated back to the Championship, to a team which stabilised themselves in the Premier League and eventually finished sixth in 2004–2005. Prozone is now used in most football clubs and the information gained is used to evaluate the effectiveness of a player's technical and tactical ability.

Performance analysis is carried out using a computer program. Due to technological advances performance analysis can be carried out using high-tech equipment. The use of this equipment can support player development as live performance can be slowed down and technical faults spotted. Most team games use this form of analysis and this has developed much more statistical data which can be used to assess the effectiveness of their performance. Also the data obtained can be used to compare performances and assess improvements as appropriate.

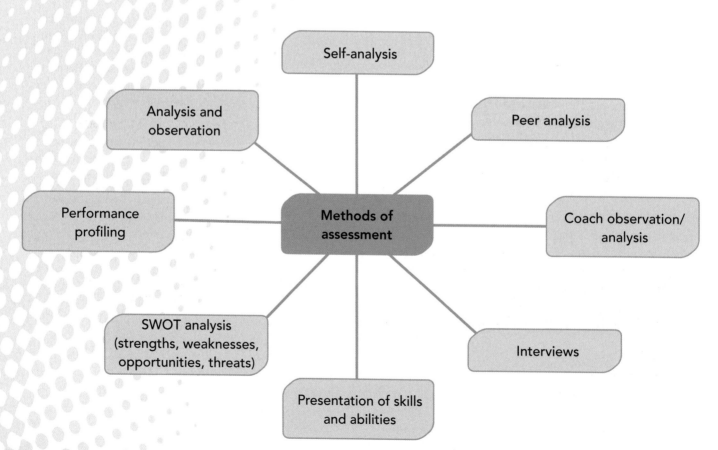

Figure 8.2: Which methods of assessment do you use? Which should you try to use more?

3 Plan and undertake a programme to develop your own technical skills and tactical awareness

Once you have carried out the analysis of your own performance and evaluated it, the next stage of the performance analysis model is to plan. You are required to complete a six-week training programme. Your plan must have clear **aims** and **objectives** and each of these should be based on the evaluations made by you and your coach regarding your technical and tactical strengths and weaknesses.

3.1 Target setting

You should use targets to develop your technical and tactical weaknesses and assist your personal development. These targets should be set around your strengths and areas for improvement. The targets should be realistic and achievable. The targets set within your six-week programme should be SMART targets (see Unit 3, page 89 for an explanation of SMART).

Key terms

Aims – what you want to achieve in your training programme.

Objectives – how you are going to achieve your aims in your training programme.

Case study: Tom Dawson, amateur golfer

Tom has been playing golf for five years. He has been a member of his local golf club for four years. He plays golf twice a week all year round. The biggest improvement of his game came during his second year as a member of the golf club. He moved from having a handicap of 32 to 24 through one season. During this season Tom was having regular lessons with the club professional. Since this development Tom has stopped having regular lessons and now chooses to have a yearly lesson where the professional analyses his performance and provides him with targets and development plans to improve his performance for the season ahead.

Tom is now currently playing off a sixteen handicap. After his most recent analysis at his golf club by the club professional he was told that if he improves and develops on the following components of his game he could reduce his handicap further:

- The technique of his mid-range putting (about 2–3 metres).
- His short play around the green (within 50 metres of the pin).
- Use of long irons (3–5 irons).
- Swing consistency (currently 7 out of 10 of Tom's swings display a slight inconsistency which produces a slight slice on his shots).

1. If you were the professional at Tom's golf club how would you prioritise targets for his performance?

2. Discuss what factors you think Tom could take to support the development of his performance.

3. Produce a SMART target summary for Tom to take away and develop a training programme from.

3.2 Training for technical and tactical development

When a training programme is being planned, specific activities need to be included that a sports coach and performer have agreed which will improve technical and tactical weaknesses. The coach should plan and design specific sessions for the training programme. For each session the coach will have to justify how specific activities are going to support the development of the performer's weaknesses and should include technical and tactical specific activities that will develop the sports performer's or team's performance.

Technical performance

In order to develop technical performance, a coach should consider specific practices to build on any weaknesses. For example, a footballer who has undertaken a player analysis, and received feedback after observation by a coach that his/her weaknesses were passing and tackling, should have a programme that includes specific activities to develop his/her technical weaknesses.

Do you regularly discuss your technical performance and how you can improve?

Tactical ability

To develop a team or performer's tactical ability the designer of the training programme should encourage the performer to carry out the tactics against a variety of participations of different levels. For example, a basketball team whose coach has recently carried out an observational analysis and has identified attacking as a weakness, should carry out specific practices which work on various attacking set plays. These plays could be carried out initially against performers of a lesser ability or unopposed (where the opponents do not try to defend against the performers) and as the performers' ability and application of the specific plays develop, so should the ability levels of the opponents against whom the team are training.

Recording documentation for the training programme

Sports coaches or you as a performer should record your progress throughout the training programme and keep a record of the achievements and targets when they have been met. This may be done in the form of a written, visual or audio diary.

4 Review own technical and tactical development and set goals for further development

4.1 Monitor and evaluate performance

After completing the training programme you are required to carry out an evaluation of the aims, objectives and targets that you set at the start of the programme and evaluate whether you think your technical and tactical ability has developed.

Within your evaluation you should assess each of the activities and training sessions that were developed and discuss their effectiveness. You should draw conclusions regarding which activities were effective in developing your technical and tactical ability and which activities were less effective and may need further development. Within your evaluation you should also describe which components of your technical and tactical ability have developed and which areas still require development. If there have been areas of your performance which have not developed you should also describe why these areas did not develop, if there were any factors that affected your development, e.g. injury, other commitments etc.

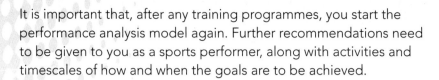

It is important that, after any training programmes, you start the performance analysis model again. Further recommendations need to be given to you as a sports performer, along with activities and timescales of how and when the goals are to be achieved.

4.2 Goals

After your training programme you should produce more long-term and short-term goals for your technical and tactical development; these should have been negotiated with your coach/tutor and be specific to you. The goals you produce should be produced using the SMART principle.

PLTS

When analysing the skills and tactical awareness of your own performance in this activity you will develop your skills as a **reflective learner**.

Functional skills

Through summarising the skills and tactical awareness of your own performance in a selected sport and identifying the strengths and weaknesses of their performance you will develop your **English** skills in writing.

Assessment activity 8.1 P3 M3 D1

1. Assess your own technical skills and tactical awareness, in your chosen sport, identifying your own strengths and areas for improvement. **P3**
2. Explain your own strengths and areas for improvement. **M3**
3. Compare and contrast your own technical skills and tactical awareness with those of an elite performer and the demands of a chosen sport. **D1**

Grading tips

- Focus on your strengths and weaknesses. Give examples and explain how you can improve your weaknesses.
- Focus on specific techniques when you compare your performance with that of an elite athlete.

Denise Sykes
Assistant cricket coach

Denise is the captain of the open-age ladies team at the club and has represented her county. She was inspired to obtain coaching qualifications after the support she gained from her club and county coach. It was through their support that Denise learnt the technical and tactical demands of her sport. Ever since she was introduced to cricket, Denise has wanted to support the development of girls' cricket at her local club as there has been a lack of girls locally who play cricket. The club has managed to increase the numbers of girls playing, thanks mainly to the publicity Denise has raised in the local media through representing the county.

Denise has been supporting the head coach of the Under 15 girls' team at Elloughton Cricket Club for two years. She is now a qualified level 1 (ECB) Cricket Coaching Assistant. The team has been playing together for three years and has been attending training sessions on a regular basis at the club in the summer and at a local school sports hall. Training sessions have concentrated this season on batting and bowling as the sessions have been based in the club's cricket nets. Denise and the head coach have been working on the bowler's technique and on each team member's batting technique. Training sessions at the club at the start of the season seemed to have paid off as the team won their first five games of the season. They won each game through scoring heavily with the bat. However, in the last three games – despite scoring highly with the bat – the team has lost.

Think about it!

- Make a list of the skills required in cricket.
- Make a list of the skills that Denise and the head coach have been working on in the girls' training so far throughout the session.
- What do you think could be the causes of the team's current losses?
- What training methods could be adopted to improve the team's performances?

Just checking

1. What is a technique?
2. What is a tactic?
3. Make a list of the skills and techniques required in basketball.
4. Make a list of the tactical demands in rugby union.
5. What methods could be used to assess the skills and tactical awareness of a sports performer?
6. Make a list of the people who can support sports performers in their development of technical and tactical application in sport.
7. What is performance profiling?
8. Draw the performance analysis model.
9. What does SMART stand for?
10. Describe why you think targets are important for sports performers.

Assignment tips

- Make a list of the technical demands and skills required in your selected sport, describe each skill and technique.

- Make a list of the tactics used in your selected sport, describe how each tactic is applied in your sport effectively.

- Produce an observation checklist that can be used to assess the performance of a sports performer in your selected sport.

- Select an elite sports performer from your selected sport.

- Record the performance of yourself and an elite sports performer.

- Observe each performance and make a list of the strengths and weakness of the application of the skills and tactics in each sport.

- Summarise your observation and each strength and weakness observed through the completion of your assessment.

- Produce a six-week training programme for your own technical and tactical development in your selected sport.

- Identify a variety of activities that could be used to enhance your skills and application of tactics in your selected sport in your training programme.

- After the completion of your training programme review its effectiveness.

- What worked well in your training programme and why do you think this worked?

- What did not work well in your training programme and why do you think it didn't?

Credit value: 10

9 Psychology for sports performance

There is more to winning in sport than just physical ability, as these examples of headlines show:

- 'He cracked under the pressure'
- 'She won because she was more determined'
- 'We kept our focus throughout the match'
- 'I always felt confident of winning'.

You obviously need to be fit and have the necessary skills for your sport, but you must not ignore the contribution made by your mind. Have you ever given any thought to training your mind for sport? Do you think you should turn up for your match without a plan, lacking in confidence and worried about your opponent's record?

Good psychological preparation is essential for you to perform at your top level and this means training your mind. In this unit you will look at the psychological demands of sport before examining how motivation, personality and aggression can influence your sporting performance. You will look at specific psychological skills such as mental rehearsal, focusing and thought stopping and assess your current abilities in these areas. You will then produce a six-week training programme in which you will develop the psychological skills needed for your selected sport.

Learning outcomes

After completing this unit you should:

1. know the psychological demands of a selected sport
2. know the impact motivation can have on sports performance
3. know the effect of personality and aggression on sports performance
4. be able to develop and review a psychological skills training programme in order to enhance your own sporting performance.

Assessment and grading criteria

This table shows you what you must do in order to achieve a pass, merit or distinction grade, and where you can find activities in this book to help you.

To achieve a **pass** grade the evidence must show that the learner is able to:	To achieve a **merit** grade the evidence must show that, in addition to the pass criteria, the learner is able to:	To achieve a **distinction** grade the evidence must show that, in addition to the pass and merit criteria, the learner is able to:
P1 describe four psychological demands of a selected sport **See Assessment activity 9.1, page 227**	**M1** explain four psychological demands of a selected sport **See Assessment activity 9.1, page 227**	
P2 describe the impact of motivation on sports performance	**M2** explain the impact of motivation on sports performance and two strategies that can be used to maintain and increase motivation	**D1** analyse the impact of motivation on sports performance and two strategies that can be used to maintain and increase motivation
P3 describe two strategies that can be used to influence motivation		
P4 describe personality and how it affects sports performance		
P5 describe aggression and two strategies that can be used to control it	**M3** explain two strategies that can be used to control aggressive behaviour	**D2** evaluate two strategies that can be used to control aggressive behaviour
P6 assess own attitudes and psychological skills in a selected sport, identifying strengths and areas for improvement		
P7 plan, carry out and record a six-week training programme to improve psychological skills for a selected sport, with tutor support **See Assessment activity 9.2, page 242**	**M4** independently plan, carry out and record a six-week training programme to improve psychological skills for a selected sport **See Assessment activity 9.2, page 242**	
P8 review the psychological skills training programme, identifying strengths and areas for improvement **See Assessment activity 9.2, page 242**	**M5** review the psychological skills training programme, explaining strengths and areas for improvement **See Assessment activity 9.2, page 242**	**D3** review the psychological skills training programme, justifying strengths and areas for improvement **See Assessment activity 9.2, page 242**

How you will be assessed

This unit will be assessed by an internal assignment that will be designed and marked by the staff at your centre. Your assignment could be:

- a written report
- a PowerPoint presentation
- a video
- an audio diary.

Student voice: Sacha – 16-year-old fencer

I was offered some work experience at the local college with the Sports Psychologist. Six weeks later, I'd discovered confidence and mental toughness. My boss worked with young tennis players whose coach was worried because they had hardly won anything over the last year. His job was to try to change what was going on in their heads. Sounds odd, but it really works.

I realised there is more to being a successful sportsperson than being good at sport. I learnt about what creates mental toughness – like controlling your anxiety and having a well thought-out routine leading up to a competition. I've learnt to control my breathing, stop negative thoughts and be positive. I've realised how personality can affect performance and training. I've also learnt ways to use my natural aggression to help me fence better. I now use strategies I developed in my training programmes.

Over to you!
- Do you think you're mentally tough enough to be successful in your sport?
- When have you felt most positive about your sports performance?
- How do you perform when you're not feeling very confident about your abilities?

1 Know the psychological demands of a selected sport

Warm-up

The power of the mind in sport

You are playing in the final of a cup competition and have been chosen to take a penalty. There is one minute left to play and the scores are level. The opposition and their fans are very unhappy with the decision. You have always been good at penalties but have missed the last two you've taken. What is going through your mind? Do you think this will affect your ability to successfully take the penalty?

Key term

Sports psychology – study of the effect of the mind in sport.

Success in sport depends on more than being skilful in our particular event or position in a team. We need to be physically fit for our sport. We also need the appropriate psychological skills if we are to achieve our potential. Most of us are prepared to spend many hours working on our techniques and skills. We also train so that we are fit enough to maintain our skill level throughout competition. However, few of us put a similar amount of preparation and training into the psychological side of sport. This could be a costly mistake during a close competition. When our physical skills are evenly matched it is usually the sports performer with the stronger mind who comes out on top. A strong psychological approach can be called mental toughness; that is, having the confidence that you will pull through in any situation.

However, if we are not careful our minds will work against us. We may find reasons to justify our failures, such as that we felt too tired or the conditions were too difficult. However, most successful sportspeople use their minds positively in order to perform well under any circumstances.

1.1 Mental toughness

When we take part in sport purely for pleasure and the result is of no importance, then our psychological approach does not really matter. As soon as the result takes on some importance for us then our psychological approach becomes vital. For example, jogging in the park does not involve the same mental toughness as playing in a competitive football match.

The stress and uncertainty of sporting competitions makes many psychological demands on us. In order to be successful, we need to be psychologically strong – that is to have **mental toughness**.

Key term

Mental toughness – being psychologically strong.

We all know that we can improve our sporting skills and fitness through regular training. In the same way we can improve our mental toughness

Case study: Jim, triathlon competitor

Jim, aged 15, has entered the Mazda London Triathlon Youth Super Sprint Competition, which takes place in one week. It starts with a 400m swim followed by a 10km cycle and finishes with a 2.5km run. Jim is a successful club swimmer but this is his first triathlon. He has been training with six friends and a coach over the last three months and is quite happy with his times for each event. In his training group he has the best times for swimming but the worst for cycling and running. He hopes to borrow a better bike for the race. His coach says that he could finish in the top 25% of the field but Jim is not confident. He has only put all the events together in one training session twice.

Both times he was extremely tired and on the first he didn't finish the run. He is anxious about:

- the sprint start in the swimming event which takes place in open water with no lanes
- pacing himself sensibly so that he has enough energy to finish the competition
- being comfortable on the borrowed bike.
- being beaten by his friends
- letting down himself and his coach.

In pairs, discuss ways in which you could help Jim to reduce his anxiety and help him feel more confident for his first triathlon.

through mental training and experience. Any psychological skills or mental toughness training programme should work on the following areas:

- anxiety control
- self-confidence
- motivation
- control of aggression
- competitiveness
- concentration
- decision making
- problem solving.

1.2 The psychological demands of sport

Anxiety control

For a professional footballer to score a goal from a penalty should be a piece of cake! However we all know that when the penalty shoot-out arrives, it is not that simple. Why do top players find it so difficult? The answer is that the situation is very stressful and this makes the player anxious. When we are anxious our sporting performance may suffer.

Anxiety is our natural reaction when we feel threatened. Our body prepares for 'fight or flight'. Sporting competition can bring on the same type of feeling. If we think our tennis match is likely to be very hard to win, our anxiety may be very high. This would affect our performance. In sport our anxiety is caused by the stress we feel.

What strategies would you use to cope with this situation?

We might find a sporting competition stressful because:

- our opponent is very good
- we feel very tired
- the weather is terrible
- the spectators are unfriendly.

However, the enjoyment of competing in sport helps us to overcome the stress and reduces our anxiety. We must look at stress in a positive way. A certain amount of stress will help our performance. We must ensure that the stress does not lead to anxiety.

Self-confidence

Modern sport is full of very confident sportsmen and sportswomen. One of these has been Jonny Wilkinson. At his very best, his absolute self-confidence helped him kick goals from all over the rugby pitch. So how did he do it? Well, Wilkinson was an extremely talented player. He had great confidence in his ability, mainly because he trained harder than anyone else.

Self-confidence is a measure of how likely you feel that you are to be successful. It is not a hope. It is what you *expect* to happen. It is how you think things will turn out in your sporting competition. Success in sport is likely to come to people who retain a confident, positive, optimistic outlook even when things are not going well. This helps to prevent them 'choking' under the pressure of competition. Positive thoughts can improve confidence, whilst negative thoughts destroy confidence. When you play in a match, against a player who is of a similar standard, your self-confidence can be an important factor.

Self-confidence can be affected by uncertainty and anxiety. Uncertainty is an important aspect of all sport. We cannot change the nature of sport. However we can concentrate on what we have under our own control. In this way we will not need to waste energy on factors beyond our control. For example, skiers should train so that they are in top physical condition for their event. They should not worry about the likely weather conditions as these are out of their control. The weather will be the same for all competitors.

Confidence is related to our personality. We would say that some people have a very confident, outgoing personality which may also be seen in their sporting performances. We know that success in sport makes sportspeople feel more self-confident and this in turn encourages them to attempt more difficult feats. Clearing the bar in the high jump is a good example. Our confidence increases as we clear each height. We can boost our self-confidence before competition by following performance routines which control our sporting anxiety.

Motivation

We all know that Chris Hoy won three Olympic gold medals in Beijing. He trained incredibly hard for four years to achieve his goal. How did he find the drive and enthusiasm to carry him through? The answer is that he was highly motivated.

Motivation is our determination to succeed. If we are highly motivated in sport we will have the drive and energy to improve our performance. We will also show determination and perseverance in our training. We will be prepared to train hard now for future success in our chosen sport. We need to be motivated to develop our ability to the full.

Our motivation may come from many different sources and may change over time. Our early introduction to sporting activities comes from play as a child and our experiences in school lessons. To the enjoyment and fun at this stage we may add the satisfaction of performing well, the praise we receive and the pride in winning as we grow up. The enjoyment of taking part with our friends is increased if we win trophies and we usually want to please teachers, coaches and parents with our success.

We will look in detail at motivation in the next section.

Control of aggression

If we open any sporting section of a newspaper, we will very soon read complaints of violent and aggressive play in a number of our national sports. In highly competitive sporting situations, where teams or individual sportspeople are in close physical contact, aggression is likely to be seen. Team games, like rugby and football, are typical examples, although bowling bouncers in cricket and hitting shots at opposing players in tennis may be considered aggressive. Forms of aggression may even be seen in non-contact sports such as netball. Aggression is much less likely to be seen in table tennis, diving, golf and gymnastics.

In a game of rugby we may describe play as rough, fierce, competitive, assertive or aggressive. However, we will only be justified in using the word aggressive if we think the behaviour intended harm of any sort to the opponent. We know that physical contact in the form of tackling is an integral part of rugby. Hostile behaviour is prohibited by the rules and punished by the officials. Team games vary in their nature and so the amount of acceptable physical contact will also vary. It will always be controlled by the rules. The way the rules are interpreted is the responsibility of the officials.

We will look in detail at aggression in the next section.

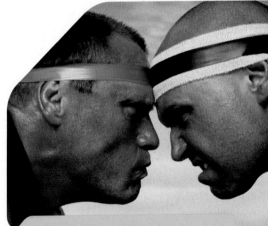

These players are behaving in an aggressive manner towards each other. Can you control your aggression when participating in sport?

Competitiveness

Competition refers to the rivalry between individuals, groups of people and teams when playing sport. It can be a highly organised competition at a professional level, a school match or the play of children in the park. The importance of the competition will therefore vary greatly.

Competitiveness refers to the ability of people to compete. A competition will be largely meaningless if one of the competitors is overwhelmingly better than the other. Although this does happen from time to time in adult sport, it is usually avoided through having competition at a variety of levels of ability. At school every effort is made to make sure competition is fair and even. This presents particular problems when children compete in age groups. Physical development can vary greatly, resulting in possible mismatches. In contact sports such as rugby, this can be dangerous.

Concentration

When we play sport there are usually people watching. If you are playing squash it may be only your opponent, if you are playing football in the park it may be the other players, the referee and a few spectators; whilst Olympic competitors may compete in front of millions of people. As sportspeople we have to cope with people watching our performance and our concentration can be affected by this. Therefore our ability to concentrate just on our sporting activity is very important if we are to be successful. In any sport our concentration will be divided between different competing demands, for example, in tennis a player will be:

- playing the game, that is making the shot
- planning the next shot or movement
- thinking about the weather, such as the effect of wind or sun
- trying to ignore any noise or comments from the spectators.

Sportspeople must concentrate on their sport. They must focus on the activity rather than their surroundings.

Decision making

When we watch a replay on television we often wonder how the player could have made such a bad decision. From the comfort of our sofa, it was obvious that he should have passed, for example, rather than have taken a shot. The ability to make correct, fast decisions is vital to all sportspeople. However, decisions are not often simple.

A vital ingredient of decision making is our perception of what is happening. In any game there is a continuous stream of information coming to our attention. This includes the position of the ball, the position of the players on both sides, the weather, the score so far and so on. We must quickly sort the information, deciding what is most important. The more experienced we are, the better and more quickly we can sort the information. Once we have the information, we can make a decision about our next action in the game. Also affecting our decision making will be our previous experience of a similar sporting situation. So it is our perception of what is happening in the game, plus our experience, which guides our decision making.

Problem solving

Whenever we play sport we have a basic problem to solve, that is how to win the competition. Our tactical skill is our ability to choose the right plan of action to succeed in our sport. We need different strategies and tactics for different sports; for example winning a trampoline competition compared with winning a squash match. Some sports, like team games, involve many players, set plays, a range of different techniques and skills and a great variety of individual responses from players. In contrast, in an 800m race there are a limited number of runners and few tactical plans to use. We need to understand the needs of our sport very well in order to develop our tactical skills.

Strategies are the plans we think out in advance of our competition. They are the methods to put us in the best possible position to defeat our opponents.

Tactics are what we use to put our strategies into action. We can work these out in advance, but they will often need to be changed during the competition. They involve planning and teamwork. The more skilful the players are, the more complex their strategies can be. Beginners need simple strategies.

BTEC **Assessment activity 9.1**

In pairs, discuss the psychological demands of a sport of your choice preferably one with which you are familiar. Choose four demands and describe **P1** and explain **M1** them in detail. You are going to present your findings to the whole group so you may wish to prepare a PowerPoint presentation or something similar.

Grading tip

Remember that in order to bring your study to life you should try to describe real situations from your own sporting experiences. Think back to an actual sporting competition and try to remember your actual thoughts and fears at the time.

 PLTS

Thinking about the psychological demands of a sport will develop your skills as a **creative thinker**.

 Functional skills

Using ICT to create your presentation could improve your skills in **ICT**.

1.3 Techniques for use in meeting the psychological demands of sport

We can use the following performance routines to help us to meet the demands of our sport:

- pre-performance
- mental rehearsal
- focusing
- thinking techniques

- thought stopping
- self-talk
- breathing techniques
- body language.

Pre-performance

In order to be in the best possible frame of mind for your sport, you need a pre-performance routine leading up to a competition. This would include such things as checking out the venue of the competition and making sure you know how to get there on time. You must also see that all your kit and equipment is ready well before it is needed.

It is important to warm up before competition. Warm-up activities prepare your body physically for the action to come by stretching your muscles and increasing the blood flow. They also help to prevent injury. The development of a regular, systematic warm-up routine also helps sportspeople to focus on their performance.

Activity: Pre-performance routines

Working in pairs, explain your own performance routine for a major competition or match using the following headings:

- Activities the day before, including any training or relaxation periods.
- Any special arrangements for diet and sleep.
- Transport arrangements on the day of competition.
- Preparation of kit and equipment.
- Practice or warm-up sessions before competition.
- Relaxation techniques leading up to the actual competition.
- Any mental rehearsal or positive self-talk patterns used before the competition.

Mental rehearsal

This is also sometimes called imagery or visualisation. Many sportspeople prepare for sporting activity by mentally rehearsing their actions. To do this we imagine in our minds that we are performing a very successful action. We make our images realistic, clear and successful. For example, a golfer may imagine how he swung the club and hit the ball. However this is not all. He will try to recall as many details as possible about the occasion, including what the weather was like, how short the grass was, how strong the wind was and if the sun was shining and so on. These details will provide some sense of the occasion. A golfer will also try to recall how he felt, his relaxation and the feeling that the shot would be a good one. The idea is that this will improve self-confidence and make sports performers feel good.

Focusing

By focusing we mean concentrating attention on every detail that will make a sports performance successful. As performers, we have a vast amount of information to consider. Some of this information is external, coming from the environment around us, such as the strength of the wind or the noise of the spectators. We also get information about our physical condition, for example whether or not our muscles feel tired or how fast we are breathing. A performer's thoughts and feelings are also important for his or her performance. They reflect their level of confidence and how relaxed or excited they feel. However, thinking about an argument we have had earlier, for instance, or what we will eat next is not helpful. To be successful we must learn to select only the information that will ensure a good performance.

Thinking techniques

These techniques can help when taking part in sporting activities such as running, swimming, cycling and rowing. Our bodies can perform these activities almost automatically, but our minds are also active. The way in which an individual is thinking can help or have a negative effect on his or her performance. There are two different techniques you could use to make sure that your thinking is positive and helpful.

- You can concentrate on the feelings you get from your body during the activity. For example, how your muscles are feeling, how fast your heart is beating, how strong your breathing is and so on. You can use this information positively to say that you are coping with the intensity of the activity very well.
- You can also think of something quite different from what you are doing. This would include imagining listening to music, planning a party, counting all the red cars you see, and so on. You can do this in order to distract yourself from the demands of the activity, for example how tired you are feeling, how your muscles are aching and how difficult your breathing is becoming.

What do you think of to help you prepare for a sporting competition?

Thought stopping

You do not want negative or worrying thoughts to distract you when you are playing. For example, imagine you have lost a point as a result of a poor shot whilst playing badminton. You must not think about this last shot, but must focus entirely on returning the next serve. To maintain concentration you can use techniques such as saying 'Stop' verbally, snapping your fingers or imagining a red light or stop sign. It is then possible to refocus quickly on positive thoughts and give full attention to our next stroke. In other words, it is essential to focus on solutions not problems in order to be successful in competition.

Self-talk

Quietly talking to yourself before, during and after a competition can be helpful. It will help you to cope with the stress of the competition and any problems with your performance. This talk should always be positive, focusing attention on the present situation – not the past. It may involve repeating a few positive, powerful words over and over again during competition. This will help to keep your focus on the important points for the performance, for example 'Power and control' when throwing the javelin. Should your concentration fail or your performance start to deteriorate, you might find it helpful to use trigger words. These are powerful reminders of the important basics of your performance and might include such words as 'Next point', 'Breathe deeply' or 'Head high'. These words can be written on your sports clothing, your equipment or even on your hands.

Breathing techniques

It is usually possible to control your breathing before, during and after both training and competition. Concentrating on breathing deeply and rhythmically allows the body to relax. This in turn helps you to concentrate solely on your performance. This can be very helpful before competition or in some sports, for example team games, during natural breaks in the performance.

Body language

It is important that your body language should show confidence and energy when you arrive at a competition. This will give you an advantage against an opponent whose posture and demeanour are not so positive. Positive body language shows that you are in control of yourself and ready for the competition. Sportspeople often use routines which allow them to stay focused and confident during competitions; for example, a routine for preparing to serve in tennis, for taking a place kick in rugby or a free shot in basketball. This helps to maintain our positive body language.

2 Know the impact motivation can have on sports performance

We take part in sport for a variety of different reasons. Most of us learn our sporting skills in school as part of a compulsory curriculum. As we get older we can choose to increase our sporting activity if we so wish. Our reasons for playing different sports may change over time, as we grow older or develop other interests. For us to continue taking part in sport we need to get something in return. Initially enjoyment of the

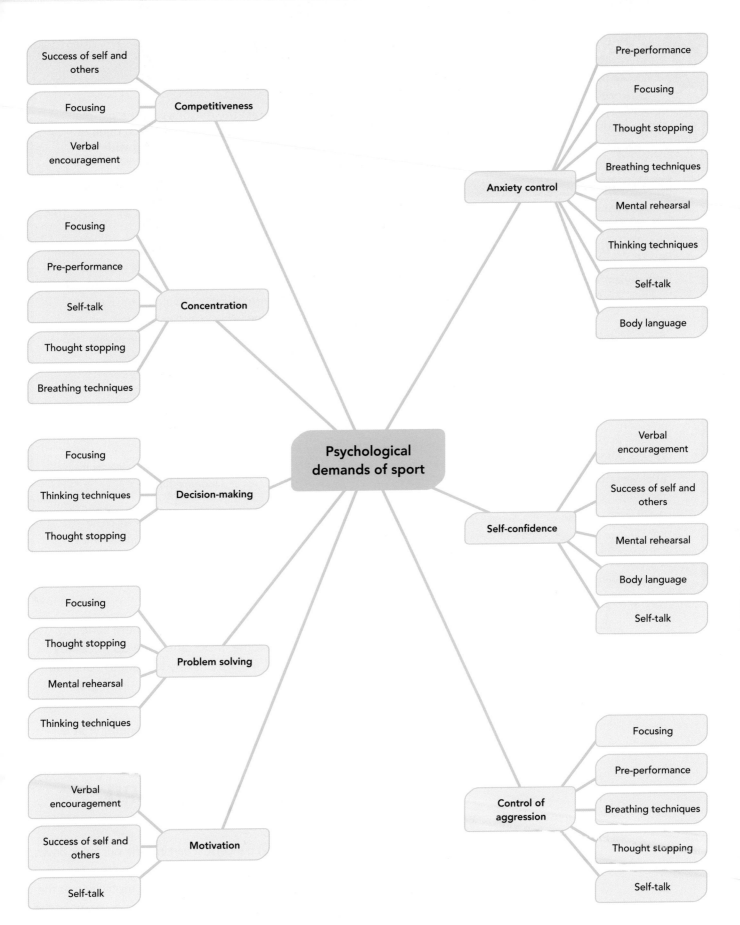

Figure 9.1: Psychological demands of sport and training techniques. Do you agree with the above analysis? Discuss with a partner.

Activity: Anyone for sport?

An exit survey at a local sports centre revealed the following answers to the question:

'Why do you come to the sports centre?'

Working in pairs, list the reasons why the people in the survey take part in sport. Can you think of any other reasons? Share your answers with the rest of the group.

Personal details	Activity	Reasons for participating
Peggy, 26 years old, one 2-year-old daughter.	Aerobics, twice a week.	To meet people, to lose weight and keep fit.
Darren, 17 years old, student at local college.	Competitive swimming training 5 times a week, with competitions at weekends. Also attends gym at least three times a week.	Has always been an exceptional swimmer from an early age. Enjoys winning trophies more than training. Has always been trained by his mother who is a coach at the club.
Aisha, 14-year-old schoolgirl.	Centre netball team. Trains twice a week with a weekend match.	Has always enjoyed playing netball and attends with three very good friends. Winning is not very important to her.
Henry, 47-year-old, competitive rower.	Trains on weights and rowing machine 4 times a week. Competitions or river work on Sundays.	Gains satisfaction from the physical action of rowing and being part of a close knit team of four. Above all he enjoys performing well.
Marika, 21 years old, who wants to join the army.	Five sessions a week including circuits, aerobics and swimming.	Failed practical army fitness test. Wants to retake test in 3 months' time.
Wesley, 23 years old, print worker	Trains once a week and plays in local rugby team at weekend.	Outstanding player in the team which he captains from scrum half. Now has girlfriend who lives 80 miles away and wants to see him more regularly.

Key term

Motivation – determination to achieve certain goals.

activity for its own sake is sufficient, but as we take it more seriously, playing well and winning also become important. If we do not enjoy the activities, or are unsuccessful, we are unlikely to want to continue. Whether we want to continue in sport or not depends upon the strength of the drive within us. This drive or desire we call **motivation**.

We all vary in our drive to succeed in sport or life in general; that is, everyone has different levels of motivation.

2.1 Definition of motivation in sport

Motivation in sport can be a difficult concept. It can include our inner drives, the external sporting factors, the energy we can produce and the way we select our activities. For simplicity, in sport, we can define motivation as the direction and intensity of our sporting behaviour. By direction, we mean the sports we choose and the commitment this involves. By intensity, we mean the amount of competition, training and hard work we put in.

Therefore, if a tennis player joins a club and plays in all the teams, practises on court regularly, works out in the gym twice a week and always gives of her best we would say she is highly motivated. If, in contrast, a tennis player plays occasionally at weekends, only practises when asked and spends much of her time talking on court, then we would think she is not highly motivated.

Personality traits

Our traits are thought to be the most permanent parts of our personality, for example our determination. They affect our motivation in sport. The socially outgoing extrovert often seems happier in team games rather than going for cross-country runs, whilst some more introverted sportspeople are often attracted to more solitary activities such as athletics or swimming.

Situational factors

All sporting events have their own situational factors, that is, they take place in different conditions. A high jump competition, a judo match, a lacrosse match and a run in the park all have their own situation depending on the activity. They may involve one or more people, they may be competitive or not; there may or may not be rewards of any kind.

Is being a team member important to you?

233

Interactional viewpoint

This viewpoint means that we believe that our motivation is influenced by both personality traits and situational factors. In other words, a sportsperson's personality does not determine his or her sporting motivation alone. The situational factors which may involve, for example, different types of skill learning, of activity, of rewards, of parental influence will all affect our motivation. A boring training session, run by an unsympathetic coach and in the pouring rain will test the motivation of the most committed of athletes.

2.2 Motives for sports participants

Intrinsic factors

Intrinsic (self) motivation comes from our own inner drives. Examples include playing for fun and enjoyment, improving fitness and losing weight, the physical pleasure of the activity, performing skilfully and being successful, and the pleasure gained from being with others.

Extrinsic factors

Extrinsic motivation comes from rewards and outside pressures. Examples include winning competitions, being praised for our achievements, satisfying the expectations of parents, teachers and coaches, and fulfilling our commitment to our team.

Achievement motivation

Achievement motivation can be thought of as our need to achieve. Some people like to test themselves more readily than others. Sport provides a great opportunity for people to evaluate and compare their performances with others. This can be done in direct competition, for example you can play a badminton match, or in reaching a certain standard, for example you can run a mile in under five minutes. We can talk of some sportspeople being more competitive or having a higher achievement motivation than others.

Attribution theory

This theory explains how both individuals and teams assess their sporting successes and failures. They will all produce attributions or causes for the result of their competitions. They may say the outcome was due to their ability, their effort, the difficulty of the competition or even luck. For example, after winning a football match we might say the opposition was poor, we worked hard in the game, the opponents were from a lower league and we were lucky to be awarded the penalty. The reasons sportspeople give for a performance may affect their future achievement motivation.

2.3 Strategies used to increase motivation

We are all motivated by a mixture of different reasons, some due to our personality and some due to sporting factors; some due to intrinsic factors and some due to extrinsic factors.

Intrinsic factors

We are all likely to continue with sport if we enjoy the experience and gain some success. The more skilful we are, the more likely we are to be successful, and this success will increase our motivation. We all want to be fit and healthy and for many people this is a starting point for physical activity and sport. Sport is usually a social activity involving close interaction with others. Most people enjoy company and being with like-minded sportspeople often encourages us to maintain our sporting activity. Therefore, motivation is likely to be improved by making people more skilful and successful, by making them aware of the value of fitness and health and by offering sport in an attractive setting.

Extrinsic factors

If we are rewarded for our sporting achievements, it is likely to improve our learning and future performances. This is called positive reinforcement. The rewards may be items such as medals, trophies, badges, certificates and money. Alternatively, the rewards may take the form of publicity, fame, approval in the community or praise from teachers, peers, coaches and parents. With rewards, there is always the difficulty of maintaining motivation when performances no longer improve or even begin to decline. At this time intrinsic factors become vital in maintaining motivation.

Goal setting

Goal setting can be highly motivating. Everyone enjoys achievement in sport, whether it is swimming a width for the first time, gaining a black belt in judo or completing that first marathon. However, goals must be SMART – specific, measurable, achievable, realistic and time-related. (see page 89) By achieving our goals we can see that we are making progress. This reinforces our motivation.

Both **mental rehearsal** and **self-talk** are important methods of reducing anxiety and increasing mental toughness. They may also affect our motivation. (See above, pages 228 and 230.)

This player has just won a medal. Is this what motivates you?

3 Know the effects of personality and aggression on sports performance

3.1 Personality

Definition

The ability to cope with the psychological demands of sport will vary from one performer to another, largely depending on his or her **personality**. We all think, feel and behave differently from one another. This is as a result of our different personalities, that is the sort of people we are. Our personality involves such qualities as our character and our temperament. Personality can be seen through an individual's behaviour, which usually reflects his or her most important and stable characteristics.

Trait approach

We can also talk about our personality traits, that is, features of our personality, for example, being friendly or shy and so on. Our traits can influence our behaviour and therefore how we prepare and perform in sport. Thus a shy person would be thought likely to be shy in all sporting situations. Some traits are thought to give us an advantage in particular sports. We should remember, however, that although we may have dominant personality traits, our actual behaviour can be affected by both our experience and our environment.

Situational approach

In this approach, behaviour is more related to the sporting situation or the environment than to any personality traits. A sports performer learns how to behave in different sporting situations, regardless of his or her traits. Imagine colliding with an opponent in a game of squash. Your reaction will depend on the actual sporting situation, that is the importance of the match, the score at the time and your relationship with your opponent, rather than just your personality traits.

Interactional approach

This approach takes the commonsense view that our behaviour is the result of our personality traits interacting with the sporting situation. This can be called the nature versus nurture approach. All sportspeople have traits which predispose them to behave in certain ways. However,

> **Key term**
>
> **Personality** – the unique qualities, character and temperament of a person.

they are also influenced by the sporting situation and their experience. In a squash collision, a quick tempered player will, hopefully, have his or her behaviour modified by the sporting situation and maintain control.

Impact of personality on sports participation and sports performance

Sports psychologists have suggested many ways of looking at the effect of personality on sport. Three of the most well-known theories follow, although no one type of personality has yet been found to predict success in sport.

Extroverts and introverts

Two extreme personalities have been described as extroverts and introverts. Most of us are neither one nor the other, but somewhere in between. Extroverts are socially outgoing and show great confidence. They are likely to prefer team sports, activities using the whole body and with a great deal of activity and uncertainty.

Introverts are less confident and more reserved in social situations. They are likely to prefer individual sports, activities with little movement, but with fine skills and sports with repetitive movements.

Type A and Type B

Personalities have been split into two types: Type A personalities have qualities such as impatience, intolerance, high levels of stress and a strong competitive drive. Type B personalities have a relaxed, tolerant approach, with lower personal stress and less competitive drive. Research has not shown that one particular personality type is preferable to another, although it is thought that Type A would be more likely to succeed in a competitive sporting context than Type B.

Do you prefer team or individual sports, or do you like a combination?

Hardiness

Hardiness is an important personality trait which has been identified recently by researchers. It refers to the ability to meet challenges and to cope with difficult times. In sport it would be likely to be linked with mental toughness. People with a high level of hardiness would be likely to have an advantage in the competitive environment of sport. Hardiness involves the ability to make an impact in all sporting situations, to refuse to give up easily and not to give way to helplessness. At the heart of hardiness is confidence, so that 'when the going gets tough, the tough get going'.

Research suggests that although we differ in our hardiness, the techniques used to improve mental toughness can be used to influence this trait.

Activity: Personality

'The success and interest shown by an individual in a particular sport is often related to his/her personality.' Discuss this statement in a small group and try to find examples from different sports in order to justify your conclusions.

3.2 Aggression

Definition

Aggression can be defined as hostile or violent behaviour or actions. It usually involves a deliberate attempt to harm somebody.

The essential competitive nature of sport ensures that aggressive behaviour will be seen. In sport, aggression, as the intent to cause harm, is quite unacceptable. The rules of each sport define what is or is not allowed.

However, the use of the word in sport to mean being assertive, very energetic or persistent is another matter. For example the serve and volley tactic in tennis may be referred to as playing aggressively, a hockey player may put in a fair but aggressive tackle and a team may be called upon to show more aggression, meaning to try harder to win the ball.

Hostile aggression

In sport we can consider an act to be aggressive if the intention is to harm a person outside the laws of the event, such as punching an opponent in basketball. This is known as hostile aggression. It involves feelings of anger. It is not allowed by the rules and is totally unacceptable in the sport.

Instrumental aggression

A player may use aggression as a means to an end, without deliberately trying to hurt an opponent. This is known as instrumental aggression. It occurs, for example, when pushing an opponent out of the way in order to catch the ball. It falls outside the accepted rules of most sporting activities and would not be allowed.

Assertive behaviour

Aggressive behaviour that is within the laws of the game is more properly called assertion and not aggression. Assertive behaviour is seen as forceful, but may be acceptable behaviour in sport. It may involve the use of legitimate physical force but does not have the intention to harm or injure anyone. Examples would include strong tackles in rugby, competing for the ball in netball and spiking in volleyball. The officials then have the responsibility to decide whether or not an action is aggressive and outside the rules or assertive and acceptable. In contact sports this can be a very difficult task.

Causes of aggression

This is another example of a nature or nurture argument. Instinct theories suggest that aggression is a natural drive and therefore in sport we may channel our aggression in an acceptable way. Social learning theories suggest that we learn to be aggressive in society by copying others and sport offers both good and bad role models. A more recent theory links both the natural drive and social learning theories. It suggests that when frustration occurs it may lead to anger and aggression. This suggests that, in sport, aggression is more likely to be seen when players are losing.

Activity: Aggression

In pairs, discuss whether you think the following are aggressive actions and give reasons to justify your conclusions:

1. Punching an opponent in boxing.
2. Holding an opponent's shirt in football.
3. Deliberately smashing the ball at your opponent in tennis.
4. Verbally abusing an official in netball.
5. Threatening your opponent with your stick in hockey.
6. Bowling bouncers in cricket.

Controlling aggression

Competitive sport brings out strong emotions, including frustration and aggression. These emotions need to be channelled into positive action. This is known as anger management. This in turn is more likely to lead to a successful performance. The following strategies can be used to manage anger and channel aggression:

- Ensure fitness and skills are sufficient to cope with the competitive demands of the sport in order to minimise frustration.
- Exposure in training to potentially aggressive situations to enable the sports performer to develop skills to cope in the competitive environment.
- Encourage the sportsperson to focus attention on the next sporting action rather than what has just happened.

- Develop performance routines which will move the player on from any recent frustration in the sporting activity.
- Develop breathing techniques to use at times of stress to encourage relaxation and to help concentration.
- Encourage thought stopping to remove negative or worrying thoughts which interfere with the sporting performance.
- Encourage self-talk to help cope with the stress of the competition and any problems with the performance.

4 Be able to develop and review a psychological skills training progamme to enhance your own sports performance

4.1 Assessment

In order to assess and improve your psychological skills you might find it useful to use a performance profiling analysis. This is an individual assessment procedure which helps you to assess your own strengths and areas for improvement in your particular sport.

First of all you need to identify the psychological qualities which you think are important for success in your sport. You can involve your coach and peers in this analysis. You now need to rate your own current ability on each of these qualities. Again you can involve other people in this process. Finally you can set yourself some realistic targets together with some appropriate strategies designed to achieve them. You should set some realistic dates for achieving each of these targets.

You might find it helpful to draw up a grid as shown in the example below for Shelley who has a very inconsistent serve in matches.

Figure 9.2: An example of a grid that might be useful for a performance profiling analysis.

Psychological quality	Current rating	Rating goal	Time frame	Strategies to achieve goal
Mental rehearsal	Not used	To use mental rehearsal before each serve.	6 weeks	Shelley to build up a mental picture of a good serve. Coach to remind Shelley to use mental rehearsal during training sessions. Review on regular basis during training and matches. Etc.

4.2 Programme

Once you have assessed your psychological attitudes and skills using a performance profiling analysis you can improve them through a six-week training programme. In order for the programme to be successful it is essential to set goals against which progress can be made. One of the most popular methods used to produce a set of goals for a programme is known as SMART. SMART target setting consists of setting goals that are: specific, measurable, achievable, realistic and time-related. (See Unit 3 page 89 for more on SMART goals.)

Your six-week programme should include some or all of the following objectives:

- Psychological skills, including
  - building motivation
  - developing self-confidence
  - changing concentration span
  - controlling anxiety
  - dealing with success and failure

- Strategies:
  - mental rehearsal
  - focusing
  - thinking techniques
  - thought stopping
  - self-talk.

4.3 Recording progress

In order to assess any progress you may make as a result of your proposed psychological skills training programme, you will need to keep detailed evidence of your current psychological skills.

Evidence which could be collected prior to the six-week programme could include:

- your performance profile
- video of you taking part in a competitive sporting situation
- comments from your coach, friends or parents about your mental strengths as well as areas which could be developed. These comments could be written or recorded on video or audio.

During the six-week programme you can record your progress using the following methods:

- diary – a personal view of each day in the programme
- logbook – a record of all relevant details of training sessions
- portfolio – a collection of information including photographs, newspaper articles, etc.
- video – a video record of key training and competition performances
- audio – comments made in real time by coach and others for later analysis
- witness statements – comments from key people including your coach, friends or parents relating to your progress.

You should ensure that all recording contains information relating to both physical and psychological performance.

4.4 Review

To carry out a review of your six-week programme it is necessary to compare your progress against the goals which you set yourself. The evidence you use for your review will depend upon your sport, the way that you recorded your progress and the type of targets and goals you set yourself.

For example if you were intent on improving your serving in tennis you could gain feedback from the following:

- Statistics from before, during and after the programme showing the percentage of successful first serves and double faults.
- Video of your serves in competitive matches before during and after the programme.
- Looking for evidence of improvements in body language, mental preparation before serves and the way emotions are displayed during matches.
- Your own personal thoughts about the training programme.
- Feedback from your coach, parents and colleagues.
- Reviewing your diary to note progress during the programme.

As a result of your review you can modify your programme accordingly. You should identify the successful aspects as well as those needing improvement.

PLTS

Researching your sport on the Internet and adding any useful information/guidance to your six-week training programme will help develop your skills as an **independent enquirer**.

BTEC Assessment activity 9.2

To achieve a pass in this assessment activity you will need to create a performance profile for your psychological skills relevant to your sport. Using this profile you will be able to prepare a six-week programme designed to improve your psychological skills. You will then follow your programme before carrying out a review at the end of six weeks. This review should identify strengths and areas for improvement. For all of this you may have tutor support. **P7**, **P8**

To achieve a merit in this assessment activity you will carry out the above process but work independently of your tutor. Your review should explain strengths and areas for improvement. **M4**, **M5**

To achieve a distinction in this assessment you will carry out the above process independently and your review should fully justify strengths and areas for improvement. **D3**

Grading tip

Try not to think of this task just as an assessment but rather as a way to improve your own sporting ability. If you can create a good personal programme and are able to use it effectively you will be a better sportsperson.

Jose Fellipe
Sports Psychologist

Qualifications: University degrees in sports psychology. Former national badminton champion who is still active in sports, particularly swimming and badminton.

Jose works on a freelance basis and currently has the following responsibilities:

- assisting two international sprinters to maximise potential
- sports psychologist to the local semi-professional town football team
- sports psychologist adviser to national swimming association
- supporting rugby club players recovering from injury
- part-time lecturing and research at local university with sports science department.

Describe your typical day

It is difficult for me to describe a typical day as each one is so varied. For instance yesterday I started early by reviewing some video of my two sprinters taken at a championship event. They want me to help them to improve their starts and I am thinking of using some relaxation and thought-stopping techniques for them. I then visited one of my rugby players who is recovering well physically from a badly damaged elbow. Unfortunately he has lost a lot of his confidence and is not yet playing to his potential. We spent some time reviewing his past performances on video and discussed his current physical conditioning which shows that he is fitter than before his injury.

I worked with my students during the afternoon and in the evening I visited the local swimming club where I am working with three national level swimmers. At the moment we are concentrating on focusing techniques which they are finding helpful, particularly during long training sessions.

What's the best thing about your job?

The best part of my job is the variety and the opportunity to make a real difference to the performance of very talented sportspeople.

Think about it!

- Do you think you need to be a good sports performer to be a good sports psychologist? Give reasons for your answer.
- Why do you think that thought stopping and relaxation techniques will help the sprinters improve their starts?
- Why do you think injured players sometimes lose their confidence?

Just checking

1. Why is being mentally tough important in competitive sport?

2. Give three examples of how stress can be generated in sporting competitions.

3. State three reasons why a performer might lose their motivation to participate.

4. Give an example of intrinsic motivation, and an example of extrinsic motivation.

5. Give three examples of activities that could be usefully included in a pre-performance routine.

6. List three factors that a performer can use to help concentrate in sport.

7. Describe how a javelin thrower could use mental rehearsal to improve his/her performance in competition.

8. Give an example of a thinking technique to use in a half-marathon.

9. Give an example of how you have used your knowledge of sports psychology to help either yourself or a friend to improve sporting performance.

edexcel

Assignment tips

A different viewpoint

Now that you understand a lot more about the psychological demands of sport you can look at sporting action from a different viewpoint. Try to focus on the reactions of sportspeople to stressful situations. For example, how does a player react when a key decision is given against him? Does he direct his anger against the referee/opposition/crowd/coach or does he find a way to use it to his advantage?

Tip: 'Focus on the reaction not the action.'

Mind games

Examples of sportspeople allowing their emotions to affect their performance can be seen in all sports. For example in tennis you can see how a player responds when she double faults, plays a set point, the ball hits the line but is called out and she is cautioned for racket abuse. Try to collect your own set of examples from different sports.

Tip: 'Appropriate examples will raise your grade.'

Self-analysis

Try to develop your ability to stand back from your own training and competition in order to fully understand how your sporting performance is affected by your mind. You will find it helpful to discuss these matters with your coach or tutor as self-analysis is difficult.

Tip: 'Your own experiences, properly understood, enrich your work.'

10 Nutrition for sports performance

Good nutrition plays an essential role in all our lives. It is important that the body is fuelled properly to make sure it can cope with the demands of sport. The body must be able to produce energy for a variety of physical activities. Not only will our diet help us cope with sport's participation effectively but it will also help with recovery after training or performance.

In order to be able to manage our diet we have to understand which foods are essential and how much we should consume and when. This may depend on how much energy we are going to expend taking part in sport. You need to include fluids in a balanced diet to make sure that the body is sufficiently hydrated. Otherwise the body will not function effectively and this may cause problems such as dehydration.

Once you have an understanding of dietary components you can start to manage diets appropriately for energy expenditure. All of this information can help plan and support an athlete's training regime, so that the body can perform as effectively as possible when required.

Learning outcomes

After completing this unit you should:

1. know the nutritional requirements of a selected sport
2. be able to assess your own diet
3. be able to plan a personal nutritional strategy
4. be able to implement and review a personal nutritional strategy.

Assessment and grading criteria

This table shows you what you must do in order to achieve a pass, merit or distinction grade, and where you can find activities in this book to help you.

To achieve a **pass** grade the evidence must show that the learner is able to:	To achieve a **merit** grade the evidence must show that, in addition to the pass criteria, the learner is able to:	To achieve a **distinction** grade the evidence must show that, in addition to the pass and merit criteria, the learner is able to:
P1 describe the nutritional requirements of a selected sport **See Assessment activity 10.1, page 255**	**M1** explain the nutritional requirements of a selected sport	**D1** evaluate the nutritional requirements of a selected sport describing suitable meal plans
P2 collect and collate information on their own diet for two weeks. **See Assessment activity 10.2, page 256**		
P3 describe the strengths of their own diet and identify areas for improvement **See Assessment activity 10.3, page 256**	**M2** explain the strengths of their own diet and make recommendations as to how it could be improved **See Assessment activity 10.3, page 256**	**D2** justify recommendations made regarding improving their own diet **See Assessment activity 10.3, page 256**
P4 create a personal nutritional strategy, designed and agreed with an adviser **See Assessment activity 10.4, page 260**	**M3** contribute own ideas to the design of a personal nutritional strategy **See Assessment activity 10.4, page 260**	
P5 implement a personal nutritional strategy **See Assessment activity 10.4, page 260**		
P6 describe the strengths of the nutritional strategy and identify areas for improvement **See Assessment activity 10.4, page 260**	**M4** explain the strengths of the personal nutritional strategy and make recommendations as to how it could be improved **See Assessment activity 10.4, page 260**	

How you will be assessed

This unit will be assessed by assessments that will be designed and marked by the staff at your centre. Your assessment could be in the form of:

- verbal presentation
- visual display
- case studies
- practical tasks
- written assignments
- report writing.

Adam, 15-year-old (studying for GCSEs and BTEC First in Sport)

At the moment we're examining our diets to see if they're balanced and if we're eating a good range of food and drinking enough water to keep the body hydrated. Understanding nutrients is important as they help your body perform and grow. I'm trying to make the first team for football but I'm not strong enough to hold off challenges made by some players. Part of my training is developing body strength while maintaining my aerobic training. Consuming the right nutrients and sufficient fluids will help increase my energy levels and complement my new training schedule. I read food labels on foods I eat, to check salt and saturated fat content. Just because something has a sticker saying it is low in fat it doesn't necessarily mean it is low – just *lower* than other products around. I like this unit as I can relate it to a lot of the issues and use it to improve my sports performance and fitness.

Over to you!
- What are the 'nutrients' that Adam is talking about?
- Can you find a food label that claims that the food is low in fat but which is not really that low?

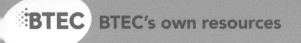

1 Know the nutritional requirements of a selected sport

Warm-up

Balancing a diet

Write down everything you ate yesterday. Divide this list into food and fluids.

Now look at the two lists – do you think this is an appropriate diet for someone your age?

Are you eating and drinking enough or too much?

Nutrients can be categorised into three main groups:

* macronutrients – carbohydrates, fats and proteins
* micronutrients – vitamins and minerals
* water.

These are all essential for a healthy diet.

1.1 Macronutrients

Carbohydrate

Carbohydrates supply the body with its main source of energy. We can divide them into two groups: **simple** and **complex**. Simple carbohydrates, sometimes called sugars, include fructose, sucrose and lactose. These can be found in food like fruit, jam and fizzy drinks. Complex carbohydrates, or starches, have a different molecular structure and are better for you, **nutritionally**, than simple carbohydrates. These include vegetables, whole grains and cereals, e.g. potatoes, bread and rice.

Carbohydrates are broken down in our digestive system into glucose and transported around the body in the bloodstream. This enables the energy to reach our active muscles. If not all of this energy is used then it is stored as glycogen in the muscles and liver. About 50 to 60% of our daily calorie intake should come from our consumption of carbohydrates.

Fat

Although a reduced-fat diet is a good idea, the body still needs **some** fat. About 25–30% of our daily calorie intake should come from fats.

Fat is the most concentrated form of energy for our bodies. Fats are composed of building blocks called **fatty acids**. There are three major categories:

Key term

Nutrition – the scientific study of food and how it is used in the processes of growth, maintenance and repair in our bodies.

Remember

The liver uses saturated fats to manufacture cholesterol therefore excessive dietary intake of saturated fats can raise the blood cholesterol level. However, polyunsaturated fats may lower your total blood cholesterol level.

- saturated fatty acids
- polyunsaturated fatty acids
- monounsaturated fatty acids.

Table 10.1: Foods the different types of fatty acids can be found in. Which type do you consume most of?

Type of fat	Found in...
Saturated fatty acids	• animal products, including dairy items, like whole milk, cream and cheese • fatty meats like beef, veal, lamb and pork.
Polyunsaturated fatty acids	• corn, soybean, safflower, and sunflower oils • certain fish oils
Monounsaturated fatty acids	• vegetable and nut oils, for example, olive, peanut and canola

Protein

Protein is fundamental to growth and development. It provides the body with energy, and is needed for the manufacture of hormones, antibodies, enzymes, and tissues. When protein is eaten, the body breaks it down into **amino acids**, the building blocks of all proteins. These amino acids are essential and non-essential.

Non-essential does not mean that they are unnecessary, but that they do not have to come from the diet because they can be synthesised by the body from other amino acids.

Other amino acids are considered essential; the body cannot synthesise them, and therefore we must obtain them from what we eat. About 10–15% of our daily calorie intake should come from proteins.

1.2 Micronutrients

Vitamins and minerals

Vitamins and minerals are the nuts and bolts of our bodies. Without them we cannot function. They are essential to the structure of our bodies, and are involved in thousands of functions, from the blink of an eye to the movement of our muscles, our breathing and the growth of our hair.

There are two types of vitamins: fat-soluble and water-soluble.

Fat-soluble vitamins

Your body needs fat-soluble vitamins in order to work properly. You don't need to eat foods containing them every day because your body stores them in your liver and fatty tissues if it doesn't need them

Key term

Amino acid synthesis – the way in which amino acids are produced from other compounds in the body.

 Did you know?

- Scurvy is a medical condition brought on by the deficiency of vitamin C. Egyptians recorded scurvy symptoms as early as 1550 BC!
- Scurvy was common with the great sea explorers of the Renaissance era.
- In 1746, James Lind, a British naval surgeon, established that oranges and lemons cured scurvy.
- Scurvy among the British sailors sharply declined when lemon juice was provided on board ship.

immediately. The stores can build up so they are there when you need them. But, if you have much more than you need, fat-soluble vitamins can be harmful.

Water-soluble vitamins

Water-soluble vitamins are not stored in the body, so you need to consume them more frequently. If you have more than you need, your body gets rid of the extra vitamins when you urinate. Because the body doesn't store water-soluble vitamins, these vitamins aren't harmful.

Water-soluble vitamins can be destroyed by heat or by being exposed to the air. They can also be lost in cooking water. This means that by cooking food, especially boiling, we lose lots of these vitamins from the food we eat. The best way to keep as much of the water-soluble vitamins as possible is to steam or grill, rather than boil.

Table 10.2: Foods the different types of vitamins can be found in. Does your diet include all the vitamins?

Type of vitamin	Found in...
Fat-soluble, e.g. • vitamin A • vitamin D • vitamin E • vitamin K	• fruit • vegetables • grains
Water-soluble, e.g. • vitamin B6 • vitamin B12 • vitamin C • biotin • folic acid • niacin • pantothenic acid • riboflavin • thiamine	• fatty foods, for example, animal fats (including butter and lard) • vegetable oils • dairy foods • liver • oily fish

Minerals

Minerals are essential nutrients that your body needs to work properly. They are found in a variety of foods such as meat, cereals, fish, milk and dairy foods, vegetables, fruit (especially dried fruit) and nuts. Minerals are necessary for three reasons:

*   building strong bones and teeth
*   controlling body fluids inside and outside cells
*   turning the food we eat into energy.

Calcium, iron, magnesium, phosphorus, potassium, sodium and sulphur are all essential minerals.

1.3 Water

Water is an essential nutrient that is involved in every function of the body. It helps to transport nutrients and waste products in and out of the body. It is necessary for all digestive, absorption, circulatory, and excretory functions. You should aim to drink at least 2 litres of water per day. **Hydration** of the body is determined by the balance between water intake and water loss.

1.4 Healthy diet

A healthy diet is important in maintaining a healthy body weight, enhancing well-being and reducing the risk of illnesses such as heart disease, stroke, cancer, diabetes and osteoporosis. A healthy diet is based on breads, potatoes and other cereals. It should be rich in fruit and vegetables and include milk and dairy products, meat and fish. Although too many fats can be bad for you, a limited amount of fat or sugar is needed. The Food Pyramid shows how we should make up our daily diet.

Key term

Hydration – process by which the correct water ratio in the body is maintained; a gain of water or moisture.

 Did you know?

Did you know the human body is two-thirds water? We can manage for a while without food but we need water more.

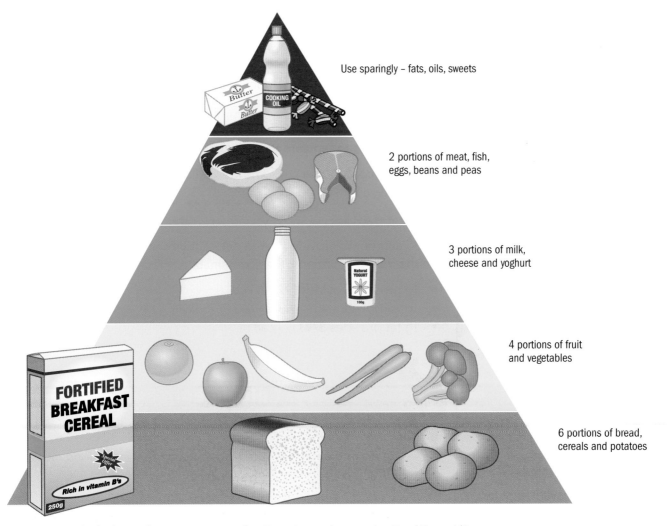

Use sparingly – fats, oils, sweets

2 portions of meat, fish, eggs, beans and peas

3 portions of milk, cheese and yoghurt

4 portions of fruit and vegetables

6 portions of bread, cereals and potatoes

Figure 10.1: Think about what you ate yesterday. Does it match up to the Food Pyramid?

Activity: Food groups

1. Copy and complete this table. Give as many examples as you can.

Carbohydrates	Fats			Minerals	Water
Bread	Butter	Meat	Fish	Milk	Tea
Rice	Cheese	Fish	Fruit	Vegetables	Soft drinks

2. Draw a circle. Show what percentage you think each food group makes up in a healthy diet.

Did you know?

About 75% of the salt that we eat comes from processed or ready-made foods, such as bread, cereals and baked beans. Even sweet things, like biscuits, have salt added to them.

Salt

Salt is made up of two different minerals – sodium and chloride. We need salt as it helps our body's cells to absorb nutrients. However, most people eat more than two and a half times the amount that is needed. Eating too much salt can raise blood pressure, which increases your risk of heart disease and stroke.

Energy levels

We eat food because our bodies need:

*   energy
*   compounds for growth, repair and reproduction
*   substances to regulate the production of energy, growth and repair.

Energy is measured in units known as kilojoules (kJ) and also in calories (kcal).

1 calorie = 4.2 kJ

Food and drinks provide us with different amounts of energy depending on the different nutrients they contain. So:

*   1g protein provides 17kJ (4 kcal)
*   1g carbohydrate provides 16kJ (3.75 kcal)
*   1g fat provides 37kJ (9 kcal).

Remember

Food needs to be digested in order to release the energy it contains. Digestion is the breakdown of food molecules into small units that can be absorbed. Digestion starts in the mouth with chewing, it then continues in the stomach, small intestines and large intestines.

Activity: Calorie content

Use the internet to look up the calories content in fast food meals and drinks.

Energy balance

Different people need different amounts of energy. The amount of energy we eat has to be balanced with the amount of energy we use. Unused energy from food and drink is stored as fat in the body so we need to eat the right amount to be a healthy weight. As we get older the amount of food we need changes.

Preparing food

How you prepare food can effect how nutritious it is. High temperatures used in cooking destroy some enzymes and vitamins. Raw foods, which hold the greatest nutritional potential, should be included in the diet every day. Cooked foods may also have nutritional advantages due to positive chemical changes created by the heating process. The key to healthy cooking is to use methods that minimise nutrient loss and maintain the natural state of food.

Steaming is a method of cooking using steam. It is a preferred cooking method for health-conscious individuals because no oil is needed, resulting in a lower fat content. Steaming also results in more nutritious food than boiling because fewer nutrients are destroyed in the water.

Boiling in water is one way of cooking, however over-cooking results in a loss of soluble vitamins from the food into the water.

Frying adds saturated fat to food being cooked so it is best not to consume too many fried foods.

Cereals

Cereals, grains, dried beans (including pulses and legumes), peas, and lentils are rich sources of nutrients, but they are difficult to digest unless properly prepared. They are indigestible unless they are soaked and cooked thoroughly; alternatively they can be sprouted, sour-leavened.

Milk and dairy products

Use semi-skimmed or skimmed milk or low-fat and reduced-fat content cheeses to reduce saturated fat intake.

Activity levels

The total amount of energy required by individuals depends on their level of activity and on their body weight. In particular, the more active they are, the more energy they can consume without gaining weight. The table opposite shows some examples of the energy expended by a person doing the following activities for 30 minutes.

Table 10.3: Energy expended by a person (weighing 60 kg) in 30 minutes.

Activity for 30 minutes	Energy used
Ironing	69 kC
Cleaning and dusting (strolling)	75 kC
Walking	99 kC
Vacuuming	105 kC
Golf	129 kC
Tennis (doubles)	150 kC
Walking (briskly)	150 kC
Mowing lawn (using power-mower)	165 kC
Cycling	180 kC
Aerobics	195 kC
Swimming (slow crawl)	195 kC
Tennis (singles)	240 kC
Running (10 minutes/mile)	300 kC

Material is reproduced with permission of The McGraw-Hill Companies

1.5 Sports-specific requirements

Pre-event nutrition

The body needs to be prepared to take part in sport so you must give it sufficient fuel so that it can provide you with sufficient energy. Aim to eat between two and four hours before a competition – this allows the stomach to settle – and choose high carbohydrate and low fat foods. For example you might have: baked potato with cheese, a chicken sandwich, lentils, fresh fruits, yoghurts or fish. Pre-exercise snacks can include fruit loaf, dried apricots, smoothies and yoghurt.

During exercise

When participating in sport most people sweat as their body tries to keep cool, so you need to take on water or a sports drink to help maintain your energy levels. You can use intervals and breaks in play to do this.

After exercise

It is important to 'refuel' after exercise and to drink about 500ml immediately afterwards. For example, about two hours after exercise, you should eat a carbohydrate-rich meal with protein, along with plenty of fluids.

Activity: Selecting your diet

The type of sport that someone trains for and undertakes will affect the type of diet that should be followed by that sports person. For example, a weightlifter will have a very different diet from a marathon runner.

Can you explain how and why?

Case study: Juliet, gymnast

Juliet is a young gymnast who has been training hard for a forthcoming gymnastics display. She is performing a floor routine and taking part in a team vaulting display.

She has been carefully monitoring what she eats in order to be fully prepared for the training and the event. She knows that she needs to take on a higher proportion of carbohydrates in her balanced diet to enable her to have sufficient energy for her performances. She has a good diet and also makes sure she has protein, fat, vitamins and minerals in the foods she consumes. However after some of the more intense training sessions she finds that she is suffering with headaches, feeling nauseous and very lethargic.

1. What do you suspect could be the problem?

2. How could this be addressed?

Supplements

For most people, a balanced diet will provide all the vitamins and minerals the body needs and supplements are unnecessary. However, due to factors such as following a special diet, e.g. vegetarian or vegan, or because of issues like wheat intolerance, supplements may be necessary.

You may need to take vitamin supplements to compensate for the food stuffs you are not getting. However, it is advisable to avoid supplements with high doses of single vitamins or minerals as these may be unnecessary and should not be taken without medical advice.

Protein powders, shakes and bars can be part of your diet if you struggle to get protein from other foods; however if you can eat a balanced diet there is no need for any supplements.

Creatine is produced by the body and helps to improve the performance of muscles during exercise. This improvement in performance will allow you to train at higher levels for certain sports and gain muscle. Foods like meat and fish provide much of the body's creatine and the rest is made in the body by the liver, kidneys and pancreas. It is stored in the muscles as phosphocreatine (you may find it referred to as PC) and contributes to the body's energy stores used during intense exercise. If you do not eat meat and fish you may want to consider a creatine supplement. At present it is still considered a legal supplement to athletic performance.

Remember

Remember that supplements should not replace a healthy diet.

Did you know?

According to Melvin Williams (*The Ergogenics Edge*, Melvin Williams, 1998) 50% of elite-level athletes are willing to take a substance that would guarantee them an Olympic gold medal, even if they knew that taking the substance would be fatal within a year.

Assessment activity 10.1

1. Consider a specific sport. Produce a report to explain what sort of nutritional requirements an individual would need in order to take part regularly in this sport.

Grading tip

Make sure that you evaluate you findings from P1 if you wish to achieve D1: remember that this means you must look at how the most appropriate dietary plan could be delivered to this sports player, suggesting suitable foods and meals, times for them, fluid intake, and when, i.e. prior, during and after participation.

PLTS

Taking into account all the information so far and utilising this in your assessment may help your skills as a **reflective thinker**.

Functional skills

Presenting your research findings in a report format you should develop your **English** skills in speaking and listening as well as your **ICT** skills.

2 Be able to assess your own diet

In order for you to assess your own diet you need to be able to do the following:

- collect and collate information
- assess your information
- report on and amend your diet in light of your findings.

PLTS

Thinking about how to record your dietary information will help you develop your skills as an **independent enquirer**.

Functional skills

Presenting your research findings in an appropriate format should develop your **ICT** skills.

 BTEC **Assessment activity 10.2** (P2)

Collect and collate information relating to your diet on an ongoing basis for a full two weeks – this includes weekends. (P2)

How might you do this? For example you might use a food diary, logbook or spreadsheet.

What information will you record? You might include: which foods, what fluids, how much, how the food is prepared/cooked, when you ate, when you took part in activity, when you rested, etc.

Grading tip

Before you start check with your tutor that your method of recording is appropriate and that you have sufficient detail in your method of recording. If not you may find later work difficult to complete.

PLTS

Your verbal presentation to your tutor will help you with your skills as a **reflective learner**.

Functional skills

Presenting your findings through a poster and the verbal presentation to your tutor should develop your **English** skills in speaking and writing. You may also be able to develop some **ICT** and **mathematical** skills in your calculations of amounts of food and calories.

 BTEC **Assessment activity 10.3** (P3)(M2)(D2)

Now you have collected your dietary information over two weeks take a good look at it. Produce a poster that identifies the strengths and weakness of your diet. (P3)

Present your dietary poster findings to your tutor in a verbal presentation and explain how and why you would make changes to it in order to improve it. (M2)

Grading tip

To achieve D2 you must be able to explain, with reasons, the changes you would make to your diet. (D2)

3 Be able to plan a personal nutritional strategy

3.1 Nutritional strategy

In order to devise a personal nutritional strategy you need to fully understand the content of this unit so far. Without the information relating to nutrients and energy production it is difficult to identify what is an appropriate diet for an individual. Every person has different requirements in relation to energy. Some people work in jobs that mean they are active all day, for example, a manual worker. Some people have jobs which mean that they are sedentary, for example, an office worker who mainly works at a desk. Both of these jobs require different amounts of energy, so they need different diets to produce the right amounts of energy for them to remain healthy.

There is certain information that a manufacturer has to give by law:

- name of the food
- weight or volume
- ingredients
- genetically modified (GM) ingredients
- date and storage conditions
- preparation instructions.

Manufacturers do not have to provide nutrition information unless they make a nutrition claim. For those that do provide nutrition information, certain rules must be followed. They should state:

- the energy value of the food in kilojoules (kJ) and kilocalories (kcal)
- the amount of protein, carbohydrate and fat in grams (g)
- optionally (unless a claim is made) the amounts of sugars, saturates, fibre and sodium.

Recent additions to the food labels include the 'traffic lighting' system, whereby nutrients are shown as:

- Red = high
- Amber = medium level
- Green = low

Do you know the nutritional values of the foods you eat?

Food labelling

Nutrition information	per 100g	per half pizza
Energy	1027 kJ	1977 kJ
	244 kCal	470 kCal
Protein	11.5g	22.5g
Carbohydrate	30.4g	58.5g
of which sugars	3.5g	6.7g
Fat	8.5g	16.4g
of which saturates	2.9g	5.6g
Fibre	2.4g	4.6g
Salt	1.3g	2.4g

Figure 10.2: For further guidance on which foods contain which nutrients you can check out food labels on food packaging.

Remember

When we consider diet this includes not just food stuffs but fluids also.

Activity: Comparing nutrients in food

Look at a bag of crisps or a chocolate bar wrapper – compare these food labels with that of a yoghurt carton or a tin of tuna.

Alternatively, compare a healthy meal option with a so-called 'low fat' option.

1. **What differences can you see in the amounts between the nutrients listed?**

2. **Which has the most salt contained in it?**

3. **Which has the most saturated fat contained in it?**

Remember

Hunger is physiological; **appetite** is psychological.

You have to take into account individual likes and dislikes. Some people will not or cannot eat meat, wheat or dairy. Some won't eat certain vegetables. There is no point in setting out a dietary plan with food stuffs that someone will not eat. Another factor to consider is cost – can they afford everything identified on the plan? If not, how can they follow it? It is vital that the person has an understanding of foods and fluids and the help they can give someone in sport as well as the negative aspects. For example, someone might eat healthy foods all day but, in the evening, could go out with friends and drink fizzy pop (or alcohol) and eat several packets of crisps; i.e. not healthy eating. So when planning a strategy you have to identify all of these sorts of issues before you can start to guide people appropriately.

Meal plans

Sports people need to ensure that they eat at the right time prior to participation; they keep hydrated and refuel appropriately after participation. The types and amounts of food required will depend on the sport; remember the comparison of the weightlifter and the marathon runner earlier.

Sports performers should seek advice regarding their diet from appropriately qualified people, for example, their coach. Their coach will have an understanding of the demands of the individual's training regime and level and amount of participation. This will help inform the coach as to what sorts of food and diet regime the individual should be following. They will be able to advise and ensure that adequate hydration takes place both during training and performance. Any deterioration in performance will be noted easily by the coach and may be linked to nutritional intake along with other factors such as injury or illness.

Plan your meals to make sure you have a balance of nutrients appropriate to your sport. Do you know what the best diet is for your sport? Talk to your coach if you are not sure.

4 Be able to implement and review a personal nutritional strategy

Identifying an appropriate nutritional strategy is essential for a sports performer so they can perform effectively. It is not possible to give the same strategy to every sports person. Every sport demands different energy levels – see Table 10.3 on page 253 which shows how many calories are used when taking part in different activities.

Many athletes fit a full-time job in and around their training and so are not able to sit and eat a perfectly balanced meal between two and four hours prior to training or an event. So compromises have to be made. If an athlete is unable to eat a normal meal due to work commitments then this has to be subsidised by eating things like energy snacks. These can help fuel the athlete. Use of energy bars and drinks can be helpful but other supplements may have to be used. Ultimately, this should not become the norm – a good balanced diet should be followed whenever possible.

PLTS

How you create your strategy and record its implementation will help you with your skills as a **creative thinker** and **independent learner**.

Functional skills

Recording your progress throughout your personal nutritional strategy and then writing your report after the strategy has been completed should develop your **English** writing skills.

BTEC ## Assessment activity 10.4    P4 P5 P6 M3 M4

Now you have identified the strengths and weakness of your own two-week diary you must devise and implement a personal nutritional strategy for yourself. First, agree with your tutor how long this will be for. Create your strategy and agree this with your tutor. **P4**, **P5**, **M3**

Produce a poster that identifies the strengths and weakness of your diet. **P6**

When you have implemented the strategy you need to complete a report that shows if your strategy worked and how, if you were to do it again, what you would change and why. **M4**

Grading tips

Make sure you agree how to monitor and record your ongoing strategy and, more importantly, check with your tutor that you have an appropriate strategy for you.

Using your own personal ideas and not just your tutor's will help you to achieve M3.

If you can identify things that you would do differently if you were to do this again and explain why you will achieve M4 also.

Kenny Anderson
Sports therapist

I work as a Sports Therapist with an amateur rugby union club and semi-professional rugby league club. I help to prepare players both mentally and physically prior to fixtures, advise about stretching/warming-up exercises, give massages and apply strappings. During fixtures I may have to give first aid if required, check injuries/strappings and make decisions about whether players can continue.

After fixtures I examine and assess injuries, treat minor injuries like bruises, strains, and blisters and if necessary refer individuals for further treatment, and accompany injured players to appointments. Outside fixtures I examine and assess injuries and provide appropriate treatment; design and implement rehabilitation programmes; advise about nutrition, diet and lifestyle issues and collaborate with trainers/coaches on injury prevention programmes.

Describe your typical day

I don't really have a typical day as my work depends very much on what has happened in training or at a fixture so I do what is needed – I have to be able to turn my hand to most things.

What's the best thing about your job?

I like being involved with helping the coaches to devise training programmes for individuals and advising them on dietary requirements. These two things go hand in hand – diet alone cannot help performance just as training can't – the two things have to complement each other.

Think about it!

- What areas have you covered in this unit that give you the background knowledge and skills a Sports Therapist needs? Write a list of these.
- What other areas might you need to develop and understand to fully use the information gained from this unit? For example, you might consider other units that relate to sports injury, anatomy and physiology or fitness testing and training but try to be specific.
- What else will you need to know to use the nutritional information you have gained? Put this next to your first list and compare, giving examples, with the rest of your group.

Just checking

1. Why is good nutrition important?
2. What are the components of a balanced diet?
3. Are food supplements necessary?
4. When might an athlete have to use supplements?

Assignment tips

Research tips

- Make sure you use up-to-date and current publications when carrying out research. There are lots of textbooks, journals, websites and CD-ROMs available for nutrition, and several are aimed specifically at sports nutrition.
- There are a number of sports publications that hold individual articles relating to nutrition for specific sports and sports performers that you could use. For example, Peak Performance is online (see Hotlinks section on page ii for a link to this website) as well as being a hard copy publication.
- There are dedicated Sports Nutrition Journals available – for further information go to the Sports Nutrition Society website (see Hotlinks section on page ii for a link to this website).
- Look at the websites of companies that manufacture food stuffs – for example, Kelloggs (see Hotlinks section on page ii for a link to this website) – as they have useful information that you can use.

Get active!

- Look at the labels on food stuff packages and containers. You should be able to clearly see what a food stuff contains, i.e. how much of it is carbohydrate, fat, water etc.
- Use one of the online free nutrition resources to work out if you are eating appropriately for the activity that you do, for example, the website for the British Dietetic Association (see Hotlinks section on page ii for a link to this website).

Key points

- There is a wealth of advertising aimed at sports nutritional supplements. Be careful that you don't use information without checking that it is accurate.
- Remember sports performers' diets will need to be balanced for the type and amount of activity that they undertake. No two performers will be the same.

11 Development of personal fitness

Designing and implementing a personal fitness training programme can be an exciting and rewarding process. A successful training programme must consider lots of factors to ensure that the design meets the sport performer's needs and goals, including lifestyle and physical activity history. The training programme should incorporate training methods that will capture the imagination of the performer. This will help them to maintain a positive interest and give them the commitment and self-motivation needed to complete the programme.

In this unit you will liaise with a sports coach, instructor or other appropriate adviser to plan, design and agree a six-week personal fitness training programme. You will cover the principles of training and programming and apply these to the design of a personal fitness training programme, with support from a coach. You will implement the programme for a period of six weeks, maintaining a training diary which documents evidence of participation. It will be important to be able to recognise factors which might prevent you from completing your training programme, since early preventative action can be taken to help overcome these factors and re-focus on your training and goals. On completion of the programme you will undertake a review to determine its success in relation to your personal training methods and goals.

Learning outcomes

After completing this unit you should:

1. be able to plan a personal fitness training programme
2. know personal exercise adherence factors and strategies
3. be able to implement and review a personal fitness training programme.

263

Assessment and grading criteria

This table shows you what you must do in order to achieve a pass, merit or distinction grade, and where you can find activities in this book to help you.

To achieve a **pass** grade the evidence must show that the learner is able to:	To achieve a **merit** grade the evidence must show that, in addition to the pass criteria, the learner is able to:	To achieve a **distinction** grade the evidence must show that, in addition to the pass and merit criteria, the learner is able to:
P1 plan, design and agree, a six-week personal fitness training programme with a coach **See Assessment activity 11.1, page 271**	**M1** contribute own ideas to the design of a six-week personal fitness training programme **See Assessment activity 11.1, page 271**	
P2 describe personal exercise adherence factors and strategies	**M2** explain personal exercise adherence factors and strategies	**D1** evaluate personal exercise adherence strategies for overcoming barriers to exercise
P3 implement a six-week personal fitness training programme, maintaining a training diary **See Assessment activity 11.2, page 277**		
P4 describe the strengths of the personal fitness training programme, identifying areas for improvement	**M3** explain the strengths of the personal fitness training programme, making suggestions for improvement	**D2** justify suggestions related to identified areas for improvement in the personal fitness training programme

How you will be assessed

This unit will be assessed by an internal assignment that will be designed and marked by the staff at your centre. Your assessment could be in the form of:

- presentations
- practical tasks
- written assignments.

Rudi, 16-year-old county-level hockey player

This unit helped me appreciate the importance of discussing and agreeing training goals with a coach before you design and start a training programme. I respected the advice and feedback my hockey coach gave me, it helped me think about my sports performance and how this could improve. I also thought about barriers which might have prevented me from completing my programme, like time available and my motivation levels and how I could overcome these.

Putting my own ideas into the design of my personal fitness training programme was important. I incorporated several training methods over a six-week period, aimed at improving speed and endurance.

My favourite part of this unit was undertaking the training programme and keeping a training diary to record progress. At the end of six weeks, it was extremely rewarding to review my personal fitness training programme and reflect on how the training had helped to improve my performance in match situations.

Over to you!
- What areas of this unit might you find challenging?
- Which section of the unit are you most looking forward to?
- What preparation can you do in readiness for the unit assessment(s)?

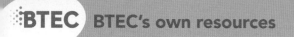

1 Plan a personal fitness training programme

Training goals

Sports coaches work with sports performers and athletes to identify, establish and agree personal training goals.

What are your current training goals?

Think about goals related to improving your sports performance, such as being able to perform a skill more effectively. Alternatively, consider goals related to your personal fitness levels and training.

Write down five personal goals in order of priority and whether these are short-term or long-term goals. Discuss and compare your goals in groups.

1.1 Plan, design and agree, a six-week personal fitness training programme with a coach

There are three main steps which need to be taken before implementing a training programme:

- setting your programme goals
- collecting supporting information to help with your programme design, such as physical activity and lifestyle history
- designing your personal fitness training programme.

The principles of setting goals

Setting goals is the first step in training programme design. You should be clear about your personal training goals and discuss and agree these with a coach or adviser before designing your programme. Goals need to be exciting, worthwhile and achievable. Goals should follow the **SMARTER** rule:

- **S** – specific
- **M** – measurable
- **A** – achievable
- **R** – realistic
- **T** – time-related
- **E** – exciting
- **R** – recorded

Activity: Goal–setting for a sprinter

Kelly is a sprinter who wants to improve her start and sprinting technique including certain aspects of physical fitness (speed and power). Her athletics coach asks her to complete a series of fitness tests so that the results can be used to develop SMARTER goals. (See also Unit 3 page 89.) Kelly needs to think about her goals for the short, medium and long term. Kelly's goals could be:

- **Specific**: I want to get away from the blocks quicker and sprint faster.
- **Measurable**: My reaction time out of the blocks, and my times for the 100m and 200m can be recorded.
- **Agreed**: I want to improve my performance on the track and my times from last season. I will discuss and agree goals with my coach.
- **Realistic**: Improving my reaction time out of the blocks will give me a better start. I know I can improve on my personal bests for the 100m and 200m.
- **Time-related**: Target dates will be set for the short, medium and longer term to help me achieve these goals. My coach will help me to plan my progress.
- **Exciting**: Improving my personal bests for these events will be challenging and I know I'm going to feel on top of the world when I have achieved this.
- **Recorded**: I'll keep a personal training diary to document my goals and monitor progress throughout my training programme.

This sprinter will have set herself goals to perform to the best of her ability. Try setting a SMARTER goal for yourself to help you focus on what you need to improve on in a chosen sport.

Types of goal

There are two main types of goal: **outcome goals** and **process goals**.

Outcome goals can be **product goals** or **performance goals**. Examples of **product goals** are when an athlete wins a race or they are selected for the relay team. Product goals can be useful for developing longer-term goals. **Performance goals** include setting a personal best or achieving a certain time for the 100m.

Process goals are usually performance-related. Examples include improving reaction time to the starter's gun or improving baton-changing technique. Process goals are usually under the sport performer's or athlete's control and can be useful in goal-setting for the short or medium term.

Collecting information

The second step when designing a training programme is to collect, record and assess information to help ensure the programme design is safe, effective and tailored to meet your needs. This includes medical, physical activity, lifestyle and dietary history and is best collected via questionnaires or data sheets, see figure 11.1.

Medical History Questionnaire

These questions are designed to identify a small number of individuals who should seek medical advice concerning the type of activity they are able to safely undertake.
Please answer each question.

SECTION 1:

1. Has your doctor ever said that you have a heart condition and recommended only medically supervised activity?	**YES/NO**
2. Do you have chest pain brought on by physical activily?	**YES/NO**
3. Have you developed chest pain in the last month?	**YES/NO**
4. Has your doctor ever recommended medication for your blood pressure or a heart condition?	**YES/NO**
5. Do you suffer from breathlessness after slight physical exertion?	**YES/NO**
6. Do you tend to lose consciousness or fall over as a result of dizziness?	**YES/NO**
7. Do you suffer from diabetes mellitus?	**YES/NO**
8. Do you have a bone or joint problem that could be aggravated by the proposed physical activity?	**YES/NO**
9. Is there any possibility that you may be pregnant or are you currently pregnant?	**YES/NO**
10. Are you aged over 65 and unaccustomed to regular physical activity?	**YES/NO**
11. Are you aware through your own experience, or a doctor's advice, of any physical reason against your exercising without medical supervision?	**YES/NO**

SECTION 2:

12. Do you have high blood pressure? (>160/100 mmHg)	**YES/NO**
13. Do you have high cholesterol levels? (>6.2 mmol/l)	**YES/NO**
14. Do you smoke tobacco? (>20 cigarettes/day)	**YES/NO**
15. Do you have a family history of coronary or other circulatory disease in your parents or siblings prior to the age of 55?	**YES/NO**

Print name: ....

Signed: ....

Date: ....

Figure 11.1: You should complete a medical history questionnaire so your medical history can be assessed.

Medical screening

It is important to collect medical information to screen an individual before they undertake a new training regime. Screening helps to:

- identify individuals with **contraindications** to exercise, these people may find exercise harmful
- identify individuals who should be referred to their general practitioner (GP)
- identify individuals with increased cardiovascular risk
- identify individuals with particular needs, like pregnancy or older age.

Some people have risk factors which mean that they should be supervised by a coach or instructor when undertaking a training regime. Here are the medical conditions for a supervised training programme:

- alcoholism, anaemia, asthma, bronchitis, cancer, colitis, diabetes, emphysema, hypoglycaemia, mental illness, pregnancy, thyroid problems
- high blood pressure (hypertension) >140–159/90–99 mmHg
- cholesterol >6.20 mmol/l
- body mass index (BMI) >30 kg/m² or <18 kg/m²
- waist-to-hip ratio >1.0
- smoking >20 cigarettes per day
- age >60 years.

Medical history questionnaire

Once a person has completed a medical history questionnaire, their results need to be interpreted.

- Answering yes to one or more questions from Section 1 of Figure 11.1 means that the person should check with their GP before starting the training programme. They will then need supervision while undertaking training.
- Answering yes to one question from Section 2 of Figure 11.1 means they should be supervised by a coach or instructor while undertaking their training programme.
- Answering yes to two or more questions from Section 2 of Figure 11.1 means they should be referred to their GP before starting the training programme and supervision during training is required.

Despite receiving advice from professionals to seek medical guidance, some people choose not to visit their doctor. In this case, a person can choose to sign a disclaimer. This means they can start their training programme (without support from their GP) and will take full responsibility for their actions and any health issues which may occur. All participants should complete a physical activity disclaimer before taking part in any activities.

Additional information can be collected concerning an individual's current physical activity levels and dietary habits, using a Health Screening Questionnaire.

Key term

Contraindications – are factors like a recent heart attack, unstable angina or abnormal heart rhythm (dysrhythmias), which result in exercise being harmful to health or recovery. If a person has contraindications to exercise, training should not be undertaken until factors are stabilised or have been reduced.

Did you know?

The five major coronary risk factors are:

1. **High blood pressure** (hypertension), where on at least two separate occasions:
   - **Systolic blood pressure** is higher than 160 mmHg
   - **Diastolic blood pressure** is higher than 100 mmHg
2. **Cholesterol** higher than 6.20 mmol/l
3. **Cigarette smoking**
4. **Diabetes mellitus**
5. **Family history of coronary heart disease** in parents or siblings prior to age 55 years.

Did you know?

Blood pressure (BP) can be measured using a digital blood pressure monitor, which provides a reading of your blood pressure as:

$$\text{BP (mmHg)} = \frac{\text{Systolic blood pressure}}{\text{Diastolic blood pressure}}$$

Systolic BP is the pressure of blood in the vessels when the heart is in systole (contracting).

Diastolic BP is the pressure of blood in the vessels when the heart is in diastole (relaxing, filling with blood).

Activity

Find an example of a health screening questionnaire on the internet, and create one of your own.

Health screening questionnaire results can be used to identify risk factors for heart disease and can highlight where lifestyle changes are needed. Health screening could include questions on blood pressure and stress levels.

Table 11.1: Health screening questionnaire results can identify individuals at risk of developing heart disease.

Factor	Risk of heart disease		
	No risk	Some risk	High risk
Smoking	None	Any	>20 per day
Dietary fibre	High	Moderate	Low
Animal fat	Low	Moderate	High
Alcohol (Males)	Up to 21 units	22–49	>50
(Females)	Up to 14 units	15–34	>35
Physical activity levels	Moderate exercise 4 or more times per week for a minimum of 20 minutes	Moderate exercise 1–2 times per week for a minimum of 20 minutes	Exercise rarely
Diastolic blood pressure	60–79 mmHg	80–90 mmHg	>100 mmHg
Self-rating of stress, tension and anxiety	Rarely feel tense or anxious	Feel tense or anxious 2–3 times per week	Extremely tense or anxious everyday

Activity: Measuring blood pressure

Work in pairs or small groups. Use a blood pressure monitor to measure and record your blood pressure.

Interpreting blood pressure results

Rating	Blood pressure reading (mmHg)
Average (desirable)	120/80 mmHg
Above average (borderline)	140/90 mmHg
High blood pressure (hypertension)	160/100 mmHg*

* A person should seek advice from their GP if BP is >160/100 mmHg on at least two separate occasions.

By assessing personal information like diet and lifestyle history, a sports coach or instructor can ensure that a holistic approach is taken to the training regime and that the programme design will target the individual's needs and goals.

Physical fitness training programme design

Once your personal fitness training goals are agreed, and you have collected and reviewed personal information to ensure training will be safe and effective, you can then move onto the programme design.

  Assessment activity 11.1 P1 M1

1. Plan, design and agree a six-week personal fitness training programme with a coach P1.
2. Contribute your own ideas to the design of a six-week personal fitness training programme M1.

Grading tips

- Clearly state your training goals for the short-, medium- and long-term.
- Provide information to show you have considered other factors in the training programme design such as your medical, physical activity and lifestyle history. This information could be in the form of completed questionnaires.
- Your training programme design should include: aims and objectives, principles of training, warm-up and cool-down, and full details of your training method(s) covering six weeks.
- Keep detailed records of the discussions you have with your coach to show that you have contributed your own ideas to the training programme design. You could keep your records in a diary or you could tape your discussions.

 PLTS

By identifying questions to answer and problems to resolve, you can develop your skills as a **creative thinker** and **independent enquirer**.

Functional skills

If you use ICT systems to plan your training programme you could improve your **ICT** skills.

1.2 Principles of training

When designing your physical fitness training programme, you need to incorporate the principles of training. These principles make sure the programme design, that is, the frequency, intensity and duration of training are set above the minimum level needed to gain fitness improvements. The training workload needs to be at an appropriate level, so that your body can adapt, enhancing your physical fitness without risk of injury.

How do you make sure the training you do is appropriate to your sport?

The principles of training are:

Type – how you train. For example, to train aerobically you could undertake training that links to your sport, like cycling, running, or swimming. Alternatively, you could select a training method to improve aerobic endurance, such as fartlek or interval training.

Frequency – the number of training sessions you will complete per week. Aim for 3 to 5 sessions per week.

Intensity – how hard you will train. Intensity can be prescribed using a number of methods including Heart Rate or Rating of Perceived Exertion (RPE).

Time – how long you will train for. Aim for 15 to 60 minutes of activity, depending on the intensity. If you have low levels of fitness, then reduce the intensity and increase the time.

Overload – in order to progress, the training needs to be demanding enough to cause your body to adapt, improving performance.

Specificity – training should be specific to your sport, activity or physical/skill-related fitness goals to be developed.

Progression – increase your training workload gradually. This can be done by increasing frequency, intensity, or time, or by reducing recovery times. But do not use all of these methods at once or the increase in workload will be too much.

Individual differences – the programme should be designed to meet your training goals and needs.

Variation – vary your training regime to avoid boredom and maintain enjoyment. Have sufficient time for recovery between training sessions, adaptation to training occurs during the recovery period.

Reversibility – if you stop training, or the intensity of training is not sufficient to cause adaptation, training effects are reversed.

Exercise intensity

In this section you will focus on the use of heart rate and rating of perceived exertion to determine your intensity of training.

Heart rate exercise intensity can be determined by calculating your maximum heart rate (HRmax) and then using this to calculate appropriate training zones.

Activity: Calculating HRmax and training intensities

1. Calculate your HRmax using the equation:

    HRmax = 220 – age (years)

    Tom is 17 years old. His HRmax is calculated as:

    **HRmax = 220 – 17
    = 203 bpm**

    For healthy individuals, undertaking cardiorespiratory training, the American College of Sports Medicine (ACSM) recommend training intensities of between 50–90% HRmax.

    Calculating HR training zones

    Tom is a fit individual and wants to improve his aerobic endurance. Tom's training intensity is 70–80% HRmax.

    70% x HRmax = Tom's lower HR range (bpm)
    80% x HRmax = Tom's higher HR range (bpm)

    $\frac{70}{100}$ x 203 = 142 bpm $\frac{80}{100}$ x 203 = 162 bpm

    So, when Tom trains he needs to ensure his heart rate is between 142 and 162 bpm.

2. Select an appropriate lower and upper % HRmax training range, according to your training goals, and calculate your HR training zones.

The rating of perceived exertion (RPE) scale

Another way of estimating exercise intensity is to use the RPE scale, developed by Professor Gunnar Borg in 1970. A sports performer uses the scale to rate their level of physical exertion during physical activity.

To give a rating, a performer needs to take into account all sensations of physical stress, effort and fatigue that they are feeling. The scale goes from '6' to '20':

*   6 – no exertion at all (at rest)
*   9 – very light exercise, like slow walking
*   13 – the exercise is feeling somewhat hard – lactic acid is starting to build up in your muscles
*   17 – very hard, strenuous exercise and you feel very tired
*   20 – maximum exertion (like how you feel during the last shuttle of the multi-stage fitness test, just before you drop out).

Warm-up and cool-down

Include an appropriate warm-up and cool-down in your training programme.

A warm-up prepares the body for physical activity. A warm-up:

*   increases heart rate and respiration
*   increases body temperature, warming muscles and connective tissues, making them more receptive to stretch in preparation for activity
*   makes synovial fluid thinner, which helps increase joint range of motion
*   helps to prevent injuries like muscle and tendon strains.

Did you know?

You can get an approximate HR value from your rating of perceived exertion, where:

RPE x 10 = HR (bpm)

So, during training, if you feel that the session is 'light', this means that your HR will be approximately 110 bpm.

A warm-up should consist of the following:

- light, continuous physical activity to increase heart rate and body temperature, like jogging, skipping or running drills
- stretching – each stretch should be held for at least 10 seconds
- skill-related activities – related to the sport or training method to follow, e.g. football drills.

A cool-down reduces heart rate and:

- removes lactic acid, helping to prevent muscle cramps and soreness
- prevents blood pooling, which can cause dizziness.

A cool-down should consist of the following:

- light, continuous physical activity to help the circulatory system remove waste products
- developmental stretching exercises – held for at least 20 seconds.

Training methods

The selection of the most appropriate training method(s) depends on your personal goals and the sport in which you participate. Discuss and agree appropriate training methods with your coach or adviser. The training methods need to be exciting and enjoyable, so you look forward to the six-week training programme.

What training method will you select?

Aerobic endurance
Can you incorporate several methods?

- Continuous training
- Fartlek or Interval training.

Speed
How about?

- Interval or Fartlek training
- Acceleration sprints
- Hollow sprints.

Power
How about a sports-specific plyometrics circuit?

- Circuit training
- Plyometrics.

Muscular strength and endurance
Could you design a circuit?

- Free weights
- Resistance machines.

Flexibility
What type of stretching could you do?

- Static or ballistic
- Proprioceptive neuromuscular facilitation (PNF).

Think of some activities you could incorporate into your training to make it more fun.

2 Know personal exercise adherence factors and strategies

2.1 Personal exercise adherence factors and strategies

Exercise adherence factors

You must be committed to your six-week training programme and see it through to completion.

What factors might prevent you from completing your training programme?

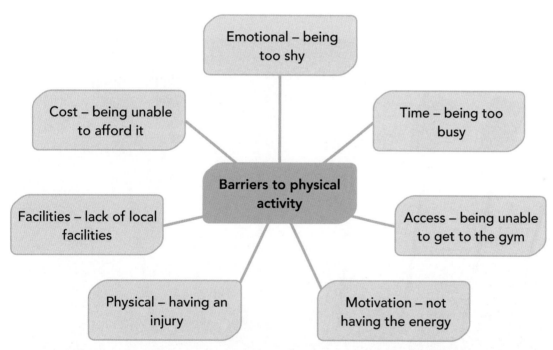

Figure 11.3: Common barriers to physical activity. What factor do you need to be most aware of?

There are ways to overcome or avoid each barrier so your training is not affected.

Time – if this is an issue, draw-up a weekly or monthly timetable of how your time is allocated. Look at opportunities to move things around. Could you do your training programme first thing in the morning or at lunchtime? Could you incorporate and design your programme to fit in with training that you already undertake at your local sports club?

Access and cost – avoid these issues by getting inventive. Design your training programme so that you are not reliant on attending a club or exercise class. For example, a simple circuit training session to build strength can be completed at home. Design each exercise station so that your own body weight acts as the resistance for developing strength. Bags of sugar or flour make good hand weights!

Motivation – being physically active helps increase energy levels. Choose training methods and a programme design that is challenging, exciting and enjoyable. A positive experience of training will help improve your motivation levels for future sessions.

2.2 Exercise adherence strategies

If you have identified potential barriers to physical activity and training, think about what action you can take to help you keep to your training regime. This might include:

- setting SMARTER targets
- keeping a training diary to log your progress and achievements
- giving yourself a reward for completing each session and the entire programme.

Incorporating another sport into your training could help to maintain your interest and exercise different parts of your body. What other sports could you try out?

3 Be able to implement and review a personal fitness training programme

3.1 Implement a six-week personal fitness training programme, maintaining a training diary

Training diary

Maintain a training diary throughout your programme. You should log the following:

- Details of your performance and achievement.
- Programme progression – include details of any modifications made to the programme, like increasing duration of training or reducing recovery times. Write down thoughts for your next training session.
- Motivation for training. How would you rate your enjoyment level and commitment? Are there changes that can be made to the programme which will keep you on track to achieve your goals, but will make it more enjoyable? Consider altering the intensity, changing the order of activities or the exercise mode.

Your diary should include the following details:

- date, time and location of training undertaken
- session duration
- resources required, for example, equipment
- main goals, aims and objectives
- session details including exercise intensity
- summary comments.

PLTS

By liaising with your coach to work towards training goals, organising your time and showing initiative and commitment towards completing the programme, you can develop your skills as a **self-manager**.

Functional skills

By using ICT systems to manage, develop and present your training diary, this activity could help you with your **ICT** skills.

 BTEC **Assessment activity 11.2**

Implement a six-week personal fitness training programme, maintaining a training diary. P3

Grading tips

- Design a suitable format and layout for your programme so that you can keep clear, detailed records of training sessions completed.
- Maintain good communication with your coach throughout the six weeks. You will need to gain agreement from them for any missed sessions.
- Keep details of your performance, programme progression and motivation for training in your diary.

3.2 Describe the strengths of the personal fitness training programme, identifying areas for improvement

After completing your six-week personal fitness training programme, the final task is to undertake a review, describing the strengths and areas for improvement.

Training programme review

Use information from your training diary and programme to reflect on your training over the six weeks. Take into account any modifications made to your programme to achieve planned goals and your motivation levels.

Activity: Programme review

Answer the following questions to help shape your review:

- Have you met your planned goals?
- How do you know your goals have been achieved? Perhaps you have improved your sports training and performance? Can you provide evidence of this? Relate improvements back to your original programme goals, aims and objectives.
- Where planned goals have not been met, what suggestions do you have for improvement?

Discuss in groups.

Lizzie Newman
Personal trainer

Lizzie works in a chain of fitness centres and is responsible for:

- working with clients to establish and agree training goals
- health, lifestyle and medical screening
- exercise programme design
- monitoring client progress and outcomes.

Describe your typical day

I'm self-employed and work in a private fitness centre. But I also advertise locally and do some freelance work. My working day will either revolve around clients based at the centre, or I'll be working with a number of clients externally.

My role involves setting and agreeing training goals with the client and designing a personal fitness training programme based on their individual needs. I monitor client progress throughout their training. Some clients choose to train alone, but others require motivation and I will lead their training session on a one-to-one basis. Leading by example is part of the job, so you need to be fit and healthy.

What's the best thing about your job?

I'm a people person and a bit of a fitness fanatic, so this job is perfect for me! I get a great sense of personal satisfaction knowing that I'm helping people to improve their health, fitness and well-being.

Think about it!

- What areas have you covered in this Unit that provide you with the knowledge and skills used by a Personal Trainer?
- What further skills might you need to develop? Think about how you would lead an exercise session with a client and the skills needed. Write a list and discuss in groups.

Just checking

1. Define SMARTER goals.
2. Name the two main types of goals and give an example of each.
3. Why is medical screening important?
4. What is hypertension?
5. What is the average (desirable) blood pressure (mmHg)?
6. If an athlete is 20 years old and wants to train at 75% to 85% of their HRmax, what will this equate to in bpm? Show your workings.
7. Describe the use of the RPE Scale.
8. Name the 10 principles of training.
9. What is the function of a warm-up and cool-down?
10. Describe one training method for each component of physical fitness (aerobic endurance, power, speed, muscular strength and endurance, flexibility).

Assignment tips

Research tips

- Check out the different types of training methods that you could incorporate into your training programme.
- Select a training method(s) that you know you'll enjoy and that will help you to reach personal goals.
- See how different training methods have worked for other people and the fitness gains they have reported.

Be proactive!

- Keep a personal training diary to log each training session and note any factors which might prevent you from completing your programme.
- Blitz the barriers to exercise! Draw up a table with two columns. In the left-hand column list your exercise adherence factors and in the other column give bullet points of what action you can take to help keep to your training regime.
- Record as much detail as possible in your training diary, for example, what you did, any changes to your training routine, e.g. altering the intensity of training to show programme progression.

Keep others in the loop

- You need to incorporate the advice of your coach/another appropriate advisor into the design of your six-week training programme.
- Discuss with your coach where your performance is currently and where you want it to be. Use their expertise and knowledge to help shape a programme that is going to meet your needs.
- Design the programme by liaising with your coach; it's a two-way process. Make sure you still bring your own ideas to the table – this will help you to meet the higher unit grading criteria.

12 Lifestyle and the sports performer

Success in sport is about more than being technically and tactically competent. Successful sports performers dedicate their whole lifestyle to their performance. In other units in this book you will have examined the importance of nutrition, psychology and training methods in enhancing performance. In this unit you will be introduced to handling the pressures of being an elite sports performer. You will investigate the work commitments of elite sports performers and the requirements of each commitment and how to behave appropriately in different situations. Sport performers are role models to thousands. As a role model you are not just representing yourself and your family but also your sport. You should understand the importance of appropriate behaviour at all times.

Sports performers set themselves career goals. In this unit you will be introduced to planning a second career. The lifespan of sports performers is limited and not all are fortunate enough to make a living from their competitive days. This unit provides you with an insight into finance and how to look after your finances as a sports performer. You will examine effective communication skills and how to use these skills. Finally you will be introduced to the different forms of the media. There will be times when you will need to plan and carry out a media interview as the interviewee; this unit will support your preparation for such an occasion.

Learning outcomes

After completing this unit you should:

1. be able to manage your own work commitments and leisure time
2. know what appropriate behaviour is for an elite athlete
3. know the factors that influence effective career planning
4. be able to participate in a media interview.

Assessment and grading criteria

This table shows you what you must do in order to achieve a pass, merit or distinction grade, and where you can find activities in this book to help you.

To achieve a **pass** grade the evidence must show that the learner is able to:	To achieve a **merit** grade the evidence must show that, in addition to the pass criteria, the learner is able to:	To achieve a **distinction** grade the evidence must show that, in addition to the pass and merit criteria, the learner is able to:
P1 produce a realistic plan for work commitments and leisure time, for one month **See Assessment activity 12.1, page 296**	**M1** explain the way work commitments and leisure activities have been planned **See Assessment activity 12.1, page 296**	
P2 describe three different pressures on elite athletes **See Assessment activity 12.1, page 296**	**M2** explain three different pressures on elite athletes and explain suitable strategies that can be used to deal with these pressures **See Assessment activity 12.1, page 296**	
P3 identify strategies that can be used to deal with pressures on elite athletes **See Assessment activity 12.1, page 296**		
P4 describe appropriate behaviour for elite athletes in three different situations **See Assessment activity 12.1, page 296**	**M3** explain appropriate behaviour for elite athletes in three different situations **See Assessment activity 12.1, page 296**	**D1** evaluate the effects and consequences of the behaviour of elite athletes **See Assessment activity 12.1, page 296**
P5 describe realistic goals in a personal athletic career plan, including second career choices **See Assessment activity 12.2, page 302**	**M4** explain goals, in a personal athletic career plan, and second career choices **See Assessment activity 12.2, page 302**	**D2** justify goals, in a personal athletic career plan, and second career choices **See Assessment activity 12.2, page 302**
P6 describe three financial issues elite athletes need to consider **See Assessment activity 12.2, page 302**		
P7 describe the skills required to communicate and work effectively with others **See Assessment activity 12.3, page 306**	**M5** explain the skills required to communicate and work effectively with others **See Assessment activity 12.3, page 306**	
P8 prepare, and be the subject of, a media interview, describing own strengths and areas for improvement **See Assessment activity 12.3, page 306**	**M6** explain own strengths and areas for improvement when participating in a media interview **See Assessment activity 12.3, page 306**	**D3** present recommendations on how to improve own media interview skills **See Assessment activity 12.3, page 306**

How you will be assessed

This unit will be assessed by a number of assignments. Your assessment could be in the form of:

- presentations
- written assignments
- role plays
- observation records and witness statements
- written training programmes
- video recordings and practical observation

Chris Armstrong, 17-year-old professional rugby league player

I completed my BTEC First during my first year as a rugby league professional at the Leeds Rhinos. Through completing this unit I learnt about the demands of being an elite sports performer away from training and competing. When I first signed as a professional at the club I thought I would just need to train and compete and then the rest of my life would be the same, I was very wrong!

This unit provided me with excellent guidance on how to deal with the extra commitments required and how to cope with the demands of playing professional sport. Through studying this unit I developed an understanding of what appropriate behaviour is and how important it is for the game of rugby league, the club, and myself that I behave following an appropriate conduct at all times.

Through learning how to communicate effectively with others I have gained confidence and now seek advice and support from coaches and senior professionals at the club. Learning how to deal with the media was fun, although at first quite scary. When I see my fellow team mates on the television now, I really appreciate what they are going through and how they have prepared for the interview.

Over to you!
- What section of this unit are you most looking forward to?
- Do you already have some experience that you could use to help you in this unit?
- How can you prepare yourself for the unit assessments?

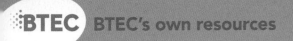

1 Be able to manage your own work commitments and leisure time

1.1 Work commitments

For sports performers who are at the top of their game and playing their chosen sport at the highest level, there is a requirement to be committed and dedicated to their lifestyle and not just their sport.

Sports performers who are fortunate enough to be employed as a sport professional need to recognise the high levels of commitment required. As with any other job, being a professional sports person has specific roles and responsibilities. In order to continue to participate in sport at a high level you have to be committed to every component of your work commitments, these include training, competition, study, other forms of employment, prioritising, informing others, flexibility and resources.

Training

As a sports performer one of the major commitments you will have to make is to be dedicated towards your own personal technical and tactical development; in Unit 8 Technical skills and tactical awareness for sport you investigated various methods of developing these elements through the completion of a six-week training programme.

When you see professional athletes compete at the highest level you are watching a perfect performance that may only last a few seconds, but which could represent many thousands of hours of training. For all elite sports performers there is a need to continually develop specific skills, techniques and tactics with the support of coaches. It is with the support of external coaches and support staff that sports performers develop. Training at the highest level needs lots of time and effort. Sports performers may have high levels of ability and skill to enable them to continue to compete at this level, but it requires constant development and concentration.

Competition

It is most important for a sports performer to apply their skills and techniques, and demonstrate their effectiveness against other performers, while they are competing. During competition is when a sports performer has the opportunity to apply the skills (learnt whilst training) against other performers. The performers who can do this consistently at a high level often succeed and gain status and reputation.

One of the most important commitments for an elite athlete is when they apply their skills, techniques and tactics in a competition. For some sports performers it may be these competitions that generate the majority of their income. For example, a tennis player like Andy Murray will rely on the earnings from competing in various competitions as a major part of his income.

For all sports performers the quality of their performance when competing will determine how long they are employed at the highest level. For example, a professional footballer who applies all the appropriate skills, techniques and tactics appropriately whilst training, but when playing in competitive league and cup matches fails to apply himself as requested by the team manager, may be dropped from the starting eleven and eventually due to lack of application during competitive matches may be seen as surplus to the club's requirements and released to seek another football club.

Which skills and techniques do you need to concentrate on in your next competition?

Study

For some sports performers, part of their employment may require an element of academic study. This is often the case for young performers as many sports clubs and national governing bodies are aware of the limited lifespan of an elite sports performer. Therefore in some sports it is compulsory for young professionals to undertake specific programmes of study that may supplement the training and competition that they are carrying out.

The commitment of study for sports performers can add an additional pressure and require them to allocate further time and effort towards academic study; on the other hand the education programme that sports performers carry out can also be an escape from the pressures of training and competition.

Not all sports performers earn millions of pounds for playing their sports and, because of this, some choose to study to provide them with options for other careers after their sporting careers are over. Other sports performers study whilst training; for example, at the 2008 Beijing Olympics many of the British Olympic team members were studying at British universities.

Sports performers should allocate appropriate amounts of time to their studies to ensure that they provide themselves with every opportunity to succeed. Many sports performers who start their careers will not generate enough money to provide them with a comfortable life after the end of their sporting career. It is therefore vital that, no matter how successful you are as a sports performer, contingency plans are also made.

Other forms of employment

Sports performers may have other ways of earning income and this can require another set of roles and responsibilities. Examples of other forms of employment that sports performers carry out include the following:

- working with the media – for example writing articles for newspapers, magazines, or journals, or providing commentary for radio or television teams
- public engagements – opening facilities in the local community or visiting schools, hospitals, etc.
- endorsement of products – advertising specific brands through written or visual media
- television appearances – interviews or appearances on chat shows.

Often sports performers may be required to carry out these roles to increase their own public image or that of the club or sport which the performer represents. Some sports performers have agents and representatives who deal with all of these engagements, including the fees which professionals charge for their services. For each of these extra forms of employment the sports performer will need to behave in a responsible and appropriate manner.

Prioritising

When a sports performer has to manage his/her own time and work commitments it is necessary to prioritise commitments appropriately. The sports performer should be able to consider which tasks and commitments are most important and which have least importance with regard to their career. When assessing these priorities it is important to have clear goals and targets. Sports performers need to carefully plan their time around training and competition schedules. For example, a professional golfer like Sergio Garcia will not choose to take a two-week holiday three weeks before the British Open as he will need the weeks before the event to prepare his body and mind for the major tournament. Garcia will also need his coaches and support network to help him in his preparation for the tournament.

Informing others

If a sports performer has to carry out other forms of commitment for any reason it is always necessary to inform appropriate members of their coaching team about the nature of the other commitment and its duration. These people would include:

- team manager
- club chairman
- coach
- team members
- agent.

A sports performer may need to gain approval before doing other activities which might require them to carry out physical exertion in case this led to undue injury and affected their ability to perform in a professional capacity.

Flexibility

A sports performer has to have a high level of flexibility in terms of their own time and personal commitments, as a coach or team manager could change their plans at any point. They must be flexible in order to support the development of their performance or that of their team. If they are to perform well at an elite level a sports performer has to be dedicated at all costs; this may include dropping personal plans to get back into training to work on a specific component of their performance.

Resources

Sports performers need the appropriate resources to enable them to play their sport at the highest level. In some instances it is the responsibility of the sports performer that they bring the appropriate equipment with them to every sports event.

Did you know?

All-in-one swimming bodysuits were inspired by the skin of a shark which is rough in texture. They support swimmers as they glide through the water and help them swim faster.

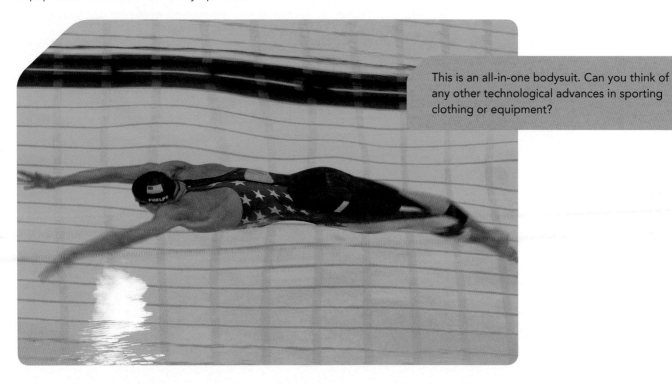

This is an all-in-one bodysuit. Can you think of any other technological advances in sporting clothing or equipment?

Sometimes it is the resources which an athlete uses that can be the difference between winning and losing. Technological advances in sports equipment design have moved so quickly that elite athletes have to be aware of which resources are available to support their performance in their selected sport.

1.2 Leisure time

After training and competing sports performers need to find time to escape from the stress and demands of their sport. Sports performers should use their **leisure** time appropriately. Modern media and technology mean the public can now have virtually continuous coverage of sports performers whatever they might be doing, e.g. through the use of mobile phones with still and motion cameras. Images of sports performers behaving badly can be easily caught on camera and the press are eager to obtain any lucrative footage of famous people behaving badly.

Social life

A sports performer needs a social life like anyone else. Many sports performers are often required to move away from their family and childhood friends to access the coaching and opportunities required to develop in their sport. Because of this, elite sportspeople often find themselves in the company of other performers with whom they have much in common.

However, the activities which sports performers participate in during their social life have to be appropriate. The suitability can depend on the nature of the activity, e.g. it would not be suitable for a professional

Key term

Leisure – the opportunity and time outside working hours to choose and take part in activities or experiences which are expected to be personally satisfying.

Activity: Leisure activities

Make a list of the activities that you enjoy in your leisure time. Discuss with your friends whether or not you consider them to be appropriate or inappropriate for a sports performer – and provide reasons for your answers.

Complete the table below with a list of what you think are appropriate and inappropriate activities for sports performers who compete in your sport at a high level.

Appropriate activities for elite sports performers	Inappropriate activities for elite sports performers

footballer to go skiing in his free time during the season as this could cause an injury to the player which would negatively affect his career.

Sports performers also need to be careful not to socialise with the wrong people, such as those who may lead them towards inappropriate behaviour, e.g. drug dealers, criminals, etc.

Inappropriate activities

If a sports performer does choose to carry out some activities that are inappropriate whilst away from their sporting commitments the effects can be very damaging to their health and well-being and possibly also their performance. Such inappropriate activities could include:

- drinking alcohol
- taking drugs
- smoking.

Alcohol

In large quantities, alcohol can damage your health. This is because of the high levels of **toxicity** found in alcohol. Alcohol can become **addictive**.

As alcohol passes through the body its toxicity can damage the throat, stomach, intestines, and blood if consumed to excess. Alcohol can cause stress on major organs such as the heart, brain, liver and pancreas. These are all long-term effects of excessive consumption of alcohol. The more immediate effects of alcohol consumption which may affect the sports performance of a professional athlete is a hangover. A hangover is caused by dehydration and it gives someone with a hangover a lethargic and nauseous feeling which has an impact on sports performance.

Alcohol consumption can slow down reaction time, affect co-ordination, balance and agility and may lead to unjustified confidence in ability or a misguided assessment of specific situations (this is one of the many reasons why it is illegal to drink and drive). These effects which occur whilst under the influence of alcohol could lead to a sports performer believing they are capable of pushing themselves beyond their physical limitations.

Smoking

Over the last few years attitudes towards smoking have drastically changed. One of the main reasons for this is due to recent changes in legislation that now make it illegal to smoke in an enclosed public space. Another reason why smoking has become less socially acceptable is because of the awareness of the effects of smoking on an individual, these include:

- an increased risk of heart disease
- an increase in blocked arteries and veins

Key terms

Toxicity – the strength of poison in a substance.

Addictive – a substance that a person can become dependent on.

- a reduction in the efficiency of the lungs and damage to the lungs
- a reduction in oxygen transportation in the blood around the body
- a decrease in gaseous exchange.

For all sports performers, smoking has many detrimental effects but some of the short-term effects for an athlete include aerobic capacity being negatively affected (although this can improve if a smoker stops early enough), halitosis (bad breath) and the smell of nicotine lingering on skin, in the hair of a smoker and on their clothes. Smokers do not just do this to themselves. Passive smoking, or inhaling second-hand smoke from a smoker, means that other people in the company of smokers can be affected in the same way.

Drugs

Illegal drugs have a detrimental effect on any member of society. Sports performers especially need to be aware of what drugs they are allowed to take which are not classed as performance-enhancing drugs. Not all substances are illegal, and some are available to the general public on prescription, but they may be banned for athletes during competitions because they unfairly enhance performance.

The use of drugs in sport is not a new issue; there is evidence that athletes were taking substances to enhance their performance during the early ancient Olympics (over 2000 years ago). Performance-enhancing drugs are taken, usually knowingly, with the intention of gaining unfair advantage over other sports performers.

In recent years there has been a big move to try to catch all the cheats and banish them from sports; this is done through random drug testing. Most sports have now introduced random testing, which has helped to uncover some performers who have tried to enhance their performance through taking banned substances.

Did you know?

The banned substance list is constantly changing as new substances are added and some contentious substances are taken off the list. It is important that you and your coaching staff are aware of these changes.

Activity: Banned substances

In the table below complete the sources of the banned substances and their effects on sports performers' performance.

Banned substance	Source (examples)	Effects on performance
Stimulants	Amphetamines	Reduce fatigue Increased competitiveness Increased aggression
Narcotic analgesics		
Diuretics		
Erythropoietin (ETO)		
Beta blockers		

There is a list of which substances can and cannot be taken by an athlete and this is produced by each sport's governing body. In some cases legal drugs, which may be taken by a sports performer to provide relief from an illness, may also be on this list so sports performers must be aware of what prescription and non-prescription drugs they are taking and whether or not any of the substances within the drugs consumed are on the banned substance list.

Appropriate leisure activities

The physical requirements of many training sessions will push athletes to extreme levels. If an athlete wants to master their sport and develop into a performer who can compete at an elite level they must be willing to put their bodies and minds through some excessive training that is both physically and mentally demanding. As they are pushed to such limits in training and during competitions, sports performers must have appropriate rest and recovery when training and after major competition or competitive situations.

All sports performers have specific training programmes planned out for them in advance and within this schedule time will be allocated for rest and recovery. This is classed as leisure time and the choice of activities selected must be appropriate and help to supplement the physical and mental recovery required for the sports performer.

Although there are recommendations of what sports performers should and should not do, every sports performer's likes and dislikes are different. The most important rule for an athlete during their leisure time is to rest and recover.

After and between training and competition, an athlete must stop playing. In order to help your muscles, joints and mind get back to a resting state you should not participate in any strenuous physical activity. Sleep is a major part of the rest and recovery process as it supports the recovery process of your muscles and joints. Sleep also allows you to de-stress and return your mind to a state of calm.

When provided with the opportunity to rest and recover, other things are important as well as sleep; for example, you should obtain appropriate physiotherapy if required, or if there are niggling injuries sports massage can support the recovery process.

Eating is an important part of the rest and recovery process. A sports performer must replenish the energy used through training and competing in a sport and ensure that the food consumed is healthy and appropriate.

To support the development of a social life, and a life outside a sport, sports performers may choose to participate in other leisure pursuits, such as playing golf, going to the cinema, reading and socialising with friends. All of these are effective methods of resting the body and mind and supporting the recovery of the body for further training and competitions.

1.3 Living away from home

Pressures

Sports performers are not guaranteed an income beyond their sport and for the majority they have to manage their own careers and monitor their own development. Although it may look like a sports performer has lots of people supporting them, in many ways they face constant pressure. A sports performer is very much in charge of their destiny and there are many different forms of pressure that can affect their development.

The people who a sports performer has constant contact with can place pressure on a sports performer deliberately or without really thinking about it. These people can include:

- friends
- family
- team mates
- coaching staff
- teachers.

It is expected that most of these people are there to provide support but sometimes they can add pressure to a sports performer in a variety of ways. For example, a family member could place pressure on a sports performer by having high expectations of their performance for their career or whilst competing. A sports performer may feel that they are under pressure to perform to meet the expectations of the family member and this may require the sports performer to try too hard and possibly under perform. This is an example of pressure that is placed upon a sports performer without the family member, for example, realising what they are doing.

Another example of how people involved in the life of a sports person can cause extra pressure on their performance might be a coach. Some coaches are very driven to succeed and may place deliberate pressure on sports performers to participate in competitions even when they are injured. In situations like this it is the coach who is concerned about their own career and rather than that of the performers who are competing for them.

Lifestyle pressures

The lifestyle choices a sports performer makes can increase the pressures they already have. Some of these choices may have a level of addictiveness that may direct attention away from the requirements of training and competition and towards the addiction. Addictions that sports performers have been affected by in the past include alcohol consumption, use of drugs, smoking and gambling.

It is often the social life of an individual, and the people who they socialise with, which affects the choices they make. Everyone can make their own choices but sometime our peers can add pressure. For example, when out socialising with friends it is hard to resist if they all want to go onto a bar or a nightclub. They might add extra pressure to go with them without any intention of harming the sports performer. As a sports performer it is important that the right choices are made with regard to what activities are suitable and not suitable in their social life. Sometimes the choices a sport performer make will have to go against those of peers to be the correct ones for the development of their career in their sport.

Another lifestyle pressure that you may have to deal with is the requirement to attain a high level of performance whilst training and competing in your sport. It is almost an expectation that an elite sport performer always performs at the best of their ability. Failure to do this often results in criticism from coaches, team mates, spectators and possibly even the press. As a sports performer you have to be open to criticisms and this high level of scrutiny can often add to the pressure.

Dealing with pressure

As a sports performer you need to be aware of the support available to you when dealing with pressure. The world of elite sport has changed dramatically over the last twenty years and this has resulted in much more support and thought about methods of dealing with the pressure. There are now support networks available for sports performers within sports clubs and national governing bodies. Clubs and NGBs have trained professionals in a wide range of areas which support performers through a variety of situations and pressures that may affect their performance when training and competing.

The pressure placed on a sports performer and the stage of their career may affect the level of support provided by a club or national governing body. Initially when a sports performer joins a sports club, or becomes part of an elite training squad, the support required may be very intense. This early stage of support may include group sessions

Figure 12.1: How do you deal with pressure?

Figure 12.2: An example of an elite performer's daily diary.

Monday 8th October – Training Day		
0800	Breakfast	Cereal milk fruit juice
0900–1030	Training	Training ground
1045	Snack	Toast with jam
1200	Lunch	Turkey salad sandwich drink
1300–1600	College – BTEC Anatomy and Physiology	Remember – folder and assignment
1700	Dinner	Pasta chicken water
1800–2000	Homework	Assessment 2
2000–2100	Free time	Meet friends

on how to plan their time appropriately and sports nutritionists may discuss what foods to eat on training days, match days and rest days and what foods to avoid. Other people may discuss what activities are appropriate and inappropriate during leisure time; other professionals may discuss the impact that alcohol, drugs and smoking can have on health and performance levels in their particular sport. At this early stage sports performers may also be given support on how to deal with the media appropriately. This may include effective methods of communicating with a variety of sources of media.

When pressures are more personal it may be more appropriate for sports performers to speak to someone on a more confidential basis. These situations may require professionals to speak to them one to one and provide advice as appropriate.

Planning aids

A sports performer has to be well organised to manage their own work commitments and leisure time and should be aware of the variety of planning aids and support available. These can include:

- a diary to manage time (paper or electronic)
- team manager
- coach
- personal assistant
- agent
- sports nutritionist
- sports psychologist
- counsellor
- teacher.

2 Appropriate behaviour for an elite athlete

Behaviour of sports performers is constantly scrutinised by the media and the public. Athletes must be aware that at any time their behaviour can be judged. The development of the 24-hour news culture means their behaviour is not just judged on the field of play or during competitions but even when away from the training ground or competitive arena.

2.1 Appropriate behaviour in different situations

Training and competing

Sports performers are judged on the field of play and during training by a number of factors and, most importantly, on their performance. A sports performer is judged on their behaviour and there is a

Activity: Good and bad behaviour

1. In small groups make a list of what you think is acceptable and unacceptable behaviour for sports performers whilst training and competing in a sport.

2. Make a list of what you think is acceptable and unacceptable behaviour for sports performers during their leisure time.

3. Discuss your results as a whole group.

certain code of conduct that sports performers are expected to follow. All sports are governed by written rules which are produced by international and national governing bodies. It is expected that all performers adhere to these rules. Failure to do so results in disqualification or removal from competitive situations. However, there are also unwritten rules which sports performers are expected to follow. These rules protect some of the oldest values in sport. We know these as sportsmanship and fair play, they include:

- respect for peers
- respect for team mates and opponents
- respect for coaches
- respect for officials
- respect for spectators
- acting as a role model
- wearing appropriate clothing
- appropriate conduct and manners at all times and in all situations.

At home

When at home a sports performer should ensure that they behave appropriately; this may include respecting family members, partners and children. Some famous sports performers have received very bad press for treating family members badly. On the other hand those who have good relationships with their family, partners and children are received very well by the press and the public. Often it is only certain sports performers who have constant media surveillance; but other sports performers receive bad press because ex-partners or friends approach the media and inform them of how badly they were treated by the sports performer when living with them.

Think about your relationships with your family. Do you behave in a respectful manner towards them?

At social functions

When they are at social functions sports performers must also act appropriately. A sports performer should remain professional at all times. Often when at social functions fans and spectators may be present, it is therefore important that the professional sports performer acts accordingly and respects all other people. It is expected that fans and spectators will have their say regarding the club's performance and the sports person's performance; however, the sports performer should respect their opinion and in no way react to these opinions.

It is also important that, when out in social situations, a sports performer keeps a low profile to reduce the attention of others.

It is important that a sports performer enjoys their time away from their work commitments and escapes from the pressures of elite sports performance; however when doing this it is important that the sports performer is constantly aware of their behaviour and actions.

Assessment activity 12.1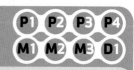

1. Produce a realistic plan for work commitments and leisure time, for one month. **P1** To attain M1 you must explain the way work commitments and leisure activities have been planned. **M1**

2. Describe three different pressures on elite athletes. **P2** For M2 you must explain three different pressures on elite athletes and explain suitable strategies that can be used to deal with these pressures. **M2**

3. Identify strategies that can be used to deal with pressures on elite athletes. **P3**

4. Describe appropriate behaviour for elite athletes in three different situations. **P4** For M3 you must explain appropriate behaviour for elite athletes in three different situations. **M3** For D1 you must also evaluate the effects and consequences of the behaviour of elite athletes. **D1**

Grading tips

- Produce a plan for a one-month period that identifies appropriate work commitments and leisure activities.
- Ensure you include your training schedule and competition schedule.
- Select three pressures and describe their possible effects on your performance.
- Consider methods that can be used to reduce the pressures on your performance.
- Select three different appropriate types of behaviour for a sports performer.
- For each type, describe how the behaviour could be applied within an appropriate situation.

3 Factors that influence effective career planning

3.1 Setting goals

When considering a career in any field you need clear goals for what you want to achieve. A goal should be something that you aspire towards and which motivates you to achieve. When setting goals you should consider appropriate targets and achievements. Goals in sport are often agreed by coaches and performers together; this enables everyone to work towards agreed targets.

The first step when planning any career is to assess your current position and where you want to progress to. Sports performers and coaches need to work towards clear goals, which should give you direction and motivation; all goals set should be achievable.

Goals and targets

Short-term goals are set over a period of time that might be between matches or periods of a season (days, weeks or months maximum). These short-term goals may be targets of what you want to achieve in the next training session or competitive situation. For example, a footballer may set themselves a target to score one goal in the next match.

Medium-term goals should bridge short- and long-term goals. These might include specific targets of where you would like to be at a specific stage of a season or training programme. These medium goals should be based around the ultimate long-term target.

Long-term goals are set with the bigger picture in mind. Some long-term goals are set towards the next big competition or completion of a competition; these are often based around a training cycle or season. For example, a middle distance runner may set a long-term goal to compete in the next Olympics. On the other hand, a rugby union player might have a long-term goal for their team to finish in the top three positions in the league and for the performer to score ten tries throughout the season. These long-term goals should contribute to your training programme and support the development of medium- and short-term targets for performance and development. Some long-term goals can be 'career goals' and these cannot be fully assessed until the end of a sports performer's career. When goals have been achieved new goals and targets need to be set to support motivation and the development of both player and team.

Athletic career

When considering how to plan an athletic career appropriate goals have to be agreed between the sports performers and their coaches. This must involve their own and their coaches' expectations for their performance and achievement. For example, a 16-year-old football scholar at a League Two football club may not have a goal to compete in a Champions League Final within the next two seasons. Obviously the footballer may have this as a career ambition but initially a more appropriate long-term goal may be to play in the reserve team at the club by the age of 18.

When setting goals for an athletic career a sports performer and coach should have regular review dates. These dates should be agreed and set at regular intervals towards the ultimate long-term goal of the sports performer. At each review date the athlete should be set medium-term goals to support their development towards their long-term goal. All reviews and targets set by a sports performer should be recorded and measured. At an elite level of participation coaches and managers can change, so sports performers must have all meetings and reviews recorded in case of a change of coach or if the sports performer moves on to another club.

Contingency planning

A sports performer needs to prepare for every scenario. Like anyone else who works and sets themselves goals and targets, a sports performer is susceptible to catching an illness. Due to the severity of some illnesses a sports performer may not be able to participate in competition and training. Because elite sports performers are constantly participating in physical activity they are more prone to injury. Some sports injuries will prevent sports performers from participating in physical activity for a period of time, which might mean that long-, medium- and short-term goals have to be modified. Sports performers must therefore ensure their plans for attaining their goals and their original timescales are adapted to support the rehabilitation needed to get them back to full fitness.

Some injuries can even end careers. When this happens a sports performer has to consider life outside their sport. There are many instances which may require you to consider a life away from elite sports participation and you need to be aware that when you are unable to play and compete at the highest level there are career opportunities beyond sport.

3.2 Planning a second career

There are many scenarios which mean an athlete needs to consider a second career. There is no guaranteed career in sport so a sports performer must have clear career plans for life after elite sport. The lifespan of an elite athlete is unpredictable. The career of a professional athlete could end for any number of reasons including illness, injury, dispute with manager or coach, or with the club; some sports performers can also be released from sports clubs as their services are no longer required. Even the greatest sports performers have to consider a second career.

Second careers

The importance of education and gaining qualifications should remain a priority for sports performers. Some sports now ensure that performers who are new to the sport have an opportunity to continue their education whilst also participating in training and competition. An example of this is the football scholarship programme, which provides all scholars at professional football clubs throughout all leagues in England, with an opportunity to carry out a set amount of hours per week towards completing an appropriately designed education programme.

Gary Lineker is just one of the professional ex-footballers who has maintained a successful career as a sports pundit. What career path would you like to follow?

Activity: Sports careers

1. In small groups discuss the variety of careers that you and your peers could pursue if you were to finish your sports career today.

2. Make a list of careers which you would like to pursue if you were not currently competing at an elite level.

3. Make a list of the qualifications and experience you would need to obtain a career in one of your selected occupations.

4. Make a list of sports performers who have gone on to other careers in other areas.

The Premier League and the Football League both administer this education programme and a variety of qualifications are undertaken. The programmes which have been developed for the majority of scholars include vocational sport qualifications such as NVQs and BTEC First and Nationals in Sport. The success rates in these qualifications are very high and students generally accept this as part of their career development. There are many ex-scholars who have completed the education scholarship programme but continued to develop as professional footballers. One of the most famous players who completed the scholarship programme successfully and obtained a variety of qualifications is Manchester United first team regular Darren Fletcher. For those sports performers who are not successful on the scholarship programme there have been many learners progressing into employment after being released from sports clubs; and some ex-scholars have progressed into higher education to study undergraduate degrees.

Many sports performers have to seek further employment when their careers end because competing even at the highest level in some sports does not guarantee large wages. Therefore as sports performers approach the end of their career they prepare themselves for careers after professional sport. Often sports performers try to seek a career in sport because it has been an area of interest that they have had all their lives. The career which an ex-professional chooses will depend on the qualifications and experience they obtained either before or during their career as a sports performer. For example, towards the end of many sports careers, professional performers try to attain as many coaching qualifications as possible to enable them to follow a career as a sports coach.

3.3 Financial management

As mentioned earlier in this chapter the **income** of sports performers can be varied. Some sports performers can earn millions of pounds per year whereas others can struggle to earn a living from competing at the highest level.

For some sports performers it may be necessary to pay for the staff who train and support their development. When a sports performer is responsible for their own income and expenses they must manage this money. Sports performers who manage their own finances have to ensure that their outgoings do not outweigh their income. Failure to do so will result in getting into financial difficulty. A sports performer often has to learn very quickly how to mange money and budget for personal living costs as well as external costs or **outgoings**, such as coaching, physiotherapy, travelling expenses and equipment costs. When income outweighs expenditure a sports performer can begin to invest money and save for the future. A sports performer should always have an eye on the future – remembering that the lifespan of a professional sports performer is limited.

Not all sports performers will have to worry about income and expenditure because they will be employed by a club or private organisation. When this is the case, all of the expenses required to compete are paid for by the organisation, meaning that the money earned by the sports performer is their own.

Taxation

Any individual who earns more than £4700 (in 2009) and lives and works in the United Kingdom has to pay tax on the money that they earn over this amount. If you are paid by a sports club or organisation your earnings will automatically be taxed by the club, so you will not have to worry about paying this or calculating the taxation on your earnings. However, if you are self-employed you will have to pay your taxes to ensure that all your earnings have been deducted accordingly. Many sports performers will seek financial advice regarding tax. This sort of advice can be from a chartered accountant. Financial professionals, like accountants, will be able to provide you with guidance on how much income is taxable and which outgoings can be claimed back against your tax allowance.

Pensions

At every stage of their career a sports performer must consider their future employment. It is also important that they think about their finances after they finish competing at an elite level. A pension is a sum of money which is made up of employee and employer contributions.

At the end of the term of the pension the payee is paid a monthly income. Everyone in the United Kingdom is entitled to a pension at the age of 65 years of age (60 years of age for women, although the pension age for women will increase from 2010 to 2020 to eventually be 65 years of age as well) but obviously most elite sports performers stop competing at the highest level much earlier in their lives than this. Because of this, some sports performers choose to pay into a private pension to supplement their income when they retire. Normally sports performers can access their private pensions much earlier than other people who contribute to private schemes.

Insurance

A professional sports performer can purchase insurance cover in the case of injury or illness during performance. If a sports performer sets up an insurance policy they may be able to claim for loss of earnings. These policies are set up with certain conditions attached and the regular payments to be made will depend upon the amount of cover provided. For example, someone who pays a dividend of £30 a month may be entitled to a lump sum payment of £15,000 in the event of an injury which could end their career. However someone who pays £60 a month may be entitled to a lump sum payment of £30,000 in the event of a career-ending injury. Cover for a sports performer may depend on age, previous illnesses and injuries and financial value regarding earnings and ranking.

Legal and contractual requirements

The length of the contract that they have with a sports club, sponsor or organisation may be an issue when some sports performers are planning the future. The longer the contract a sports performer has, the more secure they may feel about the future in their sport. However, a longer contract means it becomes harder for a sports performer to be released or obtain higher wages and endorsements for their performance. When a player is tied into a contract they are liable to act according to the terms and conditions as stated in that contract. Such terms and conditions are legally binding. Therefore if a sports performer agrees that, from any sponsorship deals they obtain, the club which they are representing gains 50 per cent of the royalties, they must abide by this or be in breach of contract – which can result in dismissal.

When agreeing contracts with sports clubs, it is essential for sports performers to seek advice. Some sports performers do this through hiring agents and solicitors to liaise with clubs and agree contracts. Sports performers need to be aware that these people can also charge a lot of money and claim amounts of a sports performer's income. It is important to be aware of all the small print in all the contracts they sign and agree to.

This player clearly needs medical attention, and, depending on the nature of his injuries, he might not be able to train or play for a while. Have you considered the implications of injury on your earnings?

Did you know?

Not all sports performers make millions of pounds for participating in their sport. Olympic Gold medallists in the Yngling sailing class, Sarah Ayton, Sarah Webb and Pippa Webb, announced losses of over £50,000 due to lack of sponsors for their boat.

BTEC Assessment activity 12.2   P5 P6 M4 D2

1. Describe realistic goals in a personal athletic career plan, including second career choices. **P5** (To attain M4 you must explain goals, in a personal athletic career plan, and second career choices. **M4** In order to attain D2 you must justify goals, in a personal athletic career plan, and second career choices. **D2**

2. Describe three financial issues elite athletes need to consider. **P6**

Grading Tips

- Identify short-, medium- and long-term goals for your athletic career.
- Describe the importance of each goal and how you are going to achieve each goal.
- Consider the support available to you to help you attain each athletic goals.
- Identify short-, medium- and long-term goals for your second career.
- Describe how you are going to meet each of your identified second career goals.
- Consider experience and qualifications that may be required to attain each goal.
- Make sure you select three financial issues that sports performers have to consider.

4 Participate in a media interview

4.1 The importance of communication when working with other people

Communication is a very important element of generating relationships. When competing in sport you must have the ability to generate and develop relationships with many other people. As a sports performer you will develop working relationships with a variety of people, including:

- coaching staff
- managers
- team mates
- opponents
- advisers
- agents
- sponsors
- and journalists.

As a professional athlete you must maintain professional relationships with the people you meet. In sport there are some individuals who have 'larger than life' personalities and these are often managers, other players, coaches, etc. In addition to this, as an elite performer in your sport you may be required to play on the same team or compete against people you would not choose to socialise with away from your sport. However, as an athlete you are required to communicate with everyone and it is important that you do this effectively.

Communication skills

There are ways to communicate verbally (talking, asking questions and so on) and non-verbally (body language, demonstrations and gestures). When developing relationships with others you need to use each form of communication effectively.

Active listening skills

When working with other people in sport you should demonstrate that you are actively listening to them. For example, when a sports coach is telling you how to develop your technical application of a skill you must listen to the instructions you are given, to enable you to make the required changes to improve your performance. When listening it is important that you:

- concentrate on what is being said by other people
- have regular eye contact with the speaker
- lean towards the speaker to demonstrate concentration and attention
- if you do not understand anything you should politely ask the speaker to repeat what they have said
- ask appropriate questions to clarify any areas you do not understand.

You will be required to ask questions of those you work with. You should ensure that the questions you ask are relevant and appropriate. Always think before you speak. Think about who you are talking to and what information they will be able to tell you before asking specific questions.

Communicating

When communicating with others verbally you need to be clear and make sure that what you say is appropriate.

First impressions are very important. Therefore, when communicating with others try to speak accurately and clearly.

Non-verbal body language is also important when developing relationships with others. The body language you display can often be easily read by those people you mix with. Therefore it is important to demonstrate very positive body language to the people you work with so that you send a positive message about yourself. Failure to do so could result in people making judgements about your attitude which could be detrimental to your future as an elite performer.

Remember

You should remember that normally you don't speak to those who you work with in the same way as you speak with friends and family. You would usually be more formal and polite with people you work with.

As a sports performer you will be required to communicate with various people who support your development and each group may require different information and different methods of communication. You have to be able to communicate with different people effectively.

Reading and writing clearly and effectively is essential. There are different methods of receiving information from those you work with and those people who can be involved in supporting your development as a sports performer. You will be required to read information when it is sent in the form of an email, letter or a performance analysis and you need to select the relevant detail from the content.

In order to read information effectively you must concentrate on the information. Read the information more than once to ensure that you take all the content in. It may be appropriate to highlight and select what information is relevant from the information provided.

Sometimes you also have to respond to information you have received. When writing back to another person it is important that:

- the information is appropriate for the respondent
- the document is checked for spelling and grammatical errors
- you have used short sentences and paragraphs throughout the document
- you have clearly expressed your own points and opinions appropriately and clearly in the document.

Reviewing and improving relationships

As you develop relationships with others you will review the relationships you already have. You should constantly strive, as a professional, to maintain the best relationships possible with those around you. It is inevitable that from time to time you will have disagreements with some people. However, you must assess the effectiveness of relationships with others and consider what can be done to develop stronger relationships.

4.2 Preparing for a media interview

Sports coverage is delivered through many different forms of media, including:

- television
- radio
- Internet
- newspapers (tabloid and broadsheets)
- magazines
- teletext
- podcasts and blogs.

Each form of media has different requirements; for example, for live broadcasts which may occur on the television, radio and/or Internet, a sports performer may be invited to participate in an interview before or after the game. When a sports performer is taking part in a live interview often they may not be aware of the questions that will be asked and because of this may have very little time to think about their responses.

When participating in media interviews you may, at times, be required to discuss your working relationships with coaching staff, managers, advisers, and fellow athletes. Remember, although a journalist might appear to be your friend, they need to write stories that sell and will do whatever is necessary to get their story.

As an elite sports performer, from time to time you may be asked to provide the media with an interview. For some athletes this will be optional; however because of the revenue that the media generates, for some sports now it can be forced upon professional sports performers as compulsory. The media is a very important tool in the development of sport but it must be used effectively and carefully to ensure that the correct messages are given to the audience.

When preparing for an interview it is important that you:

- are aware of the purpose of the interview
- try to anticipate what is going to be asked by the media professionals
- prepare possible answers in the form of a script for the interview
- prepare prompt sheets of what points you would like to cover in the interview
- research to prepare for the interview
- consider where you can seek support and advice regarding the preparation of the interview.

You should also think about what sensitive issues the media professionals may try to cover and how you could answer these questions or respond to them.

It is also important that a sports performer rehearses the interview before it takes place, either in their mind or with a family member, colleague or friend.

Delivery

When dealing with the media you need to prepare appropriately and consider how you are going to communicate – both verbally and non-verbally.

Verbally: you will need to ensure that you speak using appropriate language and pace. Your major concern should be that the information you are communicating is effectively delivered so that the audience can understand you. You should ensure that the language you use is appropriate for the audience and your tone of voice is clear and loud enough for everyone to hear. If you are concerned about the projection of your voice you could ask the media professionals to ensure that the microphones or recording equipment is switched up to its highest level to support the amplification of your voice.

Non-verbally: you need to be aware of the body language you demonstrate as this can be assessed and used by the media to make judgements on your mood and thoughts about specific points raised in the interview. You must ensure that you are aware of your posture. Crossing arms and legs can be seen as demonstrating insecurities and feeling uncomfortable, so try to show a relaxed confidence at all times. Try to sit back in a chair with your shoulders back and your arms and legs uncrossed; if possible you should also try not to fidget during the interview as this may also be assessed as a sign of weakness.

The equipment used may depend on the interview. Some interviews may require you to speak into a microphone or dictaphone, whereas others may have other equipment for you to speak into or look towards. If you are unsure about how to use the equipment effectively, or whether you are looking in the correct direction, you should ask the journalists for advice.

PLTS

Preparing to be the subject of a media interview, and describing your own strengths and areas for improvement, will help you to develop your skills as a **reflective learner**.

Functional skills

When preparing to be the subject of a media interview, describing your own strengths and areas for improvement will help you develop your speaking and listening skills in **English**.

BTEC Assessment activity 12.3

Communicating with others and the media

1. Describe the skills required to communicate and work effectively with others. **P7** For a Merit, you must explain the skills required to communicate and work effectively with others. **M5**

2. Prepare, and be the subject of, a media interview, describing your own strengths and areas for improvement. **P8** For a Merit, you must explain own strengths and areas for improvement when participating in a media interview **M6** and for a Distinction you must present recommendations on how to improve your own media interview skills. **D3**

Grading tips

- describe the effective methods of communication that should be used when communicating with other people
- make a list of your strengths and weaknesses in your sport
- consider methods of improving your sports performance
- prepare for a media interview
- consider your own presentation and appearance for the interview
- consider the delivery methods for the interview
  o use of verbal communication
  o appropriate use of language
  o pace of speech
  o tone and clarity of voice
  o ensure you demonstrate positive body language
  o be aware of the resources that are going to be used in your interview.

Jennie Dodd
Paralympion sprint swimmer

Jennie has been swimming all her life. She is a very talented swimmer and has represented her county and country at various levels. Jennie has a mild form of cerebral palsy which restricts her speech and some of her movement. Jennie's condition has meant that when out of the water her movement down one side of her body is restricting, however when swimming Jennie has been able to compete with able-bodied people of her own age and, more recently, adults who are able bodied of a much higher age.

Recently Jennie was selected to go to an institute of sport to train for the 2012 Olympics. Joining the elite talent squad has changed Jennie's life. She now has to go to regular training camps with the rest of the Paralympic swimming squad and follows a very strict diet; she has access to a large support network which she is not used to. Jennie has always been very shy and does not like to ask questions and talk to people who she is not familiar with, however she now has to regularly communicate with a variety of new and different people.

Jennie has become something of a minor celebrity in her home town of Mansfield. Due to this meteoric rise to fame she has been asked to carry out a media interview for a local radio station. The interview is going to be live on air, although Jennie will be provided with a list of questions prior to the interview by the journalist.

Think about it!

- Can you provide Jennie with some tips for how to communicate with lots of different people?
- Provide Jennie with a guide to the various forms of verbal and non-verbal communication and how she should use each to communicate with others effectively.
- Could you provide Jennie with some support for how she can prepare for a media interview and respond to the questions asked?

Just checking

1 Make a list of work commitments that an elite sports performer may have to manage.

2 Make a list of the pressures an elite sports performer has to face.

3 Describe methods of dealing with pressure.

4 Make a list of appropriate behaviour a sports performer should adhere to.

5 Make a list of second career options for a sports performer.

6 Define the following terms: income, expenditure and pension.

7 Describe the skills required to communicate with others.

8 How would you prepare for a media interview?

9 How would you deliver a media interview?

edexcel ▦

Assignment tips

- Keep a diary of your work, training and leisure commitments for a month.

- Discuss with your coach a realistic career plan as a sports performer; you should discuss specific short-, medium- and long-term goals and discuss how you are going to meet each of the goals set by your coach and you.

- Discuss with a career adviser second career options in case you do not reach the career goals for your sporting career. Discuss contingency plans and consider what actions you will have to take to ensure you meet your second career goals and what you can do in the meantime to ensure the second career goal can be achieved.

- You will need to be aware of your financial circumstances – track your income and your outgoings and select three financial issues and describe why a sports performer needs to consider each issue.

- Identify a variety of methods used to communicate and work effectively with others. Describe each method and use examples of effective and ineffective methods of communication with others.

- Take part in a media interview (real or a role play). Ensure you prepare appropriately for the interview, and analyse your performance afterwards.

14 Exercise and fitness instruction

The exercise and fitness industry continues to grow as people are encouraged to take more care of their health and fitness. Modern lifestyles are creating health issues for many people; for example, the increase in obesity amongst young children is a worrying trend. One response has been the growth in the number of health and fitness clubs which offer a wide range of services designed to help people improve their personal fitness. These facilities require well-qualified and knowledgeable staff who can safely instruct clients through exercise routines.

This unit will lead you through a variety of related areas to help you understand the knowledge and skills required by a modern-day fitness professional. You will examine the key principles that underpin fitness development and the skills and qualities that an effective fitness instructor will need to use. You will also understand how and why sessions are planned and reviewed and how to ensure the safety of clients at all times.

Learning outcomes

After completing this unit you should:

1. know the principles of exercise session design and exercise programming
2. be able to plan an exercise programme
3. be able to assist in instructing an exercise session
4. be able to undertake a review of an exercise session.

Assessment and grading criteria

This table shows you what you must do in order to achieve a pass, merit or distinction grade, and where you can find activities in this book to help you.

To achieve a **pass** grade the evidence must show that the learner is able to:	To achieve a **merit** grade the evidence must show that, in addition to the pass criteria, the learner is able to:	To achieve a **distinction** grade the evidence must show that, in addition to the pass and merit criteria, the learner is able to:
P1 describe the principles of fitness training **See Assessment activity 14.1, page 320**	**M1** explain the principles of fitness training **See Assessment activity 14.1, page 320**	**D1** relate the principles of fitness training to a range of clients with different needs **See Assessment activity 14.1, page 320**
P2 describe the health and safety issues an exercise instructor needs to consider for their clients **See Assessment activity 14.1, page 320**		
P3 produce exercise programmes for three different types of client **See Assessment activity 14.1, page 320**	**M2** produce detailed exercise programmes for three different types of client **See Assessment activity 14.1, page 320**	**D2** produce exercise programmes justifying the range of activities suggested for three different types of client **See Assessment activity 14.1, page 320**
P4 assist in instructing induction, resistance training, cardiovascular training and circuit training sessions for selected clients	**M3** demonstrate effective communication with selected clients	**D3** demonstrate competence in monitoring and adapting exercises to suit different client ability levels
P5 review three different exercise sessions identifying strengths, areas for improvement and personal development needs	**M4** justify identified personal development needs	

How you will be assessed

You will be required to complete a series of assessments which will give you the opportunity to show that you have developed both the necessary knowledge and skills to pass this unit. These assessments might include:

- practical activities
- PowerPoint presentations
- essays and reports
- multiple-choice tests
- case studies
- role plays, etc.

Antoine, 17-year-old basketball player

I want to be a fitness instructor and personal trainer in the future so this unit really grabbed me. It taught me the key areas I need to know about how we develop fitness in the correct way. To be a fitness instructor means developing knowledge and skills so that I can design training programmes, ensure clients are safe and check on how clients are feeling and performing so that any changes can be made if needed. I enjoyed the practical parts of this unit; for example, where I had to work with other people and design a programme for them and then take them through an induction where I taught them how to use different types of fitness equipment and carry out a range of exercises and activities. This linked well with the business skills unit I also covered as there is a lot of customer care involved in being a fitness instructor. I really enjoyed developing my people skills – people are what the fitness industry is all about.

Over to you!

- Can you list any skills or knowledge that you already have that would help you be a fitness instructor?
- Can any of the other units you have studied help you complete this one?
- What skills and knowledge do you need to develop to help you succeed in this unit?

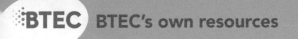

1 Know the principles of exercise session design and exercise programming

Warm-up **Expectations of a fitness instructor**

- Imagine you are a potential client who wishes to improve your fitness.
- What do you expect of the instructor?
- What should they be able to know and do?
- List three areas of knowledge and three skills you think a good fitness instructor needs.

1 Know the principles of exercise session design and exercise programming

Activity: Pushed to the limit

We can develop our bodies to enable us to complete feats such as climbing Mount Everest.

Think of your favourite sport. What physical factors are needed? Make a list of as many as you can think of.

1.1 Principles of fitness training

Developing fitness allows us to undertake and complete sporting activities at a high level. To do this well, we must follow some basic rules or principles.

The first principle is **overload**. Overload is asking the body to perform more work than normal. For instance, lifting weights or moving joints through a greater range of movement. Doing this leads to the second principle: **adaptation**.

When asked to carry out physical activities above and beyond what is normally required, the body adapts to these demands so that it can

Key terms

Overload – the body performs more work than it would usually be asked to do.

Adaptation – changes to cope with different demands being made.

better cope in the future. The body changes, or adapts, to cope. Table 14.1 opposite outlines some ways in which parts of the body might adapt.

The next principle is FITT. FITT stands for:

- Frequency
- Intensity
- Time
- Type.

Frequency refers to the number of times per day, week or month that a person exercises. Someone who trained only once a week for the London Marathon would see only a slow improvement in fitness levels. But training four or five times a week would see much greater improvement.

Intensity

Intensity refers to how hard you train and is closely linked to what you are trying to improve. One way to measure intensity is to measure heart rate: the harder the intensity, the higher the heart rate. But how do we calculate the correct intensity?

The simplest way is to first find your safe maximum heart rate. This is done by taking your age away from 220. The number left is your safe resting heart rate. The following table shows how we then use a percentage of this to calculate the intensity level of the exercise we are going to undertake. Please remember that this is only a guide. This method generally gives too high a reading for people under 30 and too high for people over 45 so perceived exertion method may be more preferable.

Table 14.1: Adaptations of the body during and after exercise.

Part of the body	Adaptation
The heart	Increases in size, works less hard at rest
Skeletal muscle	Increase in size and tone with greater definition
Joints	Allow greater range of movement
Resting pulse rate	Decreases
Bones	Become more dense and stronger

Table 14.2: Heart rate versus levels of intensity.

Intensity	What it does	% of safe maximum heart rate reserve
Long, slow runs, easy or recovery runs	• improves ability of the heart to pump blood • improves muscles' ability to use oxygen • improves body's efficiency at feeding working muscles • body learns to metabolise fat as a source of fuel	60–70%
Aerobic zone or target heart rate zone	• improves cardiovascular fitness • increases cardiorespiratory capacity • increases overall muscle strength	70–80%
Anaerobic zone (training in this zone is hard)	• increases lactate (or anaerobic) threshold, which improves performance	80–90%
VO_2 max red line zone (you should only train in this zone if you are very fit, and only for short periods of time)	• can increase your fast twitch muscle fibres which increase speed • lactic acid develops quickly as you are operating in oxygen debt to the muscles	90–100%

The client is asked to measure the feelings caused by exercising and grade them from 1 to 10. For example, sitting still in a chair would have a rating of 0. Walking at a pace where you can hold a conversation with someone would be around 3. Remember, the rating of exertion should not be linked to how fast the client is running or walking etc. It is based on the feelings caused by the exertion to the client. Increasing the pace to cause the client to run and then adding a hill or two could quickly work up to a 10.

Remember also that the higher the level of exertion, the shorter the length of time that the exercise can be carried out for. This can be seen in the way that intensity is applied to a training or exercise programme. A client training for a half marathon might need to run for two hours, so intensity should be moderate to allow this. A swimmer competing in 50m events trains at a much higher intensity.

Table 14.3: Levels of intensity of exercise and their effects.

Level of Intensity	RPE	Physical clues
Light	Easy	Does not induce sweating unless it's a hot, humid day. There is no noticeable change in breathing patterns.
Moderate	Somewhat hard	Will break a sweat after performing the activity for about 10 minutes. Breathing becomes deeper and more frequent. You can carry on a conversation but not sing.
High	Hard	Will break a sweat after 3–5 minutes. Breathing is deep and rapid. You can only talk in short phrases.

Intensity level also applies to using weights or other resistance exercise. A person looking to tone up their muscles will lift light weights, whereas a person who competes in power lifting will lift weights that are much heavier.

Client factors determine the intensity adopted. Weight loss requires low to moderate intensity to allow exercise to be carried out for a long time and calories to be burnt.

Progressive

Exercise should be **progressive** – it should get harder over time. This can be achieved by:

1. Exercising more times per week.

2. Exercising for longer.

3. Exercising at a higher intensity.

Exercise programmes must be progressive or improvements in fitness stop. You will reach a certain level and not improve further. This may be fine for someone who has reached their target weight and simply wants to maintain this level. However, elite athletes need to continue to achieve greater levels of fitness.

When designing an exercise programme, remember the aims and goals of the client. Whatever programme is designed, it must be specific to the client the activity they are working towards, any specific needs caused by disability etc. or any other particular need. A person training for a fun run should focus on developing aerobic endurance whereas a sprinter may focus on muscular strength.

Two other factors are **reversibility** and **over-training**. Reversibility means 'use it or lose it'. Stop training and your fitness will decrease faster than you can develop it. Over training is where a person trains too much, too often. Pushing your body too far means you risk injury or illness.

Health and safety for clients

The health and safety of the client is the most important aspect of an exercise programme. How do we ensure our clients are safe? The first factor is the Code of **Ethical** Practice that applies to all exercise professionals.

Always remember to ensure that you obtain consent or permission from the client. This is where you obtain written permission, or consent, from the client about all aspects of the training programme. The client is agreeing to the programme described. Remember to fully explain the programme to the client so that they understand what is involved.

The client must receive an induction before exercising. This includes being shown how to use fitness equipment, what parts of the body each type of equipment develops, and the important 'do's and don'ts' of exercising. The client should sign a form to confirm this has taken place.

The fitness instructor's role includes ensuring that clients who exercise use the correct technique. Clients who use incorrect techniques risk injury and it may mean that they do not benefit fully from the exercise programme.

Another factor is for clients to understand how moving limbs can cause injuries. All moving things have momentum. Moving arms and legs will continue to move until something stops them. Clients should not suddenly stop or change direction when exercising as they risk injury. Momentum can be used to good effect when stretching. Dynamic stretching involves gently taking limbs through the full range of movement. The key point is that the movement is gentle.

Finally, fitness instructors must ensure that clients are properly dressed for exercise.

Two final features of an exercise programme are the warm-up and cool-down. Each serves a purpose which the fitness instructor needs to understand.

Key term

Ethical – moral principles based on right and wrong.

Activity: Code of conduct

Visit the website for the Register of Exercise Professionals (see Hotlinks section on page ii for a link to this website). Give three examples of how this code protects the health and safety of clients.

Can you explain why the clothing shown is suitable?

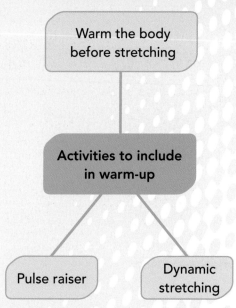

Figure 14.1: What activities do you include in your warm-up?

Warm-up

The warm-up will:

*   warm up muscles and joints ready for exercise
*   raise the pulse and breathing rate so that the body is supplied with oxygen
*   prepare the mind for exercise.

Cool-down

The cool-down takes place at the end of a session. It serves the following purposes:

*   gradually reduce heart rate and breathing
*   stretch working muscles to remove waste products and reduce soreness and stiffness
*   reduces the levels of adrenaline produced when we exercise.

The cool-down should consist of:

*   a short period of jogging / walking followed by
*   a short period of static stretching.

2 Plan an exercise session

2.1 Plan

In order that clients can experience the full benefits of exercising, the session must be properly planned. The fitness instructor needs to decide the aims and objectives of the session and then use training principles to decide what to include.

The aims and objectives for a fitness programme will be affected by:

*   what the client wishes to achieve – their goals
*   the client's current level of fitness
*   weaknesses identified in the client's levels of fitness
*   current activity level.

When planning exercise programmes, it is important to consider the type of client and their needs. For example:

*   Is it a group or one individual?
*   Do they exercise regularly or not?
*   Do they have a specific need such as a disability?
*   What is their current level of fitness?
*   How experienced are they in exercise terms?

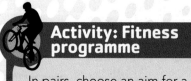

Activity: Fitness programme

In pairs, choose an aim for a client starting a fitness programme. Produce examples for each bullet point listed.

Table 14.4 shows some examples of factors to consider.

Table 14.4 Factors to consider when planning a fitness programme for clients.

Type of client	Factor to consider
Individual	Needs support and encouragement
Group	Space available, amount of equipment needed
Low fitness level	Length and intensity levels involved
High fitness level	May require fine tuning to achieve goal
Little exercise experience	Explanation of principles
High level of exercise experience	Less planning but more mentoring

Activity: Exercise

In pairs, list the types of exercise you like and dislike. What else might be important? Think about when you like to exercise and what facilities are available. What might be included in the proposed plan? What activities, exercises and training styles might be used?

Factors to consider

Below are listed some of the factors a fitness instructor should consider. First, the fitness instructor must understand the current fitness and activity levels of the client, their lifestyle pattern and what the client wishes to achieve. But how can we find this out? One way is for clients to complete a questionnaire where the client provides information about these different areas. This questionnaire will include:

- health issues, both past and present
- smoking and drinking levels
- age, height, weight etc.
- past and present exercise/activity levels.

Once you have this information, you can plan a session.

Clients

The fitness instructor will also take the client through a series of fitness tests to gather information about the client. Tests might include the following:

- body measurements using skinfold calipers
- height and weight measurements
- blood pressure
- flexibility via the sit and reach test.

Other, more specific, tests may also be carried out to measure cardiovascular fitness, strength and so on. Test results will allow the fitness instructor to identify the client's strengths and weaknesses and design a specific fitness programme for them. For instance, a client who is aiming to complete a marathon and who scored poorly on a cardiovascular test would need a programme that develops this and may include activities such as cycling, running, swimming etc., where they work at a low intensity but for at least 30 minutes. A client who has recently undergone heart surgery will need a fitness programme that starts at a very low level of intensity.

Case study: Lucy's new client

Lucy has a new client who is starting today. The client has had a major heart operation in the past few months and has not exercised for some time. The client lacks mobility in their left hip at the moment and is likely to need a hip replacement in the near future.

- **What activities would you suggest?**
- **How might you modify some activities?**
- **Give some suitable examples for different activities.**

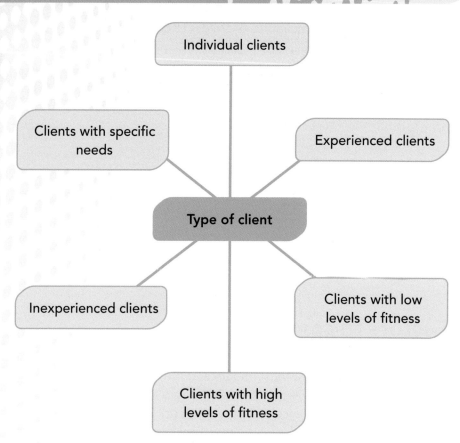

Figure 14.2: Here are some types of client you might encounter. How would you make sure you tailor a programme to suit their needs?

Activity: Clients' needs

Consider the different clients (see the diagram above) and discuss in small groups what specific issues the fitness instructor needs to think about.

Activity selection

Activities must fit into a client's routine (for example walking or cycling to work, using the stairs instead of a lift). You should also consider the following:

- Resistance training – lifting weights.
- Cardiovascular training – through running, swimming, cycling etc.
- Circuit training – either skills-based or fitness-based.
- What does the client enjoy?
- Client's goals.
- Weather conditions – being hot or cold might affect the choice of activity and the time of day the activity takes place.
- Cost – income may be limited.
- Transport – does the client have access to personal transport?
- Culture – does the client's cultural background or religious beliefs place restrictions on exercising?

3 Assist in instructing exercise sessions

3.1 Exercise sessions

The assistant fitness instructor must consider the following parts of a fitness session:

- the start and end of the session
- the main part of the session.

How you assist in a session will be affected by the type of session. A group aerobics session requires the instructor to be the focal point using clear communication, clear demonstrations and lots of encouragement! On the other hand, a one-to-one personal training session will require giving specific feedback, instruction and mentoring. All clients must be taken through an induction session. Clients must understand how to:

- warm-up and cool-down
- exercise effectively and safely
- use a range of exercise equipment.

The client must make the instructor aware of issues that might make exercising unwise and sign a disclaimer stating they have received and understood the induction process.

Start of the session

Before a session, the fitness instructor checks all equipment. Checks are carried out daily to ensure that all equipment is fit and safe to use. The client knows about what to do in the event of a fire or other emergency, what the content of each session is and the instructor may give clear demonstrations of each stretch or exercise in the session. A client for whom this may be their first session will have received a health screening and induction into exercising and using fitness equipment.

During the session

While exercising, the instructor should monitor what and how the client is doing. New clients will need advice and encouragement.

Clients will also need motivating and there are different ways to do this, which may include the following:

- Giving verbal encouragement. Clients will respond to positive encouragement and feedback.
- Setting targets for the client and helping them to achieve them.
- Regular reassessment of the client's fitness levels.
- Constantly monitoring the client. Are they over-exerting themselves? Are they performing each exercise correctly? Are they using equipment safely?

The fitness instructor should always be looking for any problems. If any are seen or heard, the instructor must act. For example, if the client is having difficulty with a particular exercise, how should the fitness instructor respond? You could adapt the exercise. For example, if a client is unable to perform a full press-up, you could suggest that they try the modified method.

Activities might be adapted because a client might have a specific need. A lack of mobility might mean that a stretch used in a warm-up might be changed. For example, a sit-and-reach exercise could be modified by instructing the client to bend their knees slightly.

Ending the session

At the end of the session, remember to gather feedback from the client. Did they enjoy the session? How do they feel? Was anything not enjoyable, difficult or uncomfortable? As the programme progresses, feedback should focus on the aims and objectives of the programme. Is the client's strength improving as planned and at the rate desired? Does the client feel the session is well managed and organised? Do they feel their needs, aims and so on are being met by the activities the instructor has planned? Do they understand the purpose of each activity?

Figure 14.3: It is important that you are able to adapt exercises for clients who have difficulty. The press-up position can be modified for clients who cannot do a full press-up. Think about how you could modify another exercise.

BTEC **Assessment activity 14.1**

You have started a new job as a trainee fitness instructor. The club is new and the management team wants to provide an atmosphere where clients are educated about health and fitness while they exercise. The club manager asks you to produce a range of informative posters to be placed around the gym about fitness principles and how they should be applied.

1. First, design a poster that explains to clients about the principles of developing fitness and then describes in more detail what each one means and involves. **P1**, **M1** Now produce some case study clients and show how the principles you have described and explained should be applied to a range of clients with different needs. **D1**

2. You have now been asked to produce an information poster for the staff room which will remind staff of the variety of health and safety issues that staff must address when dealing with the range of clients who use the club. **P2**

3. The manager is so impressed with your work that he decides you are ready to work with your own clients. Before he gives the green light for this, he asks you to produce a detailed fitness programme for three different clients who might use the club. **P3**, **M2** Finally, he meets with you to discuss the content of each programme. First he asks you to explain and justify each activity in each plan. Why is it included? What are the reasons for each programme and the chosen activities in them? **D2**

Grading tips

Imagine you are writing for or talking to a person new to exercise. For P1 and M1, tell this new client the key ideas that underpin how we need to exercise if we are to see benefit. What role does frequency and the type of exercise play? Use examples to show a new client how these ideas are applied to an exercise programme and how they will improve a person's health and fitness.

For D1, show how you would explain each fitness principle differently to a range of different clients such as young and old, male and female, a disabled person, a group and an individual.

For P2, you might adopt the role of a person giving a briefing to a new gym instructor on the key health and safety considerations. Why are warm-up and cool-down important, for example?

P3, M2 and D2 require you to produce an actual exercise programme for three different clients. Make sure you choose three different clients! You might base this on different ages, sports activities or clients who each have a different requirement.

The M2 grade requires much more detail than P3 – for example, details about your client, the way they will exercise and the precise programme they will follow.

Finally for D2, you must give clear reasons explaining why you have chosen the exercises in each programme. What will they achieve? Why did you choose them? Why did you not choose another type of activity? The reasons could well be linked to the fitness principles covered in P1.

4 Undertake a review of exercise sessions

After each training session, and once a programme has been completed, it is important that the fitness instructor gives and receives appropriate **feedback** to and from the client. This feedback should cover a range of topics which should all relate to the aims and goals targeted.

4.1 Review

Any review must focus on the feedback received from the client. Have the original aims and goals been achieved? Was the programme enjoyable? What aspects of the programme were not enjoyed? This review may take the form of a one-to-one discussion or a standard form where the client provides their feedback in writing. Whatever format is used, the activities that have been used should be assessed in terms of the effect they have had on the client.

Apart from the effectiveness of the session, the fitness instructor must also consider the management of the session. Were there any health and safety issues during the session or programme? This might highlight a need to improve the induction process. Consider whether the client was looked after in an appropriate way; for instance being encouraged to drink sufficient fluids or take appropriate rest periods.

All of this feedback has one main aim – to improve future sessions and develop the next stage of the programme. This might require a change in the content or nature of the programme. An individual who wishes to take up jogging may now wish to enter a local road race and so they need to develop greater aerobic endurance. This may mean sessions have to be more frequent or of a higher intensity.

Amendments

Once the feedback process has been completed, it is important that any changes or amendments to the programme, goals or objectives are documented in the correct way. Generally, this involves a written document which records what was discussed, and changes that are agreed, which

Key term

Feedback – information about a person's performance in a task, e.g. given to the client by a fitness instructor about how the client has done in a session or the whole programme.

PLTS

Designing your three fitness programmes will help develop your skills as a **creative thinker**.

is then signed by both the client and the instructor. Changes may involve changes to the training activities used, the number of sessions completed or the intensity of each session completed. Whatever is changed, it is important that both the client and instructor are in agreement.

4.2 Modify

At the start of this chapter, you looked at the principle of progression – gradually increasing the amount or intensity of work completed to continue to develop fitness levels. One of the aims of giving and receiving feedback is to be able to modify correctly the training the client undertakes. This might involve changing the planning method to ensure that the client completes the agreed programme or it may involve changing activities because the client is becoming bored with the current programme. In school or college you might be excited because your favourite teacher is delivering the next session. The same applies to a fitness programme. If the client is not excited about what they are going to do, they will lose interest and not try as hard as they should.

As the client's fitness develops, the fitness instructor will need to change certain aspects of the session to ensure the client's fitness continues to improve.

Activity: Modifying fitness programmes

Can you suggest ways that a client's programme could be modified to ensure their fitness continues to develop?

Development needs

A fitness programme that never changes will quickly become boring and the client will lose interest and may stop training. Feedback and constant monitoring will allow the fitness instructor to help develop both the programme and the client. Setting targets is a useful technique to use to help develop and motivate the client. Targets should be SMART: Specific, Measurable, Achievable, Realistic and Time-bound. (See Unit 3 page 89 for more on SMART targets.)

As the programme progresses, there may be opportunities to develop further so that the instructor can improve and develop their skills and knowledge. The fitness instructor may gain benefit from observing a more experienced instructor in action by attending workshops or seminars. It may involve the instructor attending training courses on specific aspects of fitness, such as developing core body strength or nutritional knowledge. All of this can help the instructor to better plan for the client's future fitness needs and provide a more effective and enjoyable service.

Carlos Rodriguez
Fitness instructor

I have recently qualified as a Fitness Instructor in a city centre health and fitness club. Having completed my BTEC First Diploma and then my NVQ Level 2 in Exercise and Fitness, I am now qualified to work independently on the gym floor.

Typical day

A typical day involves arriving at the gym and checking all the fitness equipment for safety and cleanliness. Any faults are reported to the centre manager. Water dispensers, the changing rooms and all other facilities available to clients are checked before customers arrive. I have to wear a clean uniform every day and make sure that my personal presentation is appropriate.

Today, I have a new client booked in for me to meet and induct. I have to make sure that I have the client's details to hand and am there to greet the client when they arrive.

This client is very nervous about starting to exercise and is very conscious of their body image. Remembering the knowledge and skills I developed during my college course, I take the client into a quiet room to discuss what the client wishes to achieve. I try to be friendly and supportive. I am constantly trying to encourage the client and answer all their questions honestly and expertly.

I then take the client through an induction. For each activity, I explain what the equipment is for and how to carry the task out. Gradually the client starts to relax as I build a rapport with them.

After the induction, I discuss the results with the client and point out the good points and those areas that could be improved. We then discuss what the client wishes to achieve; in this case, weight loss. I find out more about what the client likes and dislikes and then suggest a programme that will help the client to lose weight. Once this is agreed, a booking is made for the next session. The client had arrived looking fearful and apprehensive but leaves with a big smile!

Think about it!

- Why is a rapport between the instructor and client important?
- Why is it important that the client leaves feeling happy and looking forward to the next visit?
- What must the client believe?

323

Just checking

1. What is meant by overload?
2. What does FITT stand for?
3. Show how exercises can be made progressive.
4. List three checks that should be made before a person starts an exercise programme.
5. What is the purpose of an exercise induction programme?
6. While a client is exercising, what should the fitness instructor be doing?
7. How can a client be motivated by the instructor?
8. Once an exercise programme has been completed, what should the fitness instructor carry out? Why?

Assignment tips

- Make sure you include all the various principles of fitness development such as FITT, etc. Remember to explain them and give a suitable example each time to show you understand.

- When thinking about health and safety, remember to use current industry guidelines as well as the areas covered in your health and safety unit. Again, give some practical examples to help.

- When designing your three programmes, be clear about what each client needs. What do they wish to improve? What do they like and dislike? Make sure that the activities fit in with their lifestyle.

15 Sport and leisure facility operations

Participating in sport and recreation has become big business over the past few years, which means that the appropriate facilities need to be provided and operated correctly. Centres have to ensure the safety of all customers while on the premises and, as an employee, you must understand how we meet customer needs, why safety is so important and, at a more basic level, how you must erect and take down typical sports and recreation equipment.

Ensuring safety involves following procedure and good practice, while a successful sports facility will be able to attract customers who return time and again. Sport and recreation are service industries so everyone working in them must understand the reasons why people use our facilities, and make sure to provide a level of service that our customers can expect at all times. Sports centres have a staffing structure that helps to ensure the centre runs effectively. It is important that you understand this structure and the role you play in it.

Learning outcomes

After completing this unit you should:

1. know about organisational structures and staff responsibilities within a sport and leisure facility
2. know the importance of providing a safe and secure environment
3. know about customer service in sport and leisure facilities
4. be able to set up, check, take down and store equipment used for sports activities.

Assessment and grading criteria

This table shows you what you must do in order to achieve a pass, merit or distinction grade, and where you can find activities in this book to help you.

To achieve a **pass** grade the evidence must show that the learner is able to:	To achieve a **merit** grade the evidence must show that, in addition to the pass criteria, the learner is able to:	To achieve a **distinction** grade the evidence must show that, in addition to the pass and merit criteria, the learner is able to:
P1 describe the organisational structure of a selected sport and leisure facility		
P2 describe the responsibilities of four different staff teams of a selected sport and leisure facility **See Assessment activity 15.1, page 331**	**M1** explain the responsibilities of four different staff teams in a selected sport and leisure facility **See Assessment activity 15.1, page 331**	**D1** evaluate the responsibilities of four different staff teams in a selected sport and leisure facility **See Assessment activity 15.1, page 331**
P3 describe why it is important to provide a safe and secure environment		
P4 describe procedures used to ensure a safe and secure environment in areas within a selected sport and leisure facility	**M2** explain how procedures help to provide safe and secure sport and leisure facilities	
P5 identify procedures used to provide effective customer service in a selected sport and leisure facility	**M3** explain the importance of effective customer service, and procedures used to achieve it in a selected sport and leisure facility	
P6 describe the importance of providing effective customer service in a selected sport and leisure facility		
P7 set up, check, take down and store equipment for three different sports activities, with tutor support **See Assessment activity 15.2, page 338**	**M4** independently set up, check, take down and store equipment for three different sports activities **See Assessment activity 15.2, page 338**	
P8 review own performance in the setting up, checking, taking down and storage of equipment for three different sports activities **See Assessment activity 15.2, page 338**	**M5** review own performance in the setting up, checking, taking down and storage of equipment for three different sports activities, making suggestions for own development **See Assessment activity 15.2, page 338**	**D2** review own performance in the setting up, checking, taking down and storage of equipment for three different sports activities, justifying suggestions relating to development **See Assessment activity 15.2, page 338**

How you will be assessed

You will need to produce evidence that you understand typical staff structures found in sport and recreation and that you are aware of the importance and need for safety in a facility. The assignment set will also require you to show that you can put up and take down typical sports and recreation equipment safely and how to check that this equipment is safe to use. Your assignment may ask you to complete:

- written tasks
- practical tasks
- presentations
- group discussions.

Laura, 17-year-old leisure attendant

I started work at the local leisure centre after finishing my BTEC First Diploma course at college. I am part of a dynamic team of people who work together to provide a quality experience for all their customers. Working a shift system, I have an important position as a leisure attendant within a team of staff who work together each day.

This unit at college taught me that providing a quality service to all customers is vital to the success of the centre in a business sense, but also to my career prospects. I find that satisfied customers give me great job satisfaction and I really enjoy working as part of a team.

This unit also helped me to understand the different roles and responsibilities that I have to carry out each day and why they are important. Also I learned how my efforts help the business to be successful. Finally the unit showed me why customer service and health and safety are so important

Over to you!
- How many roles do you think there are in a leisure centre?
- Would you like to work in a leisure centre?
- If you currently work part time, what skills and knowledge do you have that could help you to become an effective member of staff in a sports facility?

1 Know about organisational structures and staff responsibilities within a sport and leisure facility

Warm-up

Professional conduct

Imagine you are a customer at a sport or recreation facility. You have gone ten-pin bowling with your friends or to play badminton at your local sports centre. When you arrive, and during the entire experience, what do you expect of the following:

- the facility
- the staff
- the equipment?

In order for businesses to run effectively and be successful, it is important that employees understand why each member of staff is there and what their own roles and responsibilities are. In a typical sports centre, there will be a number of different staff – each with a different role. They might include:

- lifeguards
- fitness instructors
- receptionists
- sports coaches
- cleaners
- maintenance staff
- managers.

The type of staff needed will depend on the type of facility. For example, a sports centre such as the Manchester Velodrome will need staff who have an expertise in cycling but no lifeguards as the centre has no swimming pool.

1.1 Organisational structure

All organisations, whatever the nature of the work (even your school or college), will have a staff structure. This shows the different roles of each member of staff and the 'chain of command'. Thus a staff structure at a sports centre might look like the one shown in figure 15.1 (see page 329).

Consider why it is necessary to have only one manager but three duty managers. Think about when a typical centre might be open. If a centre opens at 6am and closes at 11pm, that is 17 hours a day that the centre is open and this may apply 7 days a week or 119 hours per week. You are not legally allowed to work that many hours so it is important to have people who work at different times, to ensure the centre is properly staffed whenever it is open.

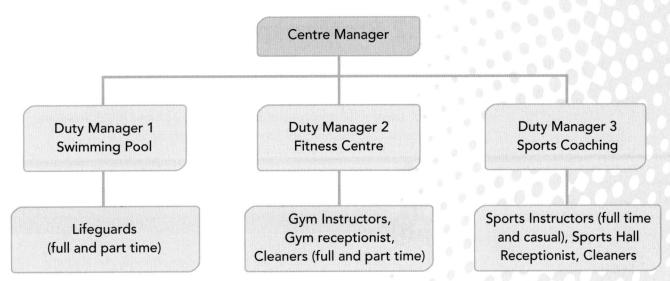

Figure 15.1: Example of an organisational structure of a sports centre. Draw up the organisational structure of your local sports centre.

Activity: Staff structure and responsibilities

1. Visit your nearest sports or leisure facility and ask for a copy or description of its current staff structure. Remember to include all the different types of employees and the number of each. Also remember to find out how many are full time, part time and casual and what these three terms mean. Look at the staff structure you have obtained, what do you notice about the staffing? Are they organised in teams? For example, a team of fitness instructors or lifeguards? Can you think why?

2. Try to match together the following teams and responsibilities:

Team	Responsibility
Fitness instructor team	Answer customer enquiries, cash up at the end of the day
Lifeguard team	Ensure all equipment is working effectively and any repairs needed are quickly carried out
Reception team	Ensure the entire centre is adequately staffed at all times, monitor all finances. Deal with appointing staff
Management team	Maintain a suitable level of cleanliness in all parts of the centre. Ensure soap dispensers, paper towel dispensers etc. are always full
Cleaning team	Supervise users and help with any questions raised. Induct new clients into safe exercising
Maintenance team	Ensure the safety of all swimmers at all times and maintain adequate lifeguard coverage

1.2 Staff responsibilities

It is important that each staff member is aware of, and understands, their roles and responsibilities – what they are expected to do – all the time the centre is open. There are some basic roles and responsibilities that apply to all employees, see figure 15.2 below. All of these are important to the smooth running of a sports or leisure centre.

Activity: Staff roles

In pairs, make a list of the basic roles you think all the staff in a sports centre would need to fulfil and list a range of sports facilities in which they would be used.

Figure 15.2: Staff have many responsibilities. Can you think of any that haven't been included?

Skills

Some staff will need specific skills to go with the more general ones we have mentioned. For example, let us consider a receptionist at a sports centre. They will need to have very good personal presentation skills since they will be the first person a customer will meet when visiting the centre. They will need to be able to communicate with customers, staff, etc. in a range of ways, for example, verbally, in writing and on the telephone. But they may also need to:

- be computer literate
- be able to use a fax machine, be able to word process and use other pieces of office equipment
- have good number skills if they are required to 'cash up' at the end of a shift
- ensure the reception area is clean, tidy and well ordered so that forms and other documents can be found quickly.

In addition, managers need to be able to open and close the centre each day, keep and maintain daily and weekly logs; for example, swimming pool water tests and results, customer numbers, staff absence records, and so on.

BTEC **Assessment activity 15.1**

1. Choose four different staff teams from your local sports and leisure centre. Draw up a poster for each team which explains to new members of that team what their roles and responsibilities are. Give some practical examples to show your understanding. **P2**

2. Why does each team need to adopt these responsibilities? Think what might happen if the responsibilities you have described are not carried out at all or to the required standard. For instance, what if a lifeguard failed to attend staff training on the new method of giving CPR? **M1**

3. Evaluate the roles you have given each team. Are there any roles that all the teams have? For example, this might include responsibilities for ensuring customer care or safety of each other. Again, how does each responsibility contribute to a successful centre? **D1**

Grading tips

Make sure you look at the responsibilities of four *different* staff teams. The greater the difference between the teams the easier it will be to show differences. For P2, describe – paint a picture in words and images – as with all Pass criteria. Assume the reader knows nothing about this topic.

For M1, give more detail and answer the question why each responsibility is needed. Use examples wherever possible.

For D1, you need to evaluate these responsibilities; for this, think about how important the responsibilities identified are. Think about what it would mean for customers and the business if staff in the various teams did *not* carry these responsibilities out.

PLTS

Completing this assessment will develop your skills as a **creative thinker**.

2 Know the importance of providing a safe and secure environment

2.1 Safe environment

The Hillsborough disaster, in 1989, showed dramatically what can happen if a safe environment is not provided at sports facilities. But how do we ensure that sports and leisure centres are safe at all times?

First of all, it is essential to ensure that the centre is complying with all relevant and current legislation that is currently in place. This includes legislation such as the Health and Safety at Work Act (HASAWA), Reporting of Incidents, Diseases and Dangerous Occurrences Regulations (RIDDOR) and First Aid Regulations. These are three examples of what is called statutory legislation – it is the law and it must be followed. All three are designed to make all workplaces safe for everybody; not just customers and visitors.

Each centre should have policies and procedures in place to make sure all staff comply with their roles and responsibilities under the law. A policy is a written statement which describes why something needs to be done and what will happen if an incident occurs; for example when the fire alarm sounds. A procedure is the actions and the order in which the policy must happen. So the procedure on discovering a fire will involve a series of steps that should be followed in a particular order. These policies and procedures will mean that different staff have different roles and responsibilities. Look at the following example of what to do in the case of a major emergency.

Major emergency

A major emergency is one where an incident occurs resulting in a serious injury or life-threatening situation. In most cases it will involve more than one member of the team and may, in extreme situations, involve all team members. If it is at a swimming pool:

- Pool attendant identifying the problem raises the alarm by using the pool alarm, whistle or hand signals.
- Pool alarm sounds in the control pod and reception to alert support staff by radio or public address system.
- Pool attendant initiates rescue/first aid procedures and removes casualty from the danger area.
- Support team members cover vacated patrol/vigilance area, clearing the pool if required.
- Duty manager summons ambulance/provides specialist equipment/ assists in crowd control etc.
- Duty manager completes incident and accident report forms and any other reports required.

Activity: Emergency procedures

As a group, discuss why it is necessary for centres to have written procedures in case of emergencies. What are the advantages of this? Why is it important for all staff to know their role?

The importance of knowing and understanding the emergency procedures cannot be overstated. All staff must know not only their own role should an emergency arise, but also that of the rest of the team.

Many recent tragedies have influenced the sports industry in recent years. The incident at Hillsborough, the Lyme Bay tragedy and others have shown what can happen when the safety of customers has not been good enough.

A safe environment is more than a legal requirement, it is important because:

- it ensures that no customer is put at risk of illness or injury while in your centre
- customers can have as enjoyable an experience as possible
- no member of staff is put at risk
- the centre gains a good reputation with its customers and so attracts more customers
- the centre is unlikely to be taken to court because of an accident, illness or injury that befalls a customer
- customers' valuables and belongings, vehicles etc. are safe at all times.

But how do we do this?

Swimming pools have a set of rules to ensure your safety. What rules does your school or college have to ensure your security?

2.2 Secure environment

Apart from safety, it is important that people and their belongings are secure from:

- theft
- fraud
- vandalism
- violence.

Areas

Sports centres have a number of different areas where safety and security is required. For example:

- changing rooms
- car parks
- reception
- sports halls and swimming pools
- fitness suites.

Activity: Equipment and environment

Consider each of these areas:

- changing room
- car park
- swimming pool.

Answer the following questions for each area:

1. What equipment is needed in each area?

2. How does the equipment help to provide a safe environment for everyone?

3. Where, and how, in a sports and leisure centre could the equipment you have listed, or similar examples, be used? You might walk around your school or college to help you here. Think about the following areas:

  - changing rooms
  - car parks
  - reception
  - sports halls and swimming pools
  - fitness suites.

4. What other equipment can you think of?

3 Customer service in sport and leisure facilities

3.1 Customers

It is often said that 'the customer is always right'. What do you think this means for a sports and leisure centre?

What is a **customer**?

So who might use a sports centre or fitness facility? You might think of families, the elderly, clubs and teams and businesses. What about you? What other customers can you think of?

The sport and leisure industry relies on repeat business. This means that people return to use the products and services we offer many times. If staff give a poor service, or the centre is dirty, unsafe or much of the equipment is broken or faulty, then people will not return and the centre will develop a poor reputation which will affect its success.

So what can we do to ensure people come back to your sports centre time and time again? Deliver excellent customer service!

3.2 Customer service

So what is customer service? It is defined as the overall activity of identifying and satisfying customer needs. It often refers to the whole process of meeting customer needs time and time again and giving them a better service than they expected.

It is then important to consider what we mean by customer needs. A customer who visits a sports and leisure centre might need some, or all of the following.

- Information – about what the centre offers, opening times and prices.
- Advice – about how to lose weight or become fitter, or what people need to improve in their chosen sport or game.
- Product information – which swimming goggles are best?
- Service information – what is provided if I take out a Gold gym membership?

If staff at a centre help with any of these requests, the information must be:

- accurate
- up to date
- unbiased.

If you do not know the right answer, you must never just make something up. You should find a person who does know the answer.

Customer service is important for a number of different reasons.

> **Key term**
>
> **Customer** – someone who buys goods or services from a business.

When you are doing work experience or if you work with customers, think about the service you would expect to receive.

Firstly, it is important to customers. If they receive excellent customer service, which exceeds their expectations, they are going to be satisfied customers. They are therefore more likely to:

- return again and again
- tell their friends and family, who may also then visit the centre.

For the centre this will mean:

- more customers
- more business and so increased profit
- a more satisfying place for all the staff to work in
- a positive image in the community
- a growing reputation for customer service which will give it a business advantage over other sports and leisure providers.

Customers are vital to the success of a sport and leisure centre. By providing excellent customer service, the centre will be able to develop positive relations with them through customer forums or user groups. All of these will help the centre to become more and more successful.

Procedures

Finally, it is inevitable that not every customer will always receive the level of service they expect or which the centre aims to provide. But it is important in these cases that the problem is quickly sorted out to the satisfaction of the customer. The way in which we deal with complaints is as important as how we deal with satisfied customers. Therefore a complaints procedure should involve the following:

1. Any complaint is handled quickly and efficiently.
2. Any promise made is carried out.
3. Any complaint is dealt with in an agreed timescale.
4. The situation is rectified to the complete satisfaction of the customer.
5. Complaints are dealt with by staff who are polite, positive and well presented.

Key term

Procedure – an official way of doing something.

Activity: Role plays

You are a sports centre manager and have to deal with the following complaints:

- Four people turn up to use a squash court which has been double booked. But there is not a free court for 40 minutes.
- A customer has had their purse stolen from their locker.
- A customer feels that one of your lifeguards has been rude to them.
- A customer has had their car damaged in the car park.
- A customer has bought a sandwich in the cafeteria and found it to be stale.

Now repeat these but imagine the staff member dealing with this does not meet suitable standards in 1, 2, 3, 4 or 5 above.

4 Set up, check, take down and store equipment used for sports activities

Much of the work of a sports and leisure centre attendant's job will involve putting up and taking down equipment for bookings etc. The key point of this chapter is that you should be assessed actually doing this yourself.

Staff at centres will need to know how to set up a range of equipment for a variety of activities, such as team games, racquet sports, martial arts, adventurous activities and so on. So team games might require goals, nets etc. to be set up; swimming might require lane ropes and starting blocks; a gymnastics club might use trampolines and vaulting boxes.

4.1 Set up

The key to handling equipment revolves around health and safety. Equipment must be chosen, carried, set up, taken down and stored so that no one is injured. This includes staff as well as customers, spectators, coaches and so on. For each activity, the centre should have a policy that describes:

- what equipment is required – nets, posts, goals etc.
- where it is stored – each should have a specific place in a sports store
- how it should be carried, set up and taken down – one person or two? Moved by one or two persons or transported by a trolley or similar
- once set up, what checks should be made when in use – tension in cables, tightness of fasteners
- how the equipment should be stored after use – upright, in cages, locked to prevent unauthorised use etc.

4.2 Check

The different checks that are needed will depend on the equipment and activity it is used for. This will include how equipment is secured to walls or the floor, whether using handles or grips and fixed properly, as well as the personal equipment that customers wear when they participate.

4.3 Review

After you have carried out choosing, setting up etc. a range of equipment, it is important you review your own performance. Can you do anything better, safer or more efficiently? Are there areas of knowledge that need to be improved? Do you need to ask for help when setting up particular types of equipment? Do you need further training?

When setting up an activity think about all the equipment you will need for it, and give yourself enough time to set it all up.

PLTS

This assessment provides the opportunity to develop your skills as a **self-manager** and **reflective learner**.

For three different sports activities, and in front of your tutor:

- select
- set up
- check
- take down and
- store the necessary equipment to play.

1. If you need help from your tutor in any of the bullet points above you will achieve P7. If you can complete this task successfully with no support you can achieve M4.

2. Once you have completed this, write a review of how you completed each of the three tasks. Could you improve anything? Could you have completed any of the tasks in a safer manner? **P8** Now give some suitable suggestions on how you might further develop your personal performance in setting up equipment etc. This might be obtaining advice on lifting in a safer manner for instance. **M5** Having made some suggestions on improving your performance, justify and give explanations as to why these suggestions will work and improve your performance. For instance, gaining some manual handling training will make your lifting safer and make you aware of how to lift safely and what to do if the load is too big. **D2**

Grading tips

For P7, you need to show that you can get three different sports ready for people to play. You must:

- select all the equipment needed – racquets, nets, posts etc.
- check all the equipment is safe and appropriate for use – no broken strings, loose handles etc.
- set the chosen equipment up correctly – with correct space around the court or table
- take the equipment down and store it safely – using help to lift or carry as necessary.

If you need the help of your teacher or lecturer, you will achieve P7. If you do this without any assistance, you will achieve M4.

When reviewing your performance for P8, think about how you could improve. Are there ways to make your performance safer? Did you erect the equipment needed in the correct order? Did the equipment comply with the necessary rules of the sport?

For M5, add some suggestions on how you could develop further. This might include working more in a team, watching other staff put up equipment, contacting sports bodies to obtain further information and so on.

Finally, for D2, look at the suggestions you have made and tell whoever is reading your assignment why these suggestions will develop you as a sports facility operator. For instance, contacting a sports governing body will give you up-to-date information on any changes to how equipment should be set up etc.

Michael Poole
Sports centre employee

Making sure that all our customers are happy with the standard of service they receive is really important. The staff here all know each other and we all know what we are expected to do.

When I take sports classes with children, I am there five minutes before the class starts in order to welcome the children. Making sure I look the part is also really important as the children and their parents are paying a lot of money for these classes and it is vital that I give the right impression.

Each week, one of the centre managers takes staff training. This is a great way of making sure we keep our skills and knowledge up to date and it really helps to build up the team spirit here. We can ask questions about a lot of things: how the centre is doing, what needs to be improved and what the customers are saying about the way we are doing things.

I communicate all the time in my job – with the children, with my manager and with parents who bring their children to my classes. As part of the Coaching team, it is important we all understand what we have to do so that all our customers can expect a great experience when they visit.

Think about it!

Consider each of the following:

- appearance
- timekeeping
- good communication
- the right attitude
- taking part in regular staff training.

Why are they so important? Try to imagine yourself as both a customer and an employee.

Just checking

1. What is a hierarchical staff structure and why is it needed?

2. What is the difference between a role and a responsibility?

3. Name three roles or responsibilities a member of staff might have.

4. List four different areas in a sports centre where security is needed.

5. What is customer service?

6. Why is customer service important to a business?

7. Explain how you would deal with a complaint from a customer.

8. Describe how a member of staff at a sports centre should be presented.

9. Choose a sport of your choice and describe to your teacher or fellow student how the equipment required should be set up and taken down safely.

10. Write a procedure for setting up the equipment for another sport of your choice.

Assignment tips

- Try to visit your own local sports centre to get information to help you with this unit.

- Talk to any of your friends who work in the sports industry.

- Ask the caretakers at your school or college about how they carry out similar tasks.

- Use the internet. The website for the Institute of Sport and Recreation Management (see Hotlinks section on page ii for a link to this website) includes guidelines for activities such as diving, play equipment and flumes and slides. What do these guidelines provide?

16 Leading outdoor and adventurous activities

Outdoor and adventurous activities are exciting, challenging and fun to participate in. In this unit you will engage in leading outdoor and adventurous activities, and reflect on your experiences to identify and extend your knowledge and skills. As with all participation in outdoor and adventurous activities, the unit will provide opportunities for self-discovery, developing self-confidence and the development of interpersonal and communication skills, as well as leadership qualities. You will spend time in the outdoors participating in adventurous activities and developing your leadership skills.

You may have transferable skills or prior knowledge associated with the Duke of Edinburgh Award Scheme, Scouts and Guides, local clubs and perhaps with family and other groups. The unit will complement Unit 3 Outdoor and adventurous activities, allowing you to use the skills you have learned in that unit in leading others.

If you have prior experience in outdoor activities you will have an opportunity in this unit to improve and expand on that knowledge and improve your skills and technique. In this unit you will focus on developing leadership skills in two outdoor and adventurous activities, especially the associated safety aspects, making you a safer and more capable leader.

Learning outcomes

After completing this unit you should:

1. know the skills, qualities and responsibilities associated with successful outdoor and adventurous activity leadership
2. be able to plan and lead, under supervision, outdoor and adventurous activities
3. be able to review own planning and leadership of outdoor and adventurous activities.

341

Assessment and grading criteria

This table shows you what you must do in order to achieve a pass, merit or distinction grade, and where you can find activities in this book to help you.

To achieve a **pass** grade the evidence must show that the learner is able to:	To achieve a **merit** grade the evidence must show that, in addition to the pass criteria, the learner is able to:	To achieve a **distinction** grade the evidence must show that, in addition to the pass and merit criteria, the learner is able to:
P1 examine the skills, qualities and responsibilities associated with successful leadership of three different outdoor and adventurous activities **See Assessment activity 16.1, page 348**	**M1** explain the skills, qualities and responsibilities associated with successful leadership of three different outdoor and adventurous activities **See Assessment activity 16.1, page 348**	
P2 produce a plan for leading two different outdoor and adventurous activities, with tutor support **See Assessment activity 16.2, page 358**	**M2** independently produce a plan for leading, and lead under supervision, two different outdoor and adventurous activities **See Assessment activity 16.2, page 358**	
P3 lead, with tutor support and under supervision, two different outdoor and adventurous activities **See Assessment activity 16.2, page 358**		
P4 review own performance in planning and leading outdoor and adventurous activities, identifying strengths and areas for improvement **See Assessment activity 16.3, page 360**	**M3** explain own strengths and areas for improvement in leading outdoor and adventurous activities, making suggestions relating to improvement **See Assessment activity 16.3, page 360**	**D1** evaluate own performance in leading outdoor and adventurous activities, commenting on own effectiveness, strengths and areas for improvement and development as a leader of outdoor and adventurous activities **See Assessment activity 16.3, page 360**

How you will be assessed

Your assessment could be in the form of:

- practical observation
- practical tasks
- presentations
- case studies
- written assignments.

Cora, 18–year–old trainee outdoor instructor

This was the best unit that I did on the programme. I want to be an outdoor instructor and in this unit I learned so much about leading outdoor and adventurous activities.

Before I did this unit I never realised there was so much planning required before we could go and do the activity. Knowing how to do the planning and what to include all made sense and made me think about what I wanted to do in the practical activity.

Leading the practical activity was the best thing I have ever done. I was nervous to start off with but really enjoyed the responsibility of being in charge of a group of six children on the lake in kayaks. Watching them progress with the skills which I had taught them gave me a great sense of achievement.

I now definitely want to improve my skills and experience and become a full-time outdoor instructor and go and work in France or Spain for a summer season.

Over to you

- Choose two different outdoor and adventurous activities and identify the skills specific for the chosen activities a leader will require.
- What skills do you think you already have which will help you to be a successful outdoor instructor?

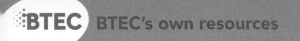

1 Know the skills, qualities and responsibilities associated with successful outdoor and adventurous activity leadership

Warm-up

Planning activities

A local youth club has approached you and asked if you can organise and deliver an outdoor activity for a group of ten 11-year-olds.

What will you need to do in the planning and delivery stages to ensure that the activity is safe and successful?

Work in pairs and make a list of all the requirements you will have to address to ensure that the activity is safe and successful.

Outdoor and adventurous activity leadership requires the leader to know the situation and context in which it will take place. Every activity needs the leader to apply different skills, for example using technical paddling skills to lead a kayak trip down a river.

In every outdoor and adventurous activity there are certain essential leadership skills. Being competent in these skills means the activities you lead will be enjoyable, constructive and safe.

1.1 Skills

Communication

Communication between the leader and the group is essential in ensuring that the activity takes place safely. Good communication means that the activity is understood by the participants and that instruction is helpful. With all communication the correct use of language is vital. As a leader you should be able to use technical language and translate this technical jargon into clear English which participants will understand. Communication is an effective tool in supervising a group and maintaining safety. Giving clear instruction provides boundaries for the activity which participants will be able to understand and adhere to.

Your role as an outdoor leader is to support the activity participants. Positive verbal encouragement and clear instruction builds understanding and confidence between participants and the activity leader, enabling you to be a successful leader.

With experience, leaders of outdoor and adventurous activities become skilled at non-verbal communication. This includes recognising a change in a participant's mood, such as someone going quiet or moving to the back of the group suggesting anxiety about the activity. Skilled leaders use their communication skills to reduce apprehension and build confidence in participants. Positive body language and clear practical demonstrations from the leader builds confidence in participants.

Decision making

Decision making involves selecting a course of action from several alternatives. Decisions may be made in advance of an activity taking place or may be dynamic, taken in reaction to a developing situation; for instance a person stuck halfway up a crag or swept away after capsizing on a river. Making the correct decision, when leading outdoor and adventurous activities, literally can mean the difference between life and death. Effective decision making is learned through observation of experienced leaders and through your own experience.

Equipment

Equipment is an important part of outdoor and adventurous activities. Leaders must be familiar with the equipment associated with the activities, capable of selecting the correct equipment for the activity, know how to use it and how to improvise the use of a particular piece of equipment if something is missing.

Improvisation

All leaders will be required to improvise the delivery of an activity at some point during their career. This could be because the equipment is not available or weather curtails the activity or prevents it from happening. For example, a planned caving activity would need to change should recent heavy rain make it unsafe to take the group to that particular cave.

Knowledge

A leader will employ knowledge when leading others. This will enable decisions to be made on safety, equipment, matching the suitability of the activity to the group, the use of appropriate skills for the activity and location of the activity. Knowledge about the activity will promote discussion with participants – enriching the experience of the activity for them.

Specific skills

Activity leaders are expected to be a coach and teacher. To progress through the national governing body award structure with a structured competitive element, like kayaking or sailing, requires the ability to coach as well as lead.

1.2 Qualities

It is often the personal qualities of the leader which make the activity enjoyable and memorable. The changing nature of outdoor and adventurous activities requires leaders to show good organisational skills and be able to work independently. Well-organised leaders eliminate many hazards associated with the activity and ensure a good experience for the participants.

Confidence shown by the leader in the activity reassures the participants that they are safe; humour also helps to reassure and makes the activity less intimidating to the participant. Such qualities should be combined with the ability to use initiative and authority and demonstrate a professional attitude to the activity and to the participants.

1.3 Responsibilities

Conduct

Leaders need to conduct themselves in a professional manner at all times when working with others. This means keeping a professional distance from the people you are working with, even if they are close to your own age. Do not become too friendly if you are a leader or lower your standards. The people you are working with will be looking to you for help and guidance; they must be able to trust you and you will need to demonstrate that you can be trusted.

Health and safety

For a detailed description on how to carry out risk assessments, see Unit 3 Outdoor and adventurous activities, page 76.

When you are leading in the outdoors you will be expected to plan and oversee the health and safety of others as well as yourself. This will include considering the following:

- aims and objectives
- knowledge of the group and its ability
- matching the activity to the ability of the group
- risk assessments
- emergency procedures
- first aid.

It is good practice, when taking a group out to do an adventurous activity for the first time, to do warm-up activities and 'ice breakers' at the beginning. This helps you get to know the group and for them to build confidence. These activities can be related to the main activity and can build skills. Due to time constraints they are often done at the start of a day's activity; but ideally they should be done in the days before the activity so that the activity can then be tailored to meet the group's needs.

Transport and travel

Young leaders will not have to transport students to an outdoor and adventurous activity venue but may have to arrange the transport. If you need to arrange transport there is very specific guidance for driving a mini bus. The most up-to-date advice can be found on the DVLA website and that of the Royal Society for the Prevention of Accidents. See Hotlinks section on page ii for links to their websites.

Equipment

Leaders should be able to select and use the correct equipment required for the activity, including any emergency equipment.

What other equipment would you take on a caving activity?

Activity: Equipment for outdoor activities

Activity	Group equipment	Individual equipment	Emergency equipment
Caving	Rope Ladders Belay equipment Caving guide/ toppo	Helmet Light Belt/harness Waterproof suit Warm clothing	First aid kit Emergency blanket and warm clothing Food/hot drink

Copy and complete the table for three different outdoor and adventurous activities. List all the equipment required for each activity.

Nutrition and hydration

Many outdoor activities need a great deal of energy. Expending energy without replacing it creates a danger of becoming very cold and tired (leading to hypothermia), thus causing safety problems for you and others. Leaders are responsible for ensuring that all those under their charge are well supplied with food and fluids. Regular stops for refreshment, where leaders can monitor everyone, are an effective way of ensuring that this happens. Leaders should carry spare food and fluids in case these are necessary. One good source is energy gels and powdered energy drinks which can be hydrated to provide a hot or cold energy drink.

Outdoor and adventurous activities

You will be assisting in delivering the following activities and the more experienced may lead them independently. For more detail on the following activities – orienteering, rock climbing, skiing, snowboarding, canoeing, kayaking, sailing, windsurfing, mountain biking, body boarding, surfing, caving – see Unit 3 Outdoor and adventurous activities.

BTEC Assessment activity 16.1

1. Consider three different outdoor and adventurous activities, with regard to successful leadership and outline the following for each:
   - Skills – communication, supervision, decision making, equipment, improvisation, knowledge, specific skills.
   - Qualities – confidence, authority, humour, organisation, initiative, style.
   - Responsibilities – conduct, health and safety, transport, equipment, contingency plans, nutrition and hydration.
2. Explain these qualities and responsibilities associated with successful leadership.

Grading tips

Choose three activities with which you are familiar and which require the demonstration of good leadership; for instance activities which require making a journey, a river trip in a kayak, or a mountain walk, or activities such as sailing where the group are spread out and the leader has to use a range of skills.

When explaining these qualities you should explain why they are needed to be a successful leader; for instance supervising a group protects the group from hazards which untrained people will not be aware of.

Functional skills

Clearly explaining your points could help to provide evidence towards functional skills in **English**.

2 Be able to plan and lead, under supervision, outdoor and adventurous activities

2.1 Plan

In order to ensure the activity runs smoothly it is essential to do all the necessary planning before undertaking any outdoor activity. Make sure that the activity is suitable for the group, that it is led by suitably experienced and qualified outdoor leaders, that you have sufficient and appropriate equipment and that correct notification and permission is obtained.

Specifics of planning

Listed below are elements of planning you may wish to consider when preparing to take a group on an adventurous outdoor activity.

- **Aims and objectives**
  Set the standards and make sure there is an educational reason for the activity taking place.

- **The group**
  The age, ability and experience in the group, the number of participants and the ratio of staff to participants all dictate the activity you plan. Never plan to do an activity just because *you* want to do it. This has led to disaster on many occasions. You must plan to meet the needs, age and ability of the group. Even if the group is experienced and capable, the ratio of staff to participants will determine the activity.

- **Activity – location and level**
  Visit the activity site and perform a risk assessment to judge whether the site is suitable for the group and to decide what equipment will be needed.

  Maps of the location help you to prepare the activity and assist in putting together contingency plans. For example, if you are leading a river trip and you have an incident, knowing where the nearest road is will help in your decision making and save time when you need to get help.

- **Permission**
  Parental consent forms, institutional consent, and medical forms are required for participants. Through stating the aims and objectives you are providing parents and senior managers at the institution with informed consent. Information about the activity allows judgement to be made about whether the activity is suitable for the child or the group.

What would you need to consider before setting off on a climbing activity?

- **Working to guidelines**

  Local authority guidelines, institutional guidelines, governing body guidelines must all be adhered to. All institutions working in the outdoor industry will have guidelines, some will be based on local authority guidelines, all will to some extent incorporate elements of the governing bodies of the activity they are involved in. Guidelines are written by very experienced and qualified practitioners with the intention to assist those with less experience and help them by suggesting what can and cannot be done.

- **Transport and logistics**

  Arranging transport can be difficult. If the activity is at a fixed location, such as a climbing crag, then it is easy. It becomes complicated when the activity is a journey; for instance for a river trip, drop-off and pick-up locations need to be arranged, two vehicles will be needed requiring a shuttle trip taking the mini bus to the finish point with a change of clothing and then a return to the start, which leaves the problem of supervision of the group while this manoeuvre takes place.

- **First aid, emergency planning and contingency measures**

  A qualified first aid person is required when leading activities; emergency plans although hopefully never needed should be included in case there are problems.

- **Allocating tasks and responsibilities**

  Delegation of tasks such as bringing up the rear and a double check of equipment, knots, etc. will take some pressure off the responsibility of leadership.

  Make lesson plans – decide which coaching methods are to be used.

  Plan to visit the activity site to assess the site and to have a 'dry run' of the planned day.

  Examine the potential hazards and how the site will influence the delivery of the activity and teaching. You need to match the site to the group.

Equipment

Being familiar with the activity and the site will help you decide what equipment is required. This is why a pre-activity visit to the site is important. Visiting the site will allow you to make an inventory of the equipment you will need.

When preparing the equipment log for all the equipment being used, good practice is to log the equipment to a person – making them responsible for that equipment. When checked back in, its usage can be tracked. If anything is lost, broken or handed back in dirty then it can be traced back to a particular person who can then be held accountable. This puts you in control of the group and the equipment.

Check that the equipment is fit for purpose before handing it out. Damaged equipment should not be used. During the activity you must remain vigilant, promoting care and respect for the equipment.

Health and safety requires a briefing and demonstration on manual handling and lifting on how to carry heavy cumbersome objects. If carrying equipment to a crag or cave, share it around.

Protection

Outdoor equipment is valuable on two levels:

1. it is expensive to replace and, in many cases, can be delicate
2. much of it is designed to protect you from harm and if damaged it may fail to do so.

Briefings on how to use and protect the equipment is important. For instance not to stand on the rope, or smoke when wearing buoyancy aids or to drop helmets.

Case study: Cadet caving

A group of young cadets who had only recently come together to form a new cadet force were on a week-long adventurous activities camp in the Mendip Hills of south west England. The group are of mixed abilities and experience; some have a good background knowledge of outdoor activities but some of the others have never participated in such challenging activities before. The main aim of the week was to use the extensive caves in the area to build teamwork and identify potential leaders within the group.

The cadet leaders all have good experience in running cadet forces but although qualified cave leaders, their caving experience is limited to group-friendly caves and they have limited experience of caving on their own in more challenging caves without groups.

As the week progressed the range of group-friendly caves became exhausted and for much of the group they are too tame. A lot of pressure was put on the leaders by the group to try more challenging caves. The leaders eventually gave in to the demands of the majority and, despite the fears of one or two others in the group, agreed to do Swildon's Hole and, if all went well, to free dive Sump 1.

All did go well on the trip and five of the group dived Sump 1 with the two staff, although one of those who

dived was pressured into doing so by both the group and the staff. Three declined the chance and stayed on the upstream side. When it came to doing the return dive one person refused to go back through the Sump and was eventually brought to the surface by the Cave Rescue team, who took six hours to reach him and bring him out.

1. Was caving a good activity to use for team building?

2. As a leader of outdoor and adventurous activities, would you allow the group to influence your choice of activity – based on what they want rather than what they are capable of?

3. Diving a submerged passage has the effect of cutting you off from an escape; was it a good idea to dive the Sump?

4. Should the leader have allowed members of the group to be cajoled into diving the Sump by other members of the group?

5. Did the party have any alternative but to call out Cave Rescue?

6. What lessons can be learned from the misadventure?

Activity: Care of equipment

Select one piece of equipment and prepare a five-minute talk on the role of that piece of equipment in the outdoors, what its properties are and how it could potentially be damaged.

Specific detailed planning

Different activities present practical differences in the activity. For example, climbing is a static activity with a static base, as is orienteering, whereas kayaking a river and mountain walking involve participants making a 'journey' as a fundamental part of that activity which could involve starting and finishing at different points. Leaders need to consider this in the planning. If it is a static activity, transport is not a problem; when making a journey, the management of transport is vital. Usually two vehicles are essential, so that you have transport at the end of the journey. This becomes even more important if the activity is in winter and could result in the participants becoming wet and cold, for instance a river trip. On such activities, as a leader you need to be busy giving instructions and making sure that the necessary clothing and equipment is there at the end of the activity.

Guidebooks and maps

There are many sources of information available to help you in your detailed planning. Guidebooks for mountain walking, caving, climbing and kayaking on both rivers and surf are available. Leaders need to understand the style and layout of these books, interpreting their

Activity: Planning an activity

You are leading a group of 10 experienced kayakers down the river Greta in the Lake District, starting in Threlkeld and finishing in Keswick – a distance of 8km.

Plan the trip by writing a brief report which highlights the key points to consider. Include:

- its length
- transport logistics
- access
- restrictions to access
- parking
- hazards
- environmental conservation and protection.

The Lake District Outdoors website could help you with this task. See Hotlinks section on page ii for a link to this website.

meaning. Map reading is a skill you will need to develop as a key part of your technical skills, not only for mountain walking but for locating caves and crags and for knowing where you are on a river.

Environmental impact

Leaders must be aware of their intrusion into the great outdoors and its impact on the environment. Activity planning should consider how the location can cope with group use; you should also consider how you can minimise the impact of group use.

Hazards

Associated with any outdoor and adventurous activity are the environmental hazards, for example, water leading to flooding in caves, rivers into spate, extreme weather which could blow campsites away or push the sailing flotilla into danger. There are also natural hazards which are there all the time, such as cliffs and rivers.

Timing

A well-planned activity with aims and objectives will have a timed structure and should be based on the aims as well as the nature and hazards of the activity. The activity will have a beginning, where you prepare the participants for the activity, provide equipment and instruction how to use the equipment, a briefing on the aims of the activity and hazards and warm-up activities which will develop skills as well as preparing the body for exercise.

The middle provides the main element of the activity; allowing participation and skill learning will make up most of the length of the activity and usually last several hours. To ensure the activity remains fun, games or break-out activities can be included; for instance if kayaking on flat water, races and tricks make a change from coaching and give participants the chance to practise their new skills in different situations.

The end or conclusion of the activity will bring together a review of the learning which has taken place and then the return and checking of the equipment.

Codes of conduct

Leaders of sporting activities must conduct themselves in an appropriate professional manner, putting the well-being of the participants at the centre of decision making and actions of the leader. You will be expected to conform to ethical standards as befits your position as leader. This will include respecting the rights of others, confidentiality and privacy, coaching with integrity and honesty and through your personal competence ensuring that the participants remain safe from harm throughout the activity.

Recent development in coaching standards has resulted in good guidance on the code of conduct for leaders.

There are several websites that provide key elements of the codes of conduct for sports coaches and governing body guidelines. See Hotlinks section on page ii for links to the websites.

Contingency

During any activity there is always the possibility of mishap and you will need to plan for such situations. Much of this planning is straightforward common sense. For instance wearing a buoyancy aid when participating in water activities is the contingency planning in case a person falls into the water; a rope when climbing does not aid the climber but it does protect them from falling.

2.2 Lead

Leading under supervision

During the practical element of the unit you will be assessed on your ability to lead others while under supervision from your tutor.

You will need to demonstrate competence in the leading of the two activities. The leading will be based on your acquisition of practical experience and to lead you will need to focus on key elements of the activity.

When planning: **who** will be the client group? **Where** will the activity take place? **What** activity will you be leading?

To do this successfully you will need a lesson plan to help and guide you and structure your session.

The following points could be included as a guide when delivering the activity:

- Introduction of session to the group.
- Setting guidelines of behaviour and gaining consensus.
- Environmental issues.
- Giving briefings – speak clearly; coping with the elements when briefing; how to say things well and what not to say.
- Equipment issue and its importance for safety and comfort. Care of equipment in use.

- A warm-up.
- Introducing a skill, using coaching methods applicable to the activity in hand, ensuring good control of safety and enjoyment for the group.
- Leadership styles while teaching: how to get success by careful observation of the individuals in the group and adapting the style to suit needs and the situation.
- Monitoring the progress of individuals during the activity in order to ensure their safety and enjoyment.
- When to stop an activity: the problems caused by peer pressure and ego. Making decisions with and without others to help.
- Concluding a session: reviews and their place, clearing up equipment.

Demonstration of skills

During the practical activity observe a specific skill fundamental to the activity being carried out by a participant. Practise and develop your coaching techniques in this skill, helping the participant improve and gain confidence to try harder skills.

Once this is mastered then progress onto another skill.

The aim is to improve your knowledge, technique and coaching skills in the activity. These skills might include:

- belaying in climbing
- using an assisted hand line in caving
- falling leaf in snowboarding
- using attack points to find controls in orienteering.

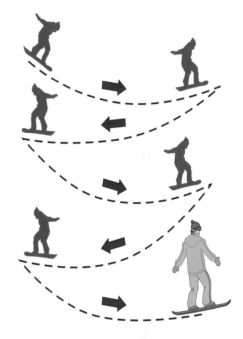

Figure 16.1: Falling leaf in snowboarding. What skills do you need to concentrate on?

Effective organisation

Before you deliver an activity for assessment, you should practise leadership roles and skills coaching with your peer group. This can be done with each group member taking it in turns to be the leader of the group and carrying out their role on the rest of the group.

You should be placed into positions of responsibility to practise the multi-roles of a leader for example:

- obtaining equipment
- demonstrating technical activity
- organising the group
- decision making.

This will help enhance your ability to organise and lead the activity.

Group management

The way in which the group is managed will influence how the individuals within the group respond to the activities.

Activity: Problem solving

In pairs, work through the scenarios listed below and identify possible solutions to the issue and styles of leadership that may fit into the situation:

- Refusal to take part in an activity.
- Student becomes stuck on a rock face.
- You and the group are lost on a mountain walk.
- A student develops a mild case of hypothermia.
- Students do not take the recommended precautions against extreme weather.
- A student refuses to move while in an underground system.
- A student/group of students ski recklessly on the slope.

At the end of the session review the solutions discussed and share them with the whole group.

Reacting to group needs

Even though thorough planning and preparation may have taken place before the activity, group dynamics will require you to react to the needs of the group as the activity progresses. How you will need to react will depend on the type of activity and the group. Examples of group needs would be dealing with the perception of danger, within the group, adapting the activity to help group members stay warm.

Qualities and responsibilities

When leading a group you must be able to adapt and use a variety of qualities to ensure that everyone in the group remains safe and the activity is worthwhile. The tables below give you some idea of what is required as a leader.

Table 16.1: Leadership skills and styles.

Leader skills	Leader styles
Motivation	Autocratic
Understanding	Democratic
Technical skills in the activity	Flat
Listening	Hierarchal
Directing	Proactive
Empathy	Reactive
Communication	Passive
Judgement	Assertive
Patience and tolerance	
Leading	
The 'sixth' sense	

Table 16.2: Leadership roles and responsibilities.

Leader roles	Leader responsibilities
Self-discipline	To participants
Good judgement	To employer
Leadership	To parents
Decision making	Other users
Delegate	To the industry
Consult	To the environment
Establish achievable aims	Landowners
Tell	To the activity
Trust	
Abdicate	

Activities

It would be very difficult to expect you to be able to lead any outdoor activity with little experience. However you should be familiar with organising kayaking, canoeing and sailing, as these are the most common water-based activities, and mountain walking, climbing and orienteering, which are the most common land-based activities.

Recording

Evidence of competence in many outdoor activities is structured through the use of a logbook to record experience in that activity, prior to taking the assessment for the qualification. To keep the qualification current the logbook is kept up to date with personal and group experience acquired in your professional capacity of leading groups.

Figure 16.1: A logbook page might look like this.

Venue	Status	Group and activity	Number of days	Date	For whom	Comments
Stanage Edge Derbyshire	Assistant leader	Rock climbing Top and bottom roping	2	26/27 May 2008	Peak District College	10 in group never climbed before Set up anchors and demonstrated climbs and how to belay
Attermire Scar Yorkshire Dales	Leader	Top roping and abseiling	1	6 June 2008	Yorkshire Dales College	6 in group Worked as leader with assistant leader. Experienced group allowing more challenging climbs to be attempted

For the purpose of your assessment, other methods of recording your experience can also be used; for example diaries, observation records, video evidence. However if you are enrolled on a governing body qualification scheme then it is important that you use the logbook you will be provided with to record your experience. This is the only valid way for that particular scheme.

Activity: Logging experiences

Using the logbook template, log all your experience in the different activities you have acquired so far in the different activities.

Logbook templates can be found on the Mountain Leader Training England website. See Hotlinks section on page ii for a link to the website.

PLTS

During this part of the unit you will have the opportunity to develop your skills as a **team worker** and **self-manager**.

Functional skills

This activity could help develop your **English** skills in reading and writing.

BTEC ## Assessment activity 16.2

1. Written class-based activity **P2**, **M2** plan two sessions for leading different outdoor and adventurous activities.

   Provide a detailed lesson plan and risk assessment for each activity.

2. Practical **P3**, **M2**

   Prepare to lead and lead two different outdoor and adventurous practical sessions.

   (Prepare feedback observation sheets for participants, observers and peers and use them to obtain feedback on your performance post activity.)

Grading tip

Your detailed lesson plan will break the activity down into stages including: meeting the group, health and safety briefing and getting to know the group, a warm-up, instructing the activity and use of equipment, and a cool-down and review of the activity. See page 76 for guidance on how to do a risk assessment.

When delivering the activity, make sure you have everything well planned; name tags for each member of the group will help you remember names and be in more control of the group. Check all equipment and make sure you have sufficient kit. Be confident and instruct the group on how to succeed in the activity.

3 Be able to review own planning and leadership of outdoor and adventurous activities

3.1 Review

In preparation for leading a session plan, consider the following:

- How you will obtain feedback from participants, peers and observers.
- How will you use this feedback to improve your performance?

The feedback sheets should be examining your performance, both in the planning and delivery stages of the activity. When considering what feedback you need, think about the following:

- Feedback should ask specific questions of the different groups. For instance, did the participants feel they were safe and well looked after, with clear educational objectives set for the session?
- Did your peers feel that you contributed to all elements of the session and that you made a valuable contribution to the activity delivery?
- Did the observers recognise that you conducted yourself in a professional, trustworthy effective manner, showing leadership and responsibility?
- From the feedback you have acquired, and your own self-reflection, identify your strengths and areas for improvement.
- When reflecting on your own performance, work through the different stages of the activity from the planning through to the preparation for review and the review itself.
- Did you meet all the targets you set for yourself and did you stay within the planning constraints you set?
- What did you do well?
- What areas do you need to improve upon?

3.2 Set targets for improvement

To develop as an outdoor leader, reflect on your performance and how it can be improved. This often requires you to practise your own skills, meaning that if you are a paddler you are going onto rivers or into the surf and playing; if you are a climber, you will go onto crags and try climbing new routes. Such activities help you develop your skills as well as knowing what the boundaries are in such activities.

There are also many training courses run by governing bodies, or approved agents of governing bodies, designed to improve your skills and assess your capabilities as an outdoor leader.

Figure 16.2 shows how to set targets to improve using SMART. See also Unit 3 page 89.

Figure 16.2: Using SMART to set targets to improve.

Areas for improvement	Specific measurable skill	Realistic actions	Realistic outcomes	Time-bound	Further work	Extension Activities
Demonstrating correct paddle strokes when kayaking	Demonstrate correct strokes giving good picture of technical correctness	Practise strokes Video self for visual feedback of self-completing stroke	Able to demonstrate technically correct strokes	September 2010	Practise advanced strokes for next stage of development	Participate in river trips and advance kayaking courses

PLTS

This activity will help develop your skills as a **reflective learner**.

Functional skills

Using ICT to present information will enable you to improve your **ICT** skills.

BTEC ## Assessment activity 16.3

1. Review both the planning and leading stages carried out in the assessment activity task 2. In the review of your performance refer to the feedback you obtained after the activity.

2. For each activity identify and explain your strengths and areas for improvement.

3. Explain your strengths and areas for improvement, suggesting valid ways of improving your performance.

4. Evaluate your own performance in leading outdoor and adventurous activities, commenting on own leadership, the effectiveness of your leadership, the strengths and areas for improvement and development.

Grading tips

When obtaining feedback, ask closed questions. For example, 'Tell me three skills which I was good at and why.'

List three skills which you think you are good at and three in which you think you need to improve.

When explaining your own strengths, and how you think you can improve further, use the feedback received. Identify key areas for improvement; for instance it may take you too long to set up anchor points for a climbing session, leaving the group unoccupied. You could improve this skill by practising placing anchors and setting up rigging ropes.

Evaluate your performance by suggesting how long it will take you to improve to the standard you would like to be at and what you will be able to do when you reach this standard. What is the timespan for improving these skills?

Mark Massey

Multi-activity outdoor instructor

In the summer I work for a holiday company in the South of France, leading school children and families on adventurous activities. The work is very mixed. Some days I am kayaking or canoeing down the Ardeche River leading a group of 10 people; I also lead walks in the local mountains, take groups rock climbing and recently we have started doing mountain bike tours.

Typical day

A typical day would require me to collect all the equipment from the stores, check and prepare it for the group. I would then meet the group and brief them on the activity. Sometimes this can be difficult because we have a mix of those who are staying with us for the week and others who just do one day of activities with us. It is on these days that I have to use all my skills and experiences to make the activities interesting and fun for everyone.

After I have briefed the group we then learn how to use the equipment before doing the activity. Leading the activity is the best part. I have to make sure that the activity is safe and keep a watch on the people all the time to make sure that they are doing it correctly. I always try to make sure that everyone has a job, which makes my job easier.

After the end of the activity, I will have a talk with the group and debrief them; I then check the equipment again and return it to the stores.

The best thing about the job

I enjoy the water activities the most, especially in the hot summer months. As a group we can all keep moving and no one minds if they fall in when paddling the fast-moving parts of the river. In fact, people are more willing to try difficult manoeuvres and tricks on the water because they do not mind falling in!

At the end of the day I can go play with the other instructors; often we go climbing and being here with other climbers has really developed my own climbing skills.

Think about it!

- Why does Mark always check the equipment out and in?
- Why would Mark want to get everyone in the group involved in activities when he can?

Just checking

1. List three skills associated with successful outdoor and adventurous activity leadership.
2. List three responsibilities a leader of an outdoor and adventurous activity will be responsible for.
3. List three factors about participants that you should know about before undertaking an outdoor and adventurous activity.
4. What should you do with your logbook and diary at the end of every activity day?
5. How could you review your planning and leadership of your outdoor and adventurous activities?

edexcel

Assignment tips

- **Communication** – When talking to a group, always ensure you have their full attention. Wait until everyone in the group is listening; do not try to give instruction if anyone in the group is not paying attention. Always check that the group understands what you have asked them to do by getting them to explain their task back to you.
- **Health and safety** – When leading an activity, play little games of Eye Spy with yourself to help you identify all the potential hazards in and around the activity. This will help develop your awareness of the environment you are using for the activity and where things could go wrong.
- **Equipment** – When preparing to lead an activity, have your personal equipment packed and ready to go, and make sure you know how to use it. Not only will this help you to look professional, but it will also allow you to concentrate on assisting the group with their needs.
- **Planning** – Make a thorough session plan, including timings, for the activity you are to lead. Take it with you in a waterproof protective case. This will help you to remember teaching points and safety briefings when required.

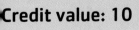

Credit value: 10

17 Expedition experience

Expeditions – 'journeys with a purpose' – have taken place for thousands of years for a variety of reasons, ranging from conquest and scientific exploration to competition. With lifestyles becoming generally more sedentary and risk averse, expeditions are seen as a valuable way of replacing risk, challenge, self-reliance, teamwork and leadership lost from everyday activity and enriching our lives. Those who already have expedition experience will have an opportunity in this unit to improve and expand their knowledge base, and improve their expedition techniques and skills.

The unit focuses on the development of skills in navigation and route planning, safety and emergency procedures including risk assessment, recognition of natural hazards, the effects of cold, heat, dehydration and exhaustion. Environmental and countryside issues are also covered, giving you an understanding of laws when in the countryside and the environmental impact of expeditions. Completion of this unit requires at least one overnight stay where the emphasis will be on a practical ability to choose the correct equipment, and demonstrate proficient use of specific expedition kit.

Learning outcomes

After completing this unit you should:

1. know the safety and environmental considerations for a multi-day expedition
2. be able to use skills and techniques required for a multi-day expedition
3. be able to plan for a multi-day expedition
4. be able to carry out and review a multi-day expedition.

Assessment and grading criteria

This table shows you what you must do in order to achieve a pass, merit or distinction grade, and where you can find activities in this book to help you.

To achieve a **pass** grade the evidence must show that the learner is able to:	To achieve a **merit** grade the evidence must show that, in addition to the pass criteria, the learner is able to:	To achieve a **distinction** grade the evidence must show that, in addition to the pass and merit criteria, the learner is able to:
P1 describe the safety and environmental considerations for a multi-day expedition	**M1** explain safety and environmental considerations for a multi-day expedition	
P2 demonstrate the skills and techniques required for a multi-day expedition **See Assessment activity 17.1, page 383**	**M2** explain the skills and techniques required for a multi-day expedition **See Assessment activity 17.1, page 383**	**D1** justify use of skills and techniques in the undertaking of a multi-day expedition **See Assessment activity 17.1, page 383**
P3 describe the equipment required for a multi-day expedition **See Assessment activity 17.1, page 383**		
P4 produce a plan, with tutor support, for a multi-day expedition [SM3] **See Assessment activity 17.1, page 383**	**M3** independently produce a plan for a multi-day expedition **See Assessment activity 17.1, page 383**	**D2** justify decisions made in the planning of a multi-day expedition **See Assessment activity 17.1, page 383**
P5 carry out, with tutor support, a multi-day expedition, demonstrating the use of relevant skills and required equipment **See Assessment activity 17.1, page 383**	**M4** independently undertake a multi-day expedition demonstrating the use of relevant skills and required equipment **See Assessment activity 17.1, page 383**	
P6 review own performance in the planning and undertaking of a multi-day expedition, identifying strengths and areas for improvement	**M5** explain identified strengths and areas for improvement, suggesting strategies to improve future performance	**D3** evaluate performance in the planning and undertaking of a multi-day expedition, suggesting strategies to improve future performance and justifying suggestions

How you will be assessed

This unit will be assessed by an internal assignment designed and set by staff at your centre specifically to match the unique situation of your programme of study. Your assessment could be in the form of:

- practical observation
- practical tasks
- presentations
- case studies
- written assignments.

Jamie, 17–year-old outdoor student

I really enjoyed this unit. We spent a lot of time outside learning how to navigate and use the equipment like tents and stoves. I'm now a good map reader. I learnt a lot about planning expeditions, especially choosing the area to go which would be best for us, how to be safe and how to get help if needed. I found out about the wildlife and environment and learned how to help conserve the area where we visited. Our motto was 'take only photographs, leave only footprints'.

At night, care was needed because it was raining and there was a danger that my tent could be flooded if I put the tent in the wrong place.

During the expedition I led the group many times and this was challenging. It was fantastic learning how to work as a group and then using those skills to complete the expedition. Discussing it at the end helped me to understand why we had done all the planning and carried out the expedition that way. I learnt a lot and there are also some things I would not do the same again.

Over to you

- What aspects of this unit do you think you will particularly enjoy?
- Which aspects will you find most challenging?

1 Know the safety and environmental considerations for a multi-day expedition

Warm-up

Health and safety

When undertaking either a one-day or multi-day expedition you must think about safety. In 1971, five teenagers and a student teacher died from hypothermia on an expedition in the Cairngorm mountains in Scotland. The jury who sat at the public enquiry made recommendations on health and safety which have developed into industry principles of good practice. Working in pairs, list what you think is good practice when participating in expeditions.

1.1 Safety considerations

Risk assessments

Risk assessments that are written in the planning stage of an expedition are designed to help you manage potential hazards. They will not eliminate hazards but can make you aware of them. During the expedition you should show vigilance, looking out for hazards like a change in the weather, swollen rivers and cliffs. This is known as a dynamic risk assessment and helps to ensure a safe expedition. For more detailed guidance on how to complete a risk assessment, and the role it plays in the outdoors, see Unit 3 Outdoor and adventurous activities page 76.

Emergency procedures

On expedition you may be alone as a group. Even if you take precautions because of bad weather, illness or poor decision making, there is a chance that an emergency could happen. The practical training you will undertake during this unit and good planning for the expeditions will prepare you.

Survival

Many emergency situations have been made worse by groups who remained where they were – when they could have left the situation before it deteriorated. However, if this is not possible, the first task is survival. Those who have survived in difficult circumstances have worked to survive, finding cover from extremes of weather, making shelter and keeping each other warm through hot food and drink and extra clothing.

Contacting emergency services

Once the situation has stabilised, and everything has been done to ensure survival, contact emergency services. Mobile phone network coverage is improving and can help to raise the alarm but there are still areas with no coverage. This means someone has to raise the alarm. Going for help is a difficult decision – who goes and how many? Is it safe to go for help? When you do go for help, you should use the safest route and note that this may not be the fastest or closest to the place of help.

When you phone 999 you must ask for the Police and then Mountain Rescue. If you are on a large body of water, explain this and be guided by the call operator as some lakes have their own rescue services. You will need to give the following information:

- Where are the group, grid reference and description of area with place names?
- How many in the party?
- Who is injured and what are the injuries?
- The experience of the party.
- How well are they equipped and what was the physical and mental state of the party when you left them?

Remain by the phone ready to answer further questions.

Distress signals

If you have to raise the alarm from where you are, the standard signalling system is six blasts on a whistle repeated every minute or, if

Table 17.1: Details of different types of emergency equipment.

Type of emergency equipment	How it is used	Different types	Advantages	Disadvantages
Emergency shelter	Provides shelter from worst of elements to casualty or whole group if required	Tent	Free-standing strong If on multi-day expedition will be carrying tents Can put up tent outer to give larger shelter	Can be heavy Cannot be put up everywhere Tents requiring inner put up first restrict how many people can be given shelter
		Emergency shelter (KISU)	Light, day expedition alternative to carrying a tent Accommodates whole group providing cohesion Provides shelter anywhere people can sit down	Requires people inside to make it work Sides made of people, those sitting against wind get cold very quickly

Table 17.1 (Cont.)

Type of emergency equipment	How it is used	Different types	Advantages	Disadvantages
Survival bag	A large plastic bag casualty can be put inside and sheltered from weather	Large plastic bag	Light, cheap and easily replaced if damaged Everyone can carry one Can be split open to slide the casualty in if too badly injured to fit in from one end Another person can also fit inside Can be used as emergency signal	Thin, may stop water but poor at retaining warmth
		'Gore-tex' bivi bag	Waterproof and warm	Expensive Tight fitting so difficult to place casualty inside Owner could be reluctant to cut open
Warm clothing	Insulates from cold, cold/injured person	Sleeping bag	Full body coverage Second person can get inside to add extra warmth Reassuring	Person cannot move when using it Bulky
		Duvet jacket	Packs down small Can still move if required	Does not provide full body coverage Second person cannot get inside to add extra warmth
First aid kit	Provides essential medical equipment for treatment of minor ailments	Can be bought off the shelf in most outdoor shops or made up to suit specific needs	Contains basic essentials to deal with minor situations Provides focus in emergencies	Tendency to put in too much equipment Lack of training in how to use them
Torch	To provide light To use as means of signalling	Hand held Head mounted Battery powered Wind up	There are torches which are lightweight, long-life and cheap. Head torches allow 2 free hands for other jobs	Hand held use a hand which could be used doing other jobs like holding a tent

Table 17.1 (Cont.)

Type of emergency equipment	How it is used	Different types	Advantages	Disadvantages
Whistle	Only used in outdoors as a means of emergency signalling	Any	Light, simple to use Can be used by individual to signal for help Effective way of signalling for help	When windy can be difficult to locate direction May not hear it
Mobile phone	Often carried	Any	Texts can be sent when signal weak or will be sent when signal is found If have signal fast and effective Advice can be given immediately	Can be used for trivial reasons, bringing out rescue services for minor reasons Lack of signal
Food	Used to give energy and revive cold tired person	Chocolate Carbohydrate Energy drinks Hot drinks	High-sugar content will give immediate boost to person tired or cold Hot drinks will revive cold tired person quickly Will prevent others deteriorating if waiting around	Can lead to complacency when person makes quick recovery If person allowed to deteriorate too far, difficult to administer any food or drink
Stoves (dangerous/combustible substances)	To heat food To heat shelter	Solid fuel	Simple to use Simple to store and carry	Gives off toxic soot Covers pans in soot Can contaminate food Slow
		Liquid fuel	Simple to use	Difficult to light when cold Fast burning requiring large amounts for long expedition Easily spilt
		Gas fuel	Simple to use Simple to store and carry Fast	Pressurised container Can leak Explosive

dark, six flashes of a light. If on a large body of open water you should have smoke flares. Setting off a smoke flare will alert those nearby that you are in difficulties.

One of the most common reasons for emergencies on expedition is lack of energy and tiredness leading to hypothermia. Having enough spare food, a stove, sleeping bag and shelter will help you manage.

Escape routes

These are pre-planned routes which lead you to lower, sheltered ground; they are designed to help you escape quickly and safely.

Governing body guidelines

For details on governing body guidelines refer to Unit 3 Outdoor and adventurous activities, page 75.

Did you know?

At 24 years of age Ellen MacArthur was the youngest person ever to complete the Vendee Globe solo, non-stop round-the-world yacht race. She was the fastest woman and the youngest sailor to sail around the world non-stop.

Case study: Dales emergency

A group of BTEC First Diploma Outdoor students are completing their final expedition in the Yorkshire Dales – unaccompanied by staff. They have undergone all the training required. The staff who trained them are confident that they have the necessary leadership and technical skills to survive in the outdoors for the length of the expedition.

To ensure they are safe, and help is close by, the leaders asked the group to do route cards with emergency escape routes should they get into difficulties. Marked on these route cards were points and times where staff would be located should help be required.

While traversing a remote ridge section of the route into a strong cold wind and rain, Harry (who suffers from diabetes) had a diabetic incident and was slipping into a hypoglycaemic coma. The group stopped, put up their tent, gave Harry some food and kept him warm by wrapping him in a sleeping bag and giving him a hot drink. After one hour Harry felt much better and felt he was able to carry on the planned route.

The ridge they were walking on had two planned escape routes to the valley and shelter and they had passed through one of the staffed help points, 3km back on the route they had just walked.

After another 30 minutes of walking on their planned route Harry felt unwell again and quickly slipped into a hypoglycaemic coma. Two other group members were now also shivering uncontrollably and felt unwell. One member of the group went for help and raised the alarm. After six hours the Mountain Rescue service reached Harry, eventually evacuating him to hospital. They had to call on the help of another rescue team to help them evacuate the rest of the group from the hill.

In small groups discuss the series of events and consider the following questions.

1. What led to the situation becoming serious?

2. What mistakes were made during the day?

3. At what point should the group have started to think about alternative options?

4. What were the alternative options the group had?

5. Could the situation requiring the mountain rescue have been avoided?

1.2 Environmental considerations

Respect, preserve and conserve

On expedition you must protect the environment. The expedition may take place in a National Park or an Area of Outstanding Natural Beauty. There may also be zones of special significance. For instance, in certain areas of the Limestone Dales, there are rare orchids which are easily damaged.

Status

Throughout Britain there are protected areas and species. Protected areas include National Parks and Areas of Outstanding Natural Beauty. There are also areas like Sites of Special Scientific Interest (SSSI). SSSIs protect smaller areas for reasons which could include unusual landscape features, such as limestone pavement or rare plants and animals, usually of international significance. See Hotlinks section on page ii for links to websites where you can find out more about the protected flora and fauna.

Legislation

In the countryside there are laws which govern where you can go and what you can do. The Wildlife and Countryside Act 1981 gives protection to flora and fauna. By-laws also exist and are used to manage the land. They can be used to close access to land if there is a danger of fire or the spread of biohazards.

The Countryside Code

There are also codes about how you should behave in the countryside. The Countryside Code helps protect the landscape and the living environment. It is based on laws which can result in prosecution if broken. For example, picking wild flowers, disturbing nesting birds, hunting animals with dogs or starting fires during drought are all offences. There are five sections of the Countryside Code, which will help you to respect, protect and enjoy the countryside.

See Hotlinks section on page ii for a link to a website that gives more detailed information about the Countryside Code.

Rights of way

Maps show footpaths, bridleways and permissive paths. These are known as rights of way. This means you can legally walk on footpaths or walk, ride a bike or horse on bridleways. In 2000 the Countryside and Rights of Way Act was passed. This gives you the right to roam off paths into mapped areas known as 'Open Access Land'.

2 Be able to use skills and techniques required for a multi-day expedition

2.1 Navigation skills

The most essential tool used for finding our way is a map.

Maps translate a three-dimensional landscape to a two-dimensional drawing. The skill is to see these features on a map and recognise what they represent on the ground and find your way. A common map scale for expeditions is 1:25000: 1cm on the map is equal to 25 000cm or 250 metres on the ground, or 4cm on the map is equal to 1km on the ground. This type of map gives walkers lots of detail. The other commonly used map has a 1:50000 scale: 1cm on the map equals 50 000cm or 500m on the ground. This map has less detail but covers a much wider area.

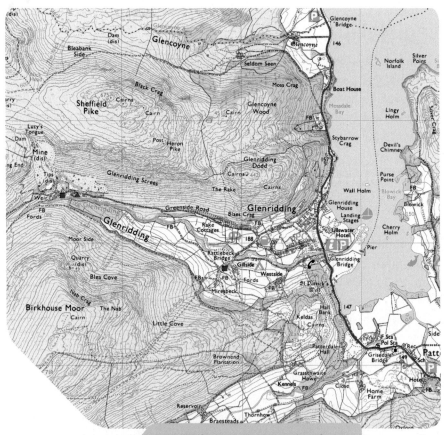

List the features you can identify from this section of map.

Grid references

Maps which are used for navigation are divided into 1km square grids made up by lines going from top to bottom of the map (called Eastings) and lines going across the map (called Northings). Eastings and Northings are all given a two number code; this code enables every square on the map to be given a unique code known as a grid reference.

The UK is divided into a grid system, known as the National Grid, which gives a reference number for any point in the UK. Figure 17.1 shows how to carry out a grid reference.

Four-figure grid references

When reading grid references, there are basic rules to follow. The first two reference numbers should be read across from left to right; these are the Eastings. The second two reference numbers should be read vertically from the bottom of the map; these are Northings. These coordinates locate the 1km square.

The square with Town A in it has a grid reference of 22 15.

Did you know?

Britain was first divided into grids 200 years ago when the first thorough mapping of this country was carried out to help the army defend the country should Napoleon have invaded! That is why they are called Ordnance Survey maps – reflecting their original military purpose.

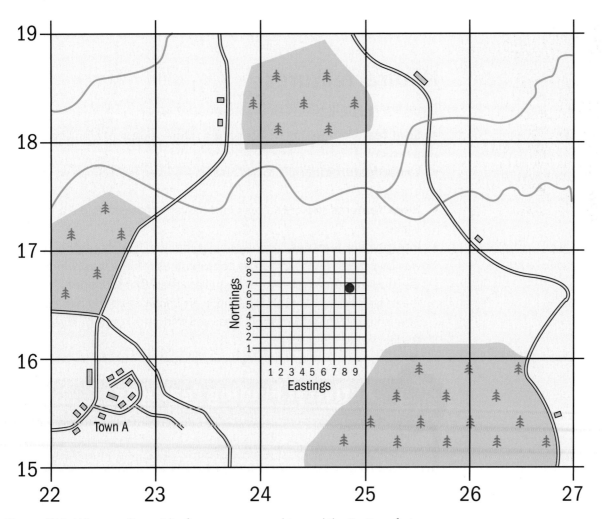

Figure 17.1: When reading grid references, you need to read the Eastings first, then the Northings. What is the grid reference for the red dot?

Six-figure grid references

A six-figure grid reference gives a much more exact and pinpointed location and is the most commonly used code when on expeditions. With a six-figure grid reference the first two numbers are the Easting number and used to locate the 1km square. The third number is used to subdivide that square into tenths. For example, if the number was 5 it would divide the square halfway between the two whole numbers. The fourth and fifth numbers are the Northing numbers and again are used to find the 1km square. The sixth number divides the square into tenths again. The red dot has a grid reference of 248 166.

Activity: Using grid references

Write down five six-figure grid references which identify a feature on the map in the book; be precise and choose a range of different features. Then swap these with another person and practise finding grid references. This exercise will also help you to become familiar with different map features.

Natural features

There are four different features shown by maps:

- **Spot features** identify points on the map – a church, a bridge, a trig point.
- **Linear features** identify long features – a river, footpath, a wall, a crag.
- **Block features** show features which cover a mass of land – a forest, a lake.
- **Interpretive features** help us look at the land in a three-dimensional way by putting lines (known as contour lines) on the map which show the shape of the land, hills, valleys, flat areas. Contour lines also show the map reader how high the land is and how steep the hillside is. This is important information when planning the route or if you have to get off the hill quickly.

Activity: Finding features

Look at a section of an Ordnance Survey (OS) map. How many examples of spot, linear, block and interpretive features can you find?

Direction determination

Navigating involves using a map to find your way from one point to another. The first task is to orientate the map.

Map orientation is achieved by lining up the features on the map to the features on the ground. When this has been achieved some facts are established. The top of the map is always north and this should point to the north.

Orientating a map to the surrounding features will help to establish where you are on the map. From this position, and by looking at the features and then reading the map, you will know which way you need to go.

Specific navigation skills include the following.

Ticking off features

When you are going along a route, a change in direction onto a different path may be required. Before getting to the change in direction you need to cross over four streams. Tick off each stream when walking the route and after four streams that would indicate you were close to where you needed to change direction.

Pacing

Pacing estimates the distance you have travelled by counting the number of steps you take to cover a set distance. You can then calculate how far you have walked. It is useful when you are walking over featureless terrain following a compass bearing. It has its limitations, however. The further you walk when pacing the less accurate it is and walking up or down hill will shorten or lengthen your stride pattern – affecting how many paces it takes you to walk a set distance.

Calculating distance through time

This measures distance travelled by knowing how long it takes to walk a set distance. The rough approximation is 1km in 15 minutes over flat ground; approximately 4 minutes to walk 250m. Knowing this and using the map you can work out where you are and when to start thinking about route choice.

Figure 17.2: Orienting a map is essential when you are trying to navigate. What features would you look out for?

Did you know?

To work out your pace for 100m, you must first measure out the 100m. Then count the number of paces it takes to walk the 100m. To get an accurate figure repeat the task. Now take the average of the two. A pace is two steps.

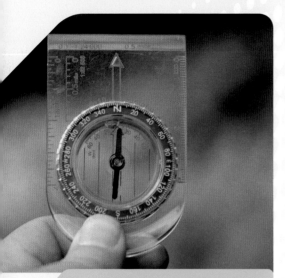

Are you confident that you can use a compass correctly?

Route choice

When navigating from one point to the next, route choice is vital. As a navigator you should look for clues – features which are going to tell you where you are – walls, streams, crags, hills and the shape of the land.

The compass

The crucial tool used in navigation beside a map is a compass.

The compass needle sits in the compass housing and floats in liquid. The needle is magnetised and the earth's magnetic field makes the arrow point to the north.

Night or limited visibility navigation

Knowing which way is north is important when navigating. It means you can always orientate the map. When you cannot see any features, because it is dark or misty, you can use a technique known as following a **compass bearing** to go in the direction you want.

Following a compass bearing is simple; more advanced techniques called 'aiming off' and 'attack points' require practice.

To use a compass bearing, place the compass on the map. Imagine it is a ruler and you are going to draw a line from where you are to where you want to go. It is important that the 'direction of travel arrow' on the compass points in the way you want to go. Turn the compass housing until the orientating lines match up with the grid lines on the map, ensuring the 'North' indicator points to the top of the map. Now take the compass off the map, add 3 degrees to what your indicator says (grid north and magnetic north are at two different points and the difference is currently 3 degrees). Line up the floating arrow with the arrow in the compass housing and then follow the direction of travel arrow to get to where you want to go.

Activity: Grid references

Practising reading grid references by identifying 10 different features on the map. Write down the six-figure grid references for the 10 features and swap with your partner who identifies them.

Using the map on page 372 and a compass, set five compass bearings for a partner by choosing two points on the map and asking them to work out what the compass bearing is.

2.2 Camping

If you are camping you must first make sure that the site is going to be free from flooding, close to water, in a sheltered area. Walls make good shelters, so do natural features like woodland. Tents should be put up so that the sides or entrance are not presented to the prevailing wind. This helps to stop the tent being flattened by the wind and stops rain blowing in the entrance.

Once in your tent, you must do your best to keep the weather out. Do not get into your tent with wet clothing and boots on. Keep the entrance closed and clear of equipment. Keep it tidy, only getting out equipment when you need it. Before you settle into your tent at night, ensure that you have everything you need. If careful you can cook in the outer part of the tent, but never inside the tent, keep any tent flaps away from flames and allow moisture to escape.

What do you look out for before you erect your tent?

2.3 Transportation

Decide the mode of transport you use for your expedition. The majority of expeditions will be on foot. Canoeing expeditions are good, if you have the skills and equipment.

3 Be able to plan for a multi-day expedition

3.1 Equipment

The correct equipment is essential. Tents, sleeping bags, stoves and personal equipment are vital when going on overnight expeditions. You must know how to use all your equipment, especially when the weather is poor.

Tents

Tents for expeditions should be weatherproof, strong and light. You will need a light mountain tent if you are making a long journey with different campsites every night. If staying at a base camp, and undertaking day expeditions, a more permanent, comfortable tent can be used. The different types of tent can be viewed on the website 'abc of hiking' see Hotlinks section on page ii for a link to the website.

Stoves

Different types of stove are defined by the fuel they use. The most common use a mixture of propane and butane gas. On longer expeditions the biggest problem is having enough fuel and this should be considered when planning which stove to take. Remember that

 Did you know?

Two people changed a gas canister inside their tent and crossed the threads of the canister – resulting in gas escaping into the enclosed space of the tent. Not realising their mistake they then tried to light the stove. The following explosion caused only minor burns. But severe burns were caused by the flames fed by the escaping pressurised gas from the leak – while being trapped inside the burning tent. If they had changed the canister outside, the incident would not have occurred.

stoves are potentially very dangerous! Most groups use Trangia stoves which are simple and effective.

Sleeping bags

Sleeping bags should be warm, small and light. Man-made insulating materials are not good at being compressed and are heavy but retain warmth when wet, are easy to wash and last a long time. Natural materials are light and offer high warmth to weight ratios, but are easily damaged. The most important personal equipment will be your boots and waterproof shell.

Boots

It is essential that boots should be comfortable and waterproof. Take care of them, clean them and re-weather proof them regularly. Cold wet feet mean a cold body.

Expedition clothing

You should wear comfortable clothing which is warm with some wind resistance. Many thin layers are better than one layer as this allows for regulation of body heat. A good pair of walking socks will reduce the chance of blisters. Windproof hats and gloves make life easier if it is cold and windy.

Waterproof shell

A waterproof outer shell protects you from the wind and rain. It is common to have a garment which allows perspiration to evaporate through a membrane while keeping rain out. This keeps you dry, warm and comfortable.

Rucksacks

Rucksacks are used to carry heavy weights as the load is carried by your skeletal frame and they keep your hands free. The rucksack should fit your frame. Use the hip belt to reduce the load on your shoulders. When packing it, you should put the equipment you are unlikely to need during the day at the bottom. Put your equipment inside a plastic bag. Put contaminates like liquid fuel in a separate pocket.

Maintenance

It is a good idea to employ a checking out/checking in system. Never put away wet equipment; always make sure it works and all the pieces are there. A drying room enables equipment, like tents and waterproof clothing, to be cleaned and dried. A washing line or store room where the equipment can be stored is as effective. When on expedition you may have to pack away when wet, but make sure you do not mix dry

Did you know?

A lot of heat is lost through contact with a cold floor when camping. A simple foam carry mat is very effective at insulating you from the cold floor.

Did you know?

Walking with arms folded or clasped behind, under the rucksack, will help rest the shoulders.

Table 17.2: Essential items to pack in your rucksack.

Essential	Desirable features	Seasoned expeditioners often...
Sleeping mat	Full length to prevent legs becoming cold	Rucksack can be used as sleeping mat for lower body
Sleeping bag	Compression stuff sack to make the bag small	Sleeping bag liners can improve warmth or can put feet inside rucksack at night
Stove, fuels and cooking utensils	Some stoves and utensils integrated Matches protected from wet or lighter Pan scrubber	For very lightweight camping tinfoil pans can be used Any type of lid helps water boil faster and saves fuel
Tent	Plastic bags to put different parts in if wet	Folding tent away properly makes it easier to put up again at night
Food for duration of trip	Snacks such as nuts and raisins	Use energy gels and energy bars to maintain energy levels Use a water pouch during the day to keep hydrated
Hygiene kit	Liquid soap Wet wipes Tooth brush	Keep hands clean so reducing chance of food poisoning
Torch	Head torch allows hands to be free	Carry spare batteries and bulb
Spare warm clothing	Many thin layers are more effective and adaptable	Pack clothing away into dry bags Put hat and gloves in small sealable plastic bags
Waterproofs	Have hood and good overlap between top and bottom	Gaiters for lower legs help prevent feet getting wet
First aid kit	Energy gels 'Compeed' blister plasters	Emergency sewing kit to repair kit. Spare duct tape and cord Sharp knife

Remember

The maximum amount of weight you should carry while on expedition is 25–30% of your body weight.

things with wet things. The tent outer may be wet but the inner dry, so keep them separate. Carrier bags are good for this. Take care of your equipment and follow care instructions. The website for outdoor gear provides an overview for care of equipment. See Hotlinks section on page ii for a link to the website.

Activity: Equipment practise

Take all your camping equipment to an open area and practise putting up the tent, arranging your equipment when in the tent, your 'housekeeping' skills and using the stove to cook food on. Then take it down again, making sure you pack it away carefully and that all parts are present, including all the tent pegs!

Plan

A through plan for an expedition helps to ensure it is successful, enjoyable and safe.

Permission, consent and access

To ensure that permission is given, you must explain the expedition's aims and objectives. Include full information on the planned area for the expedition, participants, leaders and emergency plans to enable 'informed consent' to be given by the authorities and parents of participants.

In planning you need good knowledge of the practical difficulties you may encounter, like the terrain you will be travelling over and the skills you will need. Those giving permission need to know that you are capable of achieving the planned objectives.

Route (route cards, route description, journey time, contingencies and escapes)

You should include route cards when seeking permission. This shows good planning and enables informed consent. Route cards make sure the expedition is not too difficult by making you calculate how far you will travel each day and how long it will take. Naismith's Rule is a set formula used to calculate how long it takes to walk a set distance. The formula is 15 minutes to walk 1km over flat ground, 1 minute for every 10 minutes gained in height; if no height is gained or height is lost time is not taken off. You should also put emergency escape routes on the route card.

Activity: Route cards

Route cards are used as a planning tool, to help ensure that those undertaking an expedition know where they are going. It is also an important safety tool, letting those who are not on the expedition know where the expedition is going and where to look for them should they need help.

Day Expedition Route Card

18th March 2009

Patterdale/ Helvellyn/ Patterdale

Lake District NE Explorer Map OL5

Complete the route card and plan the emergency escapes using the map on page 372.

From	To	Distance	Height gained	Time	Running total	Notes
Patterdale Church	Thornhowe Path junction 383,157	1km	50m	20 mins		Escape route return to start
Thornhowe Path junction 383,157	Ruthwaite lodge 357,135	3km				Escape route return to start
Ruthwaite lodge 357,135	Ruthwaite cove 348,139	1.8km				Escape route return to start
Ruthwaite cove 348,139	Dollywagon pike 343,131	0.8km				Walk down path to Grisedale Tarn and then to Dunmail Raise 327,117
Dollywagon pike 343,131	Helvellyn 342,152					Walk down path to Grisedale Tarn and then to Dunmail Raise 327,117
Helvellyn 342,152	Hole in the wall (via Striding Edge) 349,149					
Hole in the wall (via Striding Edge) 349,149	Patterdale 397,164					
Totals						

Transportation, logistics, accommodation

Getting to the start of the expedition and being picked up at the finish is important. You may choose a circular route, starting and finishing in the same place. When you are on expedition, you should camp near water, but far enough away so that if it rains you won't flood. Mountain huts or bothies can be used as an alternative to camping. Communication in areas where there is poor mobile phone reception also needs to be considered.

Planning meals

Having the correct food means participants have enough energy to complete the expedition. So you need to think about what foods provide the best energy source. Remember that you will be exercising for up to 10 hours a day, using twice as much energy as normal. Remember to stay hydrated. Food can be heavy, so take light food (tins of baked beans are heavy!). Pasta, rice and instant potato are effective, light and have high energy content. It is easiest to cook in small groups. Plan your daily menus before you go.

Weather information

This is one element of planning which can change at the last moment. TV and radio provide an overview of the weather; for a detailed mountain forecast visit one of the online weather forecasters. For links to the BBC and Met Office websites, see Hotlinks section page ii.

Emergency contacts

Expedition participants should have 24-hour contacts back at base who can act as emergency back-up if there are difficulties.

Remember

When packing your rucksack always ensure that equipment you will need regularly is easy to access. For example your waterproofs should always be at the top of your rucksack.

Men wanted for hazardous journey

- Low wages
- Bitter cold
- Long months of complete darkness
- Constant danger
- Safe return doubtful
- Honour and recognition in case of success

Please contact Ernest Shackleton

Figure 17.3: This is the fabled advert that Sir Ernest Shackleton placed for his 1914 Endurance Expedition to the South Pole. He is rumoured to have received 5000 applications overnight. Would you have responded to this advert?

Assessment activity 17.1

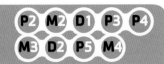
P2 M2 D1 P3 P4
M3 D2 P5 M4

You are undertaking a multi-day expedition in a mountainous area of North West Britain.

1. Describe what equipment you will need for your personal use. **P3**

2. Plan an expedition that meets the needs of the group and all requirements with respect to aims, objectives and safety requirements. When planning you should cover permission, consent and access, emergency contacts, route and route cards, journey times (contingencies and escape routes) transportation, equipment and logistics, accommodation, meals (planning, dietary considerations, nutrition for physical activity) and weather information. **P4**, **M3**

3. Undertake a multi-day expedition and demonstrate the use of relevant skills and required equipment. **P5**, **M4**

4. Using practical elements of the unit, demonstrate the skills and techniques required for a multi-day expedition, including navigation techniques and camping. **P2**

5. Having demonstrated these skills and techniques, explain why you have chosen to use the different skills and techniques you have to overcome the challenges of finding your way and camping. **M2**

6. Quite often there are many different ways to overcome the same problem when demonstrating skills and techniques required for a multi-day expedition. Justify the use of the skills and techniques you have used to overcome the challenges of finding your way and camping. **D1**

7. Having planned and carried out your expedition, reflect on key points you have addressed and justify decisions you have made. **D2**

Grading tips

When describing the equipment required for expeditions, think of the function of the equipment. Use the table on page 379 as a guide.

To successfully plan, think about what the group are capable of completing.

Set achievable aims.

Divide the tasks amongst the group.

Keep a log of who did what and when for evidence for the assignment.

When planning you will make decisions, make notes why they were made to help you justify them when reviewing the planning.

The easiest way for your tutor to assess the practical element will be with a tick sheet covering all the skills and techniques you will be assessed on. Know what is on the sheet and make sure you know how to do the skills and demonstrate them.

When explaining your use of skills and techniques, know what they are and what they are used for. If navigating, explain your route choice and the techniques you used.

When justifying skills and techniques, think about others you could have used; why were the ones you used the better ones to use in that situation?

PLTS

Planning and undertaking an expedition will help you to anticipate, take and manage risks and develop your skills as a **self-manager**.

Functional skills

This activity gives you the opportunity to develop your **ICT** skills.

4 Be able to carry out and review a multi-day expedition

4.1 Carrying out an expedition

During this expedition you will be assessed on the relevant navigation and mountain travelling skills and use of equipment required to complete the expedition successfully. You will need to show that you are competent at:

- using navigation tools to find your way
- making appropriate route choices and able to adapt the route choice if the situation demands
- living out of doors, especially erecting tents, striking tents, selecting camp site, use of terrain for shelter, cooking, waste disposal and personal hygiene
- travelling skills, including pace and rhythm, energy conservation, (craft control skills if appropriate)
- traversing difficult terrain and the avoidance of hazards
- recognising and avoiding hazards
- selecting, packing, using and caring for appropriate equipment.

4.2 Reviewing your expedition

When reviewing your expedition ask yourself a series of questions.

- Did you achieve your aims?
- Was the planning effective?
- Was the equipment suitable?
- Did your skills enable effective route choice and route finding?
- What do you feel you did well and where do you need to improve?

SMART targets are an effective way to plan to improve (see Unit 3 page 89). Table 17.3 shows how you can set effective targets.

Table 17.3: Setting targets to improve on a multi-day expedition.

Areas for improvement	Specific measurable skill	Realistic actions	Realistic outcomes	Time-bound	Further work	Extension activities
Compass work	Following compass bearing	Practise bearing in difficult conditions Enter orienteering competitions	Able to walk on bearings accurately	April 2009		Participate in advanced navigation course

Rob Steeple
Outdoor instructor

My job

I work for a town's outdoor development unit. For most of the year I run climbing and hill walking sessions and take groups like youth groups on expeditions. In the summer months I am responsible for organising and taking local secondary schools on five-day expeditions. The next development is to take groups walking to the Alps in Europe and the Rockies in America.

Roles and responsibilities

When leading an expedition my main roles are to:

- visit the participants, discuss with them the aims and objectives of the expedition and then plan an expedition to meet their needs
- inform the relevant bodies of the nature and route of the expedition
- inform the parents of the participants about the planned expedition
- plan the expedition, including having the correct number of qualified staff
- prepare the equipment
- complete the risk assessments
- lead the expedition
- review the expedition.

When leading the expedition, I transport the participants to the area where the expedition is to take place and then help them undertake the expedition. This usually means that I walk with them, helping them with their navigation, route choice and the rigours of living out of doors. If things are going really well and they are a good group I may shadow them, walking about 1km behind them. I let them make their own decisions and mistakes but I am there if they need me in an emergency. I never let the group go off alone in the hills if I have not been involved in their preparation and training for the expedition.

The best thing about the job

The best part of the job is helping a group of young people become capable of making a journey across difficult terrain in difficult conditions without any outside help. I know this will help them to become independent and self-reliant people which will help them in their life and career.

Think about it!

- Why is it important that Rob never allows the group to be alone in the hills, unless he has been involved in their training and preparation?
- How does this unit help Rob prepare for his job in leading groups on expedition?

Just checking

1. What safety considerations do you need to take into account for a multi-day expedition?
2. List five activities that need to be completed when planning an expedition.
3. Why is it so important to plan your journey, stick to it, and report your position regularly?
4. What are the CPR procedures?
5. Give three examples of how you can minimise the impact your expedition has on the environment?
6. Give five pieces of equipment that are essential on an expedition, and give a reason for each one. (Think about shelter, cooking food and keeping warm.)
7. Identify five different navigation skills and explain how you would use them when on expedition.
8. Describe three different skills you would use when on expedition and explain their importance.
9. List three ways how you can improve your navigational skills.

edexcel

Assignment tips

- Planning the expedition thoroughly will help to ensure that it is a successful trip. Plan your route with accurate timings, then add on some time. Prepare for the unexpected by taking spare food and clothing and emergency equipment such as first aid kit and torch. Always inform others of your intentions and who is in the party.

- Many groups carry an emergency shelter when in the mountains. Emergency shelters are effective for short periods, but they have many limitations. Consider carrying a tent outer with poles and a few pegs: it will be just as light but far more versatile.

- To ensure that you get your Eastings and Northings when reading or making grid references, remember the rule of 'Along the corridor and up the stairs'.

- Remember, the top of a map is always North. Orientate the map so that the features represented on the map line up with the features on the ground.

- When packing to go on expedition, check all your equipment. You may not know who used it before you and what state it is in. Pack it with the items you need least at the bottom of the back pack, and those you will need most at the top.

- Always refer to an accurate and reliable weather forecast, and be prepared to change your plans if the forecast is poor.

- Use specialist expedition food, or food which is light to carry but yields high energy and is quick to cook such as pasta, mashed potato or easy-cook rice.

18 Effects of exercise on the body systems

Taking part in some form of regular exercise, either through work-related or recreational activity, is important to maintain healthy body systems. The effect that exercise has on these systems depends on the type of exercise that is undertaken and how often it occurs. As soon as you start any form of exercise, physical activity or sport, the body automatically starts to respond. These responses will change as the body adapts and becomes used to participation over a period of time.

Anybody who is involved in advising individuals about the amount and type of exercise that they undertake, for example a fitness instructor or a coach, should be aware of the responses to short- and long-term exercise. This is essential in helping to plan and monitor appropriate fitness/exercise/training programmes and will help to prevent illness or injury occurring.

It is important for all fitness professionals to understand how the body can adapt to exercise naturally and healthily. Some individuals do not want to rely on this process and try to enhance the body adaptation process by using drugs. However, the fitness professional must be aware of the negative and positive effects such drugs can have on an individual's body.

Learning outcomes

After completing this unit you should:

1. be able to investigate the short-term effects of exercise on the body systems
2. know the long-term effects of exercise on the body systems
3. be able to investigate the fundamentals of the energy systems
4. know the impact of drugs on sports performance.

387

Assessment and grading criteria

This table shows you what you must do in order to achieve a pass, merit or distinction grade, and where you can find activities in this book to help you.

To achieve a **pass** grade the evidence must show that the learner is able to:	To achieve a **merit** grade the evidence must show that, in addition to the pass criteria, the learner is able to:	To achieve a **distinction** grade the evidence must show that, in addition to the pass and merit criteria, the learner is able to:
P1 describe the short-term effects of exercise on the musculoskeletal, cardiovascular and respiratory systems	**M1** explain the short-term effects of exercise on the musculoskeletal, cardiovascular and respiratory systems	
P2 investigate the short-term effects of exercise on the musculoskeletal, cardiovascular and respiratory systems, with tutor support	**M2** independently investigate the short-term effects of exercise on the musculoskeletal, cardiovascular and respiratory systems	
P3 describe the long-term effects of exercise on the musculoskeletal system **See Assessment activity 18.1, page 393**	**M3** explain the long-term effects of exercise on the musculoskeletal, cardiovascular and respiratory systems **See Assessment activity 18.1, page 393**	**D1** analyse the short- and long-term effects of exercise on the musculoskeletal, cardiovascular and respiratory systems **See Assessment activity 18.1, page 393**
P4 describe the long-term effects of exercise on the cardio-respiratory system		
P5 describe two types of physical activity that use the aerobic energy system and two that use the anaerobic energy systems	**M4** Explain the energy requirements of four different types of physical activity	
P6 Investigate different physical activities that use the aerobic and anaerobic energy systems, with tutor support		
P7 describe four different types of drugs used to enhance sports performance and their effects		
P8 describe the negative impact of drugs	**M5** explain the negative impact of drugs	

How you will be assessed

This unit will be assessed by assignments that will be designed and marked by the staff at your centre. The assessments are designed to allow you to show your understanding of the unit outcomes. Your assessment could be in the form of:

- verbal presentation
- visual display
- case studies
- practical tasks
- written assignments
- report writing.

Adrian, 14-year-old swimmer

In my group we have just finished looking at the short- and long-term effects of exercise. I have enjoyed this unit so far as everything we have been taught about has been accompanied by some sort of practical activity or task.

It was good fun when we all had to lie down and our partners had to find our pulse – we recorded our 'resting pulse rate' and then we played some sport. As soon as we stopped our partners had to take our pulse rate again. I could then see the difference that activity made to my cardiorespiratory system. As well as pulse rates, we looked at our blood pressure and lung capacity.

As I swim competitively for a local club my recordings were a lot better than my partner's. He only plays football once a week and doesn't train everyday like I do. It was really obvious from all my readings how much training regularly really affects how your body systems work and respond to exercise.

We're just about to start looking at the effect that taking drugs can have on performance; however I don't need to take drugs as I train hard and get good times in all my events and competitions.

Over to you
- How might Adrian have found his partner's pulse?
- How would a resting pulse rate differ from one taken immediately after playing sport?
- How might Adrian have measured blood pressure and lung capacity?

1 & 2 Investigate the short-term and long-term effects of exercise on the body systems

Warm-up

Effects of exercise

Make a list of all the physical changes you would notice after you had run up and down a flight of stairs 10 times.

1.1 Different body systems

When we start to participate in exercise there are a number of changes to our body systems that noticeably take place. These are known as the short-term effects of exercise on the body.

As we continue with our training our fitness levels increase and we can perform for longer or at a higher level; these changes are the long-term effects of exercise on the body. See also Unit 4 Anatomy and physiology, page 93, for more on changes to the body systems.

Musculoskeletal system

The musculoskeletal system is extremely adaptable; the difficulty can be finding the right balance between improving the system from training and avoiding overtraining.

A short-term positive response will be that there is an increased range of movement (ROM) at a joint. A negative response can be that small muscle fibres get torn and therefore an injury problem can occur.

A long-term positive response will include that of **muscle hypertrophy** therefore making the muscle stronger and able to function longer.

Cardiorespiratory system responses

As we start to exercise our body demands more oxygen.

This means that both our circulatory and respiratory systems have to work harder to supply oxygenated blood to our muscles and remove the waste products that build up as we exercise. To do this our body adapts by increasing the heart rate and breathing rate. Both of these effects are very noticeable in the short term.

However, as our body gets use to this type of exercise, long-term changes occur as our heart hypertrophies and our lung capacity increases, allowing us to perform at the same level but without working our heart and lungs so hard.

Key term

Muscle hypertrophy – the growth and increase of the size of muscle cells. The most common type of muscular hypertrophy occurs as a result of physical exercise, such as weightlifting.

This is because of an increase in **stroke volume** and **vital capacity**.

Cardiac output (Q) is the amount of blood per minute pumped out by each of the two ventricles of the heart.

A typical value in an adult at rest is 5 litres per minute.

The output of each ventricle is the product of the stroke volume (about 70 ml) and the heart rate (about 70 per minute). Q = SV x HR

The output increases, with muscular activity, in work or exercise perhaps to a maximum of 4–5 times the resting rate in an average healthy person, or up to 6–7 times in athletes; heart rate increases by a greater factor than stroke volume.

Activity: Calculating cardiac output

Work out the cardiac output for someone with a heart rate of 90 and a stroke volume of 65?

> ## Key term
>
> **Stroke volume (SV)** – the amount of blood pumped by the left ventricle of the heart in one contraction. It is able to do this as the heart muscle. The myocardium has hypertrophied as a result of training.
>
> **Vital capacity (VC)** – the maximum amount of air that a person can expel from the lungs after first filling the lungs to their maximum extent.

3 Be able to investigate the fundamentals of the energy systems

3.1 Energy-producing systems

There are three energy-producing systems in the human body, one of which is aerobic (using oxygen), and two of which are anaerobic (not using oxygen): ATP-PC and glycolysis.

a) ATP-PC system or alactic acid system

b) lactic acid or glycolytic system

c) aerobic system.

Each of these is suited to a particular type of exercise, and each can be improved by specific training or exercise regimes.

Anaerobic energy systems

- **ATP-PC**

For the first few seconds when you exercise you are using the ATP-PC system. This relies on stored ATP (adenosine triphosphate, the molecule that produces the energy in all living things, from bacteria upwards).

Another stored molecule, CP (creatinine phosphate), helps to restore your ATP. CP is restored aerobically (with oxygen).

The ATP-PC system allows for a short burst of energy and therefore the first few seconds of activity is usually fuelled by this system. This means that sports, such as sprints and jumping, for example, long jump and high jump, shot put, weightlifting – anything that only lasts for a short time – will utilise this energy system.

- **Lactic acid system**

When you exercise beyond the limit of your ATP-PC stores (that is, for anything more than a few seconds) the second anaerobic system kicks in, i.e. the lactic acid system.

This makes ATP from glucose (sugar) which is stored in your liver and muscles. You get the glucose from eating carbohydrates. (If you eat a reasonable amount of carbohydrate-rich food after exercising it helps to increase glucose stores.) (Note: see also Unit 10 Nutrition for sports performance, page 248.)

As there are still insufficient amounts of oxygen present, this system can only operate for a short period of time so any exercise lasting about 90 seconds will use this system as its energy system. This means sports such as 400m running, 100m swimming and so on will predominantly utilise this energy system.

When you exercise beyond the limits of your ATP-PC and lactic acid system, your body needs to start producing energy using oxygen. This is the aerobic system.

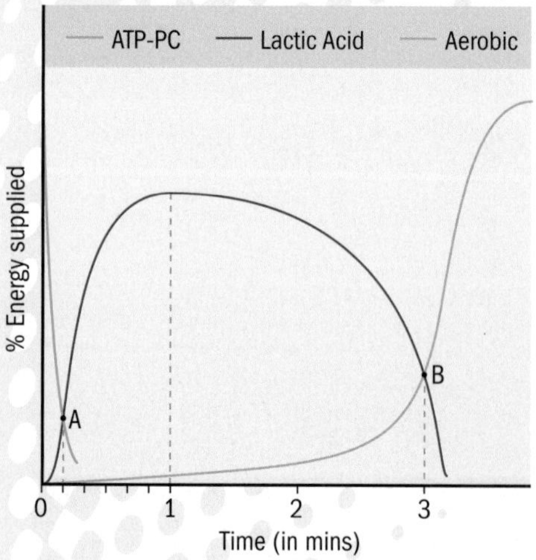

Aerobic energy system

This system is used for longer periods of exercise as oxygen helps to re-synthesise ATP. The aerobic system goes through a variety of chemical reactions, including the Krebs Cycle and the Electron Transport Chain, which produce waste products such as carbon dioxide and water. However it enables exercise to take place for a longer period of time.

This means that sports such as long distance running, long distance swimming and so on will utilise this energy system as well as supplying the energy required by the body at rest, or whilst it is recovering from any exercise.

The body utilises whichever system is the most appropriate depending on the demands placed on it. However, it should be noted that these systems are not discrete and interact with each other. For example, the lactic acid system is used between 10 seconds and three minutes, it peaks in those events lasting about one minute. It also comes into play at the end of aerobic events when the intensity increases, as it does during the sprint finish of a 5000m race.

Figure 18.1: Graph showing energy supplied against time. Do you understand what this graph is showing?

Key:

A = ATP-PC – LA THRESHOLD
The point at which ATP-PC energy system is exhausted and lactic acid system prevails

B = LA – 02 THRESHOLD
The point at which lactic acid system is exhausted and the aerobic system takes over

Assessment activity 18.1

You are on work experience at a fitness club. You have been asked to help an individual develop their fitness levels for their sport. This person has just joined the club and has not exercised on a regular basis for some time. With support, plan and implement a training programme for a sportsperson (perhaps someone in your group could act as your sportsperson) who needs to improve their musculoskeletal and cardio-respiratory systems. You will have taken sufficient measurements of their existing levels before they start the training programme.

1. You will need to identify what tests and measurements you need to take and record these.

   The training programme should last for about four weeks and at the end of it you should re-test and re-measure and record the data as you did before the implementation of the programme.

2. Once you have all of the data, produce a detailed report that shows and explains how the training programme has affected the body systems.

3. Make sure that you identify and give reasons for the major differences between the short-term effects and long-term effects of exercise on the body.

Grading tips

You should ensure that you make all the appropriate measurements *before* you start to implement the training programme. If you do not do this you will not know if the programme has been successful or not! Check with your tutor before you start that your selection is appropriate.

PLTS

Thinking about which tests and measurements that you will need to record for the correct outcome will help you develop your independent enquiring and reflective learning skills. Recording and analysing the data will also help these skills.

Functional skills

Presenting your research findings in a report should develop your **English** and **ICT** skills.

Energy requirements of physical activity

See table on page 253 of Unit 10 for energy requirements.

4 Know the impact of drugs on sports performance

Drugs in sport are generally seen as having a negative image; however some 'drugs' can have a positive and legal effect on an individual.

The use of some drugs, such as paracetamol, or painkillers when prescribed by a doctor, is perfectly safe and acceptable.

However, some other types of drugs are not necessarily safe or acceptable to use within sport.

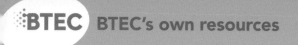

The table below shows some different types of drugs and their effects.

Table 18.1: Different types of drugs and their effects on sports performance.

Drug type	What is it?	Effect on sports performance	Negative impact
Anabolic steroids	Anabolic steroids are chemically manufactured drugs. They are a man-made version of testosterone, the male sex hormone	Increase muscle size and strength. Athletes who use anabolic steroids also claim that they reduce body fat and recovery time after injury	High blood pressure, acne, abnormalities in liver function, alterations in the menstrual cycle in women, decline in sperm production and impotence in men, kidney failure and heart disease. Can increase aggression
Erythropoietin (EPO)	Manufactured naturally by the kidneys, EPO stimulates the production of red blood cells in bone marrow and regulates the concentration of red blood cells and haemoglobin in the blood	Improves endurance performance	If EPO levels are too high the body will produce too many red blood cells, which can lead to blood clotting, heart attack and stroke
Human growth hormone (hGH)	Also called somatotrophin or somatotrophic hormone Is a naturally occurring hormone that increases the production of red blood cells, which carry oxygen	Promotes physical development – particularly the growth of bone – during adolescence Stimulates the synthesis of collagen, which is necessary for strengthening cartilage, bones, tendons and ligaments, and also stimulates the liver to produce growth factors In adults, hGH increases the number of red blood cells, boosts heart function and makes more energy available by stimulating the breakdown of fat	Too much hGH before or during puberty can lead to gigantism, which is excessive growth in height and other physical attributes After puberty, inflated levels of hGH can cause acromegaly, a disease characterised by excessive growth of the head, feet and hands. The lips, nose, tongue, jaw and forehead increase in size and the fingers and toes widen and become spade-like. The organs and digestive system may also increase in size, which may eventually cause heart failure. Acromegaly sufferers often die before the age of 40. Excessive hGH in adults may also lead to diabetes

Table 18.1: (Cont.)

Beta blockers	Beta blockers are a group of medications that are given in the treatment of angina, high blood pressure, irregular heart beats or following a heart attack	Reduce the heart rate and inhibit adrenalin production, they are often favoured by those who are nervous or require an extremely steady aim or shot	Dizziness and fainting, impotence, interfere with sleep patterns, nausea and vomiting Stopping beta blockers or sudden withdrawal can have very serious effects on health and increase the risk of heart attack
Diuretic	Diuretics are used in the treatment of: Hypertension (high blood pressure) Oedema (fluid retention, swelling or bloating) Cardiac failure Liver cirrhosis (replacement of liver cells with fibrous scar tissue, as a result of liver disease)	To lose weight rapidly in sports which require the athlete to be within a set weight limit. For example boxers and jockeys Secondly, to dilute the presence of illegal substances and aid their excretion	Dehydration Hypotension (low blood pressure) Muscle cramps Muscle weakness Seizures (or fits convulsions) Gout (caused by a build-up of uric acid) Fatigue

Table 18.1 shows some of the drugs used in sport – illegally – and the physiological consequences that individuals can experience as a result of taking these drugs.

However, there are also other aspects to the negative effect of taking drugs.

Rafael Nadal, the Spanish tennis player, has criticised tennis's new drug-testing procedures, saying they place unreasonable expectations upon players. Nadal says that is not very fair. Do you agree with Rafael's opinion?

The very fact that an individual tried to cheat others is an outrage to the concept of 'fair play' and becomes a real slur on an individual's character. Society does not like cheats and shuns them. Those athletes who have been caught taking drugs in order to win have lost their medals and, more importantly, their livelihood as a result of bans imposed from the sports governing body.

Case study: Good advice?

Paul, aged 15, is a good county and club 100 and 200m runner.

He has just started training with a new coach who thinks that he can go on to compete at a much higher level and possibly make 2012 Olympic selection.

However, after considering his training and his diet, Paul's coach suggests that he also uses a 'supplement', hGH, that may help to improve his performance more quickly than just relying on his normal training etc.

What advice would you give to Paul and why?

Diane Murphy
Swimming instructor and coach

I work at a local swimming pool. There are five swimming instructors in total employed there.

My main duties include:

- To plan and deliver swimming lessons for children and adults at all stages of swimming abilities and skills, from non-swimmers onwards.
- To determine and control the progress of customers through the various classes.
- To maintain class discipline and safety in the pool – including first aid assistance if necessary.

As well as being a swimming instructor I also help to coach the Under-14s swim team for the local swimming club.

Typical day

My 'normal' day will depend on whether or not it is in term time. In term time I have a range of different swimming classes to deliver – some just to school children and some to the general public. These classes range from beginners to advanced swimmers.

The best thing about the job

The classes I teach are mainly groups of people; however I do sometimes have individuals who book a swimming lesson. I think I find this the most rewarding as I can dedicate all of my time and attention to helping develop one person's needs and skill level in order to improve their fitness level and swimming ability.

Think about it!

- What qualifications must Diane have in order to do this job?
- Why is it important that Diane can identify when to progress a customer through to another swim class?

Just checking

1. What is the difference between the short-term and the long-term effects of exercise on the musculoskeletal system? Give examples to help explain your answer.
2. What is the difference between the short-term and the long-term effects of exercise on the cardio-respiratory system? Give examples to help explain your answer.
3. What is the anaerobic energy system? What physical activity is fuelled by it?
4. What is the aerobic energy system? What physical activity is fuelled by it?
5. Identify four different types of drugs used in sport.
6. For each drug listed above, identify an effect it has on the body in terms of improving performance and a negative effect it has on the body.

edexcel

Assignment tips

Research tips

- You can find information mainly in human physiology and exercise physiology textbooks and other similar resources.
- Websites are useful but should be used in conjunction with supportive textbook documentation in order to make sure that the web material is reliable and valid. For example, the Discovery Network website (see Hotlinks section on page ii for a link to the website).

Get active!

- In order for you to fully understand how exercise affects the human body it is important that you see the results first hand. Watch a sports performer either at a live event or on the television. Can you see the physical differences from when they start performing through to when they finish? What are the noticeable signs?
- Once you have identified the visual signs, can you now explain why they happen using the theory and knowledge that you have developed in this unit as well as in Unit 4?
- Go onto different governing body websites and find out about their latest information on drugs used in sport – both the acceptable and the unacceptable.

Key points

- Make sure you know *what* happens to the body when it undertakes exercise and, more importantly, *why* it happens.
- Remember to consider *how* different training methods and regimes can affect the energy systems (look again at Unit 1 to help support your work).
- Don't forget some drugs are acceptable and are needed by sports performers.

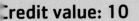

20 Planning and running a sports event

Planning and running a sports event can be a challenging and rewarding process. For the event to be a success, thorough planning, organisational and communication skills are needed as well as the ability to work as a member of a team.

In this unit you will participate in the planning and organisation of a small-scale, one-off sports event. You will then contribute to the running of the event and afterwards will undertake a review to see if it has been a success in relation to your original plans, aims and objectives.

Choosing a sports event to deliver will be an exciting part of the planning process. You will need to give a lot of thought to make sure that the event you have decided to run meets the needs of participants or customers.

Having an awareness of how to plan and organise a sports event, and gaining experience of implementing an event, will help you to develop valuable skills for potential future employment in the leisure and recreation industry.

Learning outcomes

After completing this unit you should:

1. be able to plan a sports event
2. be able to contribute to the organisation of a sports event
3. be able to contribute to the running of a sports event
4. be able to review the success of a sports event.

Assessment and grading criteria

This table shows you what you must do in order to achieve a pass, merit or distinction grade, and where you can find activities in this book to help you.

To achieve a **pass** grade the evidence must show that the learner is able to:	To achieve a **merit** grade the evidence must show that, in addition to the pass criteria, the learner is able to:	To achieve a **distinction** grade the evidence must show that, in addition to the pass and merit criteria, the learner is able to:
P1 produce a plan for a chosen sports event, outlining the planning process to meet given participant or customer requirements	**M1** produce a plan for a chosen sports event, explaining the planning process to meet given participant or customer requirements	
P2 contribute to the organisation of a chosen sports event		
P3 contribute to the running of a chosen sports event **See Assessment activity 20.1 page 408**		
P4 design and use methods for collecting feedback on the success of a sports event		
P5 assess feedback received, identifying strengths and areas for improvement	**M2** assess feedback received, evaluating strengths and areas for improvement, providing recommendations for future events	**D1** assess feedback received, analysing strengths and areas for improvement, justifying recommendations for future events

How you will be assessed

This unit will be assessed by an internal assignment that will be designed and marked by the staff at your centre.

Your assessment could be in the form of:

- presentations
- practical tasks
- written assignments.

Mark, 16–year-old college football player

This unit helped me to appreciate the importance of teamwork in the planning, organisation and delivery of a sports event. I kept a diary to record my contribution to the sports event. Looking back on my diary makes me feel proud about what we achieved.

During the planning process, we held team meetings, which were minuted, and everybody had a role. Somebody was responsible for the budget and somebody else covered resources. Parts of the planning were tackled as a team, like the risk assessments and event promotion.

We organised a five-a-side football competition for local primary schools and held the event at college, so we had access to all the resources and equipment needed. To promote the event we visited the schools and spoke to children and staff and made flyers. We charged a small entry fee for each team and organised medals for the winners and certificates for everyone.

We each had roles during the event to help things run smoothly. I was involved in setting up the equipment, taking it down, and refereeing. The event was great; everything went to plan and the children enjoyed themselves. Participant feedback showed that it had been a success. I learnt loads about myself and the rest of the team.

Over to you!
- What areas of this unit might you find challenging?
- Which section of the unit are you most looking forward to?
- What preparation can you do for the unit assessment(s)?

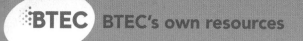

1 Be able to plan a sports event

Warm-up

Selecting a sports event

Selecting the right type of sports event to deliver will form part of the planning process.

What type of sports event could you choose?

Write a list of possible sports events and how each one would meet participant or customer requirements. Discuss your ideas in groups.

1.1 Planning a sports event

To plan, organise and deliver a sports event you need to be able to work as a member of a team. There is much to discuss in the planning process, and the best way to achieve this is to hold team meetings.

Team meetings

It will be helpful to hold regular meetings and produce minutes to document what topics are discussed and what actions arise. Team meetings could be recorded on video or audiotaped.

Minutes

Each team meeting should be minuted. You could keep your own record of the **minutes** in a personal diary. Or, as a team, agree on a rota system where each team member takes it in turns to produce minutes and issues a copy to all team members. The minutes should be a concise record and include:

- date, time and location of meeting
- names of people attending and any apologies for non-attendance
- name of person taking the minutes (if applicable)
- name of person chairing the meeting – this person steers group discussions, ensures all team members have opportunity to contribute, keeps the meeting focused on objectives and to time. It would be a good experience to take it in turns to chair meetings
- main points discussed (**agenda** items)
- actions arising – these are decisions or outcomes that the team have reached and agreed. There may be individual and/or team action points
- any other business (AOB) – any other items for discussion.

Key term

Minutes – a record of what was discussed in a meeting.

Key term

Agenda – a list of items to be dealt with.

Case study: Vikki Guy, Wedding fayre co-ordinator

Job: Wedding Fayre Co-ordinator

Vikki works for a wedding planning company and is responsible for organising wedding fayres across the UK.

Vikki says: 'Planning a wedding fayre is exciting. Organisation, communication and teamwork are key to success. Lots of companies are represented at each wedding fayre, because people planning their weddings want a 'one-stop shop'; they want to come and set everything up for their big day. The wedding fayres are held at hotels and we have stalls covering all aspects of planning a wedding, such as:

- venues: including décor
- bride: dresses, pre-wedding pampering days
- groom: suits, pre-wedding pampering days
- bridesmaids and mother of the bride: dresses and gifts
- best man and ushers: suits and gifts
- rings and jewellery
- cars
- stag and hen parties
- entertainment
- cakes
- video
- photography
- invitations and gift lists
- flowers
- hair and beauty

- lingerie
- accessories
- honeymoon packages.

My main role in organising a wedding fayre is to:

- check and book a suitable venue
- manage the budget for the event
- ensure a cross-section of companies are invited and attend the event
- organise the event promotion
- attend the event to help set-up the room(s) and ensure that everything runs smoothly.

A catwalk show of this season's outfits usually opens the event, because feedback shows this is something people want; so it is important to the success of the event.

Questions

You can see there are lots of things to consider when planning an event and how important it is to ensure that participant or customer needs are met.

- What preparation could you do to ensure your sports event is a success? Perhaps you could carry out a mini-poll to find out what sports events would be popular?
- Volunteer to help with running a local sports event to see how their event meets participant or customer requirements.
- Attend other events, to see first-hand how the event has been planned and delivered.

Personal diary

You should also keep your own record and notes of the planning process, including records of team meetings, meeting outcomes and actions arising. A personal diary is a good way to do this.

Selecting a sports event

There may be factors to consider which might affect your choice of event. For example:

- Can you get access to resources and equipment?
- Do you need a budget?
- Will the event be popular?

What type of sports event would you choose?

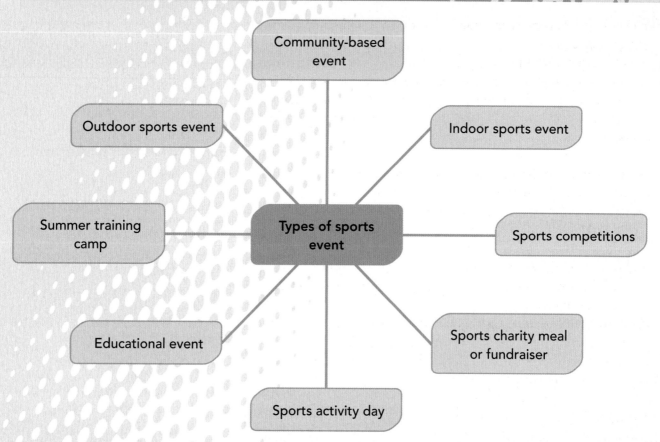

Figure 20.1: There are lots of different types of sports event. What would you like to organise?

The planning process

The following 12 questions will help with the planning process and could be used as the basis for team meetings;

- **What type of event have you decided on?** You may have chosen an educational sports event aimed at promoting fitness. Alternatively, you may have chosen a sports activity day, aimed at promoting fitness, well-being and 'sport for all'.
- **What is the event size, aims, objectives and location?** Use the SMARTER rule for setting targets and goals – see Unit 11 page 266.
- **Who is your target audience?** Are you targetting a specific age group or other type of group, for example, those with specific needs?
- **What will your timings be for the event and what resources and equipment do you need?** You need to provide an outline.
- **Have you thought about staffing, budget, costings and constraints?** Staffing levels required depends on how many participants or customers you are aiming for and the nature of your event.
- **Have you carried out a risk assessment for the event?** Produce your records. Refer to Unit 5 Injury in sport, for details of how to carry out a risk assessment.
- **Have you prepared informed consent/disclaimers for participants or customers?** You could adapt the informed consent form shown

in Unit 1 Fitness testing and training so that it is fit for purpose, or design a disclaimer.

- **Have you considered contingency planning?** You need to plan in advance for the 'What Ifs....?'. If you are running an outdoor sports activity day, what if the weather is bad? What if there are staff shortages or the equipment you were promised does not arrive? Agreeing back-up plans in advance will help to reduce stress levels if the unexpected occurs!
- **Does every team member have individual roles and responsibilities?** Individuals need to work as team members. Allocating specific roles and responsibilities during the planning and running of the event will help things to run smoothly.
- **Have you thought about first aid procedures?** Are there first-aid trained individuals within your team? Is there sufficient coverage for the size of the event? Can you draw on first aid resources within your centre or externally?
- **How can you effectively promote the event?** Explore methods of promoting your event, get inventive; you need to be creative.
- **Have you decided how to evaluate the event?** Think about different methods for gathering feedback from participants and other people involved in the event.

Budgets, costings and financial planning

Your budget and costings will depend on the type of sports event you have chosen, who your target audience is and where you intend to hold the event.

During one of your planning meetings you'll need to think about costs. Sport and leisure centres use pricing systems for activities they run, which are based on how much it costs to run the activity and the level of demand. Once the activity costs have been determined, you can then work out prices. For example, will you charge an entry fee for your sports event? Are you aiming to make a profit and give the profit to a recognised charity? If so, you could use this aim to help promote your sports event.

Mark's team (see page 401), did not have a budget allocated for their sports event. So, how did they get around this?

- When Mark's team planned their indoor five-a-side football competition they knew they could hold this on the college premises, meaning that they didn't have to find a budget to pay for a hired venue.
- They charged a small entry fee per football team. This covered their costs of buying medals for the winning team and getting participant certificates professionally printed by a local company.
- Participants were asked to bring their own packed lunch (including refreshments), so the team did not have to organise food and drink services on the day. In fact, after purchasing the medals and certificates, there was money left over and the team decided to

Key term

Contingency planning – planning in advance for the unexpected.

Remember

In the planning process, you need to make sure your chosen sports event will be cost-effective. Keeping within your budget helps to contribute to a successful sports event.

purchase a sufficient number of paper cups, so that water could be given to thirsty participants using the kitchen area close to the sports hall where the event was being held.

* Additional first-aiders recruited for the event were volunteers, so no additional costs to run the event were incurred.
* The team asked for payment up-front from participating schools and the entry fee was non-refundable. This meant that they used the money they had accumulated before the event to purchase medals for the winning team, certificates and paper cups. This also meant that if any teams failed to turn up on the day, they would not have been left with a debt.

Event promotion

How you promote the sports event will very much depend on the type of event you have chosen and who your target participants/customers are.

* You could hold a mini-roadshow in your local area to publicise the event to a wide audience and help generate interest.
* If your event targets local schools, you could visit the schools and speak to children about the event you are holding.
* Producing a flyer is a great way of promoting your sports event. If you do speak to your target audience about your event, then it is a good idea to take flyers with you and hand these out, because they will help to remind people about your event (date, time, venue etc.) after you have left.

Designing a flyer

When designing a flyer it is useful to remember the following points.

* Keep the message clear and concise. Your flyer should contain the important details of the event like the date, time and venue, plus any other relevant details like how to book, how to find the venue etc.
* Don't put too much text on your flyer – it needs to contain the relevant information but must still look attractive!
* Keep to one sheet of paper (A4, A5), or poster size (A3).
* Think about the layout. What would make you want to read the flyer rather than put it in the bin? Should you include pictures?
* Think about the content. Grab your audience with an interesting opening statement like – 'How fit are you?' Providing an exciting opening statement will make people want to read on and find out more about your event.

Figure 20.2 shows a flyer that Mark's team used to promote their indoor five-a-side football competition for local primary schools. They visited local primary schools and spoke to staff and children. Their flyer is aimed at informing parents. They left flyers at the schools so that teachers could contact parents/guardians, give them a copy of the flyer, and gain their consent for their child to attend the event.

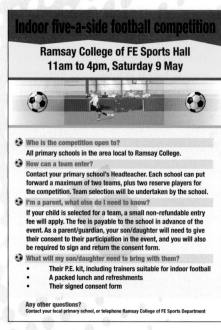

Figure 20.2: An example of a flyer. What information would you need to include for your sports event?

2 Be able to contribute to the organisation of a sports event

2.1 Meeting participant or customer requirements

Having selected a sports event and identified your target audience you need to ensure that the event meets participant or customer needs.

Activity: Participant requirements

Identify and predict how needs could vary between different types of participants or customers and what individual participant needs will be. Use role play within your team to discuss and explore these points.

Event organisation

Much of the event organisation will be discussed within team meetings. This includes the following:

- Resources for the event, such as financial, staffing, equipment and catering or entertainment (if applicable).
- Contingency planning for unexpected occurrences, such as the weather, staff shortages or accidents.
- How each team member will participate and contribute to the event. For example: by attending team meetings, by being allocated a specific role (such as to check availability and access to equipment required for the event).

Before running the sports event, you need to decide as a team how you will work together to ensure the event runs smoothly. Discuss and agree roles and responsibilities and contingencies for unexpected occurrences.

Make sure you are aware of what is expected of *you* and the timings for the event. Is everyone in your team clear about their duties during the event?

If the team is to work effectively to run the event, all team members need to be clear on their roles and responsibilities and must rise to the challenge of supporting the work of the team.

Remember

It is a good idea to maintain a personal diary and/or portfolio of evidence throughout the planning, organisation and delivery stages of the event. Record individual and team tasks completed in the run-up to the event and your personal roles and responsibilities during the running of the event itself.

3 Be able to contribute to the running of a sports event

It may seem a long way off during the planning stages, but the day for implementing your sports event will soon arrive. This will be your opportunity to work as a team member and contribute to the running of the event.

How will you and your team members contribute? The table below gives examples of roles and responsibilities for the running of a sports event.

Table 20.1: Roles and responsibilities for the running of a sports event.

Timings	Examples of roles and responsibilities
Setting up	Signs, sports equipment (including equipment checks and ensuring equipment is set up safely and securely), drink service areas, food service areas, seating
During the event	Communicating with participants/customers (e.g. supporting and supervising, motivating), responding to participant/customer queries, responding to emergencies/accidents/other issues, refereeing, instructing, officiating, monitoring
Setting down	Signs, sports equipment (including correct and safe storage), waste disposal, seating, cleaning/tidying, collecting feedback

PLTS

By organising time and resources, prioritising actions and proposing practical ways forward you can develop your skills as a **self-manager** and **effective participator**.

Functional skills

By maintaining a personal diary and/or portfolio of evidence to document your contribution to the running of the sports event, you could provide evidence towards **English** and **ICT** skills.

BTEC Assessment activity 20.1

Contribute to the running of a chosen sports event .

Grading tips

- Maintain detailed records of how you have contributed to the running of the event in the form of a personal diary, together with team meetings and task sheets.
- You will need to contribute throughout the running of the event i.e., during the setting up, during the event and setting down.

Your tutor will provide observation records/witness statements to confirm whether you have met this assessment criterion.

4 Be able to review the success of a sports event

4.1 Design and use methods for collecting feedback on the success of a sports event

Decide as a team how you are going to collect feedback to determine whether the event has been successful. Methods of collecting feedback could be discussed during a team meeting and include questionnaires, feedback forms, customer comment cards.

You may collect feedback as part of a team, but you will be expected to produce an individual review and evaluation of the sports event with suitable recommendations for improvement.

Think about the style of questions you could use. For example:

- **Open questions** enable the participant to open up on their response. Feedback could be provided that might not otherwise be captured, for example, What did you enjoy most about the sports event?
- **Closed questions** give a specific response, i.e. Yes/No answers, which can be easier to evaluate than open questions. For example, Was the venue suitable?
- **Multiple-choice questions** provide a question or statement and a number of fixed responses for the participant to select. The responses could be in the form of a rating.

Figure 20.3 shows a customer comment card used to collect feedback following an indoor five-a-side football competition. This was used to collect feedback from team members, peers, parents and other adults who attended the event.

> **Key term**
>
> **Open questions** – questions that allow a detailed answer.
>
> **Closed questions** – questions to which a simple yes or no answer is expected.

4.2 Assess feedback received, identifying strengths and areas for improvement

You need to collect feedback from a sufficient number of different people involved in the event in order to produce a well-rounded evaluation. For example, feedback could be collected from:

- your teammates
- your classmates
- participants or customers
- your assessor
- other helpers, e.g. first-aiders, referees.

In your review include:

- **Strengths of the event** – highlight where original aims and objectives were met.
- **Areas for improvement** – where aims and objectives were not achieved and where feedback from participants/customers, your teammates etc. showed that improvements were required.

You could produce basic statistical evidence to support your review. For example, you might work out percentage responses to questions and use this data to support your strengths and areas for improvement.

Include recommendations for future sports events in your review. Feedback collected from participants may help to inform this. Your feedback forms could include questions covering recommendations for future sports events to help capture ideas.

Ramsay College of FE
Bridge Street Rd
LONDON NE01 0PP

We welcome your comments about the sports event. Please let us know your comments by using one of the following methods:

- By speaking directly to a member of the team who will pass your comment to the relevant person and it will be recorded as a verbal comment.
- By completing this Customer Comment Card. If requested, a response will be sent to you within 10 working days.
- By writing to the Head of Sport and PE at the address shown above.

Name: ....

Address: ....

....

Postcode: .... **Tel no:** ....

I would prefer to remain anonymous (*if yes, tick here*): ☐

Were you (*please indicate*):
Observing the event? YES/NO

Supporting the event? YES/NO   Other (please state): ....

Time of visit (*please state*):
Have you visited Ramsay College of FE before? (*please circle*)

YES/NO

What is your overall impression of the five-a-side football event? (*please circle a number*):

1. **I am very satisfied**   2. **I am fairly satisfied**

3. **I am not satisfied**   4. **I am not satisfied at all**

Please use this space (and reverse of this card) to highlight an issue, commend a member of the team, make a suggestion, other:

_____

Comments:

Would you like to receive a reply to your comment? YES/NO
THANK YOU FOR YOUR COMMENTS!

Figure 20.3: Example of a customer comments card. What specific features of your event would you like to get feedback on?

Pauline Pavey
Recreation Assistant

Pauline works in a leisure centre and is responsible for:

- setting up and taking down equipment
- dealing with customers
- working on poolside
- keeping the centre clean
- first aid duties
- helping to run activity events.

Typical day

I'm part of a team of recreation assistants and we help the leisure centre to run smoothly and deal with customers on a daily basis. Each day is different, depending on what activities and events are timetabled, but we usually have poolside duties and help with the setting up and taking down of equipment.

What's the best thing about your job?

I like the variety this job offers; one of my favourite parts of the job is helping to run sports activity days over the summer holidays. For example, last year I helped out with the running of a number of sports tournaments for children, which included badminton, tennis and five-a-side football. It was a great opportunity for children to keep fit, get a taster of different sports and learn new skills.

Think about it!

- What areas have you covered in this unit that provide you with the knowledge and skills used by a Recreation Assistant?
- What further skills might you need to develop? Write a list and discuss in groups.

Just checking

1. What is contingency planning and why is it important?
2. Give three reasons why it is useful to record minutes of team meetings.
3. Give two reasons why it is helpful to have someone to chair team meetings.
4. What is the main purpose of disclaimers/informed consent?
5. Why should the needs of participants be considered in event planning?
6. Team-working is important in event planning. Name five other skills that are useful in event planning.
7. What is a closed question?
8. What is an open question?
9. What is the benefit of using a closed question rather than an open question?

Assignment tips

Research tips

- Conduct research locally to see what types of sports events have been organised over the past few years and how successful they have been.
- Attend events, such as wedding fayres, concerts and fetes. Think about how the event was planned and delivered.
- Arrange in advance a time to speak to event organisers. This will give you the opportunity to ask them questions about event preparation and organisation, and provide valuable insights that you can apply to the organisation of your own sports event.

Get active!

- You and your team could volunteer to help with the running of a local event. This would be a great way to gain first-hand experience and to see for yourself how the event meets participant or customer requirements.
- After an event, review with the organisers the relative success of the event, what lessons have been learned and possible improvements for future events.

It's all about team work

- Planning and running a sports event will help you to develop valuable skills including organisational and communication skills.
- Being able to work effectively as a member of a team is extremely beneficial and a skill that is highly valued by employers. Be prepared to contribute your own ideas to the planning of the event and explore the possibilities available.
- A well-planned event means less stress on the day and makes for a more enjoyable and successful event.

Glossary

Abduction – movement away from the body i.e. moving a limb away from the trunk. For example, when a gymnast pushes out their legs to do a star jump, abduction occurs at the hip joint.

Adaptation – changes to cope with different demands being made.

Addictive – a substance that a person can become dependent on.

Adduction – movement towards the body i.e. bringing a limb towards the trunk. For example, arms pulled back together during breaststroke – adduction at the shoulder joint.

Agenda – a list of items to be dealt with.

Aggression – intention to dominate others forcefully.

Aim – something you want to achieve – a goal.

Aims – what you want to achieve in your training programme.

Amino acid synthesis – the way in which amino acids are produced from other compounds in the body.

Anxiety – a negative form of stress. Can reduce a sport performer's level of confidence and concentration. Expectations of success are also reduced and the performer experiences a greater fear of failure.

Barriers – factors which prevent or make participation more difficult.

Circumduction – movement in which flexion, abduction, extension and adduction movements are combined in sequence. Any joint at which flexion, abduction, extension and adduction may occur is a joint at which circumduction may occur. For example, the shoulder joint during an over bowling action in cricket.

Collagen – the main protein in connective tissue, it is fibrous and its molecular structure provides strength and elasticity to tissue, skin, cartilage, ligaments, tendons and bones.

Closed questions – questions to which a simple yes or no answer is expected.

Conduction – heat loss by direct contact with a cooler body.

Contingency planning – Planning in advance for the unexpected.

Contraindications – are factors like a recent heart attack, unstable angina or abnormal heart rhythm (dysrhythmias), which result in exercise being harmful to health or recovery. If a person has contraindications to exercise, training should not be undertaken until factors are stabilised or have been reduced.

Contusion – another name for a bruise.

Convection – heat loss is facilitated by moving air or water vapour.

Customer – someone who buys goods or services from a business.

Elite sports performance – those who compete at sports at a professional level or the highest level available in their sport; this includes professional athletes, national representatives, national record holders, world record holders, national champions and Olympians.

Ethical – moral principles based on right and wrong.

Eustress – a positive form of stress. Can occur when a sports performer enjoys testing their own sporting ability, pushing themselves to reach their full potential.

Evaporation – heat is lost by turning liquid (sweat) into vapour (the skin's major heat loss mechanism).

Extension – straightening the joint i.e. increasing the angle at a joint. For example, a basketball player straightening their arm in order to block a shot.

Extrinsic motivation – external rewards such as trophies, external praise or money.

Extrovert – loud, excitement-seeking, easily distracted.

Feedback – information about a person's performance in a task, e.g. given to the client by a fitness instructor about how the client has done in a session or the whole programme.

F.I.T.T. principle – this acronym stands for Frequency, Intensity, Time and Type.

Flexion – bending the joint i.e. decreasing the angle at a joint. For example, when a football player is preparing to kick a ball.

Fulcrum – the pivot point of a lever.

Hazard – anything that has potential to cause harm to a person.

Hydration – process by which the correct water ratio in the body is maintained; a gain of water or moisture.

Hypoglycaemia – abnormally low level of sugar in the blood.

Impact – an effect or influence on something or someone.

Income – the money you earn and receive for playing sport – may be in the form of wages, sponsorship or prize money.

Individual sport – a sport in which a sole performer competes towards a set goal.

Intermuscular haematoma – type of bruise formed when blood has seeped some distance away from the point of contact. This shows that the muscle bundle sheath has been damaged and has allowed blood to seep out and away from the area.

Intramuscular haematoma – type of bruise where blood has not seeped very far away from the point of contact because the muscle bundle has not been disrupted, so the blood is retained in the muscle bundle sheath.

Intrinsic motivation – internal rewards (self), love of the game or health benefits.

Introvert – quiet, not seeking excitement, high concentration levels.

Joint – a joint, or articulation, is the interface (coming together) of two bones.

Leisure – the opportunity and time outside working hours to choose and take part in activities or experiences which are expected to be personally satisfying.

Liable – required according to the law.

Loading – the overload principle is the body adapts to stresses. The more you do, the more you are capable of. This is how training adaptations occur in exercise and training. When you stress the body by lifting a weight the body is unaccustomed to, it reacts by causing physiological changes so that it can handle that stress in the future.

Mental toughness – being psychologically strong.

Midline – direction referring to a vertical, invisible line through the middle of the body.

Minutes – a record of what was discussed in a meeting.

Motivation – determination to achieve certain goals.

Muscle hypertrophy – the growth and increase of the size of muscle cells. The most common type of muscular hypertrophy occurs as a result of physical exercise, such as weight lifting.

Mystery shoppers – a way of measuring quality in an organisation; shoppers adopt the role of a customer unknown to the facility being sampled and use the services offered to assess quality.

Negligent – failing to produce the care expected of a sports leader.

Non-verbal communication – communication not using words e.g. pointing, signals, body language.

Nutrition – the scientific study of food and how it is used in the processes of growth, maintenance and repair in our bodies.

Objectives – how you are going to achieve your aims in your training programme.

Objective analysis – analysis based on the measurement and comparison of numbers and performance data.

Open questions – questions that allow a detailed answer.

Outdoor and adventurous activity – physical activity that stimulates and challenges participants and is done outside, often in a hostile environment.

Outgoings – the money you have to pay out – including coaching fees, entry fees, equipment, etc.

Overload – the body performs more work than it would usually be asked to do.

Over-use injury – inflammation of tendons, muscles, joints or bones resulting from long periods of overuse.

People skills – skills you need when dealing with customers, such as empathy for others and a desire to provide a high-quality service at all times.

Performance – the level at which a skill or technique is completed.

Personality – the unique qualities, character and temperament of a person.

Private organisations – businesses and private clubs who undertake their business for profit for either the owners of the business or for the benefit of the business and its members.

Procedure – an official way of doing something.

Proprioceptive Neuromuscular Facilitation (PNF) – a stretching technique for developing flexibility. PNF is performed with a partner. If completed regularly, it can improve mobility and joint range of motion.

Public organisations – organisations whose role is to benefit the general public.

Quality – the standard of something, for example, the standard of the services and experience provided to each customer.

Radiation – heat is directly lost to the atmosphere.

Reliability – consistency of results; repeatability.

Risk – a risk is the chance that a hazard may cause harm to someone.

Rotation – movement which moves a limb towards the body. For example, when a golf player performs a drive shot, the hip moves towards the body.

Skill – an ability that can be learned or developed to allow an activity to be completed.

Sport – an activity involving physical exertion and skill that is governed by a set of rules or customs and often undertaken competitively.

Sports psychology – study of the affect of the mind in sport.

State anxiety – a performer's response to a changing situation.

Strengths – personal attributes that you may have developed over the course of many years of playing the sport, specific skills, components of fitness that develop your ability to play a sport.

Stroke volume (SV) – the amount of blood pumped by the left ventricle of the heart in one contraction. It is able to do this as the heart muscle. The myocardium has hypertrophied as a result of training.

Subject analysis – analysis based on observational judgements, personal interpretations, and opinions.

SWOT analysis – strengths, weaknesses, opportunities, threats.

Tactic – plan taken by sports coaches and sports performers to achieve a desired goal, which in sport is usually winning.

Team sport – a sport in which more than one player competes towards a set target or goal.

Technique – the way in which a movement is performed, or equipment is used. Techniques are always specific to the activity and environment.

Thermoregulation – keeping the body at a constant temperature.

Toxicity – the strength of poison in a substance.

Trait anxiety – a performer's response as a result of their own unique characteristics.

Validity – accuracy of results.

Vasoconstriction – when the blood vessels close.

Vasodilation – when the blood vessels open.

Verbal communication – communication using words e.g. team talks, shouting instructions to players/team from the side line.

Vital capacity (VC) – the maximum amount of air that a person can expel from the lungs after first filling the lungs to their maximum extent.

Voluntary organisations – people or groups who undertake activities for no payment.

Weaknesses – flaws in your performance, the skills or components of fitness which require developing to enhance your performance.

Index

A

abduction 104
accident report form 139
achievement motivation 234
Achilles tendon 125
active listening 303
activities 193–5, 318
  structure of 176–7, 194–5
Activity Centre (Young People
  Safety Act) (1995) 185
adaptation 312–13, 387
adduction 104
Adventurous Activities
  Licensing Authority 74–5, 185
aerobic endurance 4–5, 7, 8, 9, 274
  tests 17–21
aerobic energy system 313, 392
age of participants 189–90
aggression 225, 231, 238, 239–40
agility 5, 8
aims and objectives 213, 349
  of sessions 192, 193, 316
alcohol consumption 289, 292
alignment, incorrect 123
amino acids 249
amphetamines 290
anabolic steroids 11, 394
anaerobic energy systems 313, 391–2
anatomy and physiology 93–116
  cardiovascular system 110–12
  muscular system 105–9
  respiratory system 113–16
  skeletal system 96–105
antagonistic muscles 109
anxiety 11, 28–9, 223–4, 231
appearance of leader 179
application forms U13 9
arousal 28–9
assertive behaviour 238–9
assessment of performance 56–63
  goal setting 62–3
  improvement 61–2
observation checklist 57–61
  your own 178
asthma 130
ATP-CP system 391–2
attribution theory 234
awards and certification 71

B

back injuries 98, 129
balance 5, 8, 9
banned substances 290–1
barriers to participation 275–6
basketball 7, 44, 46–7
behaviour, appropriate 294–5
beta blockers 11, 290, 395
blisters 128
blood circulation 111, 112
blood pressure 269, 270
blood vessels 111
body composition 5, 6
  Body Mass Index 26
  skinfold testing 24–5
body language 230, 303, 306, 345, U19 7
Body Mass Index (BMI) 26
body types 6
bone/s 31, 100–2
breathing 114–15, 230, 240
breathing rate 115, 390
bruising 127–8
business skills U19 1–15
  customer information U19 4
  financial skills U19 9–10

C

camping 377, 382
carbohydrates 248
cardiovascular disease 26, 269, 270
cardiovascular system 110–12, 390–1
cardiovascular training 318
career planning 296–301
cartilage 100
caving 82, 347, 351
child protection 150, 186
Children Act (2004) 146, 150, 186
children, development of 189–91
circuit training 274, 276, 318
clients 316–17, 318, 335
  use of facilities U19 5
  see also participants
climbing 82, 84–5
clothing, expedition 368, 378, 379
co-ordination 5, 8, 9
coach case study U13 17
coaches 284, 287
codes of conduct 315, 353–4
communication 51–2, 175, 177–8,
  193, 302–4, 305–6, 344–5
  outdoor activities 83, 85
compass 376
competition 71–2, 194, 225–6, 285
competitiveness 225–6, 231
complaints procedure 336
concentration 28, 29, 190, 226
concussion 128–9
conditioned game/activity 194
consent form 13–14, 315, 349, 404–5
contingency planning 192–3, 298, 354, 405, 407
contracts 301
cool down 142, 195, 273–4, 315, 316
coronary heart disease (CHD) 26
COSHH Regulations 146, 148
Countryside Code 371
CPR (cardio-pulmonary
  resuscitation) 138
creatine 255, 392
cricket 38–9, 40, 41, 49
cricket coach, assistant 217
cultural backgrounds 318
curriculum vitae (CV) U13 7, 8
  covering letter U13 8–9
customer service 334–6, U19 7–9

D

decision making   226, 231, 345
dehydration   131–2, 245
demonstration of skills   193, 355
development plans   201
diabetes   133
diary keeping   41, 87, 241, 403
    training diary   276–7
diet   12, 251, 253, 256–9
disability   166, 185
Disability Discrimination
    Act (1995)   185
dislocation   125
distress signals   367, 370
diuretics   11, 290, 395
drugs   393, 394–6
    illegal   11, 166, 290–1, 387

E

effect of exercise   387–98
    energy systems   391–3
elite performers
    56, 159, 211, 281, 284, 285, 294–5
emergency equipment   367–9
emergency procedures
                               137–8, 332–3
    expedition   366, 370
emergency services, contacting 367
emergency shelter (KISU)   367
employment   U19 1
    extra forms of   286
    outdoor activities   72
endurance   9, 83, 85
energy in diet   252–3
energy drinks/gels   348
energy expended by activity   253
energy systems   391–3
environmental impact   371
    outdoor activities   79–80, 353
EPO (Erythropoietin)   290, 394
equality   186
equipment 52, 176, 184–5, 337–8
    calibration of   15
    consumer expenditure on   U19 1
    emergency   367–9
    expedition   377–80

outdoor activities 345, 347, 350–1
    regulations   46
erosion   79
escape routes   370, 380, 381
ethics and values   187
evaluation of sessions   178
exercise adherence factors   275–6
exercise sessions   321–2
    assisting   319–20
    planning   316–18
    reviewing   321
    structure of   319
expedition experience   363–86
    and environment   371
    equipment   377–80
    permission   380
    planning   77–83
    route cards   380–1
    safety considerations   366–70
    skills and techniques   372–6
extrovert personality 181, 233, 237

F

fair play   44–5, 55, 187, 295
Fartlek training   8, 274
fats   248–9
feedback 41, 63, 88, 178, 193, 242
    formative and summative   U13 16
    from clients   321, 322, U19 5–6
    sports event   199, 409, 410
financial management
                       300–1, U19 9–10
first aid   137–8
first aid kit   368, 379
First Aid Regulations (1981)
                       146, 147–8, 332
fitness   4–6, 7, 8–10
fitness instructor case study 323
fitness testing   1–32
    aerobic endurance   17–21
    body composition   24–6
    muscular endurance   22–3
    pre-test procedures   13–15
    recording results   14–15, 27
    reliability and validity   15
    speed: 35m sprint   21

your own   13–27
fitness training   6–7, 271, 312–16
FITT principle   123, 142, 313
flexibility   5, 7, 8, 9, 16, 287
flexion/extension   103, 104, 108
flyer design   406
focusing   229
food, expedition   369, 379, 382
food labelling   257–8
Food Pyramid   251
football   10, 44–5, 174, 187, 212
    scholarship programme   298–9
Forestry Step test   18–21
fractures   125–6
frostbite   132

G

gaseous exchange   114
gender and sport   191
goal setting
    62–3, 177, 215, 235, 266–7, 296–7
golf   8, 9, 213
grazes   128
grid references   373–4
grip strength dynamometer   16–17
group management   355–6
guidebooks   352–3
gymnastics   8, 49
gymnastics coach case study   117

H

hardiness   237
Hawkins, Sue   181–2
hazards: outdoor activity   75–6, 77
health fitness instructor   31
health and safety
            46, 54, 196, 315, 346
    leader's responsibility   184–5
    outdoor activities   74–8, 353
    skills for   U19 10–11
Health and Safety at Work
Act (1994)   146–7, 332
Health and Safety Executive
                       75, 147, 150
health screening
                142, 269–70, U19 5

heart 110–11, 112, 313
  hypertrophy 390
heart attack 130–1
heart rate 272–3, 313–14, 390, 391
heat imbalance 131–2
  heat stroke 131
hockey 5, 59–60
human growth hormone (hGH) 394
hydration 251, 348
hypoglycaemia 133
hypothermia 132, 348, 370

I
illnesses, types and signs 130–4
improving performance 61–2
induction session 315
information about clients
  189, 317–18, U19 4
inhalation/exhalation 114–15
injury in sport 119–54
  causes of 122–4
  dealing with 135–40
  types of 124–9
instruction, exercise and
  fitness 309–24
insurance 185, 301
intensity of exercise 313–14
interviews U13 10
introvert personality 181, 233, 237

J
joints and movement 102–5, 313
judges, role of 49–50

L
lactic acid 273, 313, 392
language, use of 177–8
leadership 172–204, 354–8
  qualities 178–83, 346, 356
  responsibilities
    183–7, 346–8, 356–7
  skills 174–8, 344–6
leadership styles 179–80, 356
legal obligations 185–6
legislation 145–50, 185–6, 332, 371
leisure centre case study 153, 203

leisure time, managing 288–91
lesson plan 354
levers 124
Lewis nomogram 22
lifestyle 1–13, 166, 281–308, 317
  pressures 292–3
listening 175, 303
loading injuries 122–3
local organisations 164–5
log book 41–2, 87, 241, 357–8
lungs 113, 114

M
map reading 352–3, 372–6
  grid references 373–4
marathon running 40
media 166, 293, 294
  interview 304–6
medical screening 268, 269
mental rehearsal 228, 235
mental toughness 222–3, 235, 237
minutes of meetings 402
momentum 315
motivation
  182–3, 224–5, 235, 275–6, 319
  and performance 230, 231, 232–4
  extrinsic and intrinsic
    28, 182–3, 234
multi-stage fitness test 17–18
muscle hypertrophy 390
muscle movement 106–9
muscle tissue 105–6
muscular endurance 5, 7, 8, 9, 274
  tests 22–3
muscular strength 5, 7, 8, 9, 274
muscular system 105–9, 390
  skeletal muscle 107–8
mystery shoppers U19 6

N
Naismith's Rule 380
national governing bodies (NGBs)
  11, 43–4, 46, 70, 75, 293
navigation skills 372–6
  calculating distance 375
  natural features 374, 375, 376

needs of clients 191, 316–17, 335
nomogram 22
non-verbal communication
  175, 303, 306, 345
notational analysis 211
nutrition 12, 245–62, 348
  after/during exercise 254
  macronutrients 248–9
  micronutrients 249–50
  planning a strategy 257–60
  pre-event nutrition 254
  preparing food 253

O
obesity 12, 309
observation analysis 210–12
observation checklists 57–61, 87, 211
occupations in sports U13 5, 6
officials 48–55
  fair play 53–4, 55
  on- and off-field 49, 50
Olympic Games 155, 158, 167
organisational structure 328–9
organisations in sports industry
  U13 4–5
  dual-use U13 4–5
orienteering 81
outcome goals 62, 267
outdoor and adventurous activities
  67–92, 353
  environmental impacts 79–80
  equipment 350–1
  leading 341–62
  local/national provision 72–3
  organisation of 70–2
  permission 349
  planning requirements 349–54
  reviewing 88–9, 359–60
  techniques and skills 83–6
  timed structure 353
  unit assessments 68–9, 342–3
outdoor instructor 361, 385
over training 143, 315
over-use injuries 123, 124–5
overload 122–3, 272, 312

P

paralympion swimmer case study 307

PARQ (Physical Activity Readiness Questionnaire) 142

participants 73, 161–3, 189, 317–18

    motives of 160, 234

pensions 300–1

people skills U19 7

performance 56–63

    goals 62, 267

    profiling 59, 240

    routines 240

performance analysis 57, 210–12

performance enhancing substances 255, 290

personal fitness training

    programme 263–80

    collecting information 267–71

    goal setting 266–7

    implementation and review 276–8

personal trainer case study 277

personality 28, 29, 180–2, 224, 233, 236–8

planning and leading activities 172–204

    exercise session 316–18

    factors to consider 188–93

    sports event 196–201

plyometric training 7, 274

police checks 186

policies and procedures 332, 336

    equipment 337

pollution 80

portfolio 87, 241

posture 230, 306

power 6, 7, 8, 22, 274

practical sport 33–66

pre-performance routine 228

press-up test 22–3

pressures on performers 292–4

PRICE treatment 127, 136

prioritising commitments 286–7

private sector U13 4

problem solving 226–7

process goals 62, 267

professional conduct 183–4, 295, 353–4

progressive exercise 314–15

project, work experience U13 12–16

    feedback U13 16

    reviewing U13 14–16

    skills U13 13

promotion of event 406

Proprioceptive Neuromuscular Facilitation (PNF) 9, 274

protein 249

Prozone 212

psychology for sports performance 27–30, 219–44

    psychological demands 222–30

    psychological skills 240, 241

    reviewing 6–week programme 242

    techniques 227–30, 231

public sector U13 4

Q

qualifications of officials 53

quality of service U19 11–13

    standards U19 12

R

reaction time 6, 8

reception and induction U19 5

recording evidence 41–2, 195, 214

    outdoor activities 357–8

    psychological skills 241

recreation assistant case study 411

referees 49, 52, 55, 65

reflective cycle 178

relationships 302–3, 304

Reporting of Incidents, Diseases and Dangerous Occurrences 332

resistance training 9, 124, 318

resources 192, 287–8

'Respect' campaign 44–5, 187

respiratory system 113–16, 390–1

responsibilities of staff 329, 330–1, 346–8

rest and recovery 291

reversibility 315

rights of way 371

risk assessment 150–2, 346

    outdoor activities 76–8, 366

risks 141–5, 184–5

role models, performers as 281

route cards 380–1

RPE (Rating of Perceived Exertion) 272, 273, 314

rucksacks 378, 379

rugby 44, 46, 225, 239

rules and regulations 43–7, 145–50, 187, 295

    space and facilities 45–6

    unwritten rules 44–5

S

safety 325, 331–4, 366–70

Safety of Sports Grounds Act (1975) 146, 148–9

sailing centre case study 91

salt in diet 252

scoring systems 47–8

secure environment 333–4

security skills U19 11

self-confidence 224, 231

self-talk 230, 235, 240

shin splints 125

sit-and-reach test 16, 320

sit-up test 23

skeletal muscle 313

skeletal system 96–105, 390

    axial and appendicular 99

    joints and movement 102–5

    types of bones 101–2

skill-related fitness 5–6

skills 37–8, 39, 142–3, 194

    hard and soft skills 83–6

    open and closed 38

    simple and complex 38

skinfold testing 24–5

skull 97

sleep 12, 291

sleeping bags 378, 379

SMART targets 89, 192, 213, 235, 241, 322, 359–60

SMARTER goal-setting 62–3, 266–7
smoking 12, 289–90
snow skiing 81, 86
social life 288–9, 291
soft tissue injuries 126–8
speed 5, 7, 8, 21, 274
spinal column 97–8
spinal cord injuries 129
Sport Development Officer 162, 164, 169
sport and leisure facilities 325–40
    customer service 334–6
    equipment 337–8
    organisational structure 328–9
    safe environment 331–4
sports centre case study 339
sports development 155–70
    key issues 166–7
    local and national organisations 164–5
sports event 199–201, 403–4
    budgets 405–6
    customer comment card 410
    organisation 407
    planning considerations 404–5
    planning and leading 196–201
    planning and running 399–412
    promotion 406
    reviewing 199–201, 409–10
    roles and responsibilities 408
    tasks flow chart 197
    team meetings 402
sports and leisure manager U19 14
sports provision 158–60, 162–3
    local and national 159–60
sports psychologist 243
sports therapist case study 261
sprains 126
starters, role of 50
stimulants 11, 290
stoves, outdoor 369, 377–8, 379
strains 126–7
strength testing 16
stress 11, 223–4

stroke volume (SV) 390
studies: allocating time 285–6
suggestion boxes U19 6
supplements, dietary 255
support networks 293–4
survival bag 368
survival, expedition 366
swimming instructor case study 397
SWOT analysis 88, 212, U13 14–16
synovial joint 102–3

T
tactics 39–41, 226–7
target setting 89, 177, 192, 213
    outdoor activities 359–60
taxation 300
team selection 40
teamwork 83, 85
technical performance 214
technical skills and tactical
    awareness 205–18
    planning a programme 213–14
    reviewing/goal setting 215
    tactical ability 214
    tactical demands 209–10
    technical demands 208–9
techniques 38–9, 83–6
    risk from incorrect 142–3
technological advances 55, 288
television replays 49, 52, 55
temperature 131–2, 143
tendons 106–7
tents 367, 377, 379
thermoregulation 112
thinking techniques 229
35m sprint 21
thought stopping 229, 240
time restrictions 46–7
torches 368, 379
training 71, 284
    intensity of 272–3
    methods 6–8, 274
    principles of 271–2
training centres 70–1

training diary 276–7
training programme 1, 266–78
    adherence factors 275–6
    see also personal fitness
transport and travel 347, 350
    expedition 377, 382
Type A and Type B personality 237

U
umpires, role of 49
unwritten rules 44–5, 295

V
values 44, 187
vasodilation/vasoconstriction 112
vertebral column 97–8
vertical jump test 22
video analysis 210–11
viral infections 133
visualisation 228
vital capacity (VC) 390
vitamins and minerals 249–50, 255
VO_2 zone 313
voluntary organisations U13 4

W
warm up 141–2, 194, 228, 273–4, 315–16, 346
water 251, 254
weather information 382
whistle 369
Wildlife and Countryside Act (1981) 371
wildlife disturbance 79
windsurfing 81, 85–6
witness statements 241
Woods, Tiger 8, 56, 205
work commitments 284–8
work experience U13 1–18
    placement U13 6, 7
    project U13 12–16
    using documents U13 7–9
work-life balance 12